# THE
# HILLARY RAIMO
# SHOW
# TRANSCRIPTS

CONVERSATIONS ON TECHNOLOGY, TIME TRAVEL,
ET'S, 9/11 AND CONSCIOUSNESS

# DEDICATION

For all the Earth Angels who guard the future and heart of humanity.

# CONTENTS

# THE
# HILLARY RAIMO
# SHOW
# TRANSCRIPTS
### CONVERSATIONS ON TECHNOLOGY, TIME TRAVEL, ET'S, 9/11 AND CONSCIOUSNESS

# FORWARD

When I was asked to write the foreword to this book, I felt it was my duty to let you know something right up front.

Hillary Raimo is a force of nature.

She is the very embodiment of the four fundamental forces that affect the basic structure of the universe which are gravitation, electromagnetism, strong force, and weak force. In short, she is a nucleus of power that people all over the world gravitate to, are magnetized by, and where the weak become strong again.

Hillary is a serious truth seeker and and warrior when it comes to expanding human consciousness, a formidable being who pushes the envelope of conversation that informs, entertains and inspires all at once more than anyone I know. She is diligent, disciplined and determined to make the highest use of her presence and insists that each of us become responsible for our place in the connect-a-dots of life. She is relentless in her pursuit of heaven on earth and has zero problem going through hell in order to get there.

This work distills over thirteen years and seven hundred plus hours of thought provoking, belief challenging, breath taking, and mind-bending conversations with some of the most important news makers, risk takers, earth shakers, and ground breakers on the planet into bite sized easy-to-swallow chunks of illumination. As you take this literary journey you quickly realize that this is far more than a book, it is in fact more of a roadmap for the incredible challenges humanity faces in the 21$^{st}$ century. By reading this book we begin to broaden our minds and consider the messages and musings as only Hillary and her guests can present them.

I've watched Hillary's path for more than thirteen years, and being witness to this highly intelligent, incredibly gifted, and deeply inquisitive Renaissance woman "find her voice" behind a microphone is confirmation of what the great poet, Henry Wadsworth Longfellow stated, "The human voice is the organ of the soul." Hillary shines like a beacon of light over the dark waters of ignorance and apathy, as she just doesn't talk the talk, she walks the walk. That authenticity is a rare commodity in our times. In the end, just as in the beginning, perhaps that is what matters most.

So, as you press onward with the "Hillary Raimo Show Transcripts" make sure that you set aside some extra "brain bandwidth" to absorb what is being offered and should you find yourself reading this book over and over again, please consider the possibility that you are experiencing a case of "transformation by association" by simply being privy to and mentally engaging in the incredible conversations that this book offers.

Onward.

John St. Augustine

Award winning talk radio host and producer. Author of "Living An Uncommon Life" and "Every Moment Matters."

# AUTHOR'S PREFACE
## REFLECTIONS BY HILLARY RAIMO

When I decided to write this book, I had made the decision to retire from alternative media as a radio host. I felt the industry had become something different than its original intention when it first started. Like many things in life, it starts out well, but sometimes fades into something else, at which point the good is lost, mangled, or perversely turned into something hideous. Greed, ego, and shrewd business habits behind the scenes have dismantled those good intentions of the original truth seekers. I can say with a clean conscious that I held my integrity through all my years on the air. I treated my guests well, created a safe space for them to share their knowledge, and an audience to do it in front of.

For the sake of integrity, I once again release their words into the world, in hopes of lighting up minds, so people can make their own connections. I know what I see, and I am ready to share that point of view.

But first, I want to address how this book should be perceived because it is an offering into a time frame. Through the years of post-9/11, the changing of privacy laws, the rise of terrorism, government spying on its citizens, collecting data without consent, and manipulating every aspect of our digital lives as if we were in a petri dish being studied by some unfathomable force. The double edge sword of all of that is the system is not hack proof. Cue the rise of the computer minds smarter than the governments. Throughout the years that this was all happening and the foundation being set, I talked about it on the airwaves with some of the most credible minds available to get the facts, because at this point disinformation was running rampant through alternative media. Guests were manipulating hosts, content was being scripted, questions had to pass through publicists, and it was becoming a pseudo hodge-podge of Hollywood type "wannabes" that were buzzing around the scene like celebrities expecting the red-carpet treatment at every turn and snubbing the shows that they deemed unlikable. Alternative media was quickly infiltrated by distrust, scandal, and was falling to pieces.

During this time, I was mentoring new radio hosts, writers, and artists to help them find their voice and spread their wings. In a Trump-era, where opinions run bold, and no one is afraid to speak up and give their thoughts to everything, it is important to remember how to express yourself, but to also be kind in listening to others. The ability to be empathic is learned, and I am not so sure social media is doing a good job.

I am a part of the generations that grew up without social media or cell phones. My childhood was not filled with electronics, it was filled with time outside in nature, eating homemade food, and television was only for special times, limited to one hour a week. My imagination had time to flourish, and the innocence of my childhood was kept pure.

During the years I was on the radio I traveled often to the Southwestern United States to work with native American elders and was involved in a series of ceremonies at sites considered sacred. Many people were talking about twin flames, we are all one, it was a global chant of light, and many had found a container for that on social media. It was bringing people together in many wonderful ways. I myself met people, had experiences and was grateful for all of it. But knowing when to cut and end things is a trait that many struggle with, myself included at times. As I have got older over the years, this has been easier to do. Deciding to stop doing radio after 13 years is another example of knowing when to end things.

I worry about the world my grandchildren will grow up in. The ground work is being laid for a very grim future, if one is to consider only the technology advances that have grown tenfold over just the last decade. I often wonder have we considered the evolution of human consciousness that has to understand, use, and change with today's technology?

Most likely we haven't because we aren't having the right conversations.

Rarely are citizens left to think for themselves, let alone critically together.

But since 9/11 we did meditate together by organizing 13 global meditations from 2014-2017. Through the rare blood moon tetrad, I watched how people could use the energies around them to better themselves. Suddenly we became aware of our intricate relationship with nature and how love really does stimulate a biochemical state of being within the human body that all life forms can respond too.

As a trained healer and non-denominational ordained minister, it is my belief that demons are real. The good side of this is that if demons are real, so are the angels.

I hope this book stirs your genetic memories of a time less violent and more nurturing. It is with that thought in mind that I offer difficult information to break down the established story, so people can think for themselves.

The magic that has been woven through all of this material, time will seed the blooms. We need to prepare all of humanity, not just those we like, but all people! The time of being special, the one better than your family members, friends, and co-workers is over along with the selfish judgments of others which keeps all of humanity from rising.

The healing work is done here, on Earth. And if you are here, you are doing the work. Taking notice of the astrology, the macro and micro environments, who you attract or don't, and how your heart weighs in light of your pain, is all relevant.

My years on the air taught me to question better. To seek the bigger picture, even if I didn't like what I saw. A true psychic never only tells happy visions. That is their ego filtering out the true spectrum. Some visions are not pleasant, and in a time when the sky may seem to be falling, could it really only be the veil lifting from our eyes to find what lives already inside of us? Hope and faith are triggers of a better world. If man can build the tower of Babel, he can certainly bring it down.

My hope is that you find value in the hindsight this material offers. To see the growth in the industries since these conversations took place, is incredibly valuable. Think about what you were doing through these years.

The big question of course, is what are the odds that you have been manifested out of the entire universe to be here?

*Astronomical.*

Make good use of it.

Hillary Raimo
Altamont, New York 2018

# 1

# DAVID ICKE
# THE PERCEPTION DECEPTION

*Lynn Andrews told me to read all of David Icke's work while I was her apprentice in her mystery school in the early 2000's. If the request had not come from her, I would have ignored it and moved on. But because she was my spiritual teacher at the time, and being a good student, I did. That included every book in his body of work, and even his sources, book for book. There was something going on in the world that needed to be exposed. This deep urge inside me rose up and I started my radio show. Little did I know that day that over the next few years, I would do four shows with David and the information we discussed always coincided with world events and relevant information for my listeners.*

*Is the world being run by a dimensional race of beings that seeks to control mankind?*

RECORDED AUGUST 5, 2010

**Hillary Raimo:** David Icke and his research discusses a fantastic web of global manipulation, orchestrated by things beyond this physical realm. His work exposes the hidden bloodlines, through which other-dimensional entities live and operate unseen among us; and he shows how the bloodlines of the royal, political, and economic rulers of today are the same as those who ruled as the kings and queens of ancient times. Welcome David, thanks so much for joining me.

**David Icke:** Pleasure Hillary.

**Hillary Raimo:** What is your take on what is happening on the world stage right now?

**David Icke:** Well, I've been writing for 20 years about something I call the truth vibrations. *The Truth Vibrations* was funnily enough the name of the first book I ever wrote so after I started to awaken myself in 1990. What I learned two decades ago was that a vibrational change was coming, which was going to increasingly act like a spiritual alarm clock and wake people up from their coma, from their deep sleep that we've been in. The more that I've understood this as the years passed, what is happening is that we are at the cusp of an epoch change. In my new book, *Human Race Get Off Your Knees*, I go into the fact that this is reality, it goes through a cycle and that cycle is dictated by a vibrational cycle that comes out of the black holes.

In our case, the black hole at the center of this galaxy, which scientists are now identifying and it is suggested there's one in the center of every galaxy, but it's a vibrational cycle. As the vibrational change happens, it elicits different information in the form of photon energy coming from the suns and we decode this through what I call the body computer. We've discussed this before in this reality that we are experiencing and you can liken it, not just symbolically, but in very many ways in actual terms to the wireless internet. I'm sitting in a room now and if it had the wireless internet, I could look around and I would not see it. It would just be a room to me and just what appears to be empty space.

If I turn on a computer out of the ether, out of the unseen without any wire connections or anything, I can pull a whole collective reality out of that wireless internet, that unseen realm onto a screen. What we're doing through what I call the body computer, the biological body computer system in the sense that it has the ability to assess information and make decisions for itself, not just react to the way it's programmed, I mean I'm sitting here now, you're sitting in there now, everyone's listening to this program sitting or wherever they are, and their immune system is working and making decisions constantly on how to react to this situation or that situation or that potential threat or whatever.

You're not aware of that, I'm not aware of that, we're just chatting. There's a heck of a lot going on within the body computer system that we are simply not aware of but it is actually up to its own level of awareness making decisions based on the information that it's receiving. What is happening is the human body computer is decoding this photon information and it's turning it from the vibrational into the electrical, into the digital, and finally into the holographic, and it's the holographic reality that we experience what we call the physical world. Now this vibration, which changes over a period of time or what we call time is in effect creating what I've called in my books before the time loop.

One of my books is called *Tales from the Time Loop* where you start at a certain point and then you go around, and then you basically come back to the same point, not in every detail but in theme. It's not actually a time loop because there is no time. What we call time and space are information constructs that we decode through the body computer into the illusion of time and space. This vibration is happening in what we call the now, this only moment that exists. As it changes as it moves through its cycle, it appears because of the way we decode reality, it appears to change and it appears to go through presence of future in this time loop. What it actually is, is a vibration in the now that just goes through a cycle.

It's not going through a period of time at all, it's only illusion. Anyway, the point is that there are certain points in this cycle, which in Asia and the Ancient Indian world they call YUGAs. We note the Mayan concepts of cycles of time and it's something that appears in all the ancient cultures, this concept of going through a loop, of going through a time loop, a time period and then coming back to the start. We're at the point now where the cusp is between a period of what people would call a dark period of suppression, of the limitation or sense of limitation.

That's what it is, and we're now at the cusp of a massive fundamental change to a period in this cycle, which is about expansion of consciousness, the end of limitation and the opening of massively greater potential for creation, self-creation, and the ability to manifest whatever you want to manifest. At this point now and what I call the truth vibrations are this new energetic change moving in and it's changing the information, but we're receiving and therefore and those that are starting to tune into this and more and more people are, they start to dramatically in many cases now change their perception of the world, their sense of reality, who they are, what they are, the nature of their own possibility.

This is what is happening now and of course some people are still closed. Most people at this minute are still closed and shutting off from this new vibe, this vibrational change, these truth vibrations and they're clinging onto the old epoch, the old energy. The control system that I've been writing about and exposing all these years, it's a manifestation of that previous epoch, the dying epoch, one of control and suppression and imposition and limitation. We look at the control system now and I understand why. My goodness me I do and for a few years it's going to still look like this, that it's actually gaining more and more and more power, and more and more and more control, and more and more domination.

What we're seeing I would suggest is the last desperate throw of the dice, the last desperate attempt to hold on to the control that it has had. Because the truth vibrations are coming in, because people are starting to awaken, because people are being affected more and more by this vibrational change, at this cusp of YUGA change if you like, they are having to throw more and more efforts to keep us in the state of suppression that we were before and thus, it is becoming more and more obvious to people that there is a control system going on because it's becoming more blatant as they throw more and more things at us.

In the next few years, it's going to seem that everything is lost, that the control system can't be stopped and all the rest of it, but there's going to come a point in a few years, not a few decades, where that cusp point, that tipping point comes where the new energetic epoch, the truth vibrations become the dominant information force in this reality. At that point, the control system will start to lose its power very, very rapidly and eventually collapse.

**Hillary Raimo:** David, I have to ask you this question. In exposing all that you do about the elite power structures that run the current global world, how are you still alive?

**David Icke:** Well, I've been asked this question many, many, many times over the years and it's even got to the point sometimes Hillary where I've seen myself on a "blacklist" as a dis-informer because if what he was saying was true, he'd be dead and alongside me are listed people who've died, who'd been putting out certain types of information. My response to that is well, let's all line up now, put our hands out for the handcuffs and our ankles out for the ball and chain because what you're telling me there for, and I'm talking about the people who say that is that we're doomed because anyone that speaks out and has anything valid to say is going to be taken out.

Indeed, being taken out is their license to credibility, and so what's the point? Let's just all line up and walk in the prison camp and just accept it. Now what I'm saying is that we create our own reality and we are decoding a collective reality from the unseen like I say the cosmic internet as I call it, the equivalent of the wireless internet, but just as you go online and we can go to the same websites, we'll see the same graphics, we'll see the same words, we'll see the same colors, we'll see the same pictures because we're experiencing a collective reality. We won't all have an opinion, a reaction, or a response to what we see that's the same.

That's where we as unique expressions of it infinite consciousness put our own spin on reality and where I'm coming from is that there are forces at work, which are expressions of these truth vibrations, and there are large numbers of them and more and more all the time who are beyond the ability of the control system to take them out because if I do not let the fact that I could be taken out into my reality, I cannot decode it into physical experience. I can't do that. I'll tell you an interesting story. What I think is interesting. When I first came to America in 1996, what I did was met a lot of whistleblowers and I saw a lot of whistleblowers from government and other areas speaking.

What I saw again and again, not in every case but a significant number, were people wearing the attacks upon them as like a war medal. I'll tell you even another. I won't mention his name, but I was in someone's house one day back in 1996. It was up in New England and I was waiting to talk in that person's house. That's how big the audiences were that time for this information. He went out and I put a video in and I saw this man talking. He was saying some very, very interesting things, but he kept repeating, "I don't know how long they're going to let me keep saying this. I don't know how long that I can keep saying this before they take me out."

I sat there that day Hillary and I thought you want to be careful mate because you're going to be a self-fulfilling prophecy if you're not careful. The guy came back home and I said, "Oh that's a very interesting video, a lot of interesting things to say." I say, "What's happened to Disco? Where is he now?" He said, "He's dead. He was murdered." I thought well to be honest I'm actually not surprised because we either manifest our power here or we run around posturing our inability to continue to do it as for as long as we want as some kind of confirmation that we're speaking the truth. I mean it's like going round and round and round in circles and I just wake up every day.

I'm doing this 12 hours a day after day after day, and I will till I keel over it's my life, it's my passion, it's the only thing I'm interested in doing. I put one foot in front of the other and what tends to happen is you get somewhere. Now I've had a number of efforts to undermine me financially, people being put in my life to undermine me. In fact, the people that have caused me most at my work, my health, and everything, most difficulty, most stress, and been the biggest challenges have been people who have expressed their love and support for me more than anybody else.

There are many, many different ways to undermine someone or attempt to without actually pulling a trigger, but what you do is no matter what is thrown at you, you get up off the floor, you brush yourself down, and you carry on. When you do that, when you keep being the rubber ball who you can undermine, you can cause stress for, you can cause difficulties for, and all the rest of it, but the rubber ball keeps bouncing. It's not that I've had 20 years where I've just been left alone. I mean I've gone through the most extraordinary gathering levels of ridicule and abuse in this country, Britain particularly.

I've had efforts to undermine me all over the place, but what you do is you get up, you brush yourself down, and you start all over again. When you do that, you cannot be stopped.

**Hillary Raimo:** David, there's some proof out there that there are electromagnetic weapons, things that can interfere with people's consciousness, their electromagnetic field as a form of stopping people, making them sick, giving them cancer, those kinds of things. What's your take on that?

**David Icke:** I think there's no question that's true. Yes. I mean I've gone through some electromagnetic attacks myself that have actually pretty much stopped now interestingly enough. Around the end of 2009 right around January and February, every night, I would virtually every night I would wake up and there would be these tremendous electromagnetic fields in the bedroom. They sometimes look like spider metallic like spider things and all the rest of it, but it wasn't that you could just see them, you could feel them very powerfully too. I remember one night they were disrupting my sleep so much that I got up out the bedroom and I walked into my lounge.

I'd lay on the sofa and I fell asleep there, and I woke up again and I looked across at the television set and it was this like ... You know Catherine wheels, (pinwheels) these fireworks Catherine wheels?

**Hillary Raimo:** Yes.

**David Icke:** There was a spinning kind of Catherine wheel of sort ... It wasn't colored energy and it was spinning with extraordinary speed and in the middle was again a metallic spider-like thing going out, like a core of it. I watched it. It wasn't that it was just there for a few seconds and then went. I watched it for about minute, minute and a half, and then I got up and I thought I'm going to see what is going on. I walk towards it and as I walked very close towards it, it had gone. This went on for weeks and weeks and weeks, and then just suddenly stopped. I have it kind of maybe two or three times a month now, but nothing like as intense as I did then. What that was all about I have no idea.

That at the time when I was going through that experience, it was disrupting my health, my rheumatoid arthritis, which is not good at the best of times. It was very, very bad then and I had one or two other health situations. Again, I'll be honest, what I used to do, I used to wake up, turnover, see all this metallic electromagnetic stuff around me and I would shall I say give it the finger, and then I would turn over and go back to sleep. It was quite funny because instead of all they're out to get me or whatever, it's like okay, whatever, whatever, whatever, throw anything at me, I'm not bothered because I'm ok.

**Hillary Raimo:** Do you think the fear equation is also included in this? because if you're afraid that they can get you, then that changes the whole game, doesn't it?

**David Icke:** Well, that's a very important point because what we're dealing with here is frequencies that are either compatible or not compatible. If someone is vibrating to the frequency of radio one, when radio two tries to attack it, it can't do it, you can't do it because radio one or radio two are on different frequencies. Of course, the base frequency of the control system is fear, it's low vibrational emotion.

An interesting thing that I've noticed in my life over the years is one of the ways that the attempt has been to undermine me and it's going on at this time funnily enough, not that it will work, is to create situations and people around me that will pull me in to that low vibrational emotional state because once you've pulled into that, you're actually thinking with the vibrational frequency of the control system, and then they can start to make an impact upon you. If you can stay outside of that, then you're vibrating at one frequency, the control system is vibrating at another, never the twain shall meet. This is why it's so important and I'm speaking to myself here as I say this.

I'm not the guru, Buddha sitting on a mounting cross leg saying this is what you must do, I've softened it. We're all in this and we're all kind of working to get ourselves in a certain state me included. When you're aware of it, it makes it more easier and what we need to do is to just hold this understanding that we are infinite consciousness, having an experience. We're not the experience. I'm not David Icke. David likes my experience. I'm infinite consciousness having an experience as David Icke. When you come from that perspective, it helps you hold perspective on the experiences that we have.

Instead of being pulled into them so that you are the experience as well as having the experience, which means that you're pulled into a vibrational state where if it's an unpleasant experience in a stressful and fearful experience, well then, you're being pulled into the stadium in which the control system plays at home. It's important that we hold this understanding and it's a real challenge because all the five sense influences are telling us that you are David Icke, you were born in Leicester in 1952 and you are just one person, just Joe public, you have no power.

If we can resist getting pulled into that to realize the reflection in the mirror is the reflection of the experience, it's not a reflection of who we are but you can see who we are through the eyes often, then you're in this world as I've said many times before. You're in this world having any experience, but of this world in the point of that you're perceiving the experience, and that can have a very powerful impact on not getting pulled in to interfere and stress and all the rest of it, which allows you to enter the control systems stadium, which it wants everybody.

That's why it's created a society, which is there to generate maximum fear, maximum worry, maximum anxiety, maximum conflict is because they want us in a certain vibrational frequency range because that's the one that they can lock into us through.

**Hillary Raimo:** Thank you. In your work you described how the

New Age movement is manipulated towards a new world order with the 'we are all one' motto. Can you explain that for those listening how that's being done now?

**David Icke:** Well, I looked at the New Age movement a lot when I first started to awaken because it was my first port of call when I was trying to get an understanding of what the heck was happening to me 20 years ago. I've observed it and I don't want to sit here now and say the New Age is a load of rubbish and all the people in it rub it. No, I'm not saying that. There are some wonderful, wonderful people that are operating what people would call the New Age movement and enormous numbers of genuine people. What I'm saying is that there are elements of it and I would say significant elements of it that I think they've rejected religion in general but have actually just accepted another one.

If you give your power away Christian heroes or Jewish heroes or Muslim heroes, that's considered by many people in the new age as absolutely wrong, you must take the power back, you must be in your own power, you must create your own reality, you must express your uniqueness. I agree with all of that, but then I see for instance you can go to Sedona, you can go to Glastonbury, or you can go to India as I did a couple of years ago, and you can see a new age from yards by what they're wearing. Then I've been into these ashrams in India and I've seen new age people going through religious rituals that are absolutely straight out of Hinduism and Islam and Judaism and Christianity in the way that they're performed.

I see people wearing the same type of clothes. I see people having their own kind of heroes or divine figures to give their power away to. I mean it used to be a star commander for some people a long time ago or it's Sunanda or it's the great white brotherhood. For me, there was a great song years ago. It wasn't actually a great song, but the theme was. It was by a guy called Val Doonican, an Irish singer when I was a kid and it said walk tall, walk straight, and look the world right in the eye.

That's what my mom had told me when I was about knee-high, and if we are infinite consciousness and we are expressions of the infinite one, then we should be looking each other in the eye, oh yes respects other aspects of consciousness for what they're doing, what they stand for, what they're expressing, yes good, but don't get a crick in the neck looking up because you are them, they are you, I am you, you are me. I still see hierarchical structures big time often within the New Age movement and a hierarchy is illusion. Hierarchy is the control system. We cannot have a situation of hierarchy and then claim that everyone is an expression of the one.

We either are or we're not and because hierarchies are the way that the control system imposes itself in so many ways because hierarchies are the few dictating to the many. That can be a few bankers dictating to the entire banking system, a few politicians dictating to an entire nation, or it can be a few heroes in the new age dictating or allowing people, allowing them to be themselves to be taken to when they are the vast majority. As for me, these blueprints structures of the control system you find them everywhere if you look for them and hierarchy is the old limitation. I'm above you, you're above me, I know my place. That's the old epoch, that's what's coming down.

The pyramids of power, they're coming down because that's an expression of the old energy. It's a shame that so much of the new age or significant sways of it anyway are still into hierarchies. It's not the way it is. I would suggest anyway, but everyone must believe what they want to believe of course.

**Hillary Raimo:** Let's talk about the alien agenda. What is your take on this whole good, bad, us versus them kind of thing? Are the ETs good, are they bad? What do we believe? There's so much conflicting information out there.

**David Icke:** Well, Hillary I don't see things in terms of good or bad. I see things in terms of conscious and unconscious. There are conscious human beings, there are unconscious human beings and it takes you about 30 seconds to see the difference if you're in their presence. Because everything is an expression of this one infinite awareness, this all possibility that I call it, then if you are dealing with an infinite all possibility, then all possibility must be able to manifest. I mean the two go together, so therefore anything is possible. When you're dealing with non-human entities or non-human expressions of awareness, then you must of course have the great tapestry, the great spectrum of possibility among them.

There are non-human entities that let's call them ETs for simplicity that are conscious and they will have a benevolent supportive view of humanity. Indeed, they will have a benevolent supportive view of all existence. You will have other ETS that are not conscious and probably not terribly bright. You'll have other ETs, which is what I would suggest we're dealing with in terms of the control system who are not conscious in terms of infinite consciousness because anything that is conscious does not want control over. It does not want to impose its will upon, but they are extremely technologically advanced compared with humans at this point.

They are shall we say clever because they have this intellectual advanced state of mind, but they are not wise in the sense that they are conscious and when you have a technological possibility coming from a developed intellect, a developed mind but you do not have that balanced by consciousness wisdom, then you can get yourself into a very destructive situation because I've said in my books all 20 years ago nearly, cleverness without wisdom is the most destructive force on earth. It's very clever to understand how to make an atomic bomb, but it's not wise to do it and this is the difference between the two.

What we're dealing with I would suggest Hillary with it in terms of the control system is extraterrestrials or not even extraterrestrials, I call them other dimensionals that are advanced intellectually, therefore very technologically advanced compared with us. They have an understanding of how to manipulate energy as part of that intellectual understanding of the way reality works, but they do not have the open consciousness, the connection to the greater awareness to balance that understanding and use it in a compassionate, loving, balanced way. For instance, the same technology that can cause great destruction can give people free energy indefinitely, no utility bills, none of it. It's like a microphone.

Microphone is not negative or positive. It's how you use it there's negative or positive, and this intellectually dominated extraterrestrial group, which I feel overwhelmingly takes a reptilian form, this is the mentality behind what we call the illuminati, these bloodlines, which are hybrid interbred blood lines, which acts as vehicles within this reality you might call visible light for the reptilian and other "demonic type entities" operating outside of this reality to actually manipulate this reality. It's like when you see scientists who are working with material that is dangerous, you'll see the material in a tank and you'll see the scientist on the outside of the tank, and then he puts his hands through these gloves that go inside the tank and then he can work the material.

Now he's outside the tank. What is manipulating is inside the tank and if you take that symbol, that analogy, that's basically what we looking at I would suggest after two decades researching this around the world in terms of the control system. These bloodlines are like the gloves, they're in the tank. They are the vehicle within this reality that allows these entities operating just outside of this reality to manipulate through them into this world. The reason they're so obsessed with interbreeding and holding a certain genetic DNA state is because everything in this reality when you come down to it, whether it looks just like a solid wall or its DNA or a glass of beer, its base state is vibrational wave form.

That's where the information is that we decode into what we see as physical objects, so therefore DNA is in its base form a vibrational field. Now if you are wishing to "possess" another body if you like and take over its mental and emotional faculties, then the closer your vibrational state is to it, the more influenced you're going to have over its mental and emotional state and so they interbred with humanity. They're probably still doing it, no doubt, they are to create a hybrid bloodline and the hybrid bloodline is quite simply a hybrid vibrational field, which allows them to lock into it much more powerfully than the general run of the human population, which is not as vibrationally compatible to them as the hybrid bloodlines that they have created and they perpetuate through fierce interbreeding.

This is the reason that the aristocracy, for instance, and royalty of not just Europe but the world has been incessantly interbred over the years with each other. It's not right snobbery just to keep the genes up. Yet, it is to keep the genes up. It's to keep a certain genetic state, like a computer software program. This is why the eastern establishment families of the United States incessantly interbred. It's because they're trying to hold this vibrational field, which will be diluted very, very fast if it's interbred with people that are not compatible with it.

**Hillary Raimo:** David if somebody is compatible with that kind of vibration and they are a hybrid, is it possible for them to overcome that strong kind of controlling energy that can attach to them? Can they evolve past that?

**David Icke:** Absolutely, they can. It's called consciousness. See, I've got a computer in front of me now and if I go to my documents, there are files below all over it. Within the DNA are endless files, information files, experience files, programmed behavior files all over it but just as with my documents, if I don't open the file and put it on the screen, it's not going to influence the reality of the computer. It's just going to sit there in a dormant state. What these people do, and this is again one of the key reasons that they bring their children up in a certain way and one of the ways they bring them up is overwhelmingly with no human parental child bonding, with no love, with no warmth.

I mean people have noted over the years the lack of warmth between each other of the House of Windsor, the British royal family. I mean I saw this extraordinary black and white film the other day where the queen is walking off a plane back in the days of black and white. She's been to an overseas visit with Prince Philip the chap. They walked down the steps and there's a line of dignitaries at Heathrow Airport waiting to meet them and she goes along and she's going hello, hello, to these dark suits, hello mom and bowing their heads. Then there's a gap and then you see what the gap is, and it's the fact that there's not a man standing there in line, it's Prince Charles who's a little boy.

He's coming in line with the dignitaries. He puts his hand out to his mother and shakes hands like the other dignitaries, and she goes on to the next one. Now that's part of the way that these people are brought up. They're also sent to what we call in Britain public schools, but they're actually private schools, fee-paying schools. You have different name for them in America, same thing and they go to these schools where they are brought up and looked after for want of a term in a certain way, and then there's the other thing. They're eventually put through rituals and these rituals are designed specifically to create vibrational fields that open the files to the deeper levels of this hybrid state, to open the deeper levels of the hybrid program.

As these files open, these kids start to change in terms of their attitude to life themselves and the world because the program has been activated, and it starts to influence their sense of self and reality more and more powerfully. When you are conscious, when you allow consciousness in, it can override any of these programs. I've met people from these bloodlines who are lovely people, wonderful people. Because of their own state of being, they have not allowed these files to be opened and so they're not influenced by them, and then they're seen within these illuminati families as cuckoos in the nest. I know one. I know one very, very well and she's a remarkable, staggeringly remarkable woman.

She's right in the middle of some of these bloodlines and she couldn't be less like them and they don't know what to do with her. Consciousness can overcome anything, but it's got to be open. I mean it's simple things like is it right, is it just, is it fair. If people just keep asking that question, instead of what is right for me and my perception in a moment, what is right, fair, and just in these circumstances. If we keep making decisions, whether we're in the bloodline or not, if we keep making decisions based on that criteria as we go through our daily life, then we are not going to be in the vibrational state of the entities and the control system.

We're not because the control system says what do I need to do to get the outcome that I want for me. That's its whole criteria, that's the whole criteria of these entities. Because one of the key traits, which explains a lot about the world Hillary, one of the key traits of these hybrid bloodlines when the files are open is a lack of empathy, no empathy, the inability to empathize with the consequences for others of our actions. Once you have no empathy, the fail-safe mechanism of human behavior has gone because anything goes 3000 people on 9/11 and we got to invade the countries, he wanted then, what's the problem. Hundreds of thousands of dead and injured people in Iraq, so what? We got to control Iraq, I mean what's the problem.

This is the mentality that they go through when you have no

empathy because it's whatever is right for me. This is why they lie all the time. They have to lie of course because if they told the truth, then they'd be saying it's all a control system and there's a few controlling the many. They're not going to do that. They have to lie all the time. They have to lie about everything they do on the stepping stones of the agenda because if they told the truth, they'd say well we're only doing this now because it's leading to this and it's leading to that and the outcome we want is total human control. They're not going to say that which means these people are lying all the time, but to them lying is not a problem, it's the means to an end.

You told a massive lie then but I've got the outcome I wanted, what's the problem? This is the mentality once you have no empathy. Anyone who has empathy with the consequences for others of their actions who does what they believe to be right and just and fair when they're making decisions over whatever situation they're facing, they are by that definition alone going to pull themselves vibrationally or hold themselves vibrationally outside of the control systems clutches.

**Hillary Raimo:** David, why do you think the positive contact experiences are withheld so frequently and not shared often enough within the subculture?

**David Icke:** Well, I think there's a tremendous amount of information about non-human activity around this planet that's kept from us, and one of the reasons is that the fact that there is a non-human element to the control of humanity. That is prime to them to keep under wraps, to keep from people. The other thing is that once you start talking in any way about life beyond this planet, what are you doing? You're immediately expanding people's perception of themselves in the world and reality. No longer is it just one race of people on one planet in a dead solar system and apparently dead galaxy, now suddenly bang, hey your expansion of a sense of possibility and the reality you are a part of suddenly massively expands once you accept that these expressions of life exist.

Not just exist, but exist in enormous abundance, so there are many different reasons for it. Of course, they don't want people to perceive any positive kind of benevolent connection to an extraterrestrial force because that by definition takes their power away, because they want to control by being the only force, the only source of control and information and all the rest of it. They don't want anybody else being looked at as hey, it's not just about governments and people like that, there's benevolent non-human entities visiting the planet crikey, what can they tell us.

It's like that they have a process of what I call defend the first domino because you see these situations sometimes where they have thousands and thousands and sometimes millions of dominoes, and they push the first one down and then it hits the next one and suddenly they're all going down right at the end. They have this system and like I say I call defend the first domino for this reason. If you start to encompass, for instance, alternative methods of healing instead of really curling and rejecting them as the system does, then you are pressing the first domino because okay, this first domino has gone down which is okay yeah, well there's something in this alternative view of healing.

Okay next Domino is a question, well how do they work then, and now you've started dominoes falling in terms of changing the perception of the nature of the human body, the nature of who we are, and all the rest of it once the first domino's gone, which is yeah well there could be something in this alternative healing the system says. They defend the first domino fiercely, so bang we must not let alternative healing get any credibility because of what comes from that and in the same way, we must shut the door on the whole ET thing, especially the benevolent part of it because of what will come from that if we let the first domino fall.

I do feel that as you indicated earlier Hillary that there is a plan, which has been talked about for a long time by various researchers and what have you, that there is a plan at some point to introduce the fact that there is a possible threat to humanity from an extraterrestrial force. It won't be the force reveal that's really behind it, but if you want to see through it there is this technique that I call problem reaction solution create the problem, get the reaction, do something oh my God, and then you offer the solution to the problems you have created, which changes societies how you want it.

If you want to change the global situation, if you want to change the world globally in terms of everyone at the same time, then you need global problems through which you can offer a global solution. You have for instance the global war on terror, so you can offer global solutions to that. You have a global financial problem, so you can offer global solutions to that, like a world central bank but it takes the war global finance to everywhere in the country. You have global warming problem they have created in the public mind on increasingly less mine, but still enormous amount of people, so you can offer global solutions to that.

Of course, if you're dealing with a global threat from an extraterrestrial race perceived, manufactured, whatever, then you have the ability to put a global solution to that, which is bringing all the military and political kind of systems together as one. I mean what you have in a country if there's a threat to a country, you have a war cabinet, you have a few people sitting around the table making the decisions, not the rest of the government anymore. Of course, if you had a perceived threat to the world from an extraterrestrial external force, then bingo you would have the equivalent of a global war cabinet, a few people making decisions for the world.

I'm not saying this is definitely going to happen, but I'm saying it's a possibility through something that's been talked about for years called Project Blue Beam, which was written about many, many years ago that this was one of the plans, one of the possibilities that would be introduced to manipulate humanity to accept an immense centralization of power in the world.

**Hillary Raimo:** David what about all of the people that are coming forward recently about time travel and exposing the fact that governments all over the world have been funding this for quite some time and researching this, and that they have in fact been using the technology, what are your thoughts on that?

**David Icke:** I think that technology in the underground bases and the secret projects is light years ahead of anything we see in the public arena, and this is a very important point because if you want to suppress people's sense of what is possible, in other words potential, then what you need to do is suppress their perception of possibility. Now this seems like an incredibly obvious statement, but sometimes we miss the obvious what I'm saying by this is if you suppress through suppression of science and such things, suppression of technological development in the public domain, what is actually possible, then you create a sense of limitation in the public mind because the public's mind's basic perception of what's possible is what they can see is possible because it's happening.

This is why when people talked about flying in spaceships or even flying at one point, they will laugh at that, that's not possible, you can't fly with a heavier than air machine, you can't do this. Yeah, how many things that we take for granted today before people's eyes and was suggested that this is possible that the general population said you're mad, you're crazy, that's not possible. Once they see it then their sense of possibility expands. Oh, you can fly in a heavier than air machine, oh I've just been on the holidays in one, I know it's true, I experienced it. The more you suppress what's possible, the more you suppress perception of possibility.

When people come out like researchers and say this is what they're doing and this is the technology they're using to do it, people said that's crazy, that's not possible. No, your perception is that it's not possible, it's not that it's actually not possible, it's your perception that is telling you that. Beyond the public arena are fantastic technologies to give us free energy, to keep people alive and healthy for immensely longer than we are now. Many different things are being used, not always being used often not being used positively, being used negatively, but being used in another way with a benevolent loving force could bring tremendously positive changes to the human experience.

This is another interesting area along with what we've got, but this is another interesting area Hillary that I've talked about in this new book *Human Race Get Off Your Knees*, and that is that these extraterrestrials, these reptilian, manipulating non-humans, they operate outside of this reality overwhelmingly, and therefore they operate to a different perception of time, which is just a construct. They can see down our timeline to a certain extent, but we can't see down because we're in it. Interestingly when you look at prophetic books that have been written in novel form like George Orwell's *1984*, Aldous Huxley's *Brave New World*, and if you put those two books together, then you've pretty much got what the control system wants to impose on planet earth as well and then some, but just in theme, they're absolutely right.

Then you say hold on a second, how do they know that? Huxley's book was written in 1932 and Orwell's book was written in 1948 or published in 1948, how did they know, how do some of these other books, prophetic books know and how could they talk about technology and the use of drugs, et cetera that didn't even exist at the time but do now.

It's interesting when you look at those two books because George Orwell's real name was Eric Blair who was a pupil at Eton college where the Royals go, one of the elite colleges in Britain just outside Windsor, in fact literally just outside Windsor, where Windsor Castle is, one of the main homes of the royal family. His teacher, French teacher for a time at Eton College was Aldous Huxley and Huxley introduced Orwell, Eric Blair to the Fabian Society, which is one of the major strands in the illuminati network of secret societies. It was the organization that created the British Labour Party of Tony Blair, the start of the 20th century.

When you can access this secret society network at some deep level, you can access the projected future that these guys want to impose upon humanity and you can therefore write novels, which appear to be from imagination but with the passage of decades now, we can see stunningly accurate in terms of what's actually happening and is planned to happen. Then you ask the question, well how could they write about technology that we have now but was not even thought of then, because when you are interacting with these non-human entities through these the deep, deep levels, not Fred and Joe down the Free Masons Lodge, I'm talking the deep, deep inner core levels of this global secret society network.

You can access the projected future through though those non-human entities, and you know things like nanotechnology and computer systems and all this stuff that's coming out now, it has been known about and used by these non-human entities, these reptilian entities I would suggest for eons.

What is the use of introducing nanotechnology in our timeline of 1640 or 1820, waste of time. It's introduced as we reach the point where it can be used as part of the control system and if you can have access to that information way back through the secret society network, then you can write prophetic novels including technology that was not there at the time but you know is coming.

**Hillary Raimo:** We are out of time David, thank you for sharing this important perspective with us.

**David Icke:** It's my pleasure. Thank you, Hillary, for your show and the work you do in the world.

# 2

# DR. DAVID LEWIS ANDERSON
# TIME TRAVEL TECHNOLOGIES

*I was introduced to Dr. Anderson through Peter Moon, author and owner of SkyBooks Publishing in Montauk, New York. Intrigued by his knowledge of time travel technology and his work in making it a reality I was eager to do our show together. Looking back, I see how precious our conversation was, as he would soon disappear from the public circuit. Even still today I get an occasional request on his location, so many people want to talk to him about the information he shared on my show.*

RECORDED JULY 29, 2010

**Hillary Raimo:** I want you to take a moment and close your eyes and imagine traveling in time. Imagine some process, or technology, that would let you go backward in time to witness the events that changed history or into the future to see if mankind survives and then to return to the present with the knowledge of what will happen tomorrow. The thought is intriguing, even mind boggling, but the science is more real than imagined. Explore the possibilities on the exciting new frontier of time control and time travel with the Anderson Institute, which is dedicated exclusively to advancing the study and development of time control capabilities. Joining me today is the founder of the Anderson Institute, Dr. David Lewis Anderson. He's going to be talking about what I just said and the reality of it and how it can change the world. Welcome, David.

**David Anderson:** Hello, Hillary. Thank you for the nice greeting. It's such a pleasure to be here on the Hillary Raimo Show.

**Hillary Raimo:** I'm glad to have you here. David, how did this journey begin?

**David Anderson:** My journey actually began by accident. I've been working now for more than 25 years in the field of studying the physical nature of time. It began actually a little more than 25 years ago when I entered the United States Air Force as a scientist working for Air Force Systems Command and also doing some projects with ARPA.

What I wanted to say, through the work I did in the Air Force, I accidentally discovered some relationships with regards to time and space that fascinated me. I actually left the Air Force and formed an

34

organization called the Time Technology Research Center and eventually, what has become today the Anderson Institute.

My background, just so people know a little bit about me, my focus is really in space time physics and special relativity. I do also focus on global community services, an ambassador for the United Nations Educational Scientific and Cultural Organization. My educational background is primarily in the area of science with degrees in engineering, physics, and philosophy from universities in West Virginia, California State, and Minnesota.

**Hillary Raimo:** What is the difference between time control and time travel?

**David Anderson:** There's two differences. First off, when you work as a physicist like I do and the colleagues we work with, many times people will chuckle at the words when you say, "Time travel," even though we've known for decades that time travel is possible within the laws of our math and physics. People tend to chuckle to discuss it without that unnecessary label but it also, when we look at what's happening around the world, which is absolutely remarkable right now, the first applications of this new technology will be for time control applications, not necessarily for sending people backwards and forwards in time.

For example, some of the first products that time control technology will be deployed for will be, for example, in medical fields, for the development and sale of stasis fields for medical applications, for chambers to accelerate test research for different types of research and development applications, perhaps for viewing and recording history, not as much as sending people backwards and forward in time. The first products that will hit the market are more time control devices versus time travel devices.

**Hillary Raimo:** You are working in the Air Force and they let you leave to pursue this work privately. The government is not necessarily involved in your work but do you feel that they're waiting for you to develop this technology to use it for themselves?

**David Anderson:** That's a complicated question. Actually, I wanted to pursue my work in the United States Air Force. I was working as a scientist at Edwards Air Force Base on the Air Force Flight Test Center. I had presented my findings to the Flight Test Center and Air Force Systems Command. At the time, it was outside of the scope of the mission. I actually decided to leave.

Two weeks prior to leaving, the Air Force finally realized what I was proposing. They declined my separation. I actually had to go to request a Congressional inquiry with Senator Rockefeller in West

Virginia to leave the Air Force because by that time, I had actually been already taking the first steps to set up the Time Technology Research Center. I would have liked to have done the work in the military. I'm very grateful because as a young person, they gave me great opportunities I never would have had anywhere else but I couldn't do it.

Today, our work includes work, partnerships with both private agencies and governments, not just in the United States but also in the Japan and South Korea, and hopefully very soon in the former Soviet Union and China.

**Hillary Raimo:**  Is the technology itself a Pandora's box? If you do create the technology that allows this to happen, can it be used for the wrong reasons?

**David Anderson:**  Yes. That's one of the greatest challenges. It's actually one of the reasons why we've stepped forward and many of our colleagues around the world working in this research every day are beginning to step forward. It's because, when you look at time control technology, we're really talking about a technology that can change our concept of reality in ways that are very difficult for people to even begin to comprehend. When we look at how the unprecedented acquisition of the capabilities in this technology, it really puts us in a critical position as a human society.

If you really look at the past, for example, with nuclear energy or any other technology, the higher the level of knowledge we as a human society have developed, the greater we were able to develop our sense of moral responsibility. If we look at human ethics, we've always seen that there's a clear principle that says, "The greater our knowledge and power, the greater the need for more responsibility as a foundation to guide how we use it." Until recently, even though many would say we've danced on the edge of the razor blade, that principle has been highly effective.

But the problem is now today being that our human capacity for moral reasoning why it has kept pace with these developments in the past is not keeping pace with the possible ramifications of time control technology. That's one of the reasons why we've stepped forward. The gap has grown too big. Too many agencies are now experimenting with time control technology, not the low-power variants that began back in the 1960s but the power and capabilities of technology have grown so much, they're being used without

understanding the possible ramifications of using them improperly and without the ability to predict what the results will be. Doing that without understanding the impact on human society, whether it be human society as a whole or one individual really is not a wise thing to do.

**Hillary Raimo:** Basically, if somebody gets a hold of this, there has to be a sense of transparency in order to keep the ethics involved on a higher level, don't you think?

**David Anderson:** Absolutely. As a matter of facts, one of our campaigns in redeveloping a strategy with several of our colleagues in India and Japan is the first step. Number one is exactly what you said, Hillary, is transparency and disclosure. We need to take this out of the arena of private funding and bury deep in these different government research initiatives, bring it into the public eye.

We, of course, have to educate because as we've been going through this for the last several decades, we've learned some remarkable things and actually many of the things we've learned have less to do with the technology but more about understanding what really is the true makeup of this universe we live in and the opportunity that that knowledge has to help us grow individually but after that education, we need then to determine as a human society how do we guide not just the use but the development. After that, of course, we have to monitor to make sure the technology is used prudently.

**Hillary Raimo:** When you talk about this topic what comes to my mind is Nikola Tesla's work, where he had the best intentions to come out with something that would provide free energy for people and people would be able to live better lives. The intention was good but what happened is exactly what you just described, where it went into private funding and government control and has not done the intended good. What are the dangers of this technology and how would you suggest that the world regulate it?

**David Anderson:** If I talk about the dangers, I'd also like to talk about the possible benefits. The dangers first, the first would be time line contamination. Actually, we have a motto on our website that talks about the Anderson Institute where history is becoming an experimental science. It's wrong. Actually, since the 1960s and especially since the 1990s all around the world, history has become an experimental science.

One of the challenges as we use it, one of the things we've learned that's remarkable is that when you alter events in time or you create fields where you accelerate time or slow down time or move information faster forward in time or backward in time, you not only affect that object, you actually affect the construct of reality. There's a risk without understanding that complex web of interdependencies is that using time control technology can actually redefine individual lives and consciousness.

Using it unwisely can also cause transcription errors is what we like to call them where unsafe technologies are used where body parts or even consciousness doesn't fit back together because it moved across a boundary layer in time or the technology was just unstable.

Believe it or not, the other thing, there are so many people that look at the good. I work with the people that I admire, that are becoming my personal heroes because when they look at this technology, not just in their word but in their hearts and minds, they see the opportunity. The opportunity for the application, the technology in medical fields to save lives. The opportunity to perhaps view and record history to learn from it, the potential to develop more quickly cures for diseases that cause great disaster and suffering on the Earth or maybe even retrieve future cures to alleviate that disaster and suffering.

But also, at the same time, we have the other interests and there are concerns. For example, and we can't fight it because this is the function of nations. They tend to want to keep technology as a strategic advantage. Many people who I meet talk more about weaponization of time control technology and even get into discussions about how to prepare for the Earth's first great time war, to use a very dramatic statement but essentially that's what people look at. How can they use it?

We even have in two countries, we have active programs where people want to run battlefield situations sending information from the future back to the past to understand the results or to tweak decisions made today, even if it's in a short time frame in the future, they feel having that feedback loop can actually help them better succeed in warfare, which is not the area where we really want to see the technology applied.

**Hillary Raimo:** I can feel my listeners thinking, "Well, this is all fascinating, but is it real?" because most think it's science fiction, something from a movie or a book, but what is the reality of this technology being applied now? Are we able to do this now? Have we been for a while? Are we tweaking things and theories and equipment that we've already been experimenting with?

**David Anderson:** Most of this remained theoretical until about the 1960s. Before that, we had the work of Einstein, a work of an obscure mathematician ... not obscure. Not in my world but he's very well known, Kurt Gödel, a German mathematician who proposed that you could time travel to the past at speeds slower than the speed of light.

In the 1960s is where it really began. In the 1960s, in Russia, they began using at the Moscow Aviation Institute, their advanced research institute at the time, they began sending information faster than the speed of light essentially backwards in time. Of course, they also did many experiments in antigravity remote viewing. They had a very different outlook on what was acceptable research and development there versus perhaps what we do today.

What's really happened is quite interesting, the US government has been involved in this since the 1970s to some degree. As a matter of fact, I would thank your listeners and they should thank themselves because, believe it or not, for the last three decades, they've been paying for this research.

To be very specific for your listeners who might be skeptical, you have to take a look at the projects that are funded. For example, take a look just at one location, Princeton University in Dr. Lishan Wang. He actually was given funding for a project that was called superluminal propagation of information. What does it really translate to? Sending information faster than the speed of light backwards in time.

These projects go on. These projects have been funded at all different kinds of levels. Some of it a little bit visible to the public. Some of it invisible. Sometimes, we just don't take the time to look.

But Hillary, what's really exciting now today is that this work is funded on a very wide scale. It's not just the Anderson Institute, NS4 and what's happening at Princeton University and Nile Tech and the University of Connecticut, all places where the government is funding activities today in time control research.

It's also Japan. Japan has taken the work at Princeton University and they've added two orders of magnitude of the ability to send information through time. In South Korea, actually, believe it or not, tomorrow we open up officially our new research facility just outside of Seoul. Korea enters the game.

In India, what a remarkable story, Hillary. Their effort is larger than the rest of the world's combined. It's absolutely amazing what's going on around the world. It's not just theory anymore. It's actual, practical application and use of time control technology techniques. They're all very different at these different locations but they're all very real.

**Hillary Raimo:** What is your personal vision for all of this technology, David? What do you hope to see happen with all of this?

**David Anderson:** In my heart, I see tremendous opportunity for human society. On one hand, I see the opportunity. This technology is, let's call it dangerous. There's a great potential for suffering to be created by this technology as equally as there's great opportunity for good.

What's different about this technology versus technologies like nuclear energy, for example, is that you may not be aware that the technology is being applied. There are those 2%, let's say, of the population that are sensitive to alterations in historical timelines but generally speaking as a population, we're barely aware of the work that's going on let alone the majority of us are not in tune to sensing these things.

What's very different, one of the great things we've learned through our experiments, not just at the Anderson Institute but these other locations are that when experiments are run, you actually change the construct of reality, even at outside of the range of the experiment, which is very difficult to sense or understand.

Our hope with the technology maybe perhaps is the tremendous good it can bring. Also, the possibility because of the tremendous risk that human society faces with the technology that it might give us the opportunity to unite and grow together and maybe help raise our collective efforts to work together as a human society and to stop using technologies without understanding the consequences of them.

Time control technology is just one but again, what's different about it is the use of the technology why it can be scientifically verified to effect reality in ways that you can't predict are very, very difficult for our limited human senses to perceive. That's a concern today. People ask about, "Well, how is this going to happen?" It already is happening. The power levels and capabilities of the technologies are growing quickly.

**Hillary Raimo:** Describe for us a typical experiment that you would run with this technology.

**David Anderson:** Okay. Typical situation. Let's talk about the Anderson Institute specifically. We have a system called a time warp field generator.

We're on our third generation. We've been active with these for about 18 years now. Essentially what we do is we can create in the laboratory, using a high energy laser array and a lot of other equipment and different types of fields, we can actually create a spherical field where within which, we can control the rate of time. We can accelerate it. We can slow it down. In some special situations, we actually can reverse the time rates.

Essentially, what we do is we can put objects, whether it be reference instrumentation or living organisms inside this field and accelerate or slow down the time. Some things that we've learned and this is work that we've been doing for the last 15 years, since about, let's say, 1993 or 1994.

We've learned some remarkable things. One of them is that this notion popularized in the media today about parallel universes is wrong. In India and at the Anderson Institute, we do not see the concept of parallel universes. What we see are multiple dimensions of one reality that we can't sense but we don't see parallel universes.

A good example would be what does it mean when you travel

through time? What is the impact if you move backwards in time and then forward again? I like to use the analogy with listeners. Imagine if you walked out your front door and say you had a flower bed in your front yard. If you were to start at one side of your flower bed, walk across the flower bed and walk back again, you would return right to that exact point in space. However, you've changed the construct of reality. You've actually trampled on some plants that will no longer bloom.

You've disrupted some seeds that will now spring into living organisms. You've changed reality and the construct of reality.

Believe it or not, I'm drawing very simple analogy but it's a very insightful one in what we're seeing in our experiment. We actually have the ability to, say, take a group of plant seedlings, put them inside the chamber, move them backwards in time and forwards again. When we move them backwards, we trigger an event that destroys the parent generation of those seedlings. Those seedlings come back with the same DNA footprint but the reference set of seedlings that was outside of that, those plant seedlings that are in the laboratory separately, the DNA construct of those seedlings changed. It's very, very fascinating. What it tells us is that the process of moving through time, no matter how small it is, you actually can change the construct of reality.

Okay. We have this very interesting experiment. A lot of people were very familiar with paradoxes when we talk about time control or time travel. One of the most popular is the grandfather paradox. What would happen if I traveled backwards in time and killed my grandfather? My father would no longer be born, so I wasn't born. Therefore, I could not travel back in time. Since I didn't travel back in time, my grandfather was born and now I am alive so I can go back.

These types of paradoxes, Hillary, really are places where our rational minds bump into their own limitations. What we actually see is when we do experiments, when we move an object backwards in time. If the parent generation or grandfather of that living organism is destroyed, say, in the case of a plant seedling and that living organism that was sent backwards in time does not cease to exist, it continues to live with the same consciousness and energy and genetic makeup, destroyed for example in an occasion base, a living plant organism. That's one of the things we've learned is that this concept of the grandfather paradox simply does not hold up in laboratory experiments.

**Hillary Raimo:** Very fascinating.

**David Anderson:** That's kind of you.

**Hillary Raimo:** You know what's fascinating to me David? is this concept of what you're discovering, the theories that are breaking down in your research such as the parallel universes and how those things aren't exactly what we thought. It gives me hope.

I'm going to ask you this question. I don't know exactly if this runs into the work that you do but what about a phenomenon like crop circles, or ET contact, those kinds of things. In this perspective of what you're doing, how do those things fit in? Could they be time travel instances and if so how does it relate to your technology?

**David Anderson:** The short answer is absolutely yes. How does it relate? At the Anderson Institute, we're a group of computer scientists, physicists, mathematicians, and games. We're not experts in these other areas but I'm pleased to offer an opinion. I would say that one of the first things that we do recognize, there's a lot of ways we do this in testing but one of the things we recognize and it's one of our favorite quotes that we use with college students is we remind them, we do not see our universe as it is. We see the universe as we are. We have to understand how we see it first before we can really answer that question. We are functions of our biological and cultural evolution. That blinds up to truly understanding and seeing the universe. Actually, with our senses and our human mind the way it operates, we only see a very microscopic part of this beautiful macroscopic universe. While we don't believe in parallel universes, we do clearly see that there are dimensions, many, many dimensions and parallel realities, if you will, that we cannot sense.

For your listeners to make it simple, let's move back 15 years and put the old television set on front of the table in front of us. That old television set, what it would do, before the days of cable TV and the internet, there would be information and energy waves flying through the air. If I wanted to tune into a channel, I'd reach up and I'd grab the tuner. I'd move it to a channel. As I did that, that television set and tuner would tap into that information and energy flying through the air. It would make me able to view and understand it. That's what our human minds are. Our human minds are like a television tuner. We see clearly out of our experiments that the universe truly is a dynamic web of information and energy. Absolutely yes, everything is interconnected. The challenge is that our senses our limited. Our senses number one, sense only a very, very small part of that macroscopic universe.

The other thing that's very difficult is the human mind. This is the greatest challenge when we work with college students is to teach them that they have to overcome their limitations. The human mind's function, if you ask a scientist in that field, is to rationalize with body sense is perceive with its own belief system. By nature, the function of the human mind is limited. To grow and to become a good scientist in this field, we have to be able to recognize that limitation. Once you do, you begin to grow from there, but those are two the biggest things we've learned from our work.

**Hillary Raimo:** Thank you. Now, about what you said before, that other countries are experimenting with the use of sending information through this time control capabilities, what exactly does that mean and how do they do that?

**David Anderson:** It really is a great question. For your listeners, I'll use an example. There's this phenomenon and I'll explain it a little more basically. It's called quantum tunneling. Essentially, what it is in physics, it's called an evanescent wave coupling effect. It occurs in quantum mechanics. Essentially, when you use the correct wave length to carry information and you use the right type of medium or material to pass it through, it actually is possible to pass parts of signals faster than light, essentially backwards in time.

This is very real, by the way. This first was done in the Soviet Union back in the 1960s. In the 1990s, actually, the NEC funded under US government funded, again, thank you tax payers who are listening to this show, an experiment where Princeton University actually set up a 10-centimeter cesium chamber, a chamber filled with cesium. They injected a signal into one side of the chamber. As the information entered and passed through the chamber, what was fascinating is the information actually finished leaving the chamber before it finished entering. That's an effect that occurs from a phenomenon called quantum entanglement or quantum tunneling. This actually is another proof that in many ways, we are connected even when objects or people or consciousness are separated in distance even that require greater than the speed of light communication.

Ostensibly, what that allows to do at that time was to pass information faster than the light backwards in time. What Japan has been doing at a facility north of Kyoto city is really expanding the capability. There's a lot of value in that if you think about it. The ability to send information from the future to the past. Imagine if you had a radio receiver that could tune one minute into the future or maybe not so impressive but what if you could tune 10 minutes into the future or 10 days into the future? How could you use that type of technology for good or how could you use that type of technology for selfish gain?

**Hillary Raimo:** What's the difference between doing this with technology and using our own psychic abilities to do this in the sense of remote viewing or tapping into our intuition? Can we achieve the same thing?

**David Anderson:** We get into an area of opinion because unlike you, Hillary, I'm not an expert in this area but I will share you an opinion. We truly believe that first off, when we see a convergence happening, we truly believe that while many people sit and they talk about metaphysical abilities to control time, views of time and religion or art or spirituality, talk about different technologies and different applications of technologies, of different philosophical views of time. They all seem that they have their own different little islands or camps.

What we truly believe, number one, is that as the true nature of time and our place in it begins to unfold more quickly, number one, what we're going to see is that all those islands and groups are looking at the same reality, just from a different perspective. We believe it's all one and the same, that the true nature of time manifests itself in many different ways. There's many ways to looking at it. For your listeners, what I encourage them is please don't judge. If you want to truly understand and become a student of the nature of time, you have to study from every perspective, from the aspect of culture and technology and philosophy and religion and art.

**Hillary Raimo:** It feels to me like this is an actual evolution of our abilities to be able to understand and navigate these things, not only from a scientific perspective but also from a spiritual perspective. You have a lot of people in this world right now who are very divided because of religious beliefs. Not only that but political differences, racial differences and all the things we're still struggling with as a culture globally. What are the implications and ramifications of the spiritual side of this, positive and negative?

**David Anderson:** Positive and negative. Let's talk about one negative that many people might sense or see but it's a negative that's discussed by many government agencies as they talk about disclosure plans or processes for the technology. One of the biggest is social unrest, believe it or not. One of the concerns is that many of these religious beliefs today are based upon very, very critical events in history.

Believe it or not, India in the state of Maharashtra, their facility there is actually completing their development of a systems of drones, that they actually want to send drones back in time to study and record history. What happens if they record key moments in the history of certain religions and they're proved to be false or they're proved to be true? There's the social unrest and the ramifications from that that could be quite profound. But at the same time, let's talk about the spiritual implications from a positive standpoint. One of the things we're seeing, one of the reasons not only do we have differences across religions, we have differences in our daily lives here. Let's just talk about this country here. We have people who've become very engrained, where science has become their religion. Only if they can touch it, see it or stand on the TV, they don't believe it's true. They've basically shrunk all the magic in the world to the size of their daily routine of material possessions.

What's really happening is fascinating to me. Science now today, what's coming out of the laboratories, not just in time control technology facilities around the world but in the particle accelerators and supercolliders has more in common with the ancient beliefs of Buddhism, Hinduism, and Taoism than it does with the classical science that we all studied in school. What's amazing, for the first time, the spiritual implication to me is we see science, religion, and spirituality converging where basically, they're coming to that single point where science is now demonstrating that those crazy ideas that the world is a dynamic web of energy and that we're all connected. They're proving it's true. It's becoming now together to a single answer in truth about our reality and place in this universe that both scientists and spiritualists can understand on common ground.

I do believe it has an opportunity to unite. At the same time, to reach that point, we have to be able to forget about these artificial lines we create across the borders of nations, across geography and religious beliefs and start working together as a single human society as we look for that. That's a very difficult path for the people of this planet to walk.

**Hillary Raimo:** Yes. I agree. I see that it's a beautiful thing. I also believe there is a moment in time when the scientific and spiritual aspects were divided intentionally so that we wouldn't get to that point necessarily. Maybe we could send a drone back and find that? Is truth being revealed by disproving the existence of "God"?

But I want to bring it back to a practical level, David. For a typical person, an average person just going about their day, headed to work, driving through the highway, could this happen to somebody in an instant? From what I've been listening to, the picture I get in my mind is when we have synchronistic moments or when we have déjà vu experiences, are these examples of maybe our time reality around us being affected? Have we been changed by way of these events?

**David Anderson:** I think in many cases; our belief is that that a lot of these phenomenon … First off, yes, we do believe that there are special situations, though very rare, where the naturally-occurring energy that allows us to create these fields could actually occur not in a man-made fashion but in a natural fashion. We do believe it could naturally occur. When you talk about these other phenomenon and awareness's, do we believe that it's possible people have viewed time travelers from the distant future? Yes.

Also, a lot of these other phenomenon like déjà vu and others, we have to remember the discussion about our senses. Our senses are flawed. We're walking around blind for the most part, sensing a very,

very small fragment of a much greater universe with many, many other dimensions of reality within this single universe. Many of these moments are places perhaps where we grow. As a matter of fact, I met with a spiritual leader, must have been about two months ago. We had a discussion about a déjà vu. He said it's considered to be in their beliefs to be considered a great gift. It's a step in growth when you have those moments because essentially, it allows your mind to tune into other dimensions.

We do believe that many of these phenomena and I hate to say it this way because I don't like the words, will be described and shown to be very, very rational and proven using the scientific method. Why it may take several years, it will come and we're seeing some of those proofs already today.

**Hillary Raimo:** For the average seeker, looking into all of these things with the age of information that we're in, what would be the intention of sending information back? You explained about the learning aspect, but what about an event like 9/11, something drastic that changed reality for people on a worldwide level. Is it possible that using this technology, we could go back in time to avoid that kind of situation or change it?

**David Anderson:** Absolutely, yes. With the one provision, which brings up the risk is that when you change an event, many people are familiar with the term ripple effect or butterfly effect, a phenomenon that when a butterfly beats its wings on one side of the planet, it creates a change reaction event that turns into a hurricane on the other side of the world, causing great disaster and suffering.

This is our concern. We see tremendous opportunity. For example, how about the opportunity to send information, to retrieve information to the future to bring back here for diseases like diabetes, AIDS, and cancer? It could avoid so much disaster and suffering. To retrieve information to avoid man-made disasters like 9/11 or naturally-occurring disasters that cause great human suffering. We can do that.

At the same time, the challenge becomes every single time a time control technology's activated, not just at the Anderson Institute but at these other facilities, the construct of reality is affected. Why we like to think and our colleagues like to think that they're doing it in controlled manners? Every action they take can cause dramatic ripple effects or butterfly effects.

People talk about sending drones in the past to record history or into the future to do the same. What about the possibility of bringing back harmful microbes or viruses, either introducing them to the past or future or bringing them back from the past or the future? Potential risk for extinction of the human race. It comes back to the basic principle that while an action may seem good, we need to understand the results. That is a very complex web of interdependencies that have to be considered that's probably beyond our capacity for thinking and reasoning today, which brings up the danger in the use of the technology.

**Hillary Raimo:** Yes.

**David Anderson:** This is why as a human society, we need to decide this as a whole. Where do we take risks and what types of risks are acceptable?

**Hillary Raimo:** That's a big step, David. I have to say, I'm a little skeptical of trusting this kind of technology in today's governments hands because we've seen what they've done with different technologies. They have definitely steered it away towards a more military purpose versus raising the consciousness and helping humanity. There's a whole lot of suffering on this planet. There's a lot of technologies out there that can help that aren't released and aren't disclosed and aren't transparent.

The money we pay as taxpayers that we think is funding certain projects are going off to black budget projects that are funding research and things like this that we don't know is happening. The average person out there isn't aware that this is happening. The reality of what's happening in the world and the research and the levels of things we're actually creating, we just don't have a clue.

**David Anderson:** This is important. It's not just of the money hidden on the black projects. Of course, that happens. You know that happens. That's a fact of life but it's also happening in a public eye and that's one of the reasons why they're stepping forward. I agree with you.

**Hillary Raimo:** You're breaking up there. I'm sorry. David, we didn't catch that last part. You broke up on me. I'd like you to repeat that, please.

**David Anderson:** Sure. We do see that people don't recognize this. It's not just the black projects that are being funded. There are projects that are being funded closer to the public eye but this is really the challenge. As individuals, this is a technology that we may not see the effect of. We talked about the fact that using the technology can change the makeup of reality and that we don't understand the impact on individuals, the human race, or the entire planet. Like you said, there are many benefits but who's going to judge what is really useful? This complex web of interdependence is beyond our capacity to predict the impact today. We don't know every time we use the technology; will it affect human evolution? When we manipulate history, are we going to force a very natural and a quick rate of change that causes harm and suffering or good?

We can't turn our back on this now, Hillary. So many people ask us, why don't you just stop? Because it's not just the Anderson Institute. We simply now have to take on this challenge, the one that you raised. It's easy to drive transparency and disclosure. Okay. It's not easy. It's hard work. We have to educate people and make people aware and, Hillary, to work with others like your show we have to make people want to be aware of what's going on.

**Hillary Raimo:** David, let me interrupt for a moment. Who is going to be in charge of this technology? Is it going to be you and your company or is it going to be all these other places out around the world? Who calls the shots?

We're fighting over the technology in the Gulf of Mexico to stop an oil spill. One oil spill on the planet. Nobody can get their act together and everybody's keeping quiet. There's so much secrecy and there's so much disinformation, it's like a giant PR campaign. What makes this kind of very incredibly powerful technology that much more able to be managed with ethics?

**David Anderson:** This is the greatest challenge. Who controls the technology, which I almost don't even like the statement or the question but it's one that has to be answered is what do we do with this new knowledge? We have the ability to look in the future to change the past. What do we do with this? How do we handle it? Who should be given access to it? These are just a few of the questions that needed to be asked. We need very serious answers because people's life choices, and indeed, maybe even their self-identity in human existence can be significantly affected.

Who should be afforded access to this technology and knowledge? One of the challenges is in transparency and disclosure, of course, are governments and nations. Just like a human mind, the nation has a function. It's number one to survive and number two to prosper. I might not like that but that's reality of the present situation in society today. One of the fundamental tenants of strategy, whether you talk about military warfare strategy or business strategy or government strategy is you keep your technology a secret.

We got to get it out in the open but what do we do? This is the challenge is we can get transparency and disclosure. We can drive an education with it. We can even later monitor the technology but what we need now is to form a global moral compass is what we like to call it, one that'll be used to guide not just the future use of the technology but the future development. It has to stand line of religion, of politics, of nations and governments and private enterprise. It really, truly has to be guided by human society as a whole and human consciousness as a whole. That's something we've never been able to accomplish in the history of human society on planet. I agree it's a very difficult challenge. At the same time, why we might have to go through some pain to get there, it's something we have to do.

By the way, it's not just about time control technology. We experiment as a human race with technologies all around the world that could force a very unnatural rate of change on human society with profound negative, catastrophic impacts. We have to stop as a human society using technologies without first understanding what the consequences of are using them, number one and number two …

**Hillary Raimo:** David, an average person like myself wouldn't have access to this technology unless of course, I was studying with you in your Institute or making an active effort to get into the field but what's the practical use to an everyday, ordinary person?

**David Anderson:** First off, I think driving the awareness is key. By the way, that's the whole point of the Hillary Raimo Show. You're driving awareness and understanding of these issues. When you ask me, "How are we going to solve this problem," I'm simply going to defer to you, Hillary. I'm going to go out and take a nice long walk in the desert. But no, awareness is such a key.

What does it mean to individuals? If, as a human society as a whole, we can learn as an individual, what's the benefit number one? As an individual, we can learn. Most people don't even understand how much they don't know about time. Just a quick exercise for your listeners, I know we're running out of time but one of my favorite philosophers about time is St. Augustine. He talked about time being an illusionary product to your mind. You talk about your listeners early, Hillary, walking to work or driving to work.

I will challenge them. When they're walking down the street, do St. Augustine's experiment. Walk up to somebody, your friend or a stranger and ask them if they know what time is. They're going to say, "Yes." Then, ask them to explain it. A simple little experiment. Simply ask them to explain time to you. You'll see them babble with a total loss for words. This is something that dominates our culture.

By the way, it's not just one answer within culture. We have cultures on this planet that believe all time exists, past, present, and future at the same point. We have time cultures even here in the United States like with the Navajo Indians where, in their culture, they have no reference in their language to the past and the future. They don't talk about an event happening in time. They only talk about the quality of that event, not it's temporal quality.

Cultures have evolved. Just because we in the United States are saying that time is linear, we've scoffed a people who say, "Past and present and future don't exist. They're all here at once," or that, "Time is a circle." Many people in Asia laugh at our concepts that time is believed to be linear.

Even within our culture and I'm sharing this because I want your listeners to really challenge themselves, first to understand how remarkable our lack of understanding of the true nature of time is and our place in it. That's the first to becoming interested to want to learn. We'll do our best at the Anderson Institute to make information available for free to people to study and learn.

That's the first thing they need to do. How it'll benefit them. I think only the future will tell or maybe the past.

**Hillary Raimo:** Thank you David. David's website is andersoninstitute.com. He gives a lot of information there. David, I see two very distinct paths developing out of this. I hope that we take a higher road because there are so many different possibilities for where this could go. I think it's important for people to understand the risks and I hope my listener's talk about how awareness really is the key.

David, I want to commend you in your research and your work. Did you expect to get into all this at this level when you started to work into this field? Did you think it was going to go global and that you would have so many different operations in different countries?

**David Anderson:** Actually, I would say, "No." When I started as a scientist with Air Force Systems Command, I did not even have a desire to get into this field. I actually stumbled into it by accident through the course of other projects that I was assigned to. I'm very happy to walk this path. It means a lot to me. I've grown a lot personally and the people around who experience the work that's being done. This is why I really appreciate your words around encouraging your listeners to learn and study.

One of the greatest benefits for everybody, I didn't answer the question well, is that when you study this and you really learn what is coming out of this, it really opens the door for so much personal growth and awaking on a spiritual level or even a scientific level. It's a great opportunity.

It's been a great course. It's been difficult. You can imagine and I have to tell your listeners, you can't ever underestimate the power and the influence that private enterprise and government interests wants to exercise on technologies like this. Their aspirations are very high. They want to control it for specific goals, some of them very noble. Some of them we might say are maybe not optimum for human society as a whole, to say that very kindly.

**Hillary Raimo:** That is putting it lightly David.

**David Anderson:** Yeah. I could use other words, Hillary.

**Hillary Raimo:** I could, too.

**David Anderson:** But, you know what? Actually, maybe we talk about that just for a second because it be very easy to put labels of good and evil or good and bad on some of the different positions but if we really accept the ancient wisdom and what many spiritual practitioners believe today and now what science is proving today that we're all connected. We're all one part of the great whole. There's not one thing that anybody can do that doesn't affect another component of reality. When we think of that, both good and evil become part of all logic as a whole.

Many times, human society if you look at history and it's tragic. Human society has used labels of good and evil to justify doing very bad things. It's good to avoid it. At the same time, we really try not to support and try to convince people who see using the technology for deeper personal or commercial profit or for weaponization not to do that.

**Hillary Raimo:** See now, my first gut instinct would be that the military would be so wonderfully supportive of this kind of research because they want to understand how it can be used as a weapon because that is the paradigm and mindset for that kind of organization. It's almost like you would need a very wonderfully evolved wisdom-filled kind of council of people who have a higher level of integrity when it comes to these kinds of things to be in control of this. I don't know if I really believe that the military's capable of taking over some kind of technology like this and using it for its highest good.

I think the highest good that this stuff has is extraordinary, profound, and it has a lot of potential to wake things up. Again, I go back to my original statement at the beginning of this show with Nikola Tesla's intention in working with these wonderful things. I'd hate to look into the future, David, 200 years down the road and say, "David Lewis Anderson was another Nikola Tesla. He had these incredibly high hopes and did these amazing things." Then, all of a sudden it goes underground. People have to fight for your information to come out so that the higher level, the higher integrity of your research is able to do that. Have you been able to see into the future to see if that's going to happen for you?

**David Anderson:** I tell you. Our solution right now is we actually have a concept that we're putting together with scientists in three other countries for the proposal for an international world time council. That's a good question. Who leads on that council? I think maybe we should tap into the global network you have on the Hillary Raimo radio show here.

You have some very interesting spiritual leaders I know who follow your work but it's a tough question and I am concerned.

Have we looked into the future to see the outcome? Remember the future is not certain. Every thought, every focus we have. Not just every thought and not just every action, every thought and every focus we have actually becomes our reality and effects reality. People do have the potential to do this. I know history says that as a human society, we've had to go through a lot of pain to reach new levels of growth and society and new levels of good, safe for human consciousness but we tend to do that. I just hope that the suffering we go through to overcome this and manage these risks are not as severe as some that we've faced in the past.

**Hillary Raimo:** We are definitely going through a wonderful death dance of an old world that no longer serves us. The one thing I feel compelled to say to you, David, in the last moments of this show is to make sure that the indigenous elders from different cultures are included on that council because they have always maintained a level of very high integrity with the knowledge that they've carried. I think they would make a very wonderful addition to that council that oversees that. It may very well be the next step in our evolution that we're supposed to be but tread carefully is the warning I get.

**David Anderson:** Hillary, your comment about committee of spiritual elders, perhaps you're describing what the future new world government should be. If you think about and I don't know as many as you do. I'm lucky. I'm fortunate. I've met with some spiritual leaders and we've discussed these issues but one thing for certain. If spiritual leaders were leading the world government, many of the problems and many of the suffering and the pain that human society feels today would go away. We would see tremendous growth on personal and also on a global consciousness basis.

**Hillary Raimo:** From your lips to the ears of whatever's listening. Thanks so much for joining me, David. We're out of time. I have to say, once again, andersoninstitute.com for those interested in learning more about it. David, thanks so much for spending the last hour with me, conversating about these fabulous and wonderful topics. It's been a pleasure.

**David Anderson:** It was an absolute pleasure, Hillary. Thank you so much.

# 3

# DR. JUDY WOOD PART 1
# EVIDENCE OF AN UNKNOWN PHYSICS
# AT THE 9/11 SITE

*It is my opinion that 9/11/01 irrevocably changed our global world. It allowed for the infiltration of the key components that began the building of our current digital age. That's why the work of Dr. Judy Wood is so vital. Her area of expertise involves interferometry in forensic science. In the time since 9/11/01, she has applied her expertise in materials science, image analysis and interferometry, to a forensic study of over 40,000 images, hundreds of video clips, a large volume of witness testimony, analyses of dust samples, seismic data, and the analysis of other environmental evidence pertaining to the destruction of the World Trade Center complex.*

*Was 9/11 the result of militarized free energy technology?*

RECORDED DECEMBER 16, 2010

**Hillary Raimo:** 9/11 was an incredible event for everybody on this planet. It changed our way of life and has cost lives not only on the day of, but afterward around the world since. We have lost a lot of freedoms in wake of the event. What really happened? Tonight, we explore the theories of Dr. Judy Wood.

We are in no way doing this show tonight to be disrespectful to the people who lost their lives on 9/11, or those families who are living without their loved ones. We are compassionate to the realities of how emotional this show will be for many people.

In this episode Dr. Wood will be talking about the weaponization of free energy technology, she will explain to us what nonlethal weapons are and how 9/11 may have been an example of this technology. Dr. Wood will be presenting some pretty fascinating material, in my opinion. She is well educated and her credentials are impressive. Dr. Judy Wood holds a bachelor's degree in civil engineering and structural engineering, a master's in engineering mechanics and applied physics. She has a Ph.D. in materials engineering science from the Department of Engineering Science and Mechanics at Virginia Polytech Institute and the State University in Blacksburg, Virginia. Her dissertation involved the development of an experimental method to measure thermal stresses and bimaterial joints, and she has taught courses including experimental stress analysis, engineering mechanics, mechanics of material.

After this episode you may change your mind about 9/11, and perhaps rethink other events in this world. Her website is drjudywood.com and it offers a tremendous amount of valuable, intense and inclusive material that I think you would all find very interesting. So welcome, Dr. Wood. Thank you for joining me.

**Dr. Judy Wood:** Well, thank you so much for having me. What you said, that 9/11 was an extraordinary and incredible event, yes. Yes, it was.

**Hillary Raimo:** Please discuss for us the basics of what your theory is about and explain to us the technology. Let's just go right into it.

**Dr. Judy Wood:** Well, it isn't what I think, and actually, I'd like to read a small portion from my book that addresses this very issue. I'd like to ... For the record, I do not believe that our government is responsible for executing the events of 9/11, nor do I believe that our government is not responsible for executing the events of 9/11. It's not a case of belief. This was a crime that should be solved by a forensic study of the evidence. Before it can be determined who did it, it must first be determined what was done, and how it was done. You can't convict someone legally based on belief. If you want to charge them with murder using a gun, you'd better make sure the body has a bullet hole in it. Yet, before noon on 9/11, we were told who did it, and how they did it, why they did it, because they hate us for our freedoms, before any investigations had been conducted as to what had been done.

I also feel that if anyone declared who did it, or how they did it before they determined what happened, it's merely speculation or propaganda. The popular chant, 9/11 was an inside job, is scientifically speaking no different from the chant that 19 bad guys with box cutters did it. Neither one is the results of a scientific investigation supported by evidence that would be admissible in court. We need to determine first what happened.

**Hillary Raimo:** Okay, so in your opinion, what did happen?

**Dr. Judy Wood:** Well, often, we're led to look at false choices because that distracts us from looking at the evidence. But if you listen to the evidence carefully enough, it'll tell you exactly what happened. The trick though is to not get distracted away from looking at the evidence.

If you look at it that day, and one of my first reactions was where did the buildings go? This is nothing I trust. And before noon, there was a lot of coverup stories, like it all shipped to China, but it couldn't have been shipped to China before noon on that day. And I've got a picture,

54

you can tell what day it is because building seven is still standing, and you should have a 110-story building between you and building seven. It's just flat ground, essentially, and there's an ambulance parked in front of tower one. It's still parked there, there's just no more tower one.

It's rather incredible to think of two 500,000-ton buildings just going away. That morning, there were two buildings there, and then they went away. How they went away is a big mystery. If you think about how much material that was and what happened, it is indeed an extraordinary event. Yes, it was used for something really ugly. It was used for destructive purposes, but it shows us a technology that exists that maybe we can use for other purposes.

So, as we look around, let's see what this technology can do. So, we have an absence of debris, a very gross absence of debris, and we have what I call dustification. I established a new vocabulary to describe new phenomena. If you wanted to be scientific, you don't know the mechanism or the phenomena you want to describe, you can't use a description that applies to a known phenomenon to describe an unknown phenomenon, so what I do is use placeholders to describe that characteristic. Instead of using numbers, 279-5A, I'd call it fuzzballs, dustification, toasted cars. And what I mean by toasted cars, it isn't to apply the cause. They're toast, they're history. It means they're not repairable, something happened to 'em, they're just gone or messed up.

So, we have all these different types of categories. Round holes in windows in the outer pane from the double-paned window and the inner pane is still intact. A glass cutter can do that, and flipped cars, evidence of levitation. Some of the toasted cars are half a mile away.

There is so much dust. When you watch the materials that's coming through the air, and I call those prefab units that made up the outer part of the building, Wheat Chex because they look like Wheat Chex. Actually, a photographer first called them that. And you see one of these Wheat Chex flying through the air in the videos, and as it comes down, it's melting like ice cream. It just goes away before it hits the ground, and you see all these Wheat Chex coming down towards this particular intersection. Right afterwards, there's a picture of the intersection, people coming out of their hiding places. There's this paper dust. A few pieces of aluminum but just paper and dust.

**Hillary Raimo:** I had a chance to stand on the site a few weeks after 9/11 happened with a hard hat and all along side the fire department, literally standing on leftover pieces of building, and looking straight down through holes in the ground. I saw papers, memos littered around the interior of the building debris perfectly in tact. A gold wedding ring embedded into a steal beam perfectly in tact like it had been pushed into putty. It was an extraordinary experience. But what I found most interesting was how quickly that debris was taken offsite. Where did it all go, and why do you think they took it away so fast?

**Dr. Judy Wood:** One of the easiest traps to fall into is making an assumption at stage one as to what happened, because then when you go to stage two, if your first step is wrong, and the assumption is wrong, everything after that is going to be wrong, and it's really hard, really hard to observe without a bias. We've heard so many things, it's hard to tune them out.

**Hillary Raimo:** Very true.

**Dr. Judy Wood:** But let's look at what happened, the buildings were turning to powder in midair. How much could they have hauled away if ... I'm not saying all of the building turned to powder, but if 90% of the building turned to powder, is there anything to pick up and take out of there?

**Hillary Raimo:** When I stood there, I observed the other buildings surrounding where the towers once stood were very much intact with the exception of a few. Such destruction should've caused more surrounding damage. How did building 7 get damaged from two planes hitting the twin towers? Everyone just drops that fact as dismissive and irrelevant. Why would the buildings turn to dust? Let's get to the heart of it.

**Dr. Judy Wood:** Look at the data, the evidence leads away. Before I began this, I'd never thought of energy weapons. It just never crossed my mind, even though my area of expertise is in interferometry, but I never thought of directed energy weapons or any kind of military uses of weapons that involves energy, directed energy as opposed to kinetic energy. Kinetic energy is like if you launch a bullet, or a cannonball, or a bomb, something physically that it moves and destroys things.

But if you just keep looking at the data until you really feel that it's speaking to you, one of the things I noticed about is this, is about 15 minutes after the north tower goes poof ... I don't say collapse. It went poof, and there's no indication it went down, is this intersection, which people are standing, and there's a slight breeze that day, like eight or nine mile-per-hour breeze, and so the air kind of cleared out pretty quickly after the tower went away.

And so, you see this blue sky, off in the west, and then you notice around these people's feet, dusty fuzz rising up. I call those fuzzballs, around the feet. Maybe they're kicking it. And then, pretty soon, at the 20-minute mark, you see that the dust is rising up, all by itself. What does that tell us?

It tells us that coarse dust landed and then became fine. That fine dust could not have settled out of the air, why would it be going back up again? And the air is clear. So, if you have coarse dust land that keeps breaking down, finer and finer, that's an interesting process, and it broke down.

**Hillary Raimo:** Thank you. For most people, they wouldn't know, or notice, the dust even means anything. I just want to remind people that they can go to Dr. Wood's website at drjudywood.com, and you can see the videos for yourself. You can see the pictures that we're discussing. It does help to see the visuals along with listening to what she's saying, so I do highly encourage people to take a moment as they're listening online to go to the website now to take a look at what we're discussing and follow along.

Judy, when I saw these pictures of what you're describing ... I mean I listened to one of your lectures on YouTube first, and I couldn't get what you were describing completely until I actually saw the pictures. So, I wanted to interject here just for a moment to let people know that it is helpful to look at the images on your website as we discuss this.

**Dr. Judy Wood:** Yeah, very good. Excellent. So, if you go to drjudywood.com, that's the homepage. You'll see a yellow block, which says Cliff Notes, or you can just type in drjudywood.com/wtc, and that's sort of one-stop shopping. You've got a whole lot of different categories, and some little guys waving that you show where the link is in each section that takes you to the index, so you can always get back to the index.

And if you go to Section H, "Fuzzballs," Figure 62 shows just north of the WTC, just about a block north of the tower one, blue sky in the background. But if you start looking carefully, you see the fuzzballs around their feet, and the pictures just below that show these fuzzballs, the horrendously thick dust that could not have settled out of the air in 15 minutes.

**Hillary Raimo:** We have a question that's been submitted by a listener, Abraham, can you please ask Dr. Wood why she thinks so many people have a problem accepting the fact that steel and marble were transformed to fine dust on 9/11, when even the mainstream media, ABC News, has admitted to this fact. He then references a YouTube video.

He would also like to know when did you first learn of the University of Alaska magnetometer readings? He is referring to the iron-rich micro spheres in Hurricane Erin. We will be getting into that more later on in the hour. Thank you for your questions, Abraham. We appreciate them. Dr. Wood will address the hurricane and the weather disturbances associated with what she has found in her research and theories. For now, Dr. Wood why do you think people have had such a hard time accepting the fact that these buildings turned to dust?

**Dr. Judy Wood:** A couple of reasons. One, it takes time to think about it themselves, so they'll just grab onto what they're fed. The other thing is it's too scary. What happens if Dr. Wood is right? Ooh, you know? The implications, they get afraid, and that's why I would like to remind folks that it has good things with it too. And if you look at it that way, it's worth studying it.

But the dust is one of the most important aspects of this, the dust breaking down finer and finer. And then, studies show that the dust was so fine, it was approaching the scale of DNA. It was much finer than red blood cells, like a hundredth of the size of a red blood cell, so that was just being inhaled directly into people's bloodstreams, making people very sick. This is not like anything we've seen before.

**Hillary Raimo:** So, are we looking at what is called free energy technology? Are we looking at examples of technology that's obviously not mainstream being weaponized?

**Dr. Judy Wood:** Yes, very much. There's no way around that. You see an entire building, a 500,000-ton building in mid-flight turn into powder that's microscopic. We're not talking about a few pieces of microscopic dust. We're talking about it's not hitting anything. If you have a bomb in the building, it bombs buildings into chunks. The chunks go flying. They stay chunks until they hit something. So, you see the chunks launched into flight, they stay in chunks, but this turned into powder as it traveled.

**Hillary Raimo:** So, as it moved away from the building, it became dust-like particles, is that what you're saying? To somebody like myself, who doesn't have a degree in physics or doesn't understand the mechanics of what you're describing, is that basically the picture that we're getting? That as the material flew away from the building, it became finer dust particles?

**Dr. Judy Wood:** Right. Think of a computer keyboard, like that's flying through space, it breaks in half. Then, each of those halves break in half, and each of those quarters breaks in half. It'll keep breaking it in two, finer and finer, and just keep on going down until you have nano-sized particles. The material is just dissociating, coming apart.

**Hillary Raimo:** Do you believe this building would have fallen in the way that it fell structurally if hit by a plane?

**Dr. Judy Wood:** If a plane hit the building, see, I'm not even making that assumption. Yeah, I'd say there's a hole in it, but who knows how ... We're just going by it, one thing at a time. But if a plane had hit it, planes don't take down buildings.

The building is also built like a tube within a tube, kind of like a tree. Trees have lots of rings around them. I've caught a lot of grief for saying this, but I still think it's appropriate, talking about the Keebler Elves. They drilled a hole in the tree for the cookie oven and whatnot. You know, squirrels drill holes in trees, other things, and the tree doesn't fall over.

**Hillary Raimo:** So structurally, it's not possible.

**Dr. Judy Wood:** Correct, no. And here's something that I think everyone can understand is they saw that the buildings remained standing. That shows that whatever happened to it, it didn't cause them to fall down, and it wasn't a high-wind day. Those buildings were built to handle up to category five hurricanes. They're built to sway in the breeze. And think of a sponge, when it curls over, the inner side of the curve is in compression, and the outer side of the curve is in tension. So, these buildings being built to bend over meant that they were designed to take many times the compressive load if that's on the downwind side. In other words, they're built to withstand ... I'm just going to guess, 20 times normal load, and it wasn't windy, so those things were standing straight, so that's already showing that they're over-designed.

And also, buildings are designed with an importance factor, not just a safety factor. Safety factors take care of any statistical deviation from what the properties are, and then some. But the importance factor is a multiplier on that, it's how important it is for that building to stay standing if something happened. And if that building went, it would take out a lot of Manhattan. So, you can bet that had a very high importance factor, that whatever circumstance, that building better remain standing, so it was well over-designed. Like if it was built out in the middle of an Iowa cornfield, if it went down, it'd just hurt the corn. If it was empty, you know, no people in it. It would just hurt the corn, so it would have a lower importance factor.

**Hillary Raimo:** For those of you who may be just joining us, my guest tonight is Dr. Judy Wood. We're discussing an alternative theory on 9/11, and what she believes is the use of free energy technology that has been weaponized. She is here with us tonight to describe the evidence to support that.

So far, we've been discussing the midair pulverization of the buildings and how they were turned to dust before they hit the ground. Again, I would like to refer you back to her website, drjudywood.com, to see the pictures for yourselves, to watch the footage, and make up your own mind and what you think.

I have to say, Judy, there are a lot of connected dots in your work. I really appreciate what you're putting out there as far as what you're talking about. Thank you. What about the underground mall that survived? Now, how would that be explained with what you're discussing.

**Dr. Judy Wood:** Well actually, it's even more dramatic. I have an upcoming book, it's soon to be out, like as we speak. And in there, there's much clearer descriptions and very detailed descriptions of things, but that a picture of the mall and the floor right above it, and right below it. Right above it, you have a missing building. It's gone. You can take a broom and sweep it up almost. And the floor below that is a little bit caved in here and there, but people were walking straight up. You can read the names of the store signs. You know where you are in the mall. And the floor below that, the loading docks don't look like anything happened. It's completely intact.

**Hillary Raimo:** Now, on your website, you give out these facts and you say that the upper 80% approximately of each tower was turned into fine dust and did not crash to the earth, and that the upper 90% approximately of the inside of World Trade Center 7 was turned into fine dust and did not crash to the earth.

It is common sense that the top isn't supposed to be turning into dust before it hits the bottom, yes? Usually, the heavier stuff is coming down and crushing the things underneath it. Is this evidence to support that this was free energy technology?

**Dr. Judy Wood:** Well, the evidence goes on and on, it's kind of overwhelming actually. But one of the biggest aha moments, I call it, that Cliff Notes page started out being a listing of my aha moments. With these cars that were found over in FDR Drive, or actually under FDR Drive, about a half mile away, that were toasted in weird ways. This one car that looks like the backend just had a new wax job, and just came off the showroom floor. The front end is completely toasted, holes eaten through the metal. Very dramatic difference, like black and white.

On the right-hand side of the car, the passenger side, the front door is completely toasted, the back door is pushed in. There's an abrupt line, and I kind of wondered, they have rubber gaskets, the front from the back. On the other side of the car, there's the back door is toasted but except for a circular spot that's in pristine condition. I call it the wax spot. It's a circular spot. On that boundary, one nanometer, one side, it's toasted. One nanometer to the other side, a millimeter, is not toasted. Fire does not do that.

**Hillary Raimo:** So, we're looking at a disturbance of elements so-to-speak, something that would disrupt the normal physics of what we would expect to see?

**Dr. Judy Wood:** Yes, yes. It's a different kind of action that we're familiar with it, but we just don't know it. It's a type of interference.

**Hillary Raimo:** Interference with what exactly?

**Dr. Judy Wood:** Different kinds of energy waves. My background being in optical interference allowed me to have a mental model of interference that was a direct analogy. And after I'd tabulated all of the evidence, I was looking at something and ended up on someone's blog and found all of these photos of all of the various phenomena that I had seen at the WTC, but they had produced like on their kitchen table. That was John Hutchinson. He had demonstrated the same thing.

**Hillary Raimo:** I witnessed a gold wedding ring embedded into a steel beam in perfect form on the 9/11 site. I could never understand how that ring was able to do that without melting in the force of the fire and destruction. I wish I had gotten a picture of it because it was just so mindboggling. But I was so consumed with the emotional impact of standing where I was standing, but that just didn't add up or make any sense. You can't have a gold wedding ring embedded into a steel beam perfectly without losing any of its shape.

**Dr. Judy Wood:** On my Cliff Notes page, if you go down to Section U, the "Hutchison Effect," you'll see photos, Figure 142, 143, 144. Well, 142 and 143 are a piece of wood that's embedded in aluminum. The wood didn't burn up. Aluminum melts at 660 degrees Centigrade. Wood would pretty well be toast by then. And then, you have a copper penny that's embedded in the aluminum. How the wood got in the aluminum, the aluminum was sitting on a wooden piece of plywood and they just mushed into each other during one of Hutchinson's test.

Now, here's another interesting thing. I kind of jumped the gun here but talking about weather events. You ever see a piece of straw through a tree, through the bark in a tree?

**Hillary Raimo:** No, but I have seen some very interesting pictures on your website of wood boards, basically impaled into the center of a palm tree, which I've never seen before. As we're talking, I'm looking at pictures of the penny in the aluminum,

Which is exactly how I saw the gold ring. I'm finding all of this pretty fascinating. And like I said, you really just can't look at these pictures and ignore the fact that there is something extraordinarily odd going on here. This is not something we're taught. This is not based on the physics we're taught in school, necessarily, and to be honest with you, it's disturbing to me that this is evidence that you have on here, that nobody's looking at it. Nobody's saying, wow, this is really odd. You know, something doesn't make sense, not with what you're presenting, but with the actual story of what's happened, or the actual reality that we believe around what happened. So, looking at this wood in this tree, it's just a fascinating picture (image on website). So, describe to me, what's going on here?

**Dr. Judy Wood:** It's from Hurricane Andrew. The two by four in the tree, and the plywood in the tree.

**Hillary Raimo:** And how are Hurricane Andrew and 9/11 connected?

**Dr. Judy Wood:** Well, it got my thinking of similarities and I just look at where the data tells me to go. Again, it's puts it out of your mind because it'll bias your thinking. Just look at it and try to figure out that you need to know what went on and look at it from that perspective.

So, I was looking at this dust that goes up, that was very revealing. Also, I'd been set up in a show where the interviewer was trying to prove to me and get me to say that all the dust went down. He was trying so hard that it was clear to me this guy knew what happened and needed to cover that up, but he was kind of green at it. But that's what they needed to cover up, so I decided to go look at the dust, and how it went up.

So, hmm, they have satellite images of it going up, and let's see how far up I can get pictures. And if I look at weather satellite images, maybe I can see how far it ... What is that? It's a hurricane. You know, right outside of New York City on 9/11. And then, I got to thinking, what do hurricanes do? I'm not concluding why it's there, but it was there. That's a fact.

So, what do hurricanes do? Well, let's start looking into it, and then I found the two by four in the tree. I think we've all heard the stories about the straw on the tree. The straw must be going so fast, it goes through a tree. It didn't make sense. The straw can't do battle with a tree under normal circumstances.

**Hillary Raimo:** Right.

**Dr. Judy Wood:** And then, you get some strange things. Okay, so started looking at weird weather anomalies. You have cars sitting on telephone poles from tornadoes, from hurricanes. You get weird field effects. Birds know to leave town when they sense a hurricane is coming. They can feel it. Some people claim they can feel the storm coming. It's a different electrical energy in it. And also, look at the shape of a hurricane. It's twirling around the top, a spinning stem, kind of like a big Tesla coil.

**Hillary Raimo:** Hm.

**Dr. Judy Wood:** It operates the same way, and you get lightning coming off of it. From the top to the ground, you have a different electrical potential there.

**Hillary Raimo:** Tell us more about the Hutchinson effect that you described, are we talking about the use of frequencies to manipulate material?

**Dr. Judy Wood:** It's not so much frequency, it's an interference type of effect. It's interferometry. It's a radio frequency signal interfering in the static field.

**Hillary Raimo:** So, it's a radio wave interfering with the electromagnetic field of something, correct?

**Dr. Judy Wood:** Yes, like from a Van de Graaff generator or a Tesla coil.

**Hillary Raimo:** Okay. So, we're talking about manipulation of electromagnetic fields. We're talking about the use of frequencies, and it sounds like some alternative technologies that have been discussed in the alternative media world, floating around the internet and making a splash in certain subcultures. Are we actually looking at an obvious example of this technology being weaponized?

**Dr. Judy Wood:** Let me make something clear. John Hutchinson enjoys playing with nature. Nature being this interaction and can fiddle around and make this happen. He has no intention, whatsoever of using it as a weapon.

**Hillary Raimo:** Because the free energy technology can be used to make free energy. Clean environmentally friendly energy for everyone on the planet.

**Dr. Judy Wood:** Right.

**Hillary Raimo:** There's a tremendous positive change opportunity with this technology. But will the fossil fuel military industrial complex allow it to come out and be used for good when it means losing lots of money and control?

**Dr. Judy Wood:** And he who controls the energy, controls the people.

**Hillary Raimo:** Yes. Question is who controls the technology now?

**Dr. Judy Wood:** Yeah. I guess what I'm getting at is that it isn't my position that John Hutchinson's work was weaponized. It's my position that this technology has been around for a century, at least. Tesla had this and John Hutchinson is just replicating some of the work of Tesla, but he is doing it, here and now, and you can go watch.

**Hillary Raimo:** Yes.

**Dr. Judy Wood:** You don't have to read about it in a book, or a hypothesis, or theories, or something. You can actually see it for yourself.

**Hillary Raimo:** You are very clearly looking at the evidence and making conclusions based on what you see and comparing it to your area of expertise.

**Dr. Judy Wood:** I want to add something about Tesla. Tesla, in a recent document that was recently declassified, Tesla had apparently, I think it was 1926, had proposed to Congress that if they built towers around the entire perimeter of this country, every 200 miles or so, he would install a little box on each one that would establish a vertical plane through which anything that passed would "dematerialize."

**Hillary Raimo:** When was that?

**Dr. Judy Wood:** 1926, I think.

**Hillary Raimo:** 1926. So, in 1926, we had the capability of disintegrating planes in midair?

**Dr. Judy Wood:** Yes.

**Hillary Raimo:** Wow. I mean if that doesn't make everybody listening to this show just pause and contemplate the reality of what that means, if we were at that level of technology back in the 1920's, where do you possibly imagine we are going into 2011? It just blows my mind. Most have no clue about what's happening in this world, would you agree?

**Dr. Judy Wood:** Oh, very much, very much. We're cave men, by comparison. The technology is what we know and what is actually out there. And John Hutchinson, again, has demonstrated that issue that doing a remake of the Arc and Covenant. I think it's been around for centuries, but it stays suppressed.

One thing that I found quite interesting is that Tesla is credited for developing alternating current, hydroelectric power plants, and that's why he's the father of the Industrial Revolution. But what is so interesting is called Toledo Edison, Ohio Edison, Southern California Edison, not anything to do with Tesla, even though it's alternating current that's being sold, and Edison was about direct current.

**Hillary Raimo:** Would this technology we are discussing be able to produce the kind of disintegration at the top of the towers as you described earlier?

**Dr. Judy Wood:** Oh, yes. Yeah, for sure, easily. Easily, and we have evidence of that, that everyone is familiar with it. I became familiar with it when I was a little tyke at around 10 years old, or so, Topeka, Kansas. Our family drove through Topeka the morning after they had that horrendous tornado that destroyed a large portion of the city. It still may be to date, the highest dollar value destruction from a tornado, it's definitely one of those, of all time. This humongous tornado just destroyed everything in its path, and for several miles.

What I'll remember that I'll never forget is this bed with a white bedspread. The bed was made, it had some magazines on the bedspread. It had some books on the dresser, clothes were hanging in the closet. It was not in disarray. This apartment building was sliced down the middle with half the building just missing, and the other half, it wasn't like a big wind had blown through there. These magazines were sitting there, the bed was made. And certainly, with a half a building, people aren't going to get in there and make the bed.

I saw the same thing in building four. The main of building four went missing, and it's only the north wing that remains, sliced up with an X-ACTO® Knife, or so it appears. It just reminded me of that room in 1966, where the tornado went through. When people say there wasn't enough energy to destroy the building, that's the funniest statement because the building's gone, so obviously there's enough, so we need to figure out how it happened. But where does the energy come from for a tornado? Folks say, oh, you didn't do calculations, so you don't know if it's true or not. Well, do you sit and do calculations to determine whether or not that was a tornado? You see a tornado come and go, and then it's nothing. It's passed. The energy comes from somewhere. It's a natural force unlocked.

**Hillary Raimo:** How was the technology delivered on 9/11?

**Dr. Judy Wood:** I don't like to speculate. I can just say it has all of the parallels with this phenomenon. The round holes in the windows. The double-paned glass, the outer window has a role in it, and the inner pain is still intact. So, what lifted the cars up, and didn't take the leaves off the trees? And it's also non-self-quenching, it continues on. I was there in 2007 and 2008, in the grounds. You were mentioning all the stuff that was hauled off from there?

**Hillary Raimo:** Yes.

**Dr. Judy Wood:** More was hauled in than was hauled away. I've got pictures over there where the dirt pile gets taller. They're bringing in dirt, and dumping it on the site, stirring it around, and hauling it back out, and the dirt was fuming. It could be saturated with water, but there's these fumes coming up from the dirty.

**Hillary Raimo:** This just strips away everything we are told to believe about the official story.

**Dr. Judy Wood:** Right, and that's the key. It's like the quote my roommate had on her poster in my dorm room, see the world as a child sees it, with wonder, and with hope. And forget about everything you've been taught, and just look, what do you see? Not what you've been taught to see, and you start seeing a whole new world of things.

**Hillary Raimo:** We only have about four minutes left in this show, and I still have questions for you. I would like to invite you to come back and do a part two and discuss some of the specific details of what you have shared today.

Let's talk more about the weather connection. Now, I know we kind of touched based on that in the past hour briefly, but do you feel that this technology produces weather anomalies?

**Dr. Judy Wood:** It's all connected. There's also other interesting details with it, such as a sudden shift in the Earth's magnetic field with each one of the events happening that day, which is another interesting anomaly. The plot thickens. And it also coincides with the path of the hurricane.

**Hillary Raimo:** Sudden shifts in the Earths magnetic fields that day. We need to discuss that in more depth. How about the steel columns, the main structures of the buildings, wrapped up like carpets? They didn't just melt and fall to pieces. You have pictures here of the steel columns being twisted into weird sculpture-like looking pieces. It's really bizarre. How did that happen?

**Dr. Judy Wood:** They're wrapped around the vertical axis, not the horizontal axis. If something was buckling, it would bend around the horizontal axis, that's the crazy part.

**Hillary Raimo:** Some may not understand the physics of it all. You have live footage on your website of the dust, it just goes poof at the top, and falls. And then all of a sudden, you have all these tremendous anomalies in the structural elements of the buildings that just don't make any sense. And if I hadn't known to look for that, I wouldn't have seen that, and I think many people are not qualified to look for that. They are not even aware to look for that. They don't even understand the structural components to things like that because the physics we're dealing with is not the physics that we're taught in high school, correct?

**Dr. Judy Wood:** Correct. And my background is in observing the evidence, that's my strength. And so even before I had figured out what happened, the handlers of the coverup knew I'd figured it out.

**Hillary Raimo:** Fascinating. Now, you offer a free book online that discusses this. Is this going to be the same book that you're coming out with, or is it something different?

**Dr. Judy Wood:** The free book is one by Andrew Johnson. My book is titled *"Where Did the Towers Go? The Evidence of Directed*

*Free-Energy Technology on 9/11."* And is available in hard copy only. It's kind of like a text book but you don't need to have a science background to read it. My father, whose background is in political science and education, not engineering or any kind of physical science, read it, no problem. And it was interesting, watching the transitions as he went through, and the realization.

**Hillary Raimo:** Now, out of curiosity, Judy, because we're running out of time... Did you publish this through mainstream publishing, or did you have to fund this yourself?

**Dr. Judy Wood:** I had to fund it myself. I was contracted with a publisher, and the publisher wouldn't publish it.

**Hillary Raimo:** What a conspiracy. Get a copy of the book, guys. Read it, look at the pictures yourself. Thank Dr. Judy Wood it's been a pleasure.

**Dr. Judy Wood;** Thank you so much for having me and thank you so much for educating your

# 4

# Dr. Judy Wood Part 2
## The Jumpers, The Holes, 9/11 revisited

RECORDED JANUARY 6, 2011

**Hillary Raimo:** Hi everybody. Welcome back to another segment. I'm Hillary Raimo. Back on December 16th I had a wonderful, fabulous, very inspiring guest join me, Dr. Judy Wood, to talk about the weaponization of free energy technology and the reality of them and how 9/11 was an example of this according to the evidence that she has collected. She is a scientist. She works from data. She's not a conspiracy theorist. She doesn't get into so much the who done it, but the how have they done it.

Dr. Wood holds a Bachelors in Civil Engineering and also Structural Engineering. She holds a Masters in Engineering Mechanics and Applied Physics and a PhD in Materials Engineering Science from the Department of Engineering Science and Mechanics at Virginia Polytechnic Institute and State University in Blacksburg, Virginia.

Now before we begin I would like to very, very passionately say to everybody out there that this was a very traumatic event for everybody on the planet and this is in no way a disrespectful conversation to the people who lost their lives. I think in really looking for the truth as to what happened we are actually in fact trying to pay homage to those people who passed away. This is not about sensationalism or trying to bring the topic in to use it for any other way except for exposing the truth and really trying to find what happened because when you look at Dr. Wood's evidence and when you look at her website and you can follow along with us tonight and that's really what I suggest you do, is you get on your computers and you go to DrJudyWood.com. Look at the pictures and you follow along because the impact of looking the pictures and listening to her evidence and what she says really is just eye opening. Welcome Dr. Judy Wood. Thank you so much for joining me again.

**Dr. Judy Wood:** Well thank you for having me back.

**Hillary Raimo:** Let's start with what you call DEW, and the Hutchison Effect.

**Dr. Judy Wood:** The first big series is called Star Wars Direct Energy Weapons. Well you remember the Star Wars program in terms of the Reagan years for the strategic defense initiative. That's what it was called, but everybody knew about it. Everybody knew there were lots of dollars being poured into it. When I first started putting up this information, folks said energy weapons don't exist. That's impossible and it's Buck Rogers, or so far in the future. Well what went on all that time during the Star Wars program? A gazillion dollars or however much went into that for years and before that, was the forerunner to that program. You mean they keep pouring money into a program that's totally useless? You mean they haven't had an R & D work? You know Research and Development since 1945, the atomic bomb?

Microwave ovens came to be around 1945. Then we had lasers in the mid-50's were developed. Hasn't technology come a lot further since then? We don't hear about it, but we know we had this Star Wars program. So, the people in the Star Wars program, they were researching energy weapons. That was my kind of hint to this is real. Other countries surely have the analogous department studying energy weapons.

Energy weapons have been around for many years and so I first named it that as a way of establishing yeah, it exists, so can we move on? Energy weapons are here and now. What do you do with a remote control on your TV? It's not an energy weapon, but it's directed energy. There was a series where I focused on things so if folks want go to a nice little bit of everything page, the cliff notes page, which is drjudywood.com/wtc and from there you'll see a little guy at the top waving. It says Index. They're not the rest of the page down, but there's a little index above each section.

That shows you also when you click on that you'll see all the different categories of evidence, or most of them, and different things that need to be explained. If you want to jump to different sections you can and then hit that little index thing about each section to jump back to the section. So, it's like everything on one page.

**Hillary Raimo:** Is this a dangerous topic to talk about? Many are hesitant to discuss this publicly. Do most people find this hard to believe?

**Dr. Judy Wood:** Well yeah, you get marginalized big time and the biggest thing is the connection they don't want anyone to make with 9/11 is the connection to free energy. This is free energy technology.

**Hillary Raimo:** If it were admitted that we had this technology to use as a weapon, we'd have to admit that we also have it for the positive aspects, right?

**Dr. Judy Wood:** Exactly and if it's not the US's technology, I'm not saying who did it. If it's not the US's technology that did it, why isn't someone studying what happened because obviously it's a wonderful technology to use for good things? So, if the US doesn't have this free energy technology they would want to study this to acquire it.

**Hillary Raimo:** Well it certainly makes you stop and think because there's a lot to think about.

**Dr. Judy Wood:** Whoops, I don't hear anything. Just got cut off for a second.

**Hillary Raimo:** Oh, did we lose you?

**Dr. Judy Wood:** Yeah, I'm back.

**Hillary Raimo:** Okay well the connection is a little sketchy so we'll have to play it as we go. Welcome to live radio folks. Speaking of technology if we have all this hi-tech technology, you would think we could make the internet connections better.

**Dr. Judy Wood:** Right, right but then you take jobs away from people who need to repair problems.

**Hillary Raimo:** True. There are people who are perpetuating the funding of research for free energy technology, wanting to build free energy technology, but the fact is that it's already been built yes?

**Dr. Judy Wood:** Right, and it's been demonstrated. John Hutchison has demonstrated it but Nikola Tesla demonstrated it and John Hutchison was only replicating Nikola Tesla's work from 100 years ago. So yeah it exists but if you pour in all sorts of money into the Collider Project, all sorts of free energy development, it looks like we don't have it and you can convince people we don't have it.

**Hillary Raimo:** What is the Collider Project?

**Dr. Judy Wood:** Who knows? Maybe I should go visit them and sit there for 24 hours a day and watch them. Nobody knows.

**Hillary Raimo:** It is interesting to watch money evaporate into the funding and the wishful wanting of these kinds of things and if we already have them, makes you wonder how long we've had them and how long we could have been out of this state of the world that we're in today. So, Judy moving on into your research I have to be honest with you. When I was reading what you sent me for a preview for this show, there was a chapter in there that was extraordinarily difficult and I talked to you about this before we came on the air tonight. Your theory on the jumpers and because I think it's important to talk about let's get right into it.

**Dr. Judy Wood:** Yeah, this chapter is about opening your eyes and observing. It's toward the beginning of the book where the idea is to you know we saw these people who appeared to have jumped out and we were told they jumped out and once humans are given an answer they quit asking questions. That's something I've discovered. So, people don't go back usually and re-evaluate it.

**Hillary Raimo:** Well my mind didn't want to keep reading it and it was interesting because you had addressed that in the beginning of the chapter where you said most people when they come to this kind of topic they don't want to know. There's a denial aspect, but what I found fascinating was the parts where you pointed out where people were hanging on the side of the buildings getting undressed, taking their clothes off.

**Dr. Judy Wood:** Right.

**Hillary Raimo:** Why were they hanging off the building 100 stories up and taking their clothes off? There was a very clear picture of a gentleman taking his pants off. Why would he want to take his pants off while 100 stories up and in the middle of all that was happening?

**Dr. Judy Wood:** So, when I got into this I just collected a whole bunch of the jumper pictures, and I tried to imagine what was going through each of their minds, their facial expressions and so forth. I really felt like they were trying to communicate with us. First you want to turn away and push it in the background because you don't want to go back and relive that day again, but then when I realized they were communicating with us. These were their last words, their last thoughts. I felt an obligation and I made a promise to them to tell their story, what it was like from their perspective and that's the way I started looking at it.

Okay, this fellow who is hanging from the 105th floor taking his pants off and you notice other ones have. There are some that are falling with their pant leg trailing, but I got to thinking. If I was on the 105th floor and this fire, I'd be the first one to the bathroom, get my extra clothing that I kept in my desk and soak it down and wrap around my head. Soak my body down and head for the door. I'd be wet. Well if the water had been cut off ... If the sprinklers had gone off, we'd be wet. If the water had been cut off and there wasn't water to a floor and there was fire, we'd be hot and sweating and we'd be wet. Any which way you look at it, you'd be wet.

So, then I'm thinking of this guy who's hanging out the window by a hand and a foot taking his pants off. If there is a problem with smoke, you just hold your breath, step inside, for whatever weird reason he wants to get his pants off. Take the pants off, jump back outside or hang back outside, start breathing again. If there's some particular reason he needs to get his pants off, why is he hanging outside by a hand and a foot from the 105th floor to take his pants off?

Also, fire you know, clothes protect you from the fire. If there is fire in there and heat, why do the firefighters wear big heavy coats? To protect them from the fire. Why do you wear a mitt as you barbecue grill? It protects you from the fire, so why would you want to take your pants off or your shirt off and especially hanging outside the building? If you need to get your clothes off, why not just step inside? What could possibly be going on in there that would make wet clothes an unacceptable condition? Any which way you look at it, they're probably wet.

Also, there didn't seem to be any smoke coming out the window, or fumes of any kind especially if you're upwind. Why did they need to be outside? Well let's see. Start thinking about other things, you know we had all this paper that didn't burn. I'm not saying this is what it is, but just as an example. You put in your microwave oven something on a paper towel, the paper towel doesn't burn, but the other stuff cooks. The Active Denial System that's used for crowd control, they say it is much, much worse if your skin is wet or your clothing is wet because it fries the moisture. The water model fields are getting more excited so you're much better off to have dry skin.

If you were getting in the middle of one of these beams from an Active Denial System and you're wearing sopping wet clothes, you maybe even decide to take your clothes off. Now the guy obviously wants to live because why is he still hanging there. You know also another thing I notice is everyone who looks to be falling is empty handed. If someone had chosen to jump, wouldn't they have a picture of their loved one with them, women have their purse or have something in their hand? These are empty handed people. There's one guy flapping his wings like how did I get here? You know doesn't know how he got out there. It's like they're caught by surprise out there.

Also, if something is just intolerably uncomfortable you don't even stop to think about it. Like your hand on a burner of your stove, if you put your hand on that burner and it's hot, you don't have to decide to take it off. Your hand goes flying off of there. I wondered for a while if that's what it was, but these people didn't seem to be burning up from physical heat. It's something else. That's how I saw that situation.

**Hillary Raimo:** Most people would not know that wetness aggravates the skin with microwave exposure. It was a very powerful moment to make that connection with your proposed perspective.

You also discuss the distance from the building that they were falling, if they were just jumping they would have been falling closer to the side of the building and instead they were very far away from the building as they fell.

**Dr. Judy Wood:** Right, I used the world's record for the standing broad jump from the Olympics 1906 or so figuring that was a good number for the average person, what shoes they have in their office, for taking a leap out the window, what speed and approximated how far they would be going assuming they're going horizontally as they're falling. If

72

they jump from the highest floor, by the time they get to the lower mechanical floor which you can see in this picture maybe they could be about 100 feet from the building. Maybe if they really gave it their all. How could this person be that far? It doesn't make sense that they could drift out that far from the building. There's also body parts found even further away, but that's a different issue. There's also testimony of a body that one firefighter saw come apart and turn into a cloud of red. He kept saying, "I didn't need to see that. I didn't need to see that."

**Hillary Raimo:** The average person wouldn't know they were falling too far from the building. It would go unnoticed and surpassed by the emotional charge of it.

**Dr. Judy Wood:** Well there is actually a window washier who fell from the 47th story a couple of years ago from a building in New York. He got busted up. His brother didn't live, but he got busted up. He was in a coma for a while then he woke up and started talking. Then got his legs fixed and got back in business. It's not likely that you're going to survive, but it is possible. The same with hitting a deer. Driving at 80 miles an hour if you smack into a deer, the deer doesn't pulverize. It doesn't turn into liquid. It gets busted up. It might live a little bit depending on how things are, if you rushed it to surgery, did CPR on it whatever, it might survive. But you don't get a piece of fur here, a half a tail over here, a piece of hoof over here, a tooth over there. The deer doesn't come apart like that. You have busted up bones, but it's still kind of in the same general area.

**Hillary Raimo:** So, from the 47th floor he survived the fall?

**Dr. Judy Wood:** Yes.

**Hillary Raimo:** The gentleman that fell from the twin towers, now if we're talking another 50 floors, the chances of someone surviving that are obviously not going to happen so-

**Dr. Judy Wood:** Not necessarily, not necessarily. The likelihood decreases but there have been some interesting survivor stories of people with parachutes not opening.

**Hillary Raimo:** From 100 stories high.

**Dr. Judy Wood:** Right, that's at least 100 stories high where they're jumping from an airplane and the parachute doesn't open. You get up to terminal velocity and you don't go much faster.

**Hillary Raimo:** So, their body doesn't disintegrate the way you were describing and turn to a cloud of red dust.

**Dr. Judy Wood:** Right, right. They get busted up. There have been some survivors, but most of them would get busted up. I know that saying it sounds coarse.

**Hillary Raimo:** This is why I'm saying it was a hard chapter for me to get through because, excuse me, you have to get through the emotional impact of what you're looking at and it's a very, very difficult thing to look at the pictures that you have in your book. Once you get past that you have to just take on a scientific mind to read the data and just lay aside the emotions and just kind of breath through it. But when you look at those images, combined with your explanation, it was a very impactful moment.

I think that a lot of people on the site that day wouldn't have known that or maybe they were just so overwhelmed with what they were experiencing they didn't process it that way. So, I'm wondering if what you're saying about them being in the building and being exposed to some kind of field, some kind of radiation type field or something where they're taking their clothes off because it's more uncomfortable to be wet in that field because it perpetuates the gene etc. that their body is somehow disintegrating from the inside out.

**Dr. Judy Wood:** Yeah, yeah, there's some of that happening. I have evidence of that that's in my next book after this one, that some very strange things happened. Another reason, I'm kind of hesitant to say this. I've not said it on a radio show before, but I guess I can say this about the survival. I have personal experience that it's possible to survive. I was hit by a pickup truck going in excess of 80 miles an hour and that's about the same as terminal velocity. It's not likely you're going to survive. You end up very busted up. That's why I feel I really could relate to these people.

So, I feel like I have personal experience that you can survive. It's unlikely and really busted up, but I felt like I could really relate to these people and maybe that helped me be able to see through their eyes and being at death's door or whatever, and I felt even more obligated to tell their story because I feel that they would want their story told, what they're experiencing, what was going on in their lives at that moment.

**Hillary Raimo:** I have never seen these images of people getting undressed published on main stream media, main stream news. I don't recall ever seeing the picture that you have in the book where they were hanging out. You have to get over that emotional wave first to be able to put that logical common-sense pieces together on this piece of evidence.

**Dr. Judy Wood:** Actually, that was a very well known published piece. It was seen in most of the media.

**Hillary Raimo:** I guess I just didn't see it.

**Dr. Judy Wood:** But we didn't observe what was in the picture.

**Hillary Raimo:** Right, right and there was a person who looked like they were actually holding onto a phone trying to record what was happening. He was holding it out at arm's length in one of the pictures and it looked like he was trying to record what was going on. Is this the first time that we've seen this technology used or do you feel that this is something that has been used in other instances?

**Dr. Judy Wood:** Well on this scale seeing an entire 110 story building turn to powder in mid-air, I don't think we've seen that before. You know how many 110 story buildings are there and we've got these mega skyscrapers come apart.

**Hillary Raimo:** Why would they have to use this kind of technology to bring the building down? Why not just use explosives to do it? There are many theories out there that discuss this event being a controlled demolition.

**Dr. Judy Wood:** For one thing you don't demolish a building in Manhattan without causing collateral damage if that's what the motive is. We don't know what the motive is. We can only take observations of what we see, but one thing I will say about safety factor and design, structures are designed with a particular ... I think I talked about this last time, the safety factor and the importance factor.

**Hillary Raimo:** Yes.

**Dr. Judy Wood:** Like if it's out in the middle of a cornfield in Iowa, you know it's not going to take out anybody else if it falls, but in Manhattan you've got to worry about the adjacent buildings. I don't think there's any control demolition company that would be able to, with the most amount of skills and preparation, to be able to take these building down without demolishing something across the street. Like Building Seven didn't even spill across the street, didn't scratch the post office. But the buildings didn't collapse. They turned to powder. They just kind of went away, you know, gone with the wind.

**Hillary Raimo:** Let's talk about Building Seven for a second because Building Seven didn't even get hit by anything and there were other buildings in between it. Do you feel that that was a side effect of what was happening or was that seismic? Was there something going on? How did that fall the way that it fell?

**Dr. Judy Wood:** Well it didn't really fall. It appears to have fallen but I think that's just the facade that did that because there's no evidence that the building slammed to the ground. Various seismic stations in the area couldn't even pick out a signal out of background noise. Some of them could just barely and they said it was 0.6 on the Richter Scale, which is you know the same as a jackhammer on the sidewalk, a little bit more than a hammer on the tabletop, but it's something you could sleep through just about and in New York City for sure you could sleep through it.

To have a 47-story building where each floor is about the size of a football field ... Imagine these planes in space and about 250 dump trucks on each floor and suddenly come crashing to ground. It should sound like raining dump trucks. You hear one dump truck rumbling down the road when you're trying to sleep at night, you know bumpety, bumpety, bump, that's all a racket. The sound was not appropriate, an appropriate level in Building Seven and neither was the ground shaking. It didn't shake.

**Hillary Raimo:** Now on your website you make mention of a few things that I find interesting. You talk about the evidence of molecular dissociation and transmutation as demonstrated by the near instant rusting of affected steel. You also talk about weird fires, the appearance of fire but without evidence of heating, lack of high heat. Witnesses reported that the initial dust cloud felt cooler than the ambient temperatures and there was no evidence of burned bodies, and that columns were curled around a vertical axis like rolled up carpets, where overloaded buckled beams should be bent around the horizontal axis and you have pictures of this on your website at drjudywood.com.

One thing that I also find interesting was that office paper was densely spread throughout lower Manhattan that day and unburned alongside often cars that appeared to be burning. So, we have a lot of anomalies here with this and what I'm curious about is what kind of anomalies do these direct energy weapons create that we lay people who aren't scientists wouldn't know to look for? Are these examples of that?

**Dr. Judy Wood:** Well those are directed, it just means energy that gets directed. It's controlled as to where it affects things. What I do in my book is go through simple, every day examples that we are familiar with where we see this anomaly but we don't recognize it as being part of it. For example, something I like to say is hot things glow, but not everything that glows is hot. Folks see things glowing in the pictures in the aftermath or see something glowing and they assume it's molten metal or red hot but think of a fluorescent light compared to an incandescent light. The fluorescent light doesn't burn your hands. The incandescent one which is a resistance heating coil that's just it's so hot that it glows.

It's a different mechanism that causes fluorescent light to glow and so you know that light can be made in different ways. There's also other phenomena that we know like you notice I call it the swamp, the street where just every car was toasted and the paper got wet from the fire hoses and the dust. It looked like a swamp. Every single car was toasted.

Nothing else was. There's sign posts that were fine. There were trees with leaves still on them and buildings on the sides. Nothing else was toasted so let's see what the differences are. It wasn't that the gas tank exploded. When you start looking at what the differences are and you realize the car was on tires.

So, it's insulated from the ground. Perhaps there's something different that happens to it if it's not grounded. You start picking up different phenomena like that. You talk about molecular dissociation. My aha moment for that was noticing that soon after the dust landed, slightly upwind you could see clear blue sky. Then a little bit after that, you start seeing fuzzy stuff around people's feet. Then some of the stuff starts rising on its own. That could only be happening if coarse dust landed and then became fine, so fine that it rose up because if it's fine dust that's rising up, how could it have landed? Why would it have been on the ground?

So, it continued breaking down and then there's a continuing ongoing reaction. One of the things when I discovered the Hutchison Effect was one of the hallmark signs of it especially in large mass, non-self-quenching was the term that really got me. We had a non-self-quenching issue going on with Bankers Trust. Bankers Trust had a gash in the front. It was right across from Building Two.

**Hillary Raimo:** You mentioned that on your website. It had a cylindrical arc that was cut into it.

**Dr. Judy Wood:** Right and they replaced those beams and columns and then decided to take the building apart.

**Hillary Raimo:** So, you mean they put the building back together and then they decided to take it back apart?

**Dr. Judy Wood:** To dismantle it and I think there's like one or two stories left. They're still working on it after nine years.

**Hillary Raimo:** Well you also mentioned the vertical round holes that were cut into Buildings Four, Five, and Six and into Liberty Street in front of Bankers Trust. So, are we dealing with the same effect affecting all these buildings? Describe to me how this is important noticing vertical round holes in these particular places.

**Dr. Judy Wood:** Vertical round holes aren't natural. Well not natural as far as what you get with a building collapse. It's also you look down they're empty. There's just nothing in these and soon after the day of the event there's some people climbing down on a long ladder down to the basement and they're walking through a puddle of water. It wasn't hot there. There's just nothing down there; empty cavern. You know what's this deal with this hollow hole? How does that happen if you have a collapse? It doesn't make sense. Nothing can fall in it and then pulverize itself as well as the hole.

Then I started looking at the, when I was looking at the Hutchison Effect, he had solid aluminum bars with holes that would appear in them, like a vertical hole to the side but not all the way through and then another hole sideways. You couldn't drill it like that in a normal drilling technique at all. It's just like it tunnels a cylindrical hole. This reacts like this is a small scale, but my first inkling was okay it's tempting to say something. This is hole punched from above like a post hole digger but that's thinking of what we know with conventional methods, or somewhat conventional. It's a phenomenon that works around an axis and everything in a particular radial distance from that axis, it's destroyed. That seems like what could also be the case.

**Hillary Raimo:** So, these vertical round holes that were cut into the buildings from above are evidence in your opinion of free energy technology at work? and it doesn't add up to a typical demolition story correct?

**Dr. Judy Wood:** Right, it's not from conventional bombs in the building. It's not anything conventional that we've seen before; to see cylindrical holes with material just missing in that cylindrical cutout.

**Hillary Raimo:** Did they release the pictures of that publicly? I know you have quite a few on your website and for those of you following along on drjudywood.com you can find them on there. I don't remember seeing any of them released publicly like on the news or people that were covering it. I could be wrong. It doesn't mean it didn't happen, but I'm just curious if you feel that that was perhaps part of what was kind of not really so much part of the story.

**Dr. Judy Wood:** Oh, the funny thing is all of this stuff has been out there. It's been out there since the beginning if you looked enough, but are we still connected?

**Hillary Raimo:** Yes, we're still here.

**Dr. Judy Wood:** Okay, when I first started talking with other people about this I said, "What about these holes?" They said, "Oh that's already been taken care of. We've already ruled out that it was explosives." Like move on. Don't look back. Move on. That's when I was thinking, okay when most people when they're given an answer they quit asking questions and so if people are told that then they move on. Oh, somebody already looked into that. Who looked into that? What did they come up with and why?

There's a video I have on my book order site, which is going to be available soon where Peter Jennings is talking to George Stephanopoulos. This is at 12:30 on the 12th, the very next day. Peter Jennings asks George Stephanopoulos, "Where did the buildings go?"

George Stephanopoulos says, "Well I've been asking around. It was just such massive buildings. They all fell down and then just turned to dust and evaporated." That's what he said on the 12th. They noticed the lack of material. That was okay, he got an answer so he moved on, but how many people are going to question that.

**Hillary Raimo:** Do you think people are kind of duped into a story? Duped into the whole timeline? How do they know who did it within hours after something like that happens? Do you think the majority of people were wrapped up into the anger and scooped up into the whole traumatizing emotional aspect of this to really be settled down to look at this from a more logical perspective perhaps? Do you think that that's what happened either intentionally or unintentionally? That's pretty much what happened. People couldn't look at it from critical mind.

**Dr. Judy Wood:** You get them to act on instinct and reaction. They'll grab their pitchforks. They need to go after the bad guy. You don't stop to think innocent until proven guilty, but you know it's just because they were told this person is guilty or these people are guilty, grab your pitchfork and go after them. Once people, first impressions stick. Once people get that in their mind it's hard to undo it.

**Hillary Raimo:** Well we've spent a lot of money in other countries since and have done a lot of damage because of this event. There were a lot of consequences following this event. It's unfortunate but when we look at these things being presented here it's very difficult to not go back and take a look at it and see it from a different perspective. You mentioned some interesting facts that I'd like to read off of your website and then I'd like to ask you a question in closing what you feel is going on with some current events in the world.

You did mention here that all planes except top secret missions were ordered down until 10:31 a.m. when only military flights were allowed to resume after both towers were destroyed and only two minutes, 120 seconds after World Trade Center One had been destroyed. Why were all the planes ordered down? Was it because of what was going on or was it because something was being allowed to happen, in your opinion?

**Dr. Judy Wood:** I do not know. That was news reports that I had seen. We do remember hearing on the news that commercial flights were all grounded. Everybody had to land as soon as they could, but I didn't realize until I had seen that and then I put it in that article after ... I mean after I started drafting it. I didn't realize that even military aircraft were ordered down. But then what were these helicopters that were flying around? I still don't know. What's the story? Why weren't they ordered to? Except top secret mission, was that top-secret mission? We don't know. But one thing is you can speculate and say, well you had all these toasted cars, were they afraid of having toasted airplanes in the neighborhood?

**Hillary Raimo:** We have about 10 minutes left. I'd like to ask you; now you also say on here that the magnetic field readings in Alaska had a recorded abrupt shift in the earth's magnetic field with each of the events on the World Trade Center site on 9/11. With the current happenings of all these birds falling out of the sky and fish bubbling up out of the water on shores in many parts of the United States and also around the world. Also, the earth magnetic fields, they're shifting naturally and yet we also have technology messing around with the fields. Is it normal to see a reaction so far away from the actual site of the event? Would you care to talk about the science of that briefly? Are these things related/connected?

**Dr. Judy Wood:** It was picked up I guess around the earth in various degrees and various seismic stations, but there's a noise here and there's sometimes from space weather. I checked with space weather for that day and there wasn't any solar storm. You get weird things happening here and there, but it really when you have every single event of the five events something abruptly happening at the exact same time in the magnetometer readings, it begs the question.

For about 20 minutes before the North Tower got its hole, not making any sense in how it got its hole, but for about 20 minutes before that all of the magnetometers that had been fairly quiet started veering off and decreasing in magnitude from their norm and as soon as the North Tower got its hole, they abruptly started to change direction, started increasing. Then when the South Tower got its hole, they abruptly leveled off. Then right when the South Tower went poof, destroyed, whatever, they started going down.

Then right when Tower One went poof, they dropped off a cliff, really went down. That got me thinking. Why did it go down and up and then down, down? It was all haywire all afternoon and then it gets under control right about the time that Building Seven goes poof. I'm thinking well, let's see what the pattern is. You have the North Tower getting a hole from North to South, the South Tower getting a hole from South to North. Both towers went poof from top to bottom. Building Seven was destroyed from all around, but the final demise was bottom to top.

Could it be that one reverses the other in what's happening? I don't know but with these other, just some questions to think about. One thing that I have been thinking about was the birds falling out of the sky, think about how John Hutchison does his magic. It's magic if you don't understand it. He has a static field and within that static field he interferes different types of radio frequency signals. So, let's say in the natural environment you coincidentally have a static field and then some radio frequency signal interferes with it. What might happen? It's an interferometry type thing. It's interference of different types of energy that cause these weird things.

So, think about this planet. You have so many different kinds of energy beams and fields going all over the planet and you have different kinds of weather patterns moving around. Now we do know when we get a tornado you have the weirdest things happen. Tornadoes, where do they come from? They come out of nowhere and it's a tremendous amount of energy that they pull out of nowhere; free energy. So, I see a lot of similarities with that and a lot of things that we should think about with regards to all these different kinds of energy waves that we're sending around the planet. What are we doing to the environment? Even if you don't see them, it doesn't mean they're not causing a problem and it could be that they interfered in a particular environment.

You know static field, there was a static field there. There's evidence of that and so if you interfere these particular kinds of radio frequency signals in that and these birds happen to be flying through at the wrong place at the wrong time, poof, down they go.

**Hillary Raimo:** Instantly.

**Dr. Judy Wood:** Instantly.

**Hillary Raimo:** Now why is it just birds and fish? Is it just because they resonate with that field?

**Dr. Judy Wood:** I don't know about the fish. I haven't looked into that any, but the birds have some strange things with them. You know, bugs come pouring out of the mouth and there's this one. I saw a video of that he landed but he wasn't chirping. He was walking around in circles like his brain was messed up.

**Hillary Raimo:** Like there was some neurological damage done to it.

**Dr. Judy Wood:** Right.

**Hillary Raimo:** Now can it happen to humans?

**Dr. Judy Wood:** Well if you look at the World Trade Center, there is effects on humans.

**Hillary Raimo:** This is not a show for the light hearted.

**Dr. Judy Wood:** Sorry.

**Hillary Raimo:** No, don't apologize because you know Judy there are certain people in this world that won't stay quiet because they can't and they're not supposed to. Your research is valid and it's important for people to be able to take a look at it and come to their own conclusions both personally and professionally in whatever field they come from, and I acknowledge the fact that you are staying out of the conspiracy circles. You're not trying to jump into the who done it and all of this other stuff which I think is important and what you're presenting also because you really are giving us an opportunity to look at the science, look at the evidence of these kinds of things, these kinds of technologies that are real. They are out there. They are at work right now and they are not science fiction and people who can't wrap their minds around it are going to have to deal with the evidence of these things.

We are out of time. Judy I'd like to say thank you so much for joining me once again for Part 2. I wish you the best of luck and when your book comes out please let me know so I can make it available on my website for people to contact you to order also. Thank you for being here.

**Dr. Judy Wood:** Thank you so much again.

**Hillary Raimo:** Everybody listening it's up to you to really figure out what truth is. Use your heart and your intuition to guide you through that. That's really the only advice I have for you after such an incredible amount of information. Other then to read Dr. Wood's book *"Where Did the Towers Go? The Evidence of Directed Free-Energy Technology on 9/11."* Thank you for being here.

# 5

# ROBERT BAUVAL
# TRUMP, JERULSALUM & THE CRUSADES

*I first met Robert Bauval in Cairo in 2005 while on tour with Lynn V Andrews in Egypt. Our friendship grew over the years and we did four shows together. In 2011, he came to New York City and we toured the 9/11 memorial together. My conversations with Robert is a stark reminder that the winner of the battles usually writes history.*

*Often the full story goes untold.*

RECORDED SEPTEMBER 29, 2011

**Hillary Raimo:** Robert Bauval is founder of pioneering research linking the pyramids on Giza with the star constellation Orions Belt, as described in his international best seller, *The Orion Mystery*. His more recent books include *The Egypt Code*, *Black Genesis*, and one of my favorites, *The Master Game: Unmasking the Secret Rulers of the World*. He writes approximately 636 pages, co-authored with Graham Hancock, tracing the steps of the New World Order.

Tonight, Robert will be sharing some pertinent information that aligns the 9/11 memorial site, the war on terror, and where we are now with the Arab Spring revolutions, and the Wall Street revolts.

Welcome, Robert.

**Robert Bauval:** Hi, Hillary. How are you?

**Hillary Raimo:** I'm well thank you.

**Robert Bauval:** I must say that it's very appropriate to have the interview because I'm actually in Washington at the moment. Much of *The Master Game*, as you know, deals with the city of Washington D.C.

**Hillary Raimo:** You're doing a book tour now here in the states. You were in Atlanta. You're in Washington D.C. now and you'll be in New York soon. You are in Washington D.C. to see some of the sites that you've written about in this book, correct?

**Robert Bauval:** Correct. I've been in Washington D.C. several times before. Like I was saying, it's been an interesting and very propitious moment, because several things have happened, more or less, in this week, which deals very much with the topics that I'll be talking about in a minute. One of them of course is the Palestinian application for recognition at the UN, that took place last week. The other is I've been having a lot of fun observing the people repairing the Washington Monument, as you probably know.

**Hillary Raimo:** Yes, it was cracked in a recent earthquake.

**Robert Bauval:** It was. They've had a team right at the top and I've been in town, yesterday, watching them with a lot of people down there. It's quite an amazing thing. That's the other. The third of course is that I'm here.

**Hillary Raimo:** Quite symbolic indeed. What made you decide to write *The Master Game*?

**Robert Bauval:** Well, let me give you the background of this book. I should very quickly say that *The Master Game*, which is the book that's come out last week, is in fact an update and rewrite of another book, which I've written with Graham Hancock, called Talisman, which was published in 2004. Talisman and consequently *The Master Game*, has a history that goes down to about 15 years ago. When I wrote with Graham Hancock, *The Message of the Sphinx*, my second book, I had proposed to our publishers to write a book on the influence of Egyptian symbolism on the Western world. That's the seed of this book and invited Graham to write it with me. We're talking about 1993 approximately. When we started researching this topic, mainly we were tracking two traditions that have come out of Egypt.

We decided to track down two traditions that emerge from Egypt. One of them is the well-known Hermetic tradition, which concerns the famous books of Hermes or thoughts, that were rediscovered in Italy in the Renaissance periods in the 15th Century. Many believe it kickstarted the Renaissance, the Enlightenment, and the Industrial Age. We wanted to track this and see the influence of this tradition across the Western world, mainly because we were aware of a variety of Egyptian symbols, obelisks, and pyramids, and all sorts of odd monuments in various capitals of the world. We wanted to understand what they were doing there and if they had any deep significance.

The other tradition is the Gnostic tradition, which is in a sense the Hermetic tradition. I should explain that the Hermetic tradition is none other than the ancient Egyptian religion or cult, which was metamorphosed or converted or changed by the Greeks into a kind of philosophy. It's rather a bit complex to explain. I won't go into too much detail now.

As we said at the beginning, the book is a massive book of 630 pages or so. In great detail, we literally sort of slink through the 2,000 years of civilization, starting with the events of Alexander the Great, and leading all the way to 9/11. You can imagine the huge historical investigation we did. We actually call it, by the way, this kind of investigation, we call it archeological history. We dig below the veneer of history, below the textbooks, and we try and get to the very heart of certain events, like the Renaissance, and the French Revolution, the American War of Independence, the founding fathers, all leading to this crescendo that we're all experiencing at the moment.

Now, having said this, *The Master Game* came about a year and a half ago, when we realized that much of the research that we did for Talisman was in fact bringing us to this rather drastic and awful event, which is now in the psyche of just about everybody in the world, the 9/11 event, and what follows, the aftermath of 9/11. Reaching this point now, where there's a whole confusion and nobody seems to understand what all this is about. We set, when I say we, I'm talking about Hancock and myself, we set ourselves the task of trying to use the material of *Talisman*, our previous book, in order to clarify this situation that is going on now, which is basically this clash of civilizations, this war on terror, and this situation with Al Qaeda. Everybody seems to be confused about this.

Ask me the next question, but I would like to start at a specific point. I'm ready to go, depending on your next question.

**Hillary Raimo:** In *The Master Game*, you talk a lot about the Masonic symbols that are in these city plans. Is this a conspiracy?

**Robert Bauval:** Now okay, listen, listen. You mentioned the key word, conspiracy. What I'm about to talk now, by the way I should tell you, I've given a talk in England last week and so my answer will be very much muddled on this idea of conspiracy. There's been a lot of talk about what 9/11 is all about. Today, for example, there's been astounding news on Fox, but I tend to be very skeptical about Fox News. Nonetheless, where apparently Al Qaeda has sent a message to the President of Iran, of all people, telling him to stop accusing the United States of having been responsible for 9/11, because they're getting pissed off. It's they, Al Qaeda, who have done this, they claim. Here again, is another turn of events that will confuse things more.

Let me start where it should start. As you know Hillary, I've lived half my life in the Middle East. In terms of years, probably your whole life in terms of years. I'm 64 years old, so I've spent about nearly 35 years in the Middle East, mostly in Egypt. I've lived in Saudi Arabia for many years, and I've spent time in Sudan. I've even worked in Iran. I know the Middle East very well.

Let me tell you this, the conspiracy is really very much something, a psychosis, whether true or not, that has affected most people in the Middle East. They believe, and it's not just the fundamentalists, it's nearly everybody you talk to in the villages, they believe, Arabs believe that there is a Zionist, Masonic, American conspiracy to take over the Middle East. It may sound strange, but the belief is very fervent.

Having said this, we should come down to the year 1998, because 1998 is a crucial year. I think a lot of people missed the point. On the 23rd of February, 1998, in a newspaper called El Kutz, which is published in London, El Kutz means Jerusalem in Arabic, there was a full-page announcement by an organization calling itself Al Qaeda. It's a declaration of war. You can find this on the internet. I'm usually very surprised and amazed really that although this has been going on for the last 10 years or so, in fact 12 years, many people haven't bothered to look at this declaration. There is a translation of it on the internet. I very much recommend you read it, to have a look. This is an actual declaration of war by Al Qaeda against what they call the Crusaders. Very clearly in their mind, these Crusaders is the United States and Israel. It's very bizarre because they speak of these Crusaders as if it's an ongoing situation, starting with the ancient Crusades that took place in the Middle Ages. One needs to understand this, because if you don't understand why they believe that there is a Crusade going on, we're all missing the point of what Al Qaeda is trying to do.

Now, Graham and I have set ourselves the task to try and understand why there is this belief. Why do the Arabs, in particular Al Qaeda, think that there is some sort of Crusade going on against them? That their declaration of war is, in a sense, a Holy War against these American quote/unquote Crusaders. In order to understand this, one must go to the original Crusades, and understand what really happened and why Al Qaeda today, and the rest of the Arab world, has centered its aim, its target against the United States. The original Crusades have nothing to do with the United States. I mean the United States didn't even exist in the Middle Ages. The big question is why now the United States? I'd like to tell you that.

**Hillary Raimo:** Please do tell.

**Robert Bauval:** Yeah, okay. Well, having set the scene, one must go to the original story. Now, I need to be very clear on this matter, because I presume many of your readers in the United States, your readers, your listeners in the United States are probably from the Jewish faith, in New York certainly. I want to make clear there is a big, big difference when one speaks of the Jewish people, when one speaks of Israel, and one speaks of the Zionists. Unfortunately, there is a confusion. There's a confusion in the mind of a lot of people and they tend to make these tags. The Zionists have nothing to do with the Jewish people, other than being an organization that kickstarted the state of

Israel. Let me be clear on this. I want to be very clear, I know it sounds like a cliché, but I'm definitely not anti-Semitic in any way. I'm not anti anything. Having said this, I would like to make sure that nobody misunderstands what I'm about to expose here, because some feathers will be ruffled. Then that's what most of my books do anyway.

We need to go to the biblical times. We need, in fact, to go to 1,000 BC. This is where the story starts. The story starts with the supposed, now I say supposed because I'm a historian and I've been involved with archeology. The supposed formation of the Kingdom of Israel, or rather the Kingdom of David in 1,000 BC. Let's just assume that historically all this is correct and so forth. Now, as you may or may not know, there is a lot of doubt about this. Even Israeli archeologists are confused, because no hard evidence has come to light, to this day, about this Kingdom of David and what follows, but let's assume it did happen. There was a Kingdom of David in 1,000 BC. What follows is 50 years later, King Solomon builds the first temple on Mount Mariah or Mount Zion or the Temple Mount, as most people know it. Then about 400 years later, the Solomon Temple is destroyed by Nebuchadnezzar and most people know this biblical history. About 100 years later, the second temple is rebuilt.

We're going to go very quickly on this history, because I will bring it to contemporary times. The Romans come eventually in the 1st Century BC, they take control of Palestine and Jerusalem, and place Herod as King of the Jews. The Herodian Temple is built, but again destroyed, the second Temple, which stands on Temple Mount is destroyed by the Romans in 70 AD and that's it. That's it. That's the end of the great Solomonic Temples. What's left is still there for us to see, the Wailing Wall.

Now, I'm going to jump to the 7th Century AD. The Romans, by that time, have weakened into another weak state in Byzantium. Jerusalem falls in the hands of a Muslim army led by Khalifa Umar, and they take Jerusalem. This takes place in about 642 or 643 BC, AD, sorry. Again, check it in the book. Jerusalem now is in Muslim hands from the 7th Century. On Temple Mount, they build two of their most sacred shrines.

The two most important shrines, other than the shrine in the City of Mecca in Saudi Arabia, are built on Temple Mount. One is the famous Dome on the Rock and the other is the Al-Aqsa Mosque. They're still there, they're still there. Here starts a problem. Meanwhile, of course, after the collapse of the Solomonic Temple under the Romans in 70 AD, emerges the Christianity, the events of the Gospels. In Jerusalem, are some of the most holy places of Christiandom. That is the problem.

The problem is we have three major religions, all stemming by the

87

way from the same source, from the Abrahamic source, from the Old Testament, if you like, who claim Jerusalem as their holy city. Particularly the Muslims and the Jews, who see the Temple Mount as the epicenter of their faith. Now, why do the Muslims see Jerusalem and Temple Mount with such importance? It's not simply because they built their two shrines, the Dome on the Rock and Al-Aqsa Mosque. It's because in the Koran, it is said that Muhammad the Prophet took a journey from Mecca on a magical horse to Jerusalem, where he landed on Temple Mount, and from there ascended to Heaven. There to consult the prophets and to consult God. In Heaven, the Koran says he meets all the previous prophets, Moses and Jesus, John the Baptist, and also talks to God. When he returns, he has the doctrines and the mandates to declare Islam as the final religion of the world. This is why Jerusalem and Temple Mount, more specifically, has the significance to the Muslims.

Now we have to go to Al Qaeda, and Al Qaeda declaration of war in 1998. Not only they declare war against these Crusaders, Americans, but the purpose of this war is to liberate the holy site of Jerusalem, which are now in the hands of the Israelis. You've got to understand this. This is what this war is about. It's not about oil. It's not about democracy. It's not about anything else. As far as Al Qaeda, it is about a Crusade to liberate the holy sites. Americans need to come to terms with this, because this is what they are up against. If it's not understood and if it's not defused, we're heading towards some serious trouble.

Now, I have to move to another part of history. For a long time, the Christian world, after the capture of Jerusalem by the Muslims, fought to regain Jerusalem through the various Crusades that went on for nearly 500 years. The First Crusade in the 11th Century was what I term the first 9/11, but the other way around. Christiandom with their knights and the Knight Templars and the Knights of St. John, attacked Jerusalem, which was now in the hands of the Muslims. There were Christians still living in the city. There were Jews living in the city, and of course Muslims. They massacred ever single individual in this city. A horrible, horrible genocide took place. This is rooted deeply in the memory of the Arabs, this terrible, terrible ... Again, after the capture of Jerusalem by the Christians, it falls in the hands again of the Muslims, with the famous Battle of Saladin, Saladin, who conquers the Holy Land. Jerusalem and the Holy Land becomes part of the Muslim Empire, as from the 12th century onwards, to this modern day. In fact, when I say modern day, until 1948.

The Christians give up. They abandon the hunt, their desire to recapture Jerusalem. Everything is nice and quiet until modern times, but then something happens. Something happens that revives the whole problem all over again.

We're getting to the real core of the problem here. We're now jumping to the beginning of the 20th Century. The 20th Century begins with a problem, and that problem is the manifestation of a document that emerges from Russia. It's supposed to be a hoax, which it might be by the way. A few days ago, I was at the Holocaust Museum in Washington, and they actually talk about this. I've seen the movie that they show there. They actually talk about this document, which is known as the Protocol of the Elders of Zion. It is a document that has proved to be a fake. Unfortunately, it is taken very, very seriously by the Arab world. This document, which emerges in 1905, purports to expose a huge plot by the Jews and the Freemasons to take over the Arab world through the banking systems and through finances.

Although, like I said, this document was shown to be a fake, unfortunately it is not seen as a fake by the Arab world. In fact, it is circulated even know in many Arab countries. Egypt did a 10-part television series on this Protocol of Zion, not long ago. In Saudi Arabia, they even distribute it in schools. We've got to be aware of this. This is the beginning of the psychosis that there is some kind of Jewish/Freemason plot to take over the Middle East. Now, what follows is ...

**Hillary Raimo:** Is there a plan to take over the financial world?

**Robert Bauval:** Let me get to the point. What *The Master Game* finally brings you to a point is what seems at first to be a conspiracy, when you read *The Master Game* you end up thinking, "Perhaps it isn't a conspiracy. Perhaps it's true, because the evidence is stacking in favor of it being true." Let me just carry on because what starts with this Protocol of Zion even takes even a different shape that convinces the Arabs that this plot, this conspiracy is actually true.

Now we jump to the First World War, or rather towards the end of the First World War, when the Zionist ... I should say this, between the Protocol of Zion and the events of the First World War, is formed the Zionist Organization. It is founded by a fellow called Theodore Hertz, who founds this organization in 1897, if I'm not mistaken. By the time of the end of the First World War, it has become a rather powerful organization with its headquarters in England, headed by the famous banker Baron Rothschild.

Now the Baron Rothschild, among other Jewish bankers, were actually funding the British war efforts. Most of the money of the British war efforts came from these big Jewish bankers. Now, here is a moment in history. After the First World War, the Allies, which mainly involved

England, the French, and the Italians, but England was the superpower at the time, decides to divide the conquered world, which is mainly North Africa which was in the hands of the Ottoman Empire, which has collapsed. They were the allies of the Germans. England takes the land of Palestine in a mandate, as they call it. In other words, they become the rulers, the owners of Palestine. It's in the hands of the British and now the Zionist Organization sees its opportunity.

Through an approach by the Minister of Foreign Affairs, Lord Balfour, who approaches the King of England, and obtains from him the famous declaration known as the Balfour Declaration. Let me get the dates right. It is actually on the 2nd of February, 1917, where Lord Balfour writes a letter to Baron Rothschild, the head of the Zionist Organization in England, and announces that the King of England has favorably looked and agreed to the formation of a Jewish state in Palestine. That's the beginning of a problem. What follows immediately was that this Declaration, this Balfour Declaration is taken very seriously of course, by the Zionist Organization. The Jews are in diaspora around the world. They've been persecuted in many places, in Russia, in Germany to follow of course, later on in the Second World War.

Here is an opportunity, because the British, who are in control and they're the superpower, they're in control of Palestine, agrees to hand over, in a sense give as a gift to the Zionist Organization the land of Palestine, and starts a big immigration towards Palestine by the Jews. They come from all over the place. They come from Russia, they come from Germany, they come from Poland, they come from the States. They start populating Palestine, to the horror of the Arabs who live there, as you can imagine. One has to be realistic about this. There are these Arabs that reside in this land for the last 1,500 years, and they see this mass of immigrants coming over, rather sophisticated people from various parts of the European continent and from the States. They start taking over. One really has to understand the problem from both sides.

I do appreciate the problem of the Jewish people. There was a diaspora around the world. There was this dream to reestablish the state of Israel, but one has to understand the problem from the other side as well.

**Hillary Raimo:** Robert you lived and worked in the Middle East for a great portion of your life. Your perspective is unique. For those who have never traveled to the Middle East, is it easy for them to believe the propaganda spread by other countries?

**Robert Bauval:** Wars throughout history have been about ideas. Oddly enough, they've never been very, very clear as to what the real purpose is. Now, we have a situation where no one is clear, no one is clear. There is a whole confusion. Let me finish my story because I was going to bring it to 9/11 here, because this is where it all finally ends.

We're now going to jump to 1948. We're now in 1948 and nothing has happened in Palestine. The British are still holding their mandate and there's been now a huge import of immigration from various parts of the Jewish diaspora, and the trouble starts. The British are fed up of being in the middle. There is almost a civil war starting. The Arabs are shooting at the Jews, the Jews are shooting at the Arabs, and the British are in the middle. The crunch comes when the terrorist organization of the Irgun, the Jewish organization blows up the King David Hotel, where the British have their headquarters. A lot of people are killed, and this finally sends a signal to the British, they do not want to be responsible for Palestine anymore. They turn now to the newly formed United Nations. They say, "Well listen, this is your problem. Take the problem. We relinquish our mandate," and they give dates. They say on the 14th of May, 1948, they're out.

Here is now the huge, huge opportunity by the Zionist Organization. Now we're talking about individuals, with Ben Gurion, Golda Meir, who are now in Palestine. They form a provisional government, a provisional Jewish government, an Israeli government. They declare that they will announce an independent state when the British move at midnight on the 14th of May, 1948. Everything, everything depends on the support of the United States. Without the support of the United States, who are now the superpower after the Second World War, this cannot happen.

This is where we have to get to understand what happened on that day, that famous day of the 14th of May, 1948. It's a crucial time. Remember that Al Qaeda announces declaration of war in 1998, exactly, exactly 50 years later, on the jubilee of what happened on that date. This is what is emerging from The Master Game. It's very, very important everybody understands this. On the 14th of May at midnight, the British literally move out. The British commission, they board the ship, and off they go. At that precise moment, Ben Gurion is about to read the Declaration of Independence of the State of Israel, referring back to the Davidic Kingdom and the Solomonic Kingdom and so forth. He needs to know whether the American President is going to support this. He needs to be sure. Without that support, that state of Israel would be literally obliterated at its infancy. What has obviously happened is once this announcement has been made, five Arab states, including Egypt, Syria, Jordan, Lebanon, and Iraq form a coalition and say if this declaration is made by the Zionist Organization, they will attack Israel. They will attack and kill this nation at its birth. This is where the whole thing stood.

Now, here is the problem and here is this Masonic/Zionist cum

American supposedly conspiracy. The problem is that the President of the United States at the time is President Harry Truman. Harry Truman happens to be a 32nd degree Scottish right Freemason. The highest grade you can obtain in Freemasonry. He happens also to be the 32nd President of the United States. There is a huge lobbying going on with the Zionist Organization in Washington. They are now based in Washington, because now this is where the whole power of the world resides. They're headed by Weizmann, who will become the First President of Israel, and they lobby heavily. Now, here it is. When Ben Gurion in Jerusalem, in Tel Aviv, sorry, announces and reads the Declaration of Independence, exactly 11 minutes later, President Harry Truman, without consulting Congress, without the approval of the United Nations, indeed without the consent of the Secretary of State, George Marshall, who is totally opposed to that situation. He knows that there will be war. President Harry Truman writes a short note saying that the United States government approves and accepts and condones this newly formed state, and that's it. He personally makes the decision.

This is why the Arab world are convinced, not just with the Protocol of Zion, which we were talking earlier on, but now they see a Masonic highest degree President of United States, being lobbied by the Jewish organization, the Zionist Organization, and making the decision himself to create the state of Israel. No wonder they believe that this is a plot. Now whether true or not, this is what they believe. The danger now, it's no more Crusades with horses and [inaudible 00:43:09] and swords, this is heading towards an Armageddon because we've got Iran on the one hand, rushing towards nuclear weaponry, and we have Israel on the other hand, already armed with nuclear weaponry. God forbid if this game goes on. It's going on to recapture, re-liberate this real estate, which we call the Temple Mount. It's got to stop. It's got to stop. We're all being sucked in this mad game that's been going on since the Crusades. Really it has to stop.

This is what *The Master Game* is all about. We need to understand what this battle is about, why Al Qaeda is still seeing America as a crusading power, and where all this is heading. Do you see it Hillary?

**Hillary Raimo:** I see your point Robert, yes.

**Robert Bauval:** I've laid it down here. Coming to 9/11, coming to 9/11, because I am convinced, I have no doubt in my mind, I know a lot of people are not going to like this, but I am utterly convinced that 9/11 is purely and solely the Al Qaeda who masterminded this attack. There is something to understand here, because of what I've just said, this psychosis, this belief that there is a Masonic cum Zionist cum American plot to take over the Middle East. More particularly, because one has to bear in mind that while Harry Truman made that decision, in the mind of the Arab it wasn't just an American President making that decision, it was a very senior Freemason making that decision. The Arabs know as well as everybody else knows, that one of the objectives of the Masonic movement is the rebuilding of Solomon's Temple, so there you are.

**Hillary Raimo:** What about the new 9/11 Memorial, what does that represent in all of this?

**Robert Bauval:** Well, let me get to 9/11 itself. The targets that were chosen by Al Qaeda are rather conspicuous. I don't need to repeat them, they blew up the Two Towers of the World Trade Center, and they attacked the Pentagon. There was a fourth flight, we're not quite sure what target it had. I'm beginning to wonder if it was in fact the Scottish Right headquarters in Washington.

Let me tell you why. If you tell a Freemason, any Freemason, and you say, "Two towers," or, "Two columns and the Pentagon," what flashes in his mind is the Temple of Solomon. The reason is, is that the rituals, the initiation rituals of Freemasonry, one of the most important ones was known as the raising of the master, is performed on a strafing board, it's a sort of prayer rug if you like. On it is drawn symbolically the Temple of Solomon. It's represented by two columns and a pentagon. The choice of Al Qaeda choosing those targets immediately, to people who know symbolism and know Masonic symbolism in particular, rings the Temple of Solomon. It's as if they're attacking the American Temple of Solomon. It's kind of weird, but that's how it comes through.

The game is entirely symbolic here. The battle is symbolic. Ultimately, they're fighting over a symbol. The symbol is a rock on Temple Mount. That's what it's about. It's a huge talisman that has haunted the Western world and now the modern world, in an incredible way. You were asking about the Memorial, sorry Hillary, the Memorial you were talking about in New York.

**Hillary Raimo:** Yes.

**Robert Bauval:** That's another weird one. I haven't gone very much into that, but certainly the tower that they will raise has, let me get this right, 1,776 feet, is that right?

It's very eerie, it's very eerie because we're beginning to sense, and that's what *The Master Game* does, that is why it is such a big book because one needs to go through it very, very carefully and very slowly, because it's a very complex problem that needs to be understood and needs to be understood by everybody. We're caught in a game here. There's a game that's been being played for the last millennium and a half. It's taking a rather dangerous shape. It's heading towards, if not stopped, that's why *The Master Game* is, in a sense, an alarm bell, to somehow see if it can be stopped. It's heading towards a very, very dangerous showdown.

9/11 is a kind of turning point here, where the game takes a very, very, very dangerous turn. Where an organization calling itself, Al Qaeda declares a Holy War in the name of Islam, and takes an action to provoke these Crusaders, the people they perceive as Crusaders, into a world battle. That is what 9/11 is about. They're sending these eerie signals, these eerie messages that are very frightening, very frightening. They think in symbolic terms, that this is what it's about, their minds. It's quite possible that the other side, the other players, the other players are thinking the same. It is something that we're caught in and we need to wake up because we're all very complacent about this. We're all letting the game take place without us being involved.

Strangely enough, as you're mentioning the events on Wall Street, suddenly the people are waking up. They realize they've been manipulated, they've been part of some bizarre game involving huge funds, involving huge military action, and they're just on the sideline. They're the ones suffering.

We've got five minutes left, and I want to tap this, this is what *The Master Game* is all about. It's very difficult to do, of course, on a one-hour talk on the radio. I hope that the main point has come across.

**Hillary Raimo:** Thank you Robert. What about those who don't believe Al Qaeda was responsible for 9/11? I have my doubts too.

**Robert Bauval:** Well, we obviously are going to agree to disagree on this one. I'm very, very convinced that this is a real attack by Al Qaeda. What is important is to understand the very roots of it If not, we're going to make a mess out of this. I know there's many theories, and many, many theories suggesting even that the United States itself, or some people controlling the United States government, are involved in this. I'm not on this line of thought, but I know there's many conspiracies. Of course, maybe I'm wrong. My research and my research with Graham Hancock leads us to the conclusions we arrive in *The Master Game*.

There we are. We disagree on one thing Hillary.

**Hillary Raimo:** Just one?

**Robert Bauval:** We'll find other things I'm sure.

**Hillary Raimo:** Thank you for being here. *The Master Game* by Robert Bauval and Graham Hancock, any speaking engagements while you're in Washington or New York that you would like our listeners to know about?

**Robert Bauval:** Yes, I'm speaking tomorrow in Washington.

Unfortunately, I don't have the details here, but I'll be talking, perhaps more interesting for your listeners in New York, I'll be speaking at the Long Island University on the 9th in the evening. I'll post the information on my website. If people want to come and hear the talk, but it's not about *The Master Game*, it's about *Black Genesis*, which is another very interesting book, but it's a very different subject.

**Hillary Raimo:** Thank you for being here.

**Robert Bauval:** It was a pleasure, as always Hillary.

# 6

# JIM MARRS (RIP)
# FUKUSHIMA, LIBYA, MISSING TREASURES
# FROM WORLD MUSEUMS

*Jim Marrs was a formidable presence when it came to digging past the headlines on everything from the assassination of JFK to UFO sightings. "Truth is part of the problem" Jim insisted. "We've all trusted the government to tell us the truth and they haven't." He was a force to be reckoned with and our conversations were always enlightening. When there was something going on in our world that reeked of hypocrisy it was part of Jim's mission in life to expose it. Jim Marrs passed away in 2017 at the age of 73. As of this publishing, his website is still active.*

RECORDED APRIL 14, 2011

**Hillary Raimo:** Japan, earth changes, the Middle East, space weapons, New World Order agendas. We're going to be covering it all. Jim Marrs returns tonight for part two. He's an award-winning journalist and a New York Times best-selling author. His books include "The Rise of the Fourth Reich," "The World by Secrecy," "Alien Agenda," and "Crossfire," which served as a basis of the Oliver Stone film, "JFK" and his most recent release, "The Trillion-Dollar Conspiracy: How the New World Order, Man-Made Diseases, and Zombie Banks Are Destroying America." Welcome, Jim.

**Jim Marrs:** Hey, Hillary. It's great to be back with you.

**Hillary Raimo:** Well, I'm excited. How about you?

**Jim Marrs:** Oh, I'm always excited there's always something getting my blood pressure getting up. Today I'm finding out the authority from Texas are working with the Carlisle Group, which of course was George Herbert Walker Bush, Henry Kissinger, and before they dropped out, the Bin Laden family. And they are dealing with the Chinese to turn over the operations of the port of Galveston to the Chinese. So that's really good news for the Chinese because now they won't have to storm the beaches like we did at Normandy. They'll just land their ships here. They'll already be here.

**Hillary Raimo:** Jim, your background is in researching secret societies, elite family connections, the military industrial complex, and the UFO phenomena. Let's start off this hour with Libya, the Middle

East and Japan. What are your thoughts about what is happening on the world stage at this moment?

**Jim Marrs:** Oh boy. Well that's covering the spectrum. Well, lets start with the Middle East. I think what's happening in the Middle East is that the New World Order guys, Wall Street, City of London, the financial masters of the world, are eliminating the middle men. They've been popping up those ten horn dictators and royal families in those middle eastern countries for years now, decades. And it's becoming problematic because it's kind of hard to support a dictator. Now, they have pretty well honed their skills and the United States as far as keeping a population in servitude because they don't know they're in servitude. In fact, we talk about freedom and democracy. And yet our elections are rigged and the financial power to run this county and the corporations have taken over the state. And by the way, just for those listeners who may not know this, check the dictionary and you'll find that the very definition of the combination state and corporate power, used to be known as corporatism, but is now the dictionary definition of fascism. It's just fascism in operation.

So, they have now unleashed their insurgence and people that have been trained, armed, and supported by the United States to start the freedom, so-called freedom movements. And they're overthrowing Egypt and they're already raising cain in Saudi Arabia, and of course now we have the situation in Libya. The problem in Libya is it didn't go like Egypt. The insurgents didn't win. In fact, they started to lose. So of course, the United States is one, somebody says we have to go along with NATO nations although there weren't very many other NATO nations. Most of them have been a tense environment, but we use that as an excuse.

Obama, who just a few months before, had authorized millions of dollars in military aid to Muammar Gaddafi. Suddenly decides he's a big dictator and then links up to the side of insurgents. So, we launched hundreds of the tomahawk missiles and bombed this nation there that had actually done nothing to us. And that prompted my memory of recalling that Vice President Joe Biden was quoted as saying, "I told the President that if he bombed that country without the consent of Congress, I would personally see he's impeached." Of course, that was in 2007 and he was talking about George W. Bush, the possibility of bombing in Iran. Now, when Obama does the exact same thing, starts bombing some third-world country who's done nothing to us, without even the consent of Congress, without even consulting Congress, where's Joe Biden? He's kind of quiet on the whole thing.

So, this is obviously a move by the New World Order people trying to shift into their New World Order, which is nothing more than a return to the Middle Ages where you're going to have the super rich and then the Serfs, with not much in between. And that's why they're eliminating their costly and hard to support middle men in these countries and just going for ... Well, for instance, in Egypt, when the Mubarak administration was bounced, they put in a military one, that's running the show. And all these guys are trained, armed, and educated in the United States. And they're all probably working with or members of the CIA. So now we got direct control over these countries without having to go through these middle men. I think that's what's happening in the Middle East.

By the way, in Libya, there's an interesting sideline. Other than the oil, which of course, is the big prize, is the grand control over oil producing countries. Even though everyone with half a brain and one eye is beginning to realize that whether or not oil has peaked or whether or not there's tons of oil still in the ground, we need to wean ourselves off of petroleum because we are choking the planet on the pollution and other environmentally hazardous and dangerous things that are happening, thanks to this petroleum economy we're based on.

But of course, the petroleum economy has been a monopoly ever since John D. Rockefeller gained control over it in the 1800s. And so, they don't, they're loathed to give that up. There are lots of other alternative ways of doing things but they have been pretty successful in suppressing any innovative alternative technology. But over and above oil in Libya, we have an instance of the man-made river, which was a water project begun by Gaddafi about ten years ago. Seems there are seven huge underground reservoirs of ice age, pure clear water that is in southern Libya. And so, he embarked on this project to build these underground conduits, bi-ducts to send this water towards the coast so they could irrigate and turn the country into a self-sustaining agriculture industry. And then, not to mention the fact that he would have all this water at his disposal to sell to Europe. Which, in addition to probably making Gaddafi a very very rich person, would give him significant control or control over a significant portion of the world's potable water supply.

And this again goes against the desires of the multi-national corporations because for anyone who's been paying attention, Coca-Cola, Perrier, Nestle, and other corporate, giant, multi-nationals have been working very hard in recent years to get a total monopoly on water. So that if you want a drink of water, you're going to have to buy it from them. And even now, most people because of the fluoridation in the water and because of the pollution that's found in a lot of the city water, they are now buying bottled water. When I was a kid, if you tried to tell somebody, "Here. I'm going to sell you a bottle of water," they would have laughed at you. Nobody bought water. We drank water out of garden hoses, okay? But they've been setting the whole thing up where they're going to control the water supply.

And then whoever controls the water, just like whoever controls the food, will control all the people. And if Gaddafi suddenly ended up with all of this water, that would be a big monkey wrench in the works. Not to mention the fact that Gaddafi did all of this without the beneficence, the approval, or taking the interest-bearing loans from the International Bankers.

**Hillary Raimo:** Well that is important to know.

**Jim Marrs:** That's the same thing Hitler did and got him in trouble, too.

Of course, in the United States, the two US Presidents that's tried to bypass the International Bankers and simply issue their own interest-free money were Abraham Lincoln, with his greenbacks that financed the war between the states, and John F. Kennedy, who in June of 1963 ordered 4.2 billion dollars in currency issued not through the interest-bearing federal reserve system, a private bank. But through the Treasury Department of the United States. Money wasn't worth any more or less, but we didn't have to pay interest on it. And I don't think that it's just a coincidence that both Kennedy and Lincoln were shot in the head in public. And I don't think it's a coincidence that there were more than 25 assassination attempts on Hitler. And I don't think it's just a coincidence that Gaddafi now is suddenly the bad guy and the counties that are dominated by the Bank of England and the Federal Reserve System are now bombing him.

**Hillary Raimo:** Did we see the same thing in Iraq, Jim? Is this character assassination and propaganda?

**Jim Marrs:** Oh yeah. Exactly. That was the same thing. Saddam Hussein was just getting a little big for his britches, impacting the profit line. And besides that, he was talking about going off the US dollar as his petroleum trading basis and turning to the Euro, which is gold based. Well, see, then he was, again, attacking the bureaucracy of the wealth of these bankers. So, that got him in big trouble too. And he didn't last very long. So that's what's happening in the Middle East as they try to consolidate their grip and create their New World Order.

Now the Japan thing is a different deal. Japan-

**Hillary Raimo:** You had mentioned an interesting connection. The looting of the Iraqi museum and also, more recently, the Afghanistan museum. The Egyptian museum was also recently looted. And I'm wondering if you could talk about what you feel is being targeted for within these museums?

**Jim Marrs:** Okay. Well, I'm just going to cut to the chase here and a lot of people are going to go, "What?" Because they weren't taught this. But a lot of European listeners may go, "Oh yeah. I know about that." We all know about the fabled land of Atlantis, which is supposedly this high, technologically advanced civilization that existed prior to our written history. In fact, there are just vague mentions of it in history. Most famous, I guess is the few lines that Plato wrote. People have argued ever since, well, if it existed, it was this big island in the middle of the Atlantic. Or others say, "No it was the island of Santorini." And others say, "No, it was the island of Crete." And others say, "No, it was actually Antarctica before the poles shifted." And they argue. And I think were like the story of the blind men and the elephant. They all have a piece of the truth.

I'm beginning to come to the belief that in our pre-history of this planet, there was a world-wide highly technological civilization. And I think that one of the centerpieces of their energy system were gigantic pyramids. Only vestiges of which are left today. But they're scattered all over the world. Pyramids on the Giza plateau, pyramids in eastern Europe, pyramids in Central America and South America. And pyramids in China. And according to many researchers and scientists such as Christopher Dunn, who they see at least the great pyramid, as a power plant, power generator. And I think that there was this world-wide, highly technological civilization. Now it fell into rack and ruin due to either and or geophysical changes and cataclysms or war and warfare amongst themselves. And almost everything was upset, obliterated and we just have vestiges of it left, all around the world.

I could go down a whole long list such as the maps of Perirease, which were drawn back in the 1500s and which clearly show the correct outline of the continent of Antarctica, although the continent of Antarctica has been buried under thousands of feet of ice for at least 700 or 800 years or more. And so how could he have done that? Well, Perirease himself said he based his maps on ancient maps from the Greeks, who themselves said were based on ancient maps that predated them.

Now what's really interesting to me on these maps, I'm getting sidetracked here, but I think it's an interesting sideline. On Perirease's maps, he also traces the correct route of the Amazon River, which was not fully mapped and recognized until 1958, the geophysical year. And when he focuses on the things in the center of his map, they are absolutely, 100% correct. And yet, as his map extends out, he gets a little distorted in the shape of the line of the continent coast and all like that. Begin to elongate a little bit. Well, this of course is what happens when you get very high in the air. And the curvature of the earth begins to cause the outline of the continents and the rivers to elongate because of the curvature of the earth. Which means that somewhere back there, whoever originated these maps, apparently were working with aerial photography. Well, you know, wait a minute. Supposedly man didn't fly until 1906 when the Wright Brothers finally lifted off at Kitty Hawk. So, there's lot of things that point to this ancient civilization.

Now, this brings up back to all of these artifacts and items that are resting usually in the basement of museums all around the world. Because when they get something and they cannot classify it as belonging to conventional history's account of the slow, evolutionary climb of Western civilization, then they call it an anomaly and they stick in down in the basement so nobody can see it. The move to on the Iraqi museum, I think, was a military backed operation in search of acquiring ancient technology. Because I have in my files, mainstream news stories from Associated Press, CNN, and BBC, that under the approval of Saddam Hussein, French and German archeologists were making amazing discoveries in the ancient Samarian cities of Peri Kapoor. And of course, we know and we were told that Saddam Hussein considered himself the reincarnated Nebuchadnezzar. And that he was working hard to rebuild Babylon. And so obviously, he had an intense interest in that period and in the technology that might have been available at that period.

For example, we have the Baghdad battery, which laid around the British museum for a long time. It was just a piece of pottery and it had a copper tube and another little cylinder. Nobody really understood what the heck it was for. Until one day, they put some wine in it, which is highly acidic. And low and beyond, it produced a half volt of electricity. So, oops, they had electricity in ancient Babylon. It was known as the Baghdad battery. And so, I think as an attempt to grab future technology from the past. And we can see evidences of this technology in the Bible. For example, you got the story of King Nebuchadnezzar who built a structure of gold. Now the Bible translators, because they didn't understand energy fields or quantum mechanics or quantum physics, they called it a fiery furnace. Although, the way they described it, it was a structure. And they give all the dimensions and it was made out of gold, which is a highly conductive metal.

Once he had this structure completed, it created an energy field. And when his people would go in there, it'd kill them. They died. So, he went down to Palestine and found the three Hebrew priests, Shadrach,

Meshach and Abednego, brought them to Babylon and said, "Make it work." Because apparently, they had some of the knowledge that had been passed down through Abraham from ancient Mesopotamia because Abraham, who is the patriarch of not only the Hebrew, but also the Palestinian Arabs, which is pretty wild, because now they're fighting tooth and toenail and actually, they're cousins. They're all racially connected and they all trace back, both of them trace back to Abraham. And Abraham, according to the Bible, came from Caldea. Well Caldea was simply the ancient term for Mesopotamia. So, Abraham was not a Hebrew. He was not a Semite. He was a Samarian. And his family was Samarian royalty, so he must have had access to some of this ancient technology and some of these ancient secrets. So, did the priest then, of Israel.

So, they took Shadrach, Meshach and Abednego, and Nebuchadnezzar said, "Make it work." And they said, "Well you're not our king. You don't believe in our God. So, we're not going to work for you." So, he said, "Well, then I'm going to throw you in there and you either make it work or you're going to die." So then interestingly enough, and they didn't just immediately chunk them in, it says they donned their raiments, their clothing, their cloaks, their hats. Well, big deal? Why would that matter and why would they put that in the Bible unless they had something special about them? For instance, maybe this is their radiation suit or something. We don't know. But when they put them in there, they didn't die.

And Nebuchadnezzar, who was afraid to even get close to this thing, this energy field that was being created within his fiery furnace, asked his men, "Are they in there?" "Yes, they're in there." "Okay, well are they still alive?" They said, "Yes. In fact, you put three in there and now there's four people in there." "What? Who's the fourth person?" They said, "Well it's the son of God." Oops. Well, wait a minute. Where'd he come from? Well, I think this is evidence that they had created with their energy field, a portal. A portal into space, time. Dimensional portal. We don't know. But something happened there. They put three in and suddenly, there's four. And they said it was the son of God. And then we never hear anymore about it. We don't know who that was or what happened to him. But we do know that Shadrach, Meshach and Abednego went on and were greatly praised and lauded by King Nebuchadnezzar, who put them in charge of Babylon. Which meant they obviously knew some of these technological secrets. So, there's a lot about the past that's being kept from us.

And I think that the raid into Baghdad, because when we launched our attack on Iraq in March 2003, we violated the most basic military doctrine. Which is, you move your forces in, you set an objective, you seize your objective, and then you consolidate your winnings, pacify the countryside, and then move on to your next objective. We didn't do that. We made a beeline for Baghdad. And then left the rest of the countryside wide open with armed guys roaming around. And that's what's caused us problems ever since.

And what happened in Baghdad, the looting of the Iraqi National Museum. And Colonel Matthew Bogdanos, who inspected, investigated this looting, for General Tommy Franks, was quoted as saying, "The basement was an inside job." They knew what they were after. They had keys to some of the cases and some of the doors. Some of the guards were suspiciously missing. They bypassed very expensive looking fakes, went for the good stuff. And although a lot of the items, and they also, of course, used the cover of the street mob that just broke in and looted the museum. Of course, the street mob could be hired really easily over there for a few hundred bucks. Most of the materials that were stolen off the ground floor and upper floors by the street mob have since been found and or returned. But the basement is still missing. And of course, this is where they would have put the amazing new discoveries.

So, I think we're looking at something kind of akin to the movie Stargate, where they found some sort of ancient technology, placed it in the basement of the Iraqi National Museum and somebody in the Western world decided they needed to get their hands on that technology and that's why all of a sudden, using 9/11, the attacks of 9/11 as a pretext, we invaded Iraq. Even though a little later, President George W. Bush himself, on more than one occasion, frankly admitted that Iraq had nothing to do with the attacks of 9/11.

**Hillary Raimo:** So, you are saying we're looking at the reality of ancient technology that actually shows us how to build Stargates and manipulates energy at the sub-atomic level, yes?

**Jim Marrs:** Right.

**Hillary Raimo:** Are we at war with countries whom have lost technologies hidden in their museum collections?

**Jim Marrs:** Well, if you back off and look at everything we've discussed since the beginning of the program, I think what you find is, there's an effort to find, seize, and suppress any sort of alternative energy sources or technology that might interfere with the monopolies enjoyed by the wealthy ruling elites of this world.

**Hillary Raimo:** What is the attitude of the military industrial complex when it comes to countries treasures and antiquities?

**Jim Marrs:** Or from the standpoint of the ruling elite. We want it, but you can't have it.

**Hillary Raimo:** You had mentioned time travel technology in the interview you did on Red Ice Radio. Are we dealing with the realities of this as well when it comes to going to war?

**Jim Marrs:** That's a very real possibility because once you learn the secrets of manipulating energy at the atomic and sub-atomic level, then you are tampering with the basic building blocks of the universe, including dimensional, gravity, time, the whole thing. Quantum physics is beginning to understand that gravity and time are somehow intertwined. This is why in the UFO literature you find the stories of the UFO comes over and the car engine stops. And then when the UFO goes away, the car engine starts again and you don't ever hear anybody saying, "Well, I put the key back in and turned on the ignition and the car started." No. What it is when the energy field, which is creating an anti-gravity situation for the UFO craft, when the car comes into the range of that energy field, then the car stops because time within that energy field is stopped. And as a result, those pistons just freeze and lock up. They don't fire because time has become meaningless and in fact, held in advance. And then went the energy field moves away, then the pistons go back to clanging and the engine starts going again.

This is, of course, leading the concept of time travel. Something that most people, myself included, because I was brought up in the 50s and 60s, the scientific age when everything was about rockets and boosters and things that we can prove, left-brained things. And yet, for those of us who kept our minds open, it seems like we're getting very, very close to a time when time travel may be reality. In fact, there is a very interesting writer in England called Jenny Randles, who's written a book called "Breaking the Time Barrier: The Race to Build the First Time Machine." It's a very readable book. She has interviewed some of the top scientists in the world who are actually knowledgeable on working on time. And according to Jenny Rambles, we may be within 10 years of developing time travel.

Whoa. And of course, if some of these scientists, and if a book is allowed to be published saying that we may be within 10 years of developing time travel, then you can pretty much bet your bottom dollar that in some secret government laboratory, deep underground somewhere, they've probably already developed it. Because if you hear about a technology today, then the government has probably been working on it for 20 years.

**Hillary Raimo:** Is free energy a reality that we are living with now?

**Jim Marrs:** I think that's the reality. I think that's exactly what's going on. In fact, you can go back and through history and peel back the rose-colored glasses version and you find that the suppression of alternative energy goes way back. Rudolf Diesel, who invented the diesel engine, originally designed that engine to run on organic matter, corn, methane, who knows what. Anything. Just organic matter. But, he unfortunately fell overboard crossing the English Channel, and so now, of course, diesel engines all run on compressed petroleum, gas. Then, of course, you've got Nikola Tesla and you've got many other people, who have developed ... Thompson Brown, others who have developed alternative sources of energy and in every case it's a repetition of that movie about ... what was the name of that movie about the guy that built a good car and they just shut him down?

I want to say Brewbaker, but that's not it. Anyway, most of you listeners will know what I'm talking about. In one instance after another they have bought up, suppressed, censored, closed off, shut away any number of inventions and discoveries which could have provided us with cheap and clean energy. Instead, of course, we get nuclear power. Which is something that I've been writing about and concerned about since way back in the late '60s and early '70s when I was attending city council meetings in Dallas and Fort Worth, and they were trying to pitch the idea of building the Comanche P Nuclear Plant, and they said, "It's gonna be perfectly safe and we can do this for approximately 777 million dollars," well, the last time I checked it was already two billion dollars over budget, and only had one of the reactors working. Of course, we now see, from the terrible experience Japan, that ... I don't care how safe they say they are, they're not safe. In fact, the tragedy in Japan is much worse than the corporate controlled media is allowing us to hear.

All we've been doing is trying to dump sea water on those exposed rods and try to cool them down. And all that does is completely vaporizes the water, leaving a residue of salt which then, builds up over the rods which then prevents them from getting more water onto the rods. It's a really tragic and dangerous situation. Now, if I was in charge, what I would do is just call upon everybody in the world and say, "Everybody bring every pound of concrete you can bring," and just entomb those reactors in concrete so that they won't harm anybody, and hopefully will stay contained for the next 50 or 100 thousand years, as long as that plutonium is still active, but at least that would close it off. But they're not doing that because that means they've lost their entire investment. While they're spewing cesium and plutonium into the Pacific Ocean, into the air, which is already being picked up in foods, milk, organic produce, here in the United States even, they still have hopes that they're going to be able to somehow rebuild all that.

In fact, they head of GE assured the people of Japan, "Don't worry.

We will rebuild all this," well, I don't think we want to rebuild all this. We want to find another way of getting energy. But, this is the corporate mentality, this fascist mentality that's now in control of the world.

**Hillary Raimo:** Do you think that the radiation levels that we're facing are actually higher in the United States than what they're telling us?

**Jim Marrs:** Absolutely. For one thing, they're not even counting Plutonium, which is the most hazardous of it all. They're only counting the cesium and slezium and saying, "Well, it's a little higher than usual, but it's not real dangerous," yeah, but what about the Plutonium? And what about other stuff? And also, the tricky part is it all depends on how much you get and how much gets in your system and how much stays with it. If you're dusted with some radioactive, say particles in the air, and then you take a good shower and it's not on you anymore than a few minutes or an hour or so, you may be perfectly okay, it may not be much worse than just getting a heavy-duty x-ray. But if you ingest Plutonium particles, say in lettuce that was in the ground and it was sucked up into the lettuce and you ingest it and it's inside your body, then it can wreak havoc on you. Okay? So that's part of the problem.

That's part of the reason that they don't want to panic the public and they don't want to say anything, because they can't qualify and quantify the effects because it's all going to be different depending on where you are, what kind of exposure you have, the duration of the exposure, etc. But, I assure you none of it, any of it is not good. Okay? Not good.

**Hillary Raimo:** Why do you think so many people are so hesitant to believe this? Is it just a lack of wanting to know about it? What do you think?

**Jim Marrs:** I think it's the deer in the headlights syndrome. I think they're just stunned and they feel helpless and they don't feel like they can do anything about it. So, they just do nothing and they'd just as soon not hear anything about it, okay? But, keep in mind that NBC and many other media outlets are owned by GE, and GE built those power plants in Japan and they built the power plants in the United States, and they plan on building more. So, do you really think they're going to tell you the truth about how dangerous they are? Of course not. Then there's also this ... I'm a journalist, I simply want the truth. And I got to admit I'm having a hard time too.

It's raining down in Texas right now and I like to go out on my porch and breath in the air and go out and walk amongst the green trees, and it's kind of scary to think that it may be radiation floating around in the air. But there is according to the maps. So far, I think where I am, it's only gotten a very lose dose so I'm not too worried at this point, but it's continuing and it's going to build up and it's going to get worse. I think people need to be concerned and they need to ... the main thing is we need to demand the truth from our so-called leadership. Now, I can understand where at certain levels of the government and certain politicians who are mostly concerned with getting reelected, that there is perhaps the idea that we should not panic the public. Well, I totally understand that, and to a certain extent agree. But on the other hand, I don't think we should treat the public like children either. I think particularly pregnant women, mothers with young children.

I think they deserve to hear the truth so that they can make intelligent buying decisions at the supermarket and at the produce stand. Don't you?

**Hillary Raimo:** Yes, I do. You know, Jim, with all the books that you have written and all the truth that you share with everybody, with all the sensitive topics you discuss does that make life dangerous for you? Or is this all about creating a hyped-up conspiracy for people to get lost and confused in?

**Jim Marrs:** Well, okay. First off, I'm a reporter. All my information is through study, research, interviewing people ... I do not have first hand information, okay? So, I can't go into a court room and be sworn in under oath and say, "I saw this. I heard this. I know this." So therefore, I'm not an immediate threat. Then, since I'm only putting together information and presenting it as a reporter, as a journalist, then that opens me to, "Well, he's just trying to sell a book. Oh, he's just a conspiracy theorist. He's just trying to push his kooky ideas," and that allows me to be marginalized and they hope that people won't listen to me much. It is an uphill fight because I'm just one reporter in Texas. They may hear me say, on the Hillary show, one night, you know, but then 24/7 they hear CNN and FOX news. So, it's an unequal fight.

When they do get to listening though, I think it's interesting if you go and check my track record, you'll find that everything I've written about and everything I've talked about, going back into the 1960s has never ever been refuted. As time goes by, I've only proved more and more correct. That's because I don't speak out about things until I feel like I have the truth. Then I try to tell people the truth as I see it. I can be wrong, I can be lied to, I can be the victim of bad information. But, when I say something it's because I genuinely feel like this must be the truth and as I say, for the most part I haven't been wrong.

I said there was conspiracy who killed Kennedy, everybody now knows that's true. I said Nixon was a crook, everybody not knows that's was true. That was back in the time I was almost kicked out of Lyon's Club because I wouldn't stand and toast the President, because I said,

"I'm not toasting him, he's a crook," and I said Vietnam was going to end badly, and I was accused of being unpatriotic. Well, it ended badly. I don't know, I could just go on and on.

**Hillary Raimo:** You claim you were censored in the new book that you released recently by your publishers? Tell us about that.

**Jim Marrs:** Yes. And then I was actually censored. I mean, my editor flat told me ... and this was after I had passed the legal review of the book. In other words, there was nothing legally wrong with the book. But I was told by my editor this, if I didn't take out certain sections that he would not publish the book. The irony of that was that the biggest section I was forced to remove was how the corporate media censors the news. So, I told him, "Well, you kinda proved my point, didn't you?"

**Hillary Raimo:** Which sections of your book The Trillion Dollar Conspiracy were actually censored?

**Jim Marrs:** Well, number one, like I said, I had a whole section on the corporate media and how it sensors the news and how that of the five major corporations, that own virtually everything you see and hear, they have interlocking directorships. So, in other words, there's a handful of people that control the five corporations, and this handful of people determine everything we see and hear. Okay? So, unless you're surfing the internet and looking at alternative information sites, if you're only reading a major metropolitan newspaper and watching mainstream media, and that includes NPR, you're only getting what these five corporations want you to hear.

Even when they can't totally censor what you hear, they can leave it out. That's censorship by omission, or if they can't leave it out, then you get the spin. For example, at the Lockerbie bombing, Gaddafi was the big bad guy of the Middle East, and then oh, he did some things, well, he's not so bad, he's okay. And then we sent him some more materials, he was okay. Well, then we decided we wanted his water and we want him out the way, so he's a bad guy. So, you get the spin, and the spin just goes around and around, and most people who are too concerned with just trying to make a living and take care of their family.

They aren't aware how the spin changes as we go along. Or if they are, then we're back to your question, they're just going, "What can we do about it?" They just feel like they're powerless, and yet, they're not. Think about this, Hillary, and everyone listening; the United States of America is still a very resource rich country. We've got gas and all ... half the oil wells in Texas are capped. If we'd uncap them we'd have enough oil here in Texas to run the rest of the country for hundreds of years. Not that I think we need to do that because of pollution, but we do have it, it's there. Not to mention up through North Dakota and Canada, which is untapped virtually, and has more oil than anything they've ever found. So, oil is not a problem. The problem is that we are not told about all this, and we're not aware of all this.

So, the United States has lots of resources. We're a very rich country and we have a reasonably literate work force, we have people who really would like to work. Most people would like nothing better than to have a satisfying, nice job that pays them enough to have a comfortable living so that they can take care of their family and come home at night, watch a little TV. and be with their family. That's what most people want, and that's not asking too much. We've got all that, so why, I ask you, are we in 14 trillion dollars in debt? Why are we in such economic straights? Why is gasoline pushing four dollars a gallon, likely to go up to five dollars a gallon before the end of summer, why is the prices in the grocery store going sky high? Why is a pair of shorts at Wal-Mart, which a year ago cost nine dollars, today costs 20 dollars?

Why are we in such economic straights? And folks, I'll tell you, it's only one reason, because somewhere somebody wants it that way.

**Hillary Raimo:** You published the censored chapters on your website, Jim? Is that correct?

**Jim Marrs:** Yes, I did. I placed them on my website.

**Hillary Raimo:** JimMarrs.com.

**Jim Marrs:** Absolutely. JimMarrs.com. Before we get away tonight I got to add one more somber tone. Last summer, about August, we were told, "Oh they finally capped the well in the Gulf of Mexico," since then, there's really been nothing on the news, has there, to speak of? And it's like, oh, out of sight, out of mind. Well, let me tell you something, folks. Oil is still leaking into the Gulf of Mexico. They did not cap the right well, plus they had already cracked the sea floor and there's oil seeping out. At one point they frankly admitted there was six locations that were leaking oil. They only managed to cap one. It's still leaking, and why haven't we heard about that? Because contrary to the disinformation, they are still spraying Corexit all over the Gulf of Mexico, which makes all the oil sink to the bottom. So, you don't see it a whole lot, although it's beginning to break out in huge places now because they can't keep it covered up forever.

There are people, particularly the people who courageously signed up for cleanup work, who are now dying not because of oil, but because of the Corexit. They still will not admit to this or tell you about this, but if you truly care about human life and particularly about human life among your fellow citizens in that state, go check and see what's happening in the Gulf States. They're being decimated and all we hear about is what's happening in Japan and how many bombs we've dropped on Libya. It's really upsetting.

**Hillary Raimo:** On the national news here in New York, there was a story today about the Gulf and residents from Louisiana and around the Gulf States had actually flown to the shareholders meeting in London. They bought their own tickets and they flew just to protest the meeting and all of the happenings. But what was interesting is a lot of their signs were talking about the Gulf and it not being over and still having issues there, but that's not the story that was reported in the press. That's not what the media was saying. They were not talking about that, they were just talking about the poor people flying over there to complain about PP. They weren't talking about why.

**Jim Marrs:** They probably made them sound like this is just demonstrators, right?

**Hillary Raimo:** Yes.

**Jim Marrs:** Yeah. Exactly. Well, this is what happens. This is what happens when people who are aware show up at the DT20 meetings and try to say, "We don't want the Nazi bank of international settlements running our economy," that message is never presented. All that's presented is you saw demonstrators today who were raising cane in downtown Seattle, wherever it is, Miami, and think what happens there, and it's happened every time is that you'll have by large, the people that go to demonstrate or exercising their First Amendment rights to demonstrate, to petition the governments regresses, and then what they do is put their agent provocateurs out there, they put their hirelings, they always hire some street goons, and they go out there and they break windows and they attack people and start fist fights. Then, they go to the local law enforcement people and say, "Look, the hooligans are breaking laws," they'll send the troops in and the troops go in and by then, the guys that are causing the problem have either disappeared or have been whisked away, and they start rounding up the legitimate protestors.

I've seen this happen time after time after time. This goes back to the 1968 riots in Chicago, that has now been proven to have been instigated by the FBI, but of course, nobody hears that because the media will not report on that.

**Hillary Raimo:** Jim, how do we survive and thrive within the world that we're facing today?

**Jim Marrs:** Okay, I hear this all the time, "I'm just one person, what can I do?" I know the feeling because I have that same feeling, and I even have, you know, I can get books published and I can go make public talks. I can a little something, but I can understand how the average guy goes, "What can I do?" Well, you'd be surprised what you can do. You can go and you can begin to try to mobilize at the local level. You can take over your local city council, you can take over your local school board, you can take over your local country commissioners, you can write letters to the media. The media, believe it or not, as controlled as it is, still responds to the public, because after all, they need somebody to buy the papers, somebody to watch the programs, and somebody to build up the numbers that they can present to their advertisers.

So, believe it or not they would listen to you. If you get a bunch of people and you go to them and say, "We want the truth. We don't want to hear about this anymore. Why don't you tell us about this?" You might actually start doing some good. I cannot tell you specifically what to do, you're going to have to figure it out for yourself based on your own individual location, but what I can tell you is quit sitting around saying, "I'm only one person, what can I do?" And just get out and do something, you might be amazed at what you can do.

**Hillary Raimo:** Whether it is writing books or gathering people, whatever it is you do, if you just do that and you contribute in that way, that will definitely help.

**Jim Marrs:** Right. That's exactly right, and then keep remembering there's more of us than there are of them. There's more people of good heart on this planet and in this country than there are of the small bunch of psychopaths that want to try to run everybody's life. So just tell them no and mobilize. Get people with you and have neighborhood meetings and have a discussion, "What do you think about this?" Good thing to break them in on is 9/11. People are simply ignoring 9/11 because it's just like the 15 years after the Kennedy assassination, it's just considered impolite to bring that up in decent company. Well, forget that. Invite people in.

Show them some of the better documentaries and then ask for their opinion. And don't accept, "I don't believe that," because I don't believe that is not a valid argument. If they want to say, "Well, I think it's this because of this," fine. They're entitled to their opinion, everybody is, let's hear that. But let's have some intelligent discussions. None of this oh, he just says that because he's democrat, he just says that because he's republican or I just don't believe that. That's opinion. Which, you know, is great but opinions are like noses, everybody's got one. You know?

**Hillary Raimo:** Great words to end by. The *Trillion Dollar Conspiracy* is his latest book. All of them are available on his website, including those censored chapters. Everyone, the truth is out there. You will find it with a grounded sense of love. Thank you, Jim, for all your hard work and courage to share it with everyone you can.

# 7

# THE GULF OIL PANEL
## DR. RIKI OTT, PETER TAYLOR, GAIL SWANSON, BARBARA HAND CLOW, DR. IAN PRATTIS & BARBARA GOODFRIEND

*On April 20, 2010 The Deep Water Horizon, a floating drill rig exploded, flooding the Gulf of Mexico with millions of gallons of crude oil. The world watched as underwater cameras showed the hemorrhaging of oil into the sea, infecting marine life and costal waterways with toxic sludge. It would be known as "The BP Spill" and by the time it was "officially "sealed in September of 2010, it would claim eleven lives and leave 4.9 million gallons of oil in the Gulf. I convened an expert panel to discuss this great atrocity and the intentional destruction of our fragile ecosystem.*

RECORDED JUNE 25, 2010

**Hillary Raimo:** Hi, everybody. Welcome to a very special two-hour show. Sometimes, you just have to do something about what you see going on in the world. You can no longer sit and just watch it happen. You have to decide the best way to offer support and lend your energy into a cause. That is exactly what has inspired me to bring you this special two-hour broadcast on the Gulf oil leak situation. Many people around the world are feeling helpless. Some remain hopeful, some indifferent, and many are very angry. There has been a mixture of emotions leaking into the minds of those following and affected by this ongoing event.

Some say what has happened has not been a natural disaster. Others say it's a conspiracy that breaches our highest leadership, not only of this country, but others. Some suggest this is the end of times, prophesies being fulfilled. Others say getting mad or angry is the wrong thing to do, that we should only focus our prayers and love on the situation. What is the right thing to do? So many people struggle with the news feeds, the media blackouts, and constant barrage of information and disinformation that we are seeing on a daily basis. Some turn their heads and refuse to acknowledge, going about their day as usual and bury their heads in the sand.

Conspiracy theories, media blackouts, apocalyptic destruction, wipe-out of the human race, is it illusion or fact? There are so many theories circulating the world right now. Where is the hope? What do we do? How bad is this? Our intuition does not match up to the official stories we are being told. People are conflicted by what they feel and see, and what their leaders are telling them. Joining me these next two hours are an array of experts on a variety of different perspectives, all lending their time and knowledge to us here on the Hillary Raimo show, right here on AchieveRadio.com.

My first guest joining me is Dr. Riki Ott. She is a community activist, a former commercial salmon fisherma'am, and has a degree in Marine Toxicology with a specialty in oil pollution. She experienced, firsthand, the devastating effects of the Exxon Valdez oil spill and chose to do something about it. She is the author of *Sound Truth and Corporate Myth: The Legacy of the Exxon Valdez Oil Spill*, and *Not One Drop: Betrayal and Courage in the Wake of the Exxon Valdez Oil Spill*. She's also the founder of three nonprofit organizations that deal with lingering harm from manmade environmental disasters. Dr. Ott will be informing us of firsthand observation of a possible coverup by BP. Her recent appearance on a variety of news programs have sparked controversy and interest in underlying agendas in the Gulf. Welcome, Dr. Ott thank you so much for joining us.

**Dr. Riki Ott:** Thank you for inviting me.

**Hillary Raimo:** What is the reality of this situation that we're facing in the Gulf?

**Dr. Riki Ott:** Just like Exxon Valdez, there's two versions of reality, and one version is control by BP, and it's what the public comes to see on the media, television, radio interviews, largely. Unfortunately, it also tends to be the official story.

There's two versions of reality, one is what the people see, what's going on in their communities, and this is not the same as what the official version is. What I'm going to talk about is the official version ... I mean, the people's version. Here we go. There, let's try this. BP, I think it's pretty well-known that, right from the start, BP was underestimating the amount of oil that spilled. This happened also in Exxon Valdez, and this is basically, this is about controlling the images and controlling the story of damages, of how much damage there is. The less damage that people know about, the less liability there'll be outstanding for this giant transnational oil company to have to deal with.

Also know that, of course, BP, and actually, Exxon did the same thing, but not quite as much, pushed the media up into the air 3,000 feet, pushed the media off the beaches when the oil started coming in, and is taking an incredibly aggressive attitude with the public. I mean, these are our beaches. This is our ocean. People who are walking the beaches, and they find dead wildlife, birds, dolphins, turtles, BP workers come swooping in, or BP themselves, BP representatives, talking about, "We'll have you arrested if you touch that carcass." People are getting very confused. They're saying, "Well, we don't ... Who owns this? I mean, how can BP have us arrested?" I'm actually working with different lawyers to find out, in the different states, what are people's rights on their own beaches?

In Alaska, this was handled a lot differently. NOAA, the National Oceanic, Graphic, and Atmospheric Administration was responsible for collecting carcasses, because this wildlife is owned by us, the people. It was collected. It was put as evidence of loss. It was collected into freezer vans that were kept under lock and key. The freezer vans were maintained until October of 1991, when there was a settlement for natural resource damages under the Clean Water Act, and then, the carcasses were burned. I don't see any of that going on down here, in terms of amassing evidence for court. I kind of am seeing the opposite.

**Hillary Raimo:** In your opinion, is there a coverup happening? Are they actively trying to keep us from knowing the truth of what's happening?

**Dr. Riki Ott:** I actually have evidence to suggest that that is going on. I've got, actually, images of a dumpster incident fairly recently, where carcasses were being dumped into a dumpster, and that's kind of being investigated right now, separately. We're kind of waiting on that story, to get it further along. I mean, carcasses are not supposed to be ending up in dumpsters, they're just not.

**Hillary Raimo:** You had said in another interview, Dr. Ott, that people were actually going to the beaches at night and removing carcasses before dawn.

**Dr. Riki Ott:** Yeah.

**Hillary Raimo:** What's the truth behind these disappearing carcasses?

**Dr. Riki Ott:** I have talked to people in four different states now, that this personally happened to them, where they were on the beach at night. It's cooler. You go out early in the morning. You go out at night. People said, "Oh my god, there's a dead baby dolphin," was one person in particular here in Alabama. Within 15 minutes, down came this white, unmarked van, carcass surrounded, people told, "Stay away," flashlights out, carcass gone.

The turtle monitoring people, this is a program called Share the Beach. It's done by volunteers, and the volunteers are out on the beaches every morning from May 1st into September at six o'clock. Each person has a half a mile of beach, and they walk the beach, looking for turtle tracks. There's four or so different species of turtles that come ashore now to spawn. The idea is the monitors are out at 6:00 a.m. They walk a half a mile of beach. If they find any turtle tracks, they follow the tracks up the beach and mark out where the nest is. They flag it. They fence it, to give the eggs the biggest chance of ... Then, they monitor it, and when the baby turtles hatch, they help the turtles, to get the maximum number of turtles into the ocean.

What the turtle watch team did was they made it very clear to BP that they're going to be out at six o'clock in the morning, in the mornings, and they need to have the beaches untouched before six o'clock, so they can look for tracks. Instead, what they're finding are raked ... Basically, what that told BP was get people out there before six o'clock in the morning. So, by the time the turtle people come out, the beaches are all raked very nicely, and there's no dead anything on the beaches, but there's also no way to see whether there's turtle tracks or not, because the beaches are all raked.

**Hillary Raimo:** You also said that the animals are being beheaded. They're taking their heads off, because they cannot be autopsied without the head attached, correct?

**Dr. Riki Ott:** They need to be intact carcasses to be autopsied. I've had pictures, I have pictures of people down in Mississippi who were on a beach, just happened to be walking their beach when they saw BP-paid workers raking up birds, and the birds are a little fragile, and these were oil birds. The heads were becoming detached from the bodies. There's no way that those bodies were then going to be saved as evidence or autopsied. These animals, the wildlife needs to autopsied to prove the death, birds maybe not so much, but definitely turtles, dolphins, whales, because probably one of the primary causes of death is inhalation. This is what happened in Alaska with harbor seals, and with sea otters, even though the sea otters also got physically oiled, and these vapors just fry the brain of these animals. It's a narcotic, and they get dizzy, and they get unconscious, and then they drown. This is what happened in Alaska, and we need evidence, we need bodies, and we need autopsies to establish a case.

**Hillary Raimo:** The chemicals that are involved in this cleanup, can you explain what the side effects are on both humans and animals?

**Dr. Riki Ott:** Okay. First of all, oil itself is a hazardous substance declared after it's spilled. Obviously, there's problems with it before it spills, too, but we've got hundreds of millions of gallons of oil right now, and this is a Louisiana Sweet crude, and about 40% of it, it evaporates into the air or dissolves quickly into the water column. It's got a high proportion of light ends, what are called light ends. These volatile organic compounds, benzene, toluene, xylene, naphthalene, they cause a narcotic effect. Literally, the most toxic places to be are in the water column as the oil is dissolving, and at the air/water interface, where there's this sort of cloud of hydrocarbons that have evaporated into the air. That's a big problem.

If you go to look at the Material Safety Data Sheets for Louisiana Sweet crude, don't do Weathered Sweet crude, just Louisiana Sweet crude, primary route of exposure's inhalation and skin contact, nausea, dizziness, headaches, sore throat, alluding to unconsciousness, coma, and even death. The less severe, the headaches, the nausea, the dizziness, the sore throat, that is what people offshore and people onshore are complaining about. I think this is a problem.

Then, on top of the hazardous situation created just by the oil itself, BP's actually managed to make a bad situation worse by adding in dispersants, and these dispersants of choice that it's using have a human health hazard, 2-Butoxyethanol. That's just one of the compounds of concern. The proprietary compounds, it turns out, are a lot of inorganic chemicals that are also incredibly toxic. The dispersants break up the oil into little droplets that then go down into the water column. The dispersants that are being used are about 53 to 63% effective, so you have roughly a little bit better than half of the oil, say, that's being pushed into a subsurface state of little, tiny droplets. The dispersed oil is more toxic than the undispersed oil, and the dispersants are more toxic than the oil itself.

Now, we've got, coming ashore on these beaches, not only the hard asphalt sort of patties or chunks left over from the burn, but also mousse, which is oil and water mixed together and dispersant, the dissolved cloud-like forms, the plumes that are underwater, that are mixed oil and dispersant, surface sheen, and oil in the air. I mean, you can actually, when the wind is blowing right ... I've been in two different communities now, Venice, Louisiana, and Orange Beach, Alabama, on literally what the residents are starting to call bad hair days, where you can actually taste the oil in the back of your throat. I've had people describe it to me as, "Oh, it smells like my daughter's crayons when they melt in the sun," or somebody told me, "Oh, it's like if I go spend the weekend at the racetrack, and I come back smelling of hydraulic fluid and stuff." It is. It's crude oil in the air.

**Hillary Raimo:** What are the probabilities of this getting into the rain cycle, where it will get into the atmosphere and then come down as precipitation elsewhere?

**Dr. Riki Ott:** Huge. I mean, that's what happens. That's how the air clears itself of toxic chemicals, airborne ... It's sort of a false statement to say that the oil, once it gets into the air, it disappears. It doesn't. It goes up, and it will come down as rain. The residents down here are saying, "What about the hurricane season?" It's like, what about the hurricane season? I mean, the hurricane, like with the Prestige oil spill in Spain, it just picked the surface oil and mixed it into the air, and then it came down on people's houses, and the sheep, and the dogs. Entire communities in Spain got sick because of this.

**Hillary Raimo:** Do you think that this is responsible for the strange spotting on vegetation that has been reported in the Mississippi river bottoms, the white spots on different plants?

**Dr. Riki Ott:** I don't know about that yet, but I do know that the burning is creating, concentrating the heavy metals that are naturally occurring in oil, and there's a signature that is coming down as rain, and it's as far as Tennessee, I believe.

**Hillary Raimo:** What is your personal opinion of the political agenda here? Is this a conspiracy?

**Dr. Riki Ott:** Well, the oil industry already has one big strike against it, and that is the climate crisis. We know that burning of fossil fuels is related to destabilizing our life-giving climate. I think what the oil industry is very much about here is trying not to have a second strike against it, in terms of public health risk and worker safety. We're getting people that have classic symptoms of chemical illness from this hazardous waste oil that are being, I believe, misdiagnosed with food poisoning and heat stroke.

This would be a second huge strike against oil if people really knew that this stuff is toxic, and it's coming out the tailpipes of our automobiles, and it's a problem. We really do need to get off it, and I think that that's the big thing that industry's trying to prevent. It's trying to prevent a bigger backlash against fossil fuel use. I think it's time that we, as a people, look at the cost, the true cost, of our energy dependency here and add in those costs. It's not all about benefits from oil. There's a lot of costs, too, and I think we're seeing that in the Gulf.

**Hillary Raimo:** Some people have suggested that the oil well was drilled into the side of a natural volcano, to release pressure buildup, to protect the overall oil wellbeing and industry investments in the Gulf, claiming that if this volcano had naturally exploded, it would have destroyed all the oil industry rigs, so that this was done as a well-oiled, pun intended, operation to release the pressure, to protect the industry. The unfortunate side-effects of this decision would be the results that we're seeing now, and would also explain the lack of government intervention, the staged press conferences, huge stock selloffs prior to this event, and the overall lack of serious cleanup efforts. I'm wondering, Dr. Ott, if you agree, or if you have any insights to this theory?

**Dr. Riki Ott:** I do know that, after the Exxon Valdez, there were a bunch of ... There were theories that the Exxon Valdez had run intentionally aground. My commitment on March 24, 1989, was to work upstream of these spills, because wherever we drill, we seem to spill. I was really to focus my energy on shifting, a reasonable transition like in the 10 years, off of fossil fuels. I think we know enough to make this happen, and it's a matter of political will right now.

I'm hoping we can use this event in the Gulf, for whatever reason it was caused, to say that, "You know what? This is too much." We've poisoned the ocean. We're poisoning our local communities, upturning people's lives. There are other people on this planet besides the oil industry, and we happen to live our lives, by choice, differently, as real estate people, as commercial fisherman, as charter fisherman, as just our culture. As people said in Louisiana, "I don't want BP's money. I want my community." We have to acknowledge that these people have rights to live the way they want to live, and it's not all wrapped around oil. We need to start reigning in the oil industry as a whole, so that the rest of us can live the way we want to live, without this big threat in our backyard.

**Hillary Raimo:** We have a question submitted form Debbie in Texas. She asks, "Is it true that the administration refused, and is still refusing, the help of fleets of skimmer ships from Europe and other places? If so, if those ships had been deployed in a timely fashion, would this have diminished the environmental impact by any noticeable amount?"

**Dr. Riki Ott:** I think it's a shame, at this point. This is so big. I think we should bring all tools to bear on it, and I don't care what country owns them. I think that, in actual case, at Exxon Valdez, we had a Russian skimmer in. I think part of what's going on here is where do you put the oil once you pick it up? I think there's some reluctance to actually pick up this oil, because what do you do with it when you pick it up? It's a waste that the industry then has to deal with. I mean, I really don't know why we aren't allowing other people to help. I mean, surely, we aren't that arrogant, as a country, and no, BP obviously does not have all the solutions. Otherwise, we wouldn't be in this big of a mess.

What I think we have here is a lack of our political leadership, the federal government. It's one thing to leave the spiller in charge of the response with the boom, the burning, the dispersants, that we already know 20 years ago didn't work. Why are we doing this again? But then, it's a whole other thing to say, the federal government, "Well, okay, BP. It doesn't seem to be working so well, so we're actually going to bring in

..." I mean, we should be monitoring this, as a federal government, and if the spiller is failing, we don't just go down with the ship here. We bring in other expertise. I mean, give the spiller a chance. If they blow it, bring in help, and I'm not seeing that.

**Hillary Raimo:**  It's interesting that people keep calling this a spill, because a spill is coming from a definitive amount in a container holding a certain amount of oil, and this is still leaking right now as we're talking on the air, tonight while we're sleeping or having dinners with our family. This isn't going away. It is coming out of the ground. This isn't an eight-hour day job kind of thing. This is continuously happening every minute of every day while it leaks. Do you see any end in sight?

**Dr. Riki Ott:**  Well, I see a reservoir under the earth that is continuing to spill oil, and I don't know how big that reservoir is. I guess we could call it a leak, but there seems to be more than one leak, as well. I guess my hope is that we have this six months ban on offshore drilling, that that sticks, and that during that six-month period, not only do we find out the causes of this, but we also, as a people, insist that Congress take a hard look at the cost of our fossil fuel dependency.

I also hope that groups, while we're waiting the six months, will take the initiative to start setting up solar industries, wind industries, so that when the six months is over, and Anadarko and the other companies want to come back ... Anadarko, by the way, which went to Brazil, which does require these valves, so interesting there, so that when these companies come back, we can say, "You know what? We don't need you anymore." I mean, I would love to see that happen. I would love to see this disaster turned around and transformed, so people realize this is about a sovereignty issue. I'm not talking British petroleum. I'm talking who rules? Is it democracy with the people and our values, our lives, our quality of life counting more than corporate capitalism and corporate capitalism's drive to make money at all costs? Money's not the only thing on the planet, neither is oil, and our values, our lives need to count.

**Hillary Raimo:**  Yes, thank you. You can find out more information about Dr. Ott's cause at RikiOtt.com, Thanks so much for joining me, Dr. Ott.

**Dr. Riki Ott:**  You're very welcome.

**Hillary Raimo:**  My next guest joining me is Peter Taylor from the UK. Peter is a science analyst and policy advisor to all levels of government, the voluntary sector, international NGOs, the EU, and the UN. In 1978, he set up and directed the Political Ecology Research Group in Oxford, pioneering critical environmental review and the service of leading scientists and lawyers in the protection of communities and biodiversity. He was involved in government reviews of ocean pollution and the UN's system of oversight and protection and participated in the development of the precautionary principle and moves toward clean production technology. From 2000 to 2003, he sat on the UK government's national advisory group for the Community Renewables Initiative and has taken a longstanding interest in the environmental impact of energy-related developments.

In addition to his scientific training, Peter has a diploma in Social Anthropology from Oxford and has studied systems of thought, magic, causation, and healing among tribal peoples in Africa. He has also trained with North and South American shamans, worked within the Celtic traditions, and is a longstanding adherent of Himalayan yogic practice, where he specializes in breathing and mediation teaching for health professionals. Thank you so much for joining me, Peter. Welcome.

**Peter Taylor:** Oh, thank you, Hillary.

**Hillary Raimo:** How do you see this event in the Gulf of Mexico?

**Peter Taylor:** How do I see it? I actually see it and feel it more from a kind of consciousness perspective than a pollution perspective, even though that's my main background. There have been incidents in the Gulf, which have been bigger than this, which people tend to forget, the one off the coast of Mexico, which largely only impacted Mexico, and it was several times bigger than this current leak.

The environment, in a way, can cope with this sort of impact. It's more a question of what it really means to us, because although it's really heartening to hear people's concern, I also spend quite a bit of time in the blogosphere, talking to essentially climate activists, is what I've recently spent quite a bit of time looking at climate science. I've been quite appalled at a lot of American conversations. There is a huge middle America that actually sees limitations on oil exploration in a very different light and doesn't get the message, fundamentally, from this, which is that we are fowling our own nest, in that sense, beautiful coastlines and beautiful creatures.

For me, it's not a question of how many and whether they will recover and so forth. It's really listening to what this really means on a deeper level. We are dependent on oil, and that's not really going to change very much. The more dependent we are, the more risks we seem willing to take, including deep water drilling. I'd like to see a moratorium on deep water drilling. We have drills off the coast of Scotland just as deep as this, and there were moves in the UK parliament to have a moratorium, which was dismissed. They just simply said,

"Well, our safety procedures are in place, and we have every confidence in them." But whether it's due to negligence, or whether it's a pure unlucky event, these things are going to happen. It's the price that we pay for our dependency, really.

**Hillary Raimo:**   Why is there so much resistance to move into more 'green' energy format?

**Peter Taylor:**   I'm not sure that I would agree that the world is that hesitant. If you look at governments throughout the European Union and the Obama administration, they are embracing at least the need to develop renewable technologies. Nothing new in the way of technology needs to be developed. All the renewables are a lot more expensive than fossil fuels are right now. Wind, for example, is about twice as expensive, biofuels, roughly three times, solar, anything up to 10 times more expensive per unit of energy produced, so Western economies simply couldn't cope with that sort of price increase across the board. This hasn't really been taken on board by the green movement, really. They don't do their sums. I helped found the green movement, so I'm not kind of critical of green philosophy, but currently, they're not really being very realistic.

**Hillary Raimo:**   Do you think there's a political agenda behind the Gulf incident?

**Peter Taylor:**   I don't personally. I think it's an accident borne of cost-cutting. From what I've seen, from some distance from the events, the oil companies involved ... It was a general thing when I was working with the UN on pollution control, that the regulators and the industry, they're very close. They know exactly what's going on, and so the regulators turn a blind eye, and the companies cut costs, because they're operating on the margin, really, in this kind of deep water drilling. It's a bit of both, I think. Obviously, the US administration wants to blame the company. There's been a lot of blaming, as well as ... I actually think there's quite a big effort to try and clean it up going on, but as it's continuing to spew out, and everything's failed, this could go on for some time. Maybe a relief drilling operation would affect place in office, but it's not impossible that it could be simply irreparably damaged, and it could go on.

**Hillary Raimo:**   Some people suggest the theory that this is an underwater volcano, and this was done intentionally to release pressure from it so not to threaten the rest of the oil industry rigs in the area. Is a possibility?

**Peter Taylor:**   I'm not technically qualified to really have an opinion, but from an intuitive perspective, no, I wouldn't think so. The pressures involved when volcanoes are concerned are enormous, and a tiny, little hole in the sea bed like this, I don't think would be powerful enough to relieve any such pressures. So, I think that's just kind of not true.

**Hillary Raimo:** Does it come down to greed and incompetence?

**Peter Taylor:** Yeah, it is. I think it is sad. What saddens me more is that people are not getting the message. They're really not looking at this from a ... Like the earth actually speaking to us, that we have this oil spilling out and covering a really pristine and beautiful coastline. We are fowling our own nest. For a lot of people, this is the price we're paying of the kind of civil order that they have, but actually, that civil order is very, very unstable, and it's made more unstable by its dependency on oil, fossil fuels. You can't simply replace fossil fuels with renewables. Renewables are a very dispersed form of energy, and it's vastly expensive to collect all that energy together. It won't work unless we decentralize our systems of living and reduce our demand. The economic models that we continue to embrace don't allow for that. They're going in the opposite direction.

Unfortunately, America, in many ways, has led the world in high consumption, and private transport systems, and the whole deal, so it's very hard for a country like the US to adapt, much easier for a country like Holland, for example. But either way, the prospect, the future requires a huge shift in consciousness, not technology.

**Hillary Raimo:** Peter, you have an impressive government background, and you have an impressive spiritual background. How do you see the world of industry and consumerism? Is there hope for a higher level of love and compassion in the business world?

**Peter Taylor:** I'm working on that. I've been having meetings recently with people in the financial world, who have been very chastened by the events of the last two or three years. Their world has completely changed. I'm finding people, though, that do care and want to make amends. We've had some very strong conversations, where I've challenged them and said, "Look, there are two billion people on this planet. 75% of them are involved in subsistence agriculture, and they are in poverty and very vulnerable to climate change, and none of the development aid, none of the investments are reaching these people."

A tiny percentage of financial investment is what we would call ethical and sustainable. In fact, you have special funds labeled ethical investment, which means that the vast majority, 99.9% of the financial world is not ethical, and they admit that. They completely agree. They nod their heads. I said, "Well, what are we going to do about it?" They just say, "We're trapped. We are absolutely trapped." They don't see a way of helping the rest of the world, and they don't see a way of turning the investment policies around. What we've seen in Britain and the European Union is vast amounts of money given to the banks, and then our own industries, small businesses especially, saying, "Well, hang on. The banks are not lending it to us." Of course not. They're lending it to companies investing in China, and India, and Brazil, Indonesia, Russia, where there is still economic growth of 5 to 8%, whereas in most of Europe and North America, economic growth is stuttering along at half of 1% or whatever.

That's the system, and it has created a great deal of wealth, but unfortunately, it's also created a huge discrepancy in the world and a lot of potential instability. The question is, can that system respond to these issues, energy, the transition, peak oil and climate change, and so forth? So far, I mean, we're still meeting, and I'm still looking at it and seeing if there's anything that I can do, and I kind of hedge my bets, really, because when I talk to my Shamanic friends, the message is completely different. It can't be turned around. The earth herself will intervene, whether you want to call it Gaia, or in India, it would be Kali. It's like the mother, the creator that is our source, will intervene.

That is the message that we're getting, and I was told this 30 years ago by a Himalayan master. So far, we've had a couple of little warnings, like the volcano in Iceland and then all the airplanes disappearing out of the sky. I see this as a warning, as well, that the earth and the solar system, particularly the sun, are immensely powerful. We haven't seen much in the last 200 years of our industrial civilization.

I mean, just one event, for example, I visited the States in February to talk with climate scientists in Boulder, Colorado. It was interesting, actually, because a friend of mine, who was hosting my visit, we went up into the Rockies, and we visited a valley where his grandfather had been on some kind of Conservation Corps work program. As we went up, he showed me all the dying pine trees and said because they're suffering from beetle infestation due to global warming. I said, "Well, that's very interesting, because the hottest year in the US record was 1934." As we got to the valley, there was a plaque, which showed where the camp, the conservation camp was where his grandfather was working, and lo and behold, the plaque said 1934. What that work camp was doing was cutting down infested pine trees from the beetles. On the photograph, it looked identical. Nothing much had changed. The climate comes in cycles, and I really don't feel that humans have affected the climate that much. I think it's overplayed very, very much.

In those conversations with the climate scientists, I have a sense that science has kind of lost the plot. It's relying on kind of a virtual reality of computer models. It's ignoring some very, very basic facts about ... It's not even the cosmos, actually, just our solar system. Another synchronicity was that we visited Denver's art gallery, a Daniel Libeskind building, which I didn't like very much, but it worked inside very well. I was particularly interested to visit all the Native American exhibits, and it was amazing. The whole floor was devoted to Native American art, and obviously, that's mostly handicraft and the different tribal areas around the whole of the continent.

It's really beautiful, but they had a little bit of a gallery of the artwork of the first settlers. It could have come straight out of some Scottish castle, really, oil paintings and landscapes. There was a painting of Denver, and it was basically two rivers meeting, and a buffalo, and a tree. The painting was dated 1859. That is such a synchronicity, because in 1859, there was what we call a megaflare, a solar flare. At the time, there were hardly any electrical systems, just telegraph wires, which melted down, and telegraph operators got their fingers burnt.

Now, in 2008, the National Academy of Sciences made a report to Congress ... I don't know if you've heard of this, probably not, on something called the Carrington Event, in 1859. Most people haven't a clue about this. Everyone knows about global warming, which is a kind of computerized projection, a virtual reality projected into sort of 50 or 100 years' time, and nobody knows about the Carrington Event. If that was repeated, and NASA, at the moment, is very worried that it will be, if that is repeated, it could take down the electrical grid over the whole of the United States, in fact, the Northern Hemisphere, possibly even the globe. That would be irreparable, largely because you haven't got any machines or industry to operate, to actually carry out the repairs. The report to Congress makes very, very scary reading, because you go back to 1859, and everybody was provided, locally, with food and water. All of the pumping systems would fail, all of the transport systems would fail, and there'd be no communications. Civilization would come to a halt overnight.

**Hillary Raimo:** Some people don't realize the connection between the sun activity and the cycles of the earth. How do you see all of this spiritually?

**Peter Taylor:** I agree. It's about the shift in consciousness that's occurred over the last 2,000 years, really. In my work, I've written a book, which 3/4 of it is about climate theory. It's called *Chill: A Reassessment of Global Warming Theory*. In the last chapter, I make some comments about what I've learned over the whole computerized science world. They don't recognize cycles. They can't handle irregular periods. They don't use spiral mathematics. Any of those inputs would've altered their worldview, and those are all elements of the feminine mind. We're dealing with almost like an amputation of consciousness, that the feminine side of the brain has been put to sleep, and it shows in the nature of the science itself.

As for the disconnect, it goes deeper, I think, then the heart. In the work we do here, we focus very much on the dance, something we learned from Native American tradition, really, the way that Native Americans dance. They dance by bringing in the energy of the earth in through the base chakra, if you want to use yogic terminology. When a group of Native Americans dance, they are dancing in a very powerful way, because they're already connected to the earth and their hearts, but when we started to learn to dance here, it's a whole learning process, because A, we're not really connected to the earth. We're not free. We don't know where we belong. We don't know where our food is coming from. We don't tend to the land. There is not just a disconnect but a fear, an insecurity. Also, in the United States, it's a base insecurity. People are concerned about their mortgage, their home, their job, and that insecurity is fostered by the financial system and the governmental/political ideology. Keep people insecure and afraid, and they will do things they would not normally do, which is one, surrender their will.

**Hillary Raimo:** Which is what's happening. Thank you, Peter.

**Peter Taylor:** Well, it's very encouraging to be able to do this across a huge divide.

**Hillary Raimo:** Across the ocean.

**Peter Taylor:** Yeah, yeah. Yeah.

**Hillary Raimo:** Have a wonderful evening there in the UK. Up next is Gail Swanson. She's the author of *The Heart of Love: Mary Magdalene Speaks*. After moving from New Jersey 13 years ago to Sarasota, Florida, Gail spent many nights and days on the sands and in the water of the magnificent Gulf of Mexico. She walked the crystal sands and bathed in the healing Gulf waters, and she feels that this magical area was the catalyst that opened her to receive a life-changing vision. She was shown her connection to Mary Magdalene and soon, a communication with Mary began. She was guided to share these messages to bring forth the power of the divine feminine, and to help to heal and balance the masculine and feminine energies of the world. She speaks today to express her love for these waters and its habitants, and to discuss the extreme importance of our spiritual connection to all the waters of the earth. She joins us now with a very special message. Welcome, Gail.

**Gail Swanson:** Hi, Hillary. Thank you for having me.

**Hillary Raimo:** What message do you have to share today, Gail?

**Gail Swanson:** You know, it's just interesting, listening to your other two guests, because I feel so thankful that we have Dr. Ott, who is the voice of reason, and Peter, who was just on, who is sort of straddling both worlds, which we need more of. I'm always kind of on that higher view of, as you said, moving here and being introduced to the Gulf, which I had never even seen before. I just think that there is such a deep connection, as Peter was saying, that we truly do have with the earth and the waters, and that we have forgotten. I just think about all the people, the fishermen and all of this, and this is their livelihood, and they love these waters for many reasons.

The other side of that is just loving it simply for its beauty and for the nourishment that it gives us, and the joy that we get when ... I know when I'm swimming in that Gulf, and the pelicans fly close, low down over your head, the feeling that you get is just so incredible. Everybody always goes, "Ahhh." That's how it makes you feel, and to hear ...

You know, I didn't even want to get into all this. I mean, I watch a little bit of it every day, but I almost can't take too much of it. I think most of us can't. But to hear of the complete irreverence for life, even when they are no longer living, to be putting them into ... I mean, it's just inconceivable to me, and I do feel that what Peter was saying is true, that everyone has gotten so far away from the connection to the water, to all the living beings, to every form of life, to just making a buck and doing everything they have to do, and blindly just going forward, doing things that are just unthinkable. This is where we are now. I don't know. I was going to have a more, I don't know, sweet message, but I feel kind of ...

I feel that both of your guests touched on it, and I do feel that, hopefully, I hope and pray that we all wake up and make the changes that need to be. I don't know. I wanted to read this message for everyone.

**Hillary Raimo:** Yes, thank you. Let's do that now.

**Gail Swanson:** Okay. This is one of the messages I received from swimming with these beautiful creatures. Freedom dwells only in equality. Those who exist in the sea emanate a loving vibration of freedom, their purpose to imbue us with the joy and exaltation that freedom brings. Our hearts leap with joy as we bear witness to their majesty. Our souls remember what joy is found in unbridled playfulness.

There is spiritual nourishment where the sea and sky meet. There is magic where the sea and sky meet and the majestic ones play. There is hope and wisdom riding on their backs. There is honor and nobility in their eyes. There is love of family as they glide side by side, all elements of nature harmoniously existing and serving humanity.

As we move through this most crucial time, these keepers of light and knowledge call to us, sing to us, blessing us with all that they are.

They are calling us home. They are awakening our hearts. They speak the language of universal love. They ride the waves of multidimensionality. They beckon us to remember, we are one heart, one world, one magnificent creation, born to remember love. They are ever so joyfully willing to commune with us, connecting our hearts to the sea, and the sky, and to each one of them. They are aiding us in ways that are beyond our comprehension at this time. They call us forth now to meditate upon the sea, the sky, the sun, and the moon, to breathe in the stars of heaven, and to merge with our ancient and wise brothers and sisters of the sea as humanity strives to restore balance on earth.

**Hillary Raimo:** Gail Swanson, thank you so much for sharing those wise words of wisdom.

**Gail Swanson:** You know, I just feel that the whole event has to have a higher purpose, because I've been very fortunate to see what I call the higher view with certain events and certain times. I'm not particularly sure with this one is, it's so enormous, but I would like to just share one thing. I think that if everyone could see something like this in their own lives, it would change everything. It's very meaningful for this situation, also, as far as how we conduct ourselves, and how we feel about how what's going on, and how we just conduct our own lives.

I think I mentioned to you how this is like a, as within, without. All the things that are going on in our own lives, that we are held down in this muck, is manifested in the outer. My best friend from childhood became very ill. She had cancer, and she was becoming weaker and very sick. She was an artist, and she was a beautiful, beautiful soul. It was one of those stories that you hear about all the time, but I was blessed to see it, how she just moved through this whole thing with such grace, and she never complained, and she never said she was in pain. I would speak to her every day. I was here in Florida, and she was in New Jersey. We were having all kinds of really interesting things happen, and many things happened to us in the Gulf, both of us, when she would come to visit me in between her treatments. We had this connection.

It was the first day when she was unable to walk anymore, she couldn't get out of bed, she was told she cannot walk anymore, and I called her, and she said, "Oh, Gail. This is so terrible. I'm watching on television," and it was Katrina. I said, "Oh, honey. Turn that off. You have so much on your mind. Don't look at it." She said, "I can't help it."

I've only had this happen a very few times, but my eyes were open, and I began to have a vision in front of me. I could see that there was like a golden thread almost going from her. I could see the entire family sitting on the roof in Katrina, and what I was shown was that the grace with which she was not able to get out of the bed, but so accepting and loving towards everyone was literally, literally sustaining these people. I'm telling you that every time I tell this, I still get the chills. I tell it every chance I can, because it changed me in such a profound way, because I could see, and I was shown that what we do in our own lives with grace, and humility, and integrity, and love changes things that we may never know and never see, but it really can change the world. If everyone were more grace-filled, I really think things would be a lot better.

**Hillary Raimo:** I agree, and thank you, Gail, for sharing your beautiful message, and being a part of this today. Thank you so much for joining us.

**Gail Swanson:** Thanks Hillary.

**Hillary Raimo:** Next, Barbara Hand Clow has joined us. Barbara is an international Mayan elder, Cherokee record-keeper, and internationally acclaimed ceremonial teacher and author of many books, including my personal favorite, one of them, anyway, *The Mayan Code: Time Acceleration and Awakening the World Mind.* She will be discussing tonight the unique relationship between world events and the Mayan calendar, and of time resonation with the 102,000-year regional underworld of the Mayan calendar, and how the oil spill began at exactly the 95 hundred BC point, the time of the great cataclysm during the end of the global maritime civilization, the fall of Atlantis. Because of this relationship, Barbara claims that the oil volcano is either the beginning of a great extinction or is the trigger for the psychic processing of ourselves as a multi-traumatized species. Welcome, Barbara.

**Barbara H.C.:** Hi, Hillary. How are you?

**Hillary Raimo:** I'm great thank you. I'm so happy you're here.

**Barbara H.C.:** Good. I'm happy to be here, too.

**Hillary Raimo:** Where do you stand on this event in the Gulf Barbara?

**Barbara H.C.:** Well, that was a good summary of my own personal response to it. When the event actually happened, April 19th, 20th, 21st, I was working with time resonation factors in the calendar, and I was waiting to see what would happen at that point, because whatever would happen at that point is a trigger for us, as a species, to start processing inner trauma from the past that we have not cleared yet. Even though this situation is absolutely horrendous, and I can't imagine anything worse that could have happened, it also is a signal that we're coming to a point of major change in the consciousness of our species. You have to ask yourself, "Well, what kind of change could that be?"

In my case, I have a Cherokee background, and also some Mayan training in this lifetime, and I've had some experience in this lifetime in ceremonial work, where we've been in resonation with the planet. Then, of course, many, many thousands of years ago, all of us were in resonance with the planet. I think what's happening is we're getting kicked in the pants, in a sense, to move back into resonation with the planet, because when we're in that state of consciousness, we're profoundly different beings. I think that's what's happening to us. I think we're being forced and moved back into the actual consciousness with the planet at this time.

**Hillary Raimo:** You often talk about how people, in general, have repressed memories of the 10,500 BC event, and how it lives in our DNA. Therefore, it's in our consciousness. With so many reactive spectrums going on from people being ... fear, sadness, anger, helplessness, hope, trying to cope is this a catalyst, actually, to move us through these things?

**Barbara H.C.:** Well, I think it really is a catalyst for healing. Now, when I was a child, I was trained by my Cherokee grandfather, and for 17, 18 years pretty consistently, so a great deal of time in my life. He said that, like many indigenous people do, he said that until we remember our story, that we can never heal. He said that we were profoundly separated from the story of our species and the story of our journey on the planet. It seems that this event, the pain of this event, is what's actually taking us back into the ability to recall our story.

Then, when you know your story, then you move into consciousness and resonance with the planet itself. This event, Hillary, is much, much bigger than people, at this point, realize, as far as I'm concerned. Another thing that's in one of my books, *Alchemy of Nine Dimensions*, is a discussion of the abiotic oil theory. Abiotic oil theory is a theory about oil as a renewable resource that comes from Thomas Gold, who was a very famous scientist, who just died a few years ago. Thomas Gold actually proved that oil is a renewable resource, and that the tap into the oil is around five to six miles below the surface. We haven't just tapped into a little pocket of oil.

The other theory, the theory that we grew up with about oil was that the planet was filled with all these pockets of oil that came from rotting matter from millions of years ago. It turns out, that's not true. We haven't just tapped into a pocket, a deposit of oil. We've actually tapped into the source of the planetary blood, and that's why this is such a big deal, much, much bigger than anybody realizes at this time.

**Hillary Raimo:** Do you think, Barbara, that the Gulf was an accident?

**Barbara H.C.:** Yes, I do think it's an accident. It's an accident by corporate America. There's another issue here.

We're resonating with different night sixes of the different underworlds. There's actually a whole series of them. The night six that we're resonating with in the previous underworld, the industrial underworld, is the development of planetary control by means of corporations. This type of incident, this type of control over the planet, planetary resources itself, could only have been accomplished by corporations. From that point of view, you could almost say this is deliberate, except that none of these people really wanted it to work out this way, either. It's kind of hard sometimes to call it an accident. I mean, how do you call something an accident when it was inevitable, that it had to happen eventually, judging by the way they were using resources?

**Hillary Raimo:** What is the earth's message for humanity as her blood spills out of this tapped deep vein?

**Barbara H.C.:** I really think the earth's message is for us to tune into the inner part of ourselves that actually resonates with the planet. If you watch people closely ... It's been really fascinating to watch people. A great number of people around me have been sick for the last two and a half, three months, including myself. I've had a series of health complaints that are really bizarre. If you watch yourself closely, people are even feeling this event, to the point of their own personal health. This is teaching us that we're much more deeply connected with our home than we thought we were. We've gotten radically disconnected from our home itself.

**Hillary Raimo:** As people find and recover these repressed memories, they're realizing that these grand cycles aren't separate of them.

**Barbara H.C.:** Yeah, that's right.

**Hillary Raimo:** This event isn't separate from us. What can people do to reconnect?

**Barbara H.C.:** That's a very, very difficult one. Imagine one of the people who's actually directly affected by this. This is actually an issue of major public health issue, because another thing going on in this situation is not just the oil. Also, the other thing that's being released in gigantic quantities is methane. The methane release is potentially extremely toxic for the people who live in that region. It's actually a very, very dangerous issue. This is one of the things that there's kind of a ... You're not supposed to really talk about this, but I'll say what I want to say, no matter what.

**Hillary Raimo:** You can say whatever you want on my show Barbara.

**Barbara H.C.:**  Right. The issue would be that people who are living near the shore and down in that region are actually in danger, and I think it's significantly enough danger that I think evacuation should be looked at. I think, for instance, if you consider what China would do, I think China would be evacuating people at this point.

**Hillary Raimo:**  Intuitively, I feel the same thing Barbara.

**Barbara H.C.:**  Yeah, and I feel it's a major public health issue. I think, for those of us who are concerned, I think we need to be connected with this and prepared to assist in this situation, because this is really, truly a gigantic disaster.

**Hillary Raimo:**  It's really overwhelming. Some are sick of hearing it already, but the thing is that this isn't a spill. This is ongoing. This hasn't stopped yet.

**Barbara H.C.:**  Yeah, that's the main thing.

**Hillary Raimo:**  The effects of this are ongoing. This is a 24-hour nonstop leak that's coming into our environment on a continuous basis.

**Barbara H.C.:**  That's right.

**Hillary Raimo:**  Barbara, tell us about this important relationship between the Mayan calendar and this event in the Gulf, and how some people are taking this event and others as prophesy fulfillments.

**Barbara H.C.:**  Well, you know, the way I look at that one is we're in the middle of some major astrological cycles right now, too, and we're in the middle of a series of eclipses that are actually creating kind of a gigantic lock on reality. We're in the middle of a situation right now where it's kind of like you're stuck right where you are. The only change that you can actually effectuate is to change yourself.

As I've watched this situation continue as it is, I just continually look at the American government and Obama, and I keep screaming, "Why don't you stop the war? Why don't you stop the war?" In other words, speaking of something that people could do, it's outrageous that the United States continues to carry on wars in the world when a situation as critical as this is going on right in the country. It's unbelievable, really. I think another thing that all of us should be feeling right now is just a tremendously huge feeling of rage, that this country could go on like this. Eclipses, by the way, are saying, and the timing of eclipses are saying change, change, change, and yet nothing changes.

**Hillary Raimo:**  What do you think it's going to take for us to really get it?

**Barbara H.C.:**  Well, you'd think this would, wouldn't you, you know what I mean? At this point, I'm standing back and going, "I can't believe that this isn't causing massive levels of change right now." The earth, by the way, is very much alive and very responsive, and if there isn't some change, there's going to be more response on the part of the earth. The eclipse cycle, June 26th and July 11th in the next couple of weeks are showing that there is going to be hurricanes, and earthquakes, and solar flares, and everything, if there isn't some kind of level of change here. I think if people are feeling kind of a sense of rage, they should be. At this point, we have reason to be justifiably very angry.

**Hillary Raimo:** I think most people have a very hard time with anger. They don't have a good relationship with it. They can't express it. They're afraid of it. They don't know how to do it in a way that is productive. They don't know how to take anger and transform it into some kind of positive production. We've become very, very dysfunctional.

**Barbara H.C.:** You know, and there's just anger, and then there's anger that's coming from having not faced yourself. You see the difference? This one is pushing us right up against the edge of facing the consequences of what's going on, and then the natural, healthy response is actually very just anger. I'm hoping that people will be able to motivate themselves, then, into their own part of action in this, because there are many, many things that people can do, and there are going to be many, many things developing now that are going to enable people to do things about this. We've got to move it, at this point.

**Hillary Raimo:** What can people do, Barbara? Do they get in their car, and drive down there to help? Do they protest?

**Barbara H.C.:** Yeah. I don't think people should drive down there. I think it's exactly opposite. They need to be driving out.

**Hillary Raimo:** Away.

**Barbara H.C.:** But I think there are lots of ways that people ... People are kind of still stunned right now. First of all, when the whole thing happened in the first place, then supposedly BP was doing everything, and of course, they're not. There's a little bit of involvement, at this point, on the part of the National Guard, but you would think that you'd see more participation in the situation right from the military forces in the National Guard in the United States, in terms of response down there. But I think in terms of individual response, there needs to be fundraising. There needs to be charities and groups of people who are helping on this, because people really, really are going to need help.

**Hillary Raimo:** Jesse Hicks is putting together a wonderful documentary. I was hoping that he would be able to call in tonight. It's called Dark Horizon, a documentary about the Gulf oil disaster, and you can go to his kickstarter.com/darkhorizon. This is a kind of example,

Barbara, of what people can do.

I asked myself that question, and I said, "Okay, I have this Facebook page. I have X amount of people on here. I can post things that I'm finding in my research, but I can also make air time available, to gather a group of people who can speak on the topic and give listeners their opinions. That is how I can help. Everyone has different skills and things they bring to the table.

I encourage people who have skills, who have the ability to do things, to start doing it, because we all have something unique to offer.

**Barbara H.C.:**  Yeah, and so the issue for me, what is my personal part in this? Well, as you know, on my website, I'm using my website as a coaching device now, season by season, and new moon by new moon, to help people move through this. When this whole situation hit, meanwhile, astrologically, the astrology is saying that it's time to really go into the deepest depths of our personal character. The astrology is saying that who we each are as an individual right now matters a huge amount, and that each one of us needs to go into the deepest levels of questioning about what are our values? What are we giving? What are we creating? Because this event itself is happening in order to bring out that level of commitment and awareness on our part.

That's really what this whole thing is all about. I mean, as an individual, we can't change what's happening down there in a physical way, but our response to it involves the response to the consciousness of the planet, and that's what the planet's asking us for. It's almost like, with the planet suffering the way she is, if we didn't realize it, and we didn't see it, and we didn't feel that, then what would anything matter? How we're responding and how we feel matters, a lot. For me, it's actually been a matter of just staying on an even keel, physically. I can't believe the symptoms that my body is going through, and I'm a great distance from this thing. I'm way up in Vancouver, British Columbia, but I'm just-

**Hillary Raimo:**  Thank you for coming on the air for this segment, to share this. Barbara's website is HandClow2012.com.

**Barbara H.C.:**  Okay, Hillary. Thanks for doing this show.

**Hillary Raimo:**  Next up is documentary filmmaker Jesse Hicks, welcome Jesse.

**Jesse Hicks:**  Hi, Hillary.

**Hillary Raimo:**  Tell us about the project that you're working on.

**Jesse Hicks:**  Yeah. We're working on a documentary about this disaster, which is obviously a huge event, and it affects millions of people in lots of facets, and it's very complicated. Our documentary is a work in progress. We've been down there, and we've shot with some locals in Grand Isle. We got some great stuff and met some amazing people, and were encouraged to go down, so I'm actually on my way back down there on Tuesday.

We're just going to keep at it and try to gather more footage, meet more people, and really try to shape the documentary into something that will reach a lot of people, and impact a lot of people, and hopefully ... I guess what I really want to do is make the connection between what's going on down there and the way we live, as Americans, and globally, I guess in other First World countries. Our consumption has something to do with what's going on right now, and I think a lot of people, maybe they know that, but they don't really feel that connection. That's one of the goals of this film, but the film, of course, will develop as we continue to work on it.

**Hillary Raimo:**  What did you see down there?

**Jesse Hicks:**  When we were down there, we were there relatively a while ago. I guess it was about three and a half, four weeks. We saw lots of fisherman who were not fishing but were working with BP. They were all very closed off to us, because BP doesn't want them to talk to the media or any sort of media-related people, including independent filmmakers and reporters. We saw them, and we saw oil. There was oil everywhere, and there's oil in the water. Where we were in Grand Isle, at that point, it was before it had really come to the surface and congealed in the way that you see in a lot of the more recent news video coverage, but it was still everywhere.

Anyone who had been out in the water doing any sort of cleanup, their vessels and all their equipment was covered in oil. It was mostly, though, just at that point, the people were in shock and really worried about a way of life being destroyed and an industry being destroyed, and not really sure what was going to happen next, and I don't think they are, still. But at that point, I think there was still mostly the shock phase.

**Hillary Raimo:**  Were people willing to speak to you, or did you have a hard time getting people to talk about it?

**Jesse Hicks:**  It was a mix. I mean, anyone who was working with BP, which was quite a large number of the people down there, they were hesitant to speak to us, and most of them didn't want to. We had a couple fisherman who let us sort of shoot their boat and talk to them. We framed their faces out of our shots, so they spoke to us anonymously, essentially. There's also some people that we found, who were very upset about the efforts that were being done to protect the area and to clean up the oil, so since they were sort of at odds with BP's efforts, they were willing to speak with us.

**Hillary Raimo:** Did you find frustration in regards to being able to tell the truth about what's happening?

**Jesse Hicks:** I think there was frustration in what was being put out there on a larger scale, frustration with what was being heard in the news. There's been several videos. Ours is just a trailer, but there's some clips that support this, but then, other longer ones, a fisherman who, I don't know all their backstories, but for whatever reason were unafraid to speak up against BP and basically say that some stuff's being done, but not as much as you're made to think by the news media. I mean, this is from other sources, but that voice is definitely out there, and we perceive that, as well. That said, there's a lot of people who are working for BP. That was our perception, but the question of how effective that work is a whole other thing to be determined.

**Hillary Raimo:** Were people concerned about the health effects of what they're experiencing down there?

**Jesse Hicks:** Absolutely. I mean, for a lot of the fishermen, the only choice ... The obvious choice for employment now, now that the fisheries are essentially closed down around Grand Isle, and I think something like 20% of the water in the entire Gulf and more right around Louisiana, their obvious source of employment would be to work for BP and clean up, but some people have read reports and books, probably from your first guests, also, about how the dispersants and the cleanup has detrimental health effects, so a lot of them just didn't want to participate in that, which basically left them with few options on finding a source of income. Most people felt trapped, very understandably. Yeah. It's a pretty crazy situation. Everyone was mobilized to clean up the spill, but if you didn't want to do that, then your kind of out of luck.

**Hillary Raimo:** There's also some talk of this being an opportunity for Martial law or a military state to be put into place. Did you get the feel for that while you were down there, at all?

**Jesse Hicks:** There's definitely National Guard everywhere, which, that changes the mood in a town. I mean, this town was one that was described to us as an ... I'm speaking of Grand Isle. It's a small town. Everyone knows each other, you know? Everyone says hello. You go walking around, and you see your friends walking around, too. Then, all of a sudden, there's Humvees everywhere, and half the people ... Maybe not that many, but a huge amount of people in camp. There's a lot of National Guards. I don't know about Martial law taking over the town, but there's definitely a different vibe, and of course, if someone in a Humvee comes up and wants to do something, or stop you from coming onto the beach, or whatever it is, then chances are, they're going to have some authority, or at least be effective.

**Hillary Raimo:** Jesse, thanks so much for calling in and sharing your experiences. Where can people find out more information or help fund your project?

**Jesse Hicks:** Yeah. We have a Kickstarter page that, the best way to get to that, if you go to tinyurl.com/oilspilldocumentary. You could also find us just through Kickstarter, which is what you were saying before on the air, but that shorter URL is probably the easiest way. It's tinyurl.com/kickstarter, and yeah, you can watch the trailer, and people, if they're interested, can contribute a little and help make sure that we can keep spending time down there and keep covering this, and come out with a wonderful project that a lot of people can relate to.

**Hillary Raimo:** Good luck with your project and thank you.

Next, is Barbara Goodfriend. She's an animal communicator who is joining us to share a special message from the sea animals of the Gulf of Mexico. Animal communication is an understanding spoken between species whose hearts and minds are linked through mutual love. It is a thread that weaves interaction in the wild, and it brings us deeper levels of compassion and learning in the domesticated world. It is very tangible and beneficial for both the animal and human involved. Her website is, BarbaraGoodfriend.com. Welcome, Barbara. Thanks for waiting.

**Barbara G.:** Hi, Hillary. It's great to be on. Thank you.

**Hillary Raimo:** What is the message you have for us from the animals in the Gulf?

**Barbara G.:** Well, I think there are multiple messages here. One of the deepest messages that I feel is that the animals are bringing to us is really for us to go deeper and feel the connection, also, to the earth. You know, there's a great amount of loss of life going on with the animals, a lot of pain, a lot of suffering, but also, at the same time, what's going on is people are really feeling, they're getting within themselves, and they're feeling all their emotions. These are triggers for things going on in their lives, and I believe, also, that unless we straighten out our own emotional baggage and take care of what we need to do, we need to steward ourselves in order to steward the wildlife, in order to steward the planet, and to bring forth the planet and the earth for future generations, bring the solutions through, also.

What happens now is that people are able to talk about this. They're able to go into their emotions and speak about what's going on with the animals. I believe it's really, really important to get into our own telepathic abilities in order to really get our own guidance to know how to move forward, find solutions, work through this in the most peaceful way that we can, and come together in a way that everyone can cooperate, that we can really feel the truth. That's the thing. If you go inside, go really deep inside, and get in touch with your telepathic abilities, which is the way that the animals communicate, you can really see where the truth lies in all these situations, not only here but globally, also.

**Hillary Raimo:** Do the animals know to migrate away from this event in the Gulf? Can we help them by telepathically giving them the thoughts and the images of moving away from this area?

**Barbara G.:** Yes. I think it's possible, although some of them, of course, they're getting poisoned by the fumes, and the toxins, and the dispersants, and they can't really maneuver through this. With the dispersants, they are ingesting this. Some of

them, no, they can't get away, but others, yes, I do believe that we can speak to them and ask them to move to safer waters. Yeah. I believe that we can definitely let them know the extent of the damage, where they could go to. I've been trying to do this with the whales myself, although I feel like a lot of the whales are already at the bottom of the Gulf. But yes, I believe that we can do that. We can communicate with them. They're very, very responsive.

I feel like they're looking for our help, and as groups, they're looking for their own survival. I think that people could get together, and there's more power in a group, and send those messages out, and assist the animals in moving on. I've read accounts of flocks of birds that aren't specific to certain areas, that seem to be showing up in different parts of the country now, so yes, there is a group mind going on, and yes, we can affect it, we can communicate with them, and we can help them in this way. Yes.

**Hillary Raimo:** It's a really positive way of handling the energies that we're all feeling right now. Many feel very helpless with this. They don't know what to do. Do they take it to their social networking sites? Do they take it to their local book club? Do they talk about it in the grocery store? They don't know what to do, and so they just kind of watch the little segment on the news, and then they turn it off, and they go about their lives, and they figure it's somebody else's problem. Somebody else will fix it. Somebody else will stand up and get angry about it. Somebody else will make a big enough stink, and then something will happen from there. It's not going to work this time.

**Barbara G.:** No.

**Hillary Raimo:** You cannot just stick your head in the sand and pretend it away.

**Barbara G.:** Exactly.

**Hillary Raimo:** Have people, in general, become so complacent and docile in their reactions to things in this world that they're sleepwalking through much of their life? Many still don't have a connection to their psychic, telepathic abilities, because they don't believe in it.

**Barbara G.:** Yeah. Well, our psychic and telepathic abilities are totally innate in us. The same thing happened to me when ... April 20th, I started feeling everything that was happening with the animals. Then, I said to myself, "Well, what can I do to help them? Instead of sitting here and ripping my own hair out, and crying, and worrying, what can we do to help them?" Our innate abilities, they can create a natural response, even if you're helping an animal pass, even just comforting the animals. They don't know what to do. They're caught in this oil, but they're catalysts for all of us waking up and seeing how reckless we've been, and how reckless and how material we've been living our lives, and where we can go with this, how we can make little changes in our lives, how we can so easily feel for the animals, but do we feel for each other?

**Hillary Raimo:** Right.

**Barbara G.:** They are catalysts in this, and this is what's so important, and I feel like this is their message. Get inside ourselves, to come together, to help, even praying or helping the animals pass, or asking them to move, helping the families, feeling this, but like you said, not feeling depressed. I mean, we can feel our anger. We have right to feel our anger, but it's about where are we going to take all this? Where are we going to go with this? This will help us connect with what's really important, connect with the earth, the heartbeat of the earth, the nourishment of the earth and everything that can be renewed, or lifted, or taken care of here. I feel it's really, really important when people connect with the animals, because they reach inside themselves, and they can feel this, and this unlocks within them.

**Hillary Raimo:** Anybody who has a pet they love dearly knows that that's what you're talking about. Anyone who has a special connection with any kind of animal understands what you're saying. If somebody who may not believe in psychic abilities, or this is all a bunch of woo-woo stuff, knows that they have a special relationship with their animal. That's undeniable.

You know what I want to ask you, Barbara, is a lot of people have been saying to me, and I mentioned this to Barbara Hand Clow earlier, many people have been telling me that their animals, their dogs especially, are getting sick now, just for no reason. Just out of the blue, they're just getting sick. I said to somebody today, actually, I was seeing a client, and I said to her, "Well, you know, they're taking on a lot of the energy that's happening right now. Look at what's going on." I think animals have a tendency to physically manifest this quicker than humans do. Is that correct?

**Barbara G.:** Yeah. I do feel they're more connected to the earth, more naturally connected, or have a quicker response in a lot of times. I have been seeing a lot of dogs actually almost teetering, trying to decide, having big health issues come up but not passing, and sort of, "Am I staying, or am I going?" It's been very confusing for their owners. Yeah. You know, the animals are just very ... They can feel all of this. They can definitely feel all of this.

They're affected, and not only do they take on these energies, but I found, in the last few years, that I would say five years ago, the animals really took on our illnesses and all our emotions and all this, but what I've been finding, across my work, is that what they're doing now is more reflecting things back, so that we take responsibility for the things that are going on, not only in our lives, but in the world, also. All of this, they show us through the heart connection, and that's all kinds of healing for the planet has to come from.

**Hillary Raimo:** A need to be rewired back to the heart?

**Barbara G.:** Absolutely.

**Hillary Raimo:** Barbara, thanks so much for joining me and sharing your valuable information with us.

**Barbara G.:** My pleasure.

**Hillary Raimo:** Thank you. Next, joining me is Dr. Ian Prattis. He's a professor in Ottawa, Canada. He'll be adding to our discussion and speaking on the topics of the spin factor, consumer culpability, and spiritual guidelines and how they relate to the Gulf. He's a poet and scholar, peace and environmental activist. He has trained with masters in Buddhist, Vedic, and Shamanic traditions, and he teaches and talks at seminars and retreats around the world. He is founder of Friends for Peace, a coalition of meditation, peace, and environmental groups that work for peace and planetary care, and also, he is the resident teacher of the Buddhist meditation community in Ottawa, Canada. Welcome, Ian. Thanks so much for waiting.

**Dr. Ian Prattis:** Oh, thank you. Not a problem.

**Hillary Raimo:** What perspective do you bring to the table in regards to the Gulf oil event?

**Dr. Ian Prattis:** The perspective I bring is to first acknowledge that this particular crisis has also brought an enormous amount of spin from not just the corporations, where we expect it, but also from government, the media, and the general public. The underlying aspect I'd like to bring to the fore is that all sectors are culpable. As consumers, if we have a demand for oil and oil-based products, we drive the whole process. We have an artificial spin to justify our consumption patterns.

This crisis is huge. It's bigger than most people are prepared to take into their minds, but there are other crises like this happening in the Arctic regions, the desert regions, and so on, and we have to go beyond the crisis and look at what is really at stake here? What is at stake is the human mindset, which has to change. There's no short answer better than that one. The mindset has to change, and until it does change, we will go on destroying the ecosystem.

My most recent book is called *Failsafe: Saving the Earth From Ourselves*. This points out how we can change our mind, that we must stop, examine our patterns of consumption, and then make a commitment to do no further harm, either to the planet or to ourselves. The solution is an internal one. It doesn't matter what spiritual tradition one prefers, or yoga practice, or meditation practice, we have to come to a steady stop, look at what we do with our patterns of behavior, and change those patterns that cause harm. This is what I teach, that I've been teaching at the university and to meditation students for over 20 years, and I do see radical changes.

At my home, my response has been to give up my car, several years ago, to do a major eco retrofit on my modest home in the West end of Ottawa, and to be very careful in my consumption habits, and to be aware. If I could tell you a small anecdote, I was giving a small talk in Orlando, Florida, about environmental issues a year ago. An answer I gave to a very good question, which the question was, "Is my mindfulness enough?" This was from someone who was very aware and careful about his consumption. This was a good question. I said, "Yes, your mindfulness is enough, but are there enough of us who are mindful?" That's crucial, because I think there's a tipping point that we're not too far away from, where people are changing their patterns. They are changing their minds, but is it enough? I don't have the answer to that. I have certain speculations.

**Hillary Raimo:** Which are?

**Dr. Ian Prattis:** That it only takes around 2% of the world's population to meditate on a daily basis, to produce a tipping point. It's the hundredth monkey syndrome, whereby a quality of energy will leap from mind to mind, and we would make different kinds of decisions about what we consume, how we behave, how we interact. Those of us who are wealthy all around the world will learn how to live on less, and also live happily on less. It'll bring about a different structure of institutions and society all from taking care of the planet, taking care of ourselves, and also taking this out as action.

There's an awful lot of talk through the social networks of, "Okay, let's make everything love. Let's make everything compassion," but where is the action? The action component of taking the changed mind into the arena of everyday life, this is the challenge that faces us. The challenge of the Gulf oil spill is enormous. It's the most enormous challenge, I think, that the US has faced, and it's not just the US that faces this challenge. It's the entire world.

**Hillary Raimo:** What a beautiful thought. It's been one of my bigger frustrations, that so many have such a difficult time with the word action. Action has to be angry? Why do we need to act? It's all divine will. It's all this. It's all that. It's frustrating, because on one level, I want to see more people do it, and on another level, you're fighting an entire mindset. You're fighting ... Not fighting. Fighting's the wrong word, but you're up against several, multiple mindsets... I like how you present the, each person has their own role in this.

I tell people that they're gatekeepers of their own home, that they make the choice when they go out and they buy something to endorse it or not, to further encourage the production of that or not, regardless of where it comes from. The lack of awareness of what goes into somebody's body with the food issues that we have, I mean, we could go on and on with examples, but the problem is this lack of awareness, this lack of conscious awareness of what we're consuming.

**Dr. Ian Prattis:** Absolutely.

**Hillary Raimo:** Where do you think we went wrong? Where did it start, Ian?

**Dr. Ian Prattis:** I think we left consciousness over in one space and didn't recognize that it has to be engaged with society and with the environment in a very practical, down-to-earth manner. Eight years ago, I founded an organization called Friends for Peace, and this has grown into a coalition of over 50 groups in the city of Ottawa. This is action-oriented, in terms of actually saving pristine whitewater rivers and wetlands, actively seeing social justice occur with Aboriginal populations in Canada.

We're very action-oriented, and the former mayor of the city of Ottawa, we have an annual event in City Hall. He said publicly, this is the face of Ottawa he would like to see. I took him to one side, and I said, "Oh, no, no, no. This is the face of Ottawa now, not future." The future, which is very difficult to wrap our minds around, the future is now, because the actions we take now set in motion what our future structure and conditions will be like, and the actions we have to take now are selfless. We have to go beyond our wealth, our ego, our desires and our needs, and recognize that if we're going to have a chance, as a species, to be here by the end of this century, we have to change our ways. I get so pumped ... I think that is the word, from seeing what happens with the Friends of Peace organization, is that people are changing. The whole diversity of Ottawa comes together. There's quite a lot of change in our Northern city as a result of this.

**Hillary Raimo:** That reminds me of this quote, "Always aim at complete harmony of thought, and word, and deed. Always aim at purifying your thoughts and everything will be well." I think that, as we watch the waters become the opposite of purified, and we're going to have to go through a purification process, it's the same thing with us, isn't us?

**Dr. Ian Prattis:** Absolutely.

**Hillary Raimo:** It's the same thing with us on another level, a different level. We're going through a purification process of releasing our own vein of muck.

**Dr. Ian Prattis:** Absolutely. The muck and the mud are essential, because if you didn't have the mud, you couldn't have a lotus growing. We need the mud and the muck, but we work through it. This is work. This is internal work, and there's so many different ways of doing it, all of which are viable. That's the beauty of what's available to us, but when we do the internal work, and we become steady, and we become clear, that's when we engage with the environment, with society. Without the engagement, all of this spiritual stuff is useless. The days of the yogis meditating in caves is over. This is the 21st century, and if we want to really build a different kind of society for the remainder of this century, we must change our ways.

I have a chapter in *Failsafe: Saving the Earth From Ourselves,* which is about stopping, finding the still point, changing the patterns, and it gives very, very precise methods and procedures. I see this on a weekly basis, in terms of the community I teach. I see the transformations taking place in people, and because there's an example set of how to reduce the size of the ecological footprint that we leave, and how we engage with society, with other groups, and with the environment, with that example, people will follow suit. In a sense, all that I'm saying to you, I do my very best to actually walk that talk and put it into action. I must emphasize the word action, because without action following consciousness change we're in trouble and we will be going down the tube.

**Hillary Raimo:** Indeed. Dr. Ian Prattis, thank you so much for joining me. Your website for listeners is, IanPrattis.com.

**Dr. Ian Prattis:** Thank you, Hillary.

**Hillary Raimo:** Where is our accountability for how we live, how we consume, how we treat each other, and whether or not we come from our heart when it comes to other people? There is hope. The earth will recover. We will recover, but I can guarantee you, things will not be the same, thankfully. Goodnight, everybody.

# 8

# GAIL REX
# HEALING THE LIVING LANDSCAPE

*Not all of my guests were well known. I often sought out authors who were presenting unique material with powerful messages for the betterment of humanity. When I read Gail's book I immediately knew I wanted to talk to her. Her work sparked inspiration in me and made sense to my healing arts background. Her work applies the concept of acupuncture to the living landscape and her story is breathtaking and offers hope in an all too often dim world and the important lesson that, when the land heals, we all heal.*

RECORDED APRIL 5, 2016

**Hillary Raimo:** In this episode we will be talking about applying the principles of Chinese medicine to build healing relationships with the Earth with my guest Gail Rex author of *Earth Acupuncture: Healing the Living Landscape*. Her story is incredible and inspiring. After experiencing a powerful vision of the nuclear power plant near her home and its toxic effects on the Hudson River, acupuncturist Gail Rex was inspired to help heal the river and surrounding lands but was unsure how to begin.

Her story starts with a workshop with a 27th generation Cherokee wisdom teacher, venerable Dionee Yowahoo. She discovered the answer. She could treat the landscape just as she treated her patients by taking its pulses and treating the points of stagnant energy and pollution with acupuncture. Tracing her journey from initial vision and pulse taking to building a stone circle to opening a major energy meridian of the Hudson, Gail reveals how our rivers, valleys, and forests are capable of illness and healing just like a living being. She explains simple practices in her book for attuning with the living landscape and responding appropriately to the messages and images received from the Earth's intelligence.

By making offerings of thanks and asking the land's permission before every interaction, Gail Rex demonstrates the power of right relationship in motion. I'm really excited to talk about this tonight. Gail Rex is an acupuncturist, author, and editor. A graduate of the University of Pennsylvania, and the Tri-State College of Acupuncture. She has been practicing Chinese medicine since 1995, first in New York and now in

Vermont, and she is the author of another book called *Wood Becomes Water: Chine Medicine in Everyday Life*. Welcome Gail. Thanks so much for joining us.

**Gail Rex:** Thanks Hillary. I'm glad to be on the show.

**Hillary Raimo:** This is a really incredible story. Where would you like to start?

**Gail Rex:** Well let's start with the vision, which came as a surprise to me. I was sitting in a meditation class and all of a sudden, I had a vision. It was as if I was in the air, looking down from a mountain at the Hudson River right near the Indian Point nuclear power plant. And I saw these lines of fire moving from the power plant into the Hudson River and into the land below the river. And it just sort of was this volcanic fiery dark wound that was happening, and I realized, "Oh. The river is hurt. And it's showing me its pain." And then I heard this voice in my head that said, "What you are given to see, you can heal. Work with the hills."

And then I sort of became aware again of the room that I was sitting in and what everyone else was doing in the meditation workshop and I was stunned. I had never had such an experience happen to me before, and it changed my life.

**Hillary Raimo:** There couldn't be a better timing as far as I'm concerned to bring you on the air to share your story, to get people to understand that they too can have a role in healing the landscape.

You have done a wonderful job of showing how this energy work can be applied to the Earth. When you started to go out into the land to find your pulse points, you were looking for something called the dragon's bad breath. Could you talk about that?

**Gail Rex:** Yes. A few months after that initial vision it came to me that the way that I needed to heal this landscape was to build a stone circle. Kind of like the old Hindus in Britain, but perhaps smaller, and that that would function as acupuncture for the Earth. And I was in a workshop with venerable Dionee Yawahoo, and I just sort of announced during a question and answer period that I was thinking of building a stone circle to help heal the landscape around Indian Point, and did she have any suggestions. And lo and behold she did, and one of her suggestions was that I should find the place where the dragon exhales its bad breath, and that's where I should build my circle. And that was one of several things that she said, but that was the most absorbing thing initially because it's so poetic, and dramatic, and mythical. This dragon's bad breath. And I didn't know, once I began to look around, what such a thing would be. Where was I going to find a dragon and what would its bad breath look like?

145

But the very first day that I went exploring I went across the river, opposite side of the nuclear power plant, to just go have a look at it from the other side of the river. And as I was driving through the landscape, I suddenly got this horrible, sick feeling in my body that I didn't know how to describe, I didn't feel actually nauseous, but my stomach was pulling tight, and I got a headache across the front of my head. And in another minute, I was suddenly looking at the Indian Point nuclear power plant just across the river. And it was huge from that vantage point. And there was smoke coming out of it. And there was just this little town.

Right on my side of the river was this tiny little, must have once been beautiful, but at this point a little rundown sad seeming little village that seemed blighted for lack of a better word. But here it is in one of the most prosperous counties in the whole state, in the whole country in fact. But here's this little dark spot. And so, I realized that in fact, this was the place of the dragon's bad breath. This was where the power plant was exuding its poisons right there in the river. And there's this pool at that point in the river where the tides ... So, water comes down from the North, and rushes through the Hudson Highlands, which is a narrow and steep canyon. And the water comes through there very very quickly.

And then all of a sudden, the riverbed widens out and the water kind of comes to a crashing, not quite a stop but it's velocity really changes because it's no longer rushing through this steep and narrow canyon, it's now in this wide bay. And at the same time, Hudson Woods is a tidal river, so there's tides coming up from the Atlantic Ocean miles below. But when the tide is coming in, the water is actually coming upriver. So, it comes up the river, and meets this kind of stagnant pool right at Indian Point and there that water sits for quite some time. So, all of that bad breath that's coming out of that dragon, doesn't really move away.

**Hillary Raimo:** Interesting. You had quite the interesting time figuring out how to take the pulse of the land like you would take the pulse of the client. Tell us a little bit about that.

**Gail Rex:** Well I was really working blind because it was not something I had ever done before, it was not something I had ever heard about before. It was just a completely novel idea. So, I didn't really know what to do, but I just kind of started by looking at a map and deciding, "Well I guess I would want to look in public parks," because I didn't want to be ... I certainly couldn't go to someone's house and take a pulse there. So, I would look for places that were public parks. And Dionee Yawahoo had given me the advice to look for pulse points at three miles, and six miles, and nine miles away from the power plant which is analogous to the three fingers that I put on a client's wrist to feel their pulses. I feel a different pulse under each finger. So, the three-mile zone, and the six-mile zone, and the nine-mile zone would be roughly analogous to that.

And after a while I realized that, "Oh, water is the way to feel pulse. I need to be near water in these public parks because water moves the way that blood moves in a blood vessel. So that's where I might find a pulse." So, I identified likely spots on my map and then I started to go around to them and I would ... I didn't really know what to do once I got there because I wasn't sure how I was going to feel a pulse of a landscape. And at first, I tried to feel a real pulse the way I would feel a person's pulse, but the river itself didn't seem to be doing anything that I could identify as a pulse. So, then I just started to relax and let what came to mind come through.

And what I began to see was just images. Images sometimes of people. Sometimes weak people, sometimes an overbearing sensation. Sometimes I would have other little visions of birth and rebirth, and at each spot I came away with a pretty clear pulse reading that came to me in a different than a human pulse, but that once I began to analyze the qualities had in fact qualities that were very similar to a human pulse. Like weak and thready, or slippery, or tight. It began to ... The metaphor that I had thought was just going to be a cute metaphor about taking the pulses of the land, started to seem really very similar to taking pulses on a person.

**Hillary Raimo:** Hm. And when you were talking earlier about the dragon's breath being bad, it reminds me of how we can sometimes tell the health of the inside of a human body by someone's bad breath. Would agree with that?

**Gail Rex:** Absolutely. Yes.

**Hillary Raimo:** When you talk about the comparison between the acupuncture points, putting the three fingers on the wrist, plotting out the three circles at the given amounts of distance, finding the areas by water. I mean it's almost like you're inside of a human body and you're tracking these telltale signs of the landscape, and you know I've never lived near a nuclear power plant. But I know people who have, and I've also heard stories that the areas are often economically depleted, they have a very low status of income, and things of that sort. There's just some kind of stagnant energy there along with the humans. It makes perfect sense that we have this mirror type alignment between the two in comparison. Comparing one versus the other can often give us a diagnosis of the other, don't you think?

**Gail Rex:** But it was a new idea to me at the time. In hindsight it makes perfect sense, but mostly in Chinese medicine we do it the other way around. We use nature to help understand what's going on with the humans and vice versa.

**Hillary Raimo:** It compliments each other. And you, Gail, had the original idea to compare the art of acupuncture to the landscape. I don't think anybody has done that, officially have they?

**Gail Rex:** Not as far as I know. I have heard of people who do things called Earth acupuncture, and where they put rods or stones or whatnot, or crystals in the Earth. But I don't know of another acupuncturist who actually uses the systems, and the models, and the theories of acupuncture to do it.

**Hillary Raimo:** You mapped out around Indian Point power plant and associated places you choose as pulse points with the kidney, the lung I believe, and the heart. The liver, excuse me. The liver. I knew it was an L.

**Gail Rex:** So, they're the main organs used in Chinese medicine, and each organ has a reflection in one of the pulse positions. So, there's, well depending on what system you use, you can find 6, or 12, or even sometimes 18 different pulses reflecting different organs. I simplified for my purposes down to the main six. So, the heart, the spleen, and the lungs, and the liver, and the kidney.

**Hillary Raimo:** I was fascinated when I read your story. When this title crossed my path, I said, "Wow, that's really interesting." Because I've been working with meditation and nature through my *Love Breath for Earth* platform, and I've been taking groups of people out into the woods, into different natural areas to meditate. To talk about the effects of that.

What you're revealing is a very profound intelligence. You're actually aligning your human knowledge with the Earth's knowledge and performing a healing on the meridians of the land. You started to work with a man named James who was acting as a yin-yang. Can you talk to us about the yin-yang importance and how this affects the energy work that you were doing?

**Gail Rex:** Well in Chinese medicine yin and yang is the primary duality from when everything was just one big whole, and then things divided into these two poles. Yin and yang. And almost everything in Chinese medicine is viewed through that lens of some things are very yang and have a lot of bright effervescent energy. Some things are very yin and sort of a darker, condensing, contemplative energy. And as I set about ... As I had done a few pulses on my own, and then it was the day when I had decided I should be looking for the kidney yang pulse, and I realized that I just had no idea how to go about looking for kidney yang because I am just not a very yang personality. I'm quiet, I'm contemplative, I'm slow moving and slow talking. And that kind of burning bright yang, get a lot done energy is kind of mysterious to me.

And so, I decided that I should actually find a partner. Someone who could be the yang part of this so that we could be really doing a complete circuit of energy. It was imbalanced to just be looking from one viewpoint. We needed the other part. So, I had a friend who was also an acupuncturist who was willing to go on these adventures with me, and that made a great change and allowed a whole different kind of energy and viewpoint to come through.

**Hillary Raimo:** I think your work is the foundation of a future science.

**Gail Rex:** I certainly hope so. And in fact, it is really already happening. Maybe it's not always happening with acupuncture, but there's people like you and me, and I've met probably a dozen others at this point and I'm sure there are more, who are understanding that the Earth speaks if only we will listen. And I think it is the start.

**Hillary Raimo:** Very inspiring. How do our ancestors and megalithic sites play into all of this?

**Gail Rex:** I absolutely thought about that and I had the help of two really powerful geomancers in this project. One of them, Ivan Macbeth is a modern-day druid who has built giant stone circles all over the world. And he's really a Celtic spirit, and he more than anyone else I've ever met really understands the work involved, and the precision involved, and the cosmic conversation involved in creating something like this. And it really does tie you in to all those ancestors who ever did that before. And especially to all those ancestors who knew and understood that we are having a conversation with all of creation and that this is a way for humans, by creating something that stands and reflects the precision of the universe, this is a way for humans to speak back.

**Hillary Raimo:** You write something very interesting in your book. I'm going to read it. You write, "Our linear concept of time is thus introducing a cancerous consciousness into our dealings with each other and our environment. In contrast, circular time awareness brings us back to living in a renewable relationship in so many parts of our life and activities." Tell us what that means to you.

**Gail Rex:** I could except that in fact that particular section is from *The Forward* by Patrick MacManaway. So, it was his words, although they certainly powerful and relevant. Our culture made a big wrong turn somewhere some several thousand years ago where we started to believe that time was in fact linear, and that things kept moving forward and growing, and that somehow, we have that model for our economy as well that everything's supposed to keep growing all the times in this forward way, and to get to something and achieve something. But really, in point of fact, that is exactly what cancer does. Cancer keeps growing. Cancer moves forward and destroys everything behind it. But it's not a healthy growth. Healthy growth is growth in balance with your surroundings, and in concert with your surroundings. And so, Patrick's point in *The Forward* is that there are many traditional societies around the world who have this concept of circular time that it is not in fact the moving forward of progress, but it's a spiral in which we rediscover and repeat and reinvent our relationships every time we go around the wheel.

And so, that's a much more sustainable paradigm because it includes everything.

**Hillary Raimo:** Thank you for sharing that with us. Moving back into your work with this particular area of the Hudson River, which by the way I live in Albany so this is very close to home for me as well. So, this is a really interesting timing because as you were writing this and actually doing all of this, I look back in my life and said, "Well where was I at when she was doing this," and I was going through a very deep healing time. So, I'm curious how people are affected in ways they may not even be aware are connected.

Have you any thoughts on that?

**Gail Rex:** I have thoughts, but no real evidence. Yeah. I do think that the more tuned in people are with their surroundings, the more responsive they are to what's happening around them. So, it seems to me likely that a lot of people in that time and place would have shifted subtly or not so subtly in their thoughts, and behaviors, and experiences. And I know that there are people doing similar kinds of work around the world who actually will measure things like crime statistics or high school graduation rates, or crop yields to gauge whether a healing has had a broad effect like that across the time space.

**Hillary Raimo:** That would be a great experiment for big data to focus their positive energy on, don't you think?

**Gail Rex:** Wouldn't it? That would be awesome.

**Hillary Raimo:** You also talk about geophysics and telluric currents. Tell us about that.

**Gail Rex:** Yeah. So, these energies that I was working with in Earth acupuncture, they're ... I certainly didn't invent them. There are cultures throughout time and all around the world that have understood that there is energy in the Earth and around the Earth, and above the Earth, and people give it different names. Kind of a name that's becoming current these days is just to talk about geopathic stress as being disturbed Earth energy. But there are others ... I mean when people talk about ley lines or ... I don't know what else. Miasma, or chi, or prana, it's all the same. It's just occurs at different levels. There are Celtic traditions that identify different spirits like they'll talk about devas who are little land spirits or fairy people have relationships with humans. And so, the energies have always been there, it's just whether our language and our culture are big enough to put names to it.

**Hillary Raimo:** There are a lot of myths and stories about little people in the Native American traditions as well. They help connect you back to Earth frequency.

I enjoyed the part in your book where you talked about the shape of Indian Point energy center. You describe how it looked like a penis and testicles. I'm thinking as I read it, "Isn't that really interesting how it's the point of the dragon's bad breath, and that the overrun patriarchy on the planet now, as it is defined by mainstream culture, is a very much cancerous unsustainable kind of consciousness." So, if you are seeing and perceiving this place as a male penis phallic type symbol, and it's spewing out this negative energy, you absolutely went in and healed this toxic dragon's breath, an outdated cancerous patriarchal energy. A transformation of the divine masculine energy is indeed in order wouldn't you say?

**Gail Rex:** Well thank you. And it was a beautiful experience to live through, and I will say that since I was working on that land, the structure of the power plant has changed and they have since taken down that tall tower in the middle that looked like a penis surrounded by testicles. So now there's just two breasts.

**Hillary Raimo:** Ah. So now it's like removing the toxic feminine energy. It would make sense from a yin yang perspective.

**Gail Rex:** Absolutely.

**Hillary Raimo:** How would you describe toxic feminine energy?

**Gail Rex:** Well it can have a few different aspects, but one of them is just complete annihilation. Just that total overbearing, over protecting, taking over everything. And another ... So that sort of corruption that beautiful feminine tendency to take care of, or care about, or to think about. But when it becomes unbalanced it's over controlling and being over critical as well. I think those are the two that come to mind. Can you think of others?

**Hillary Raimo:** When women embrace their dark, and it is unhealed, they can embody the dark mother energies, the crazy woman or death eater that manifests and feeds off negative energies and drama. If they are healed I think they handle the dark in different way. It is transformed through creative energies, assimilated instead of rejected and embraced as a catalyst for growth. It's a lot different when it's handled in a healthy way versus a more traumatic, harmful way.

What did you learn about yourself in this whole process of this journey?

**Gail Rex:** A lot of it is complicated to share, and I did as best I could to describe it in the book, but for me the really profound part was just the realization that in fact we could communicate with rivers, and with mountains, and that in fact we have an obligation to do so. And that once we begin that process of creating that relationship of conversing with the world around us, it wakes them up to the possibility as well. And so that we feel that it's our duty to begin to participate in the living of this planet. This beautiful planet. And that if we don't participate in the living then we are in fact contributing to the dying, which we see all around us everyday in a thousand different horrible ways and it can make us feel very helpless with diseases and global warming, and all of these global problems, not to mention the wars and the abuses, but that in fact all we can do is all we have to. Which is to wake up and participate.

**Hillary Raimo:** That's a beautiful vision. Thank you. In *Earth Acupuncture: Healing the Living Landscape* you talk about an idea of 'spirit of place.' What does that mean exactly?

**Gail Rex:** Well this is a concept again that is found in a lot of cultures around the world and they will ... There are different names for it. But it's kind of the ... Well you can think of it as a sum total of the energies of the beings that are in a particular place. Or sometimes there's an overarching being like for instance the Hudson River running through that landscape, that river has its own spirit and it flavors the landscape all around it in myriad ways. And there's nothing like a river town, and you can tell when you are near the river or farther away from the river just from the ... Not just the species that are around you, but also just the feel of the place. So, the spirit of place includes all that goes into it. But sometimes there's just some bigger characters than others.

**Hillary Raimo:** How do you get people out of that artificial matrix, and back into the natural world?

**Gail Rex:** You just need to go outside. I mean it can't be done indoors. Even looking out a nice window doesn't get you there. But it's very simple and very hard at the same time. If you have a busy life and particularly if you're a city dweller and there's not a lot of ... It doesn't seem like there's a lot of natural world around you. But in fact, stepping outside is really the way to begin. And the more time you spend out of doors, the more of a relationship you build. It's kind of automatic because you start to replace constructions of your mind with constructions of your screen, with constructions of your job, become replaced with trees, grass, birds. Even in cities there are ... You can find these things. Parks are better, but if you don't live near a park there's

152

probably a tree or two or some birds. The more time you spend looking, the more you learn and the more you remember that you were once a part of it, and the more you long to become a part of it again.

**Hillary Raimo:** Talk to us about the birds and your work. When you were doing all of this did you notice any change in the birdsong around the places you were working on?

**Gail Rex:** That's a really good question. Only in the sense that the seasons changed, and so the bird life changed. But I wasn't really paying attention... That's an interesting question. It would have been fun to have a bird person really paying attention.

**Hillary Raimo:** How would that translate into the human body with chi? The migration of birdsong.

**Gail Rex:** Well I would say ... So, if you think of birds as a part of the greater ecology, and some birds for instance are kind of like weedy species and they can live in any environment, and then others are more sensitive and need things a little bit more stable. So, with people it's when we are ... The better our health is, the more everything begins to function more smoothly. So, when you are in fine form, perhaps you have more intuition or you're better able to recognize your intuitions, or you have really great creative ideas and are able to manifest them. So, it's the signs of a smooth functioning system that start to appear as you begin to heal.

**Hillary Raimo:** Birds fly according to the electromagnetics of the Earth. So as those change, the birds react and people can track that.

**Gail Rex:** Yeah that's true. I wasn't thinking about it but it would really be a beautiful thing to pay attention to.

**Hillary Raimo:** There's a lot more in your book about your experience. Your book is a pilgrimage of spirit.

Gail, where can people find you?

**Gail Rex:** Now I am working on acupuncturing people again. And I am starting work on another book but I'm not quite ready to talk about that yet. But it is another book about healing. And I do have a website which is GailRex.com where people can learn more about the book, as well as my first book, and you can order the book through the website. There's also information about my acupuncture practice which will only be helpful to people who live near me. But that's a good way. I have a plan to start up a kind of web clearing house of Earth healers. Like a one stop collection of sites for people who practice various kinds of Earth healing like the work that you do or the work that other people do where people can learn about what Earth healing is and all the many different ways you can practice it. That's a little bit down the line, but that's something that-

**Hillary Raimo:** That's exciting. This is going to become really important work in the future. Especially for generations coming up in such a digital world. They really don't get exposed to nature the way that some of us have been because we didn't have all the fancy technologies that are available today and it's just going to get worse. So, it worries me, as an older person looking down at younger people, that they don't forget what it is like to be out in nature and connect directly with that frequency versus not. And I wonder if some of the mental issues that we deal with now, some of the social issues, don't stem from a lack of connection to Earth. What do you think?

**Gail Rex:** Yeah. I'm sure that that's true. And there have been a couple of books about that. I'm trying to remember one of them specifically about kids losing their kind of nature literacy. But I forget what it's called and I forget the author. But there are ... I think absolutely it's true that once we divorce ourselves from the divine model of how things work in concert, in relationships then we become subject to all kinds of ills and well, we can heal those ills and we can rediscover the relationship and it just begins with stepping outside. Bring the kids outside.

Look at the stars on a cold night. I don't know. It's probably cold where you are. It's really cold here in Vermont tonight. But it's beautiful.

**Hillary Raimo:** How do see the realm of human interaction affecting that frequency of nature? Do people just miss Earth energy because they are distracted? How do we deal with seeing Donald Trump and Hillary Clinton getting caught up in all these melodramas? How do we get out of the spell? Your thoughts?

**Gail Rex:** Well they start by noticing how they feel when they are watching these people or listening to these people. There is a certain stomach-turning thing that happens when someone is not speaking truth. And you can feel that. And I think again, when you go outside nature you can see that the natural world doesn't lie. So, once you get used to realizing that it is actually possible to act with integrity, then you can start to see the people who are not and the people who are more so. I think politics is a special case where by its very nature, you're sometimes doing things you don't agree with in order to gather consensus and gather power. So, it doesn't always mean only doing the things in you believe in 100%. But it does mean speaking the truth. And you can tell who is speaking truth and who is being incendiary, and who is trying to curry favor.

**Hillary Raimo:** It is like a real livestream. You go outside, and you're connecting to the ground and the trees, and the fresh air and the sun, and the real light. There's a different feeling to that in your body and I think that creates a different biochemistry, and then we start to change how we feel inside. There's a health that returns. Wouldn't you agree?

**Gail Rex:** Absolutely. Yes. And so, then once you know what that feels like you look for it and you connect with other people who feel that same thing. And then we start to shift the character of what's going on as more and more people bond together in this sense of health and truth.

**Hillary Raimo:** Do you see that as a saving grace for humanity at this point? A change in sustainable consciousness is really what's necessary?

**Gail Rex:** Yeah. I think that's about almost the only option available to us right now. The other ones are slow moving and politically hamstrung and it's not going to be enough to just change the laws or just stop the pollution. What has to happen is that deep internal change of recognizing that this is the planet we have. And if we lose it, we lose everything. And therefore, let's save it.

**Hillary Raimo:** Right. The book is *Earth Acupuncture: Healing the Living Landscape*. I've been talking to Gail Rex. If you'd like to know more, go read her book or get a hold of her and maybe ask her your own questions. Gail thanks so much for joining me tonight, it's been a pleasure to talk to you.

**Gail Rex:** It's been a joy Hillary. Thank you so much.

# -9-

## JOHN PERKINS
## CONFESSIONS OF AN ECONOMIC HITMAN

*The health of our financial systems determines the health of our world. That being said, the systems that drive our world in terms of who wins and loses comes down to human behavior. My conversation with John Perkins was about digging to the root causes in regard to the current and ongoing global financial crisis.*

RECORDED JULY 8, 2010

**Hillary Raimo:** My Guest tonight, John Perkins first book *Confessions of an Economic Hit Man* was a ground-breaking story about corporate greed in America. It's destructive global influence on developing third world countries and the role he, himself played in that destruction. The book spent nearly a year on the New York Times Bestseller List and went on to become one of the most critically acclaimed nonfiction books of the year.

Perkins goes into even more depth in this book, *The Secret History of the American Empire*. About the Machiavellian manipulation of the global economy by what he calls the corporatocracy of America. And what we as responsible citizens can do to help put a stop to it.

In his other book *Hoodwinked*, he pulls back the curtain on the real cause of the current global financial meltdown. He shows how we've been "hoodwinked" by the CEO's who run the corporatocracy. Those few corporations that control the vast amounts of capital, land and resources around the globe and the politicians they manipulate. Theses corporate fat cats, John explains, have sold us all on what he calls predatory capitalism.

John, welcome.

**John Perkins:** Thanks, Hillary. It's my pleasure to be here.

**Hillary Raimo:** Well I have a lot of questions for you tonight. Let's start with what exactly is an economic hit man?

**John Perkins:** Well Hillary, I think it's fair to say that we economic hit men have created the worlds first truly global empire. Primarily without the military for the first time in history, with true economics. Although we have many different approaches to doing this, I think the most common one would be to identify countries with resources corporations covet like oil and generate huge loans to that country for the world bank or one of its sister organizations.

Yet the money doesn't go to the country, it instead goes to our own corporations that build power plants and highways, industrial parks. Big infrastructure projects that, of course bring in a lot of money to those corporations. And help a few wealthy families in those countries. But do not help the majority of the people, who are too poor to benefit from them. And yet those people, the citizens of the country are left holding a debt they can't possibly repay.

So, we go back to the country at some point and say since you can't repay your debt, sell your oil real cheap to our oil companies or whatever the resource is, without any environmental restrictions, vote with us in the United Nations, allow us to build military base on your land. Really be part of our empire.

And when the few cases when we fail, and I talk in my books about how I failed with the President of Ecuador, Jamie Roldos and the Panamanian President, Omar Torrijos. I wasn't able to corrupt and I wasn't able to get them to accept these deals, to play the game. They were both assassinated by people we call jackals. And these are men or women who either are with rogue governments or assassinate their leaders. They step in when, in the few instances when we economic hit men fail.

**Hillary Raimo:** So, you are saying the big corporations have become so large and have gained so much power that they are able to act like private governments and are going in and exploiting these people?

**John Perkins:** Yeah, the big corporations run the government. It's not the other way around unfortunately. I think, well I don't know if it's unfortunate or not, but it's just the way things are. And that's changed in my lifetime really. They used to be, when we looked at the world as this globe of roughly 200 countries, a few of those countries have a lot of power, the Soviet Union, the United Kingdom, the United States. But today we better envision the globe, still roughly 200 countries, but these huge clouds drifting around it. These are the big corporations. And they don't know any national boundaries or listen to any specific sets of laws. They strike deals with whatever country satisfies them, or whatever one has the resources or markets they're interested in exploiting. They're really calling the shots. They own the mainstream media. They own most of the politicians one way or another around the world. They really are the new power.

We are at a time in history, Hillary that kind of like when, the city states became nations. Except this time the nations are becoming irreverent, it's the big corporations that are ruling.

**Hillary Raimo:** John, how did you get involved in this kind of work?

**John Perkins:** Well, I was recruited by the National Security Agency when I was still in business school in Boston in the late 60's. Went through a whole series of tests, personality tests, lie director tests. And they identified me as a guy that would make a good economic hit man. I was a good con man they thought. And with credentials, from a kind of business school. And they also identified several weaknesses that would make it easy to hook me. And I talk in detail in the books about these, but I think I can summarize them by saying I think it's the three big things of our culture, sex, power, and money. I was a very young man, I was infected with all of those charges. I wanted sex, and I wanted power, I wanted money. And they offered, and they still offered all of them.

**Hillary Raimo:** They seduce you in, set you up by exploiting what they consider weaknesses. Do they actively search out people in schools? How do they find people like you to do these jobs? Are they always watching?

**John Perkins:** Well, I can't really answer that question because I don't know what their policy is. But in my particular case, I was married to a woman whose father was very high up in the Navy department. I was trying to avoid Vietnam, and this was back in the late 60's. My father-in-law's best friend was very high up in the National Security Agency, which had a potential for being drafted preferable. So, he arranged for me to go in for interviews. And once I'm in there, I'm going through the lie detector tests and the personality tests and at that point they identified me as being ideal for this kind of a job. That something else they might have identified as being the perfect guy to be spotted behind the scenes in North Korea, I don't know. But for me, this is a personality that they saw in me.

**Hillary Raimo:** So, some people would say, this is a conspiracy. You hear the word illuminati all over the internet. What are your thoughts on that?

**John Perkins:** I have no proof of that at all. And no reason to believe that. I don't suppose I have any real reason not to believe it. I certainly never been at those levels or seen anything like that. What I see instead is a fairly small group of corporate executives that I call the corporatocracy. Men primarily and a few women who run our biggest multinational corporations. All being driven by one goal, one common goal, and that is to maximize profits, regardless of the social and environmental costs. Simply put, maximize profits.

And they don't have to get together and conspire to do anything illegal, a lot of them don't even know each other. But they're all headed for that same goal. So, while you may have Exxon and Chevron, they're competing for your dollar at the gas pump, the fact of the matter is, when it comes to new regulations for example, new regulations are going to be imposed as a result of the terrible accident in the gulf. The powers are all going to come together and fight as one family in Congress. Not to have water restrictions or at to least minimize that.

And you'll say the same thing about Nike or Reebok and Adidas and those companies. When push comes to shove, they come together. Then they compete in the market. This doesn't imply that there is a conspiracy but there certainly is the common shared goal. And they all recognize that and fight very hard to preserve that goal.

And in addition to maximizing profits regardless of social and environmental costs, the other part of that is something Milton Freedmen, what I call predatory capitalism, fought very hard for. And that is to cost or reduce regulations. Businesses don't want to be regulated. So, they all fight hard not to be regulated.

**Hillary Raimo:**  To maximize their profits.

**John Perkins:**  Maximize profits and avoid regulation and privatize everything. Convince the government that private business should run basically everything, including the military in Afghanistan.

**Hillary Raimo:**  In your opinion what is going on in the gulf right now? Is this just a matter of total lack of respect for the environment and about maximizing profits? is it just that cut and dry?

**John Perkins:**  Well it tells you the power of oil companies. And you have to remember that the oil companies are by no means alone, the banking industry, the insurance industry, the health industry, and the engineering industry, all the industry that revolves around all those that I just named. Are all highly dependent on oil. And they step to the plate to defend oil. And they realize how important oil is to them. Not to mention the transportation sector or the utility sector. So many sectors are dependent on oil. So, you can see right here the power base that a company like BP has and all the oil companies.

And I think it's important for us to understand that this well, that this leak that's going on right now could conceivably never be stopped. I don't think that's likely but we have to face the possibility that such a catastrophe could happen. It could destroy the oceans. It could destroy life as we know it on earth. It's one well. It's a possibility. So, while we are all worried about Iran having nuclear weapons and what's North Korea is doing, etc, etc.

We ought to be a lot more concerned about what these big corporations are doing and it's an accident theoretically. But obviously some very poor decisions were made that were all based on greed. Or based on the idea of maximizing profits. And we really, really need to look at that and the danger to our planet.

I think the other thing we should be looking at, Hillary, is understanding that actually Texaco, which is now owned by Chevron, has a worse catastrophe in the Ecuadorian Amazon. The last I heard the amount of toxin waste that was spilled in the Amazon by Texaco were roughly 3 times more than what's got into the gulf so far. That changes everyday, so I'm not sure what the number is today. But that was intentional, Texaco did this as a matter of policy. It wasn't an accident. In the largest environmental lawsuit in the history of the world now was filed against Texaco on behalf of 30,000....

**Hillary Raimo:** How did they do it on purpose John? Can you explain that? Why would they do that on purpose?

**John Perkins:** Well it's deep in the Amazon and when a drill is drilled for oil they have a lot of oil that comes up that they never use. That they flare off, that they spill off. Under most regulations they have to take care of that and somehow, they have to manage it. But in those days in the Ecuadorian Amazon they get away without managing at all. They just dumped it into huge pools. So now you've got huge lakes out there. I've seen these that are just toxic waste oil and other toxic waste from oil producing. And at the time Ecuador was run by dictators, military dictatorship that was put into power by the CIA. And allowed Texaco to get away with this.

It was not a democratic elected government, it was a US puppet government. I was there. It was in the late 60's and the 70's I was there first as a peace corp volunteer and then as an economic hit man at the time. And the current president of Ecuador is extremely incensed over this. And there's no question that Exxon, no Texaco, excuse me, needs to pay up. The fact of the matter is people are still buying because Texaco is hard balling us and refusing to settle this case and refusing to take responsibility. And it's Texaco, and as I've said before, it's now owned by Chevron. So, it's really Chevron these days. It's a terrible catastrophe. And the executives at Chevron are doing nothing today to resolve this problem.

And yet we don't even hear about them in the United States. And that's probably my point, Hillary. That these things go on all the time in Africa, in Indonesia, in Latin America, all over the world that we don't even pay attention to. We just say, well, okay what the heck. Just keep pumping oil and give it to me cheep.

So, I hate to say this, and I want to be very careful that I don't get misunderstood. If there has to be such a terrible oil spill. I'm sorry there is. But if there has to be I think the world is blessed that it happened off the shores of the United States. Because we are the largest consumer of oil in the world. We are the most powerful and wealthiest nation in the world. And now we are understanding the implications of things that have been happening on many different scales throughout the rest of the world, the third world for years and years and years and we haven't even noticed.

**Hillary Raimo:** Very sad. Do you think this will wake people up?

**John Perkins:** Yes, I think that should be a very strong positive benefit that comes out of this. I fear, however is that the oil companies and many other powerful interests, many politicians will tell us that all we need to do is ban off shore drilling in the United States. And that would be a terrible mistake because if we don't cut back demand for oil that means that we'll just take the same disaster some place else. We'll go back deep into the Amazon, we'll go into the deadest of the Middle East, we'll go into the jungles of Indonesia.

And that's not a solution. So, we have to be very careful, I think, that we don't just say, well the solution is no more off shore drilling in the gulf or any place in the United States. We have to truly understand this as being a message that there's a virus around the world. I call it the mutant viral form of predatory capitalism. And very much symbolized by this oil spill, is spreading throughout the gulf and could spread throughout the oceans of the world. There is this spreading viral capitalism that is very, very destructive and is a failed system really. And it's a system in essence threatening to truly destroy our planet whether it's oil or something else.

You know we had the disaster in Nepal in India back a number of years ago. We've had many of these sorts of things around the world. It's time we really woke up and said, you know we've got to change our consciousness. We've got to take as our first priority creating a just and peaceful world for every child on this planet.

**Hillary Raimo:** These companies have become so gigantic, they have so much power and so much influence in the current system. How does an average person change anything?

**John Perkins:** Well I think, Hillary, we have a lot more power than we realize. And my most recent book, *Hoodwinked*, is the devoted to addressing that. What can we do? What can you do? What can all of your listeners do? And obviously I can't cover the whole book in this radio program. So, I suggest people read the book if they're really interested.

But to summarize it. There's five different areas and perhaps the most important one is that we as consumers have a great deal of power. These big corporations exist only because we support them one way or another. We buy their goods and services or our tax dollars do. Now this is a global empire, but it's the first one in history that hasn't been created by the military. Nobody is forced to buy from Nike, or from Exxon, or from BP. Nobody is forced to buy any of these things. And if we recognize the market place is democratic and that every time we buy something or choose not to, we're casting a vote. And if we express our opinions to the bias...

Let me give you an example. If everyone of your listeners when we get off this program, goes to their computer and sends an email to Nike and says I'm not buying anymore Nike products because I know you still have sweat shops and slave labor in Indonesia. I'm not going to buy any of those products until you pay those people fair wages and give them decent working conditions. I'm not asking for you to get out of Indonesia and turn those people out of jobs. I'm asking you to give them fair wages and give them decent living conditions and health insurance. If we all did this, Nike would have to come around.

We have that power. We got rid of apartheid in South Africa by boycotting businesses that supported it. We got companies to clean up terribly polluted rivers all over the United States back in the 70's. More Recently we got them to get rid of trans fats in foods and very recently antibiotics in chickens. But now we need to ratchet this up a notch and say, we're not going to buy from any company that is not committed to creating a sustainable just and peaceful world. That's got to be the commitment. In order to be perfect at it, that has to be their commitment. I'm only going to buy from companies like that and I have made that commitment we can do that. And send them emails. Let them know because they do read those. Somebody reads them, the CEO's don't read the emails, but he does get a matrix once a week or so. To tell him what kind of emails are coming in and it matters. It's important to them.

**Hillary Raimo:** We're going to go to the phone lines. We have a caller on the line from Alberta, Canada. Jay thanks for calling in. You have a question?

**Jay:** Yes, I do Hillary. Thanks so much. Hey John, I just wondered, regarding the oil in the gulf, when this thing, if they can't cap this and all these gallons and gallons of oil going to actually be leaking out of there. I just wonder if it's going to shock the oil futures market because, like the Saudi's need $55 a barrel over and above what's going on right now in order to keep their countries sustainable and going. And if they find out that there's more oil than their creating a shortage for and it goes down and it effects the Saudi's plus our economy in Alberta too is based on oil. And just wondered what it's going to do to the American economy too. I just find that there's more and more stuff than oils going to do even environmental effects in Florida and the pan handle there. It's going to devastate the economic, you know the fruit and vegetable market and the tourism market. I just wondered what your views on that.

**John Perkins:** Well certainly, yes. We don't know the full impact at this point. And I was involved in a discussion a few days ago, on that point we were talking about peak oil. And this whole idea that there's this unlimited supply and in a way, people were saying on this channel that this endless well is showing us that there is no limit to the supply of oil. There's a lot of oil there gushing away. That's one thing that may be coming out of this. And certainly, BP stocks have fluctuated a lot since this has happened.

The creditability of the industry is being challenged, but I think we also have to remember that it's an incredibly powerful industry. It's so much of the world economy depends on oil one way or another that it's always been a very resilient industry. But I think we the people must speak out. And we must say, one of the things we must say is we got to get off oil. And there's no question, it's a terrible substance to be dealing with. And we sometimes talk about the limited supply, the possibility of a very limited supply of oil, the peak oil idea. To me what's perhaps more of a concern than whether we run out of oil or not. I wish we would run out of oil in a way.

But the bigger concern is can the carrying system of the planet handle this much carbon dioxide. And I think that's a more limiting factor than the amount of oil that we have. Whether we can handle the green house effect that comes out of this, so hopefully this terrible catastrophe that going on in the gulf combined with what's going on in Ecuador and other places will shake us awake to realize we have got to get the oil economy. We simply have to get off, it's a terrible, terrible addiction. Like any addiction, the only way to get rid of it is essentially go cold turkey.

**Jay:** I have another question. Is that okay?

**Hillary Raimo:** Absolutely Jay, go ahead.

**Jay:** Yeah, we have like, in the world, an economic pyramid. That means it's all interconnected in some way. So, if we take out one way of doing things, it's still there and I'm wondering is that we have no..... Like when you buy a product, okay, let's say you buy something that's has plastic wrapping or something like that. There's no way of doing something useful with that plastic. You can do something with cardboard, but not really with plastic because it's made of petroleum. And there's really no reasonable resource to turning that into a reusable product again. And turn it around again and close the loop. We really have no way of going back to a way of making a close loop system. It's just a one-way system.

**John Perkins:** That's exactly why we have to get off oil. I mean, what's done is done. We can't go back and get rid of all the plastics and all the other oil residue around the planet, but we can stop creating more. And we need to do that. We really need to make a commitment. Like I said this is an addiction that we have to go cold turkey on.

**Hillary Raimo:** Thanks Jay. Great questions. Thanks for calling in tonight. We have another question from John in Vancouver. John asks, is there any governance to the common property of the planet? Tribes in Pakistan took a stand against Coca- Cola and Pepsi over water for beverages contracts made by the government. How can citizens of the world take similar actions?

**John Perkins:** Well we're seeing a lot going on and incidentally in Vancouver, I'm speaking and doing a workshop in Vancouver in late July, The Tipping Point Conference. It's the 22nd through the 28th of July. I'd love to meet the listener there and other people. You've been getting calls from all over, Hillary, this is wonderful. But go to my website, johnperkins.org and you can find out where I'm going to be. I'd love to meet some of your listeners. I travel around speaking a lot.

Yeah, this whole thing of international governance, we don't have any and the UN has proven to be a paper tie area. It pushed hard against the Iraqi war to begin with that totally habilitated. The world bank is in the pocket of the economic hit men and corporatocracy. We need a world governing organization to watch out for these things. And we don't have it. And the big corporations will resist it. They'll fight it.

So, I would really encourage that the listener who wrote in about this, to go out there and fight for it. The internet gives you a tremendous forum today. We need to push for these things. It needs to come from we the people around the planet. We have to take back our planet. I feel that the United States, our country, has been stolen. Canada also has been stolen. The world has been stolen by these robber barons, by these modern-day robber barons.

We must take it back and we the people are going to have to do this. Just as we've had to do everything in the past. We're the ones that had to get rid of apartheid. We're the ones that had to shout out against racial bias and bias' against gender in United States, Canada, and around the world. We must do it now. We really need to take back our country. And there is no international body that supervises these things. We're it. And how we shop does matter. Go after those international companies, arrange boycotts, start letter writing campaigns, email writing campaigns. This is so easy. And we must go after these people, we have to do it.

**Hillary Raimo:** Let's talk about Monsanto. How do we take a stand to a corporation like that?

**John Perkins:** Well, you boycott everything that Monsanto produces. Everything that they produce. And Whole Foods, for example, won't sell any products that have GMO's in it. I think that's wonderful. I know a lot of people have a problem with Whole Foods and some of their labor policies. I have a problem with those too. But one thing they are doing right is staying away from GMO's. And you, as I understand, when you buy things there and many other stores. Let Monsanto know, send them emails and let the stores that you buy from that don't use GMO's know.

Europe has had a fantastic success record. You don't get things with GMO's in Europe. So, you can buy something that's make by Kellogg's in the United States that has GMO's in it and in Europe that same product doesn't. So, they've been able to make this happen in Europe. We can make it happen here too. But we have to have the resolve, you know. We the people have to get off our fannies, stop looking at television for long enough to get on the computer and make it happen. And God, it's so easy today. You know, if you go to my website, johnperkins.org there's a whole link there for starting petitions and there's hundreds of petitions and you can sign one of... it's very, very easy. All you have to do is click on it and put your name and address in and then once you're done continue to stay in and all you have to do is go back when new petitions go up. They are important. We have a great media here now. We're casting votes constantly. But we all need to take an active role in this.

**Hillary Raimo:** Speaking of media, John. President Obama just issued a media black out for the Gulf of Mexico where people can be fined up to $40,000 for getting closer than 65 feet to the boons or anything related, the ships. What do you have to say about that kind of action taken by our government when there should be transparency? Do you think that is a result of BP demanding that, that happens?

**John Perkins:** Absolutely, it shows you the power that BP has, that the oil industry in general has. They're all stepping up behind BP now. You know, any good journalist should get out there and defy those orders and be taken to jail if necessary.

Imagine Walter Cronkite coming back from Vietnam and saying it isn't how it looks over there. We're losing that war and shouldn't be there. Had a huge impact. I think if Walter Cronkite were 40 years old today he'd be down there with a CBS crew going, breaking the law. And we need to have that happen.

It's terrible, it's also terrible in the United States, the ban on showing caskets and bodies coming back from Afghanistan or Iraq. The media should not stand for these things. It's a sign that our mainstream media is totally sold out. They're either owned by the corporatocracy directly or through advertising budgets. But thank God there are programs like this Hillary. We do have a free press and it's coming in through programs like this and through streaming, through the internet, through blogging. It's an amazing thing going on out there. And most of the bloggers and steamers and people doing these kinds of programs like yours don't have the finances or the staying power to cross those lines and go in and get arrested. You probably wouldn't get that much attention. We need a few bold journalists out there that are in the limelight. The Walter Cronkite type that will do this. I just hoping one will emerge. I think it's disgusting that the Obama administration would yield to something like this. Our presidents are not very powerful anymore. And they are very vulnerable.

**Hillary Raimo:** I see a lot of anger towards Obama and I try to stress to people that it's not necessarily him making these decisions, it's a product of a system. Speaking of Afghanistan, John, I recently found out that they have discovered, a $14 trillion mineral resource deposit that's in Afghanistan. Now with your background, is the war in Afghanistan really over this?

**John Perkins:** Certainly, and that's one of the reasons that we did go in. This may be news to most of us, these mineral deposits. But it's not news to the corporatocracy. They've known all along. They may have not known the value of it, they shouldn't know the value of it. They're just throwing numbers around now. But they've known it was there for a long time. And they've known Afghanistan is in a critical strategic location geographically. The Soviets knew that, that's why they basically, Afghanistan basically brought down the Soviet Union. But the Soviet's were determined to win in Afghanistan, that's why they stayed in so long cause they knew about these minerals. And they knew about the strategic location.

The other thing that I think it's important for us to understand Hillary, that our economy is very, very based on war. It's based on oil and war. And the two go together. There's a movie out that Oliver Stone just released called South of the Border, I think is the name of it. I saw excerpts from it before it was released. It's about some of the major presidents in South America. And he interviews President Kirchner, the former president of Argentina, who talks about a meeting he had with the second George Bush president. In which Bush said, you know the economy in the United States is based on war, we have to keep going to war.

And that's true, at this point. That you and I, and all your listeners have to turn this around too. We have to look for a new kind of economy. I wrote extensively about that in Hoodwinked. How we've got to come up with an economy that serves the world, rather than serves the war machines. And let's get all those brilliant minds today who work for General Dynamics and General Motors and General Electric and all the other generals racing on out all the military industries whose supported by our tax dollars. Let's insist that our tax dollars pay them to instead of making missiles and anti aircraft and so on and so forth. To come up with technologies that will clean up the terribly polluted lands of the world. We've polluted the world. We've polluted the earth. We've polluted the water. We've polluted the air, all over.

Let's devote ourselves to coming up with technologies to clean it up. Let's devote ourselves, let's pay Cargo and Kraft and Chiquita and all the other agriculture businesses, Monsanto. That are doing so much damage, to instead come up with ways for the starving people of Africa to produce food more efficiently. To store it at a local level and distribute it locally and efficiently. So, they no longer have to starve.

We talk about sustainable energy and that's very important but there are so many other things we can do too, to create a new economy. And I go over in detail, in Hoodwinked how each of us should be participating on one level or another. Get out of the military economy, get into a new economy that's earth friendly.

**Hillary Raimo:** John, do you think 9/11 was an inside job? Do you think it was something that happened so that we could use it as an excuse to go into Afghanistan to go to war?

**John Perkins:** Your bold, aren't you?

**Hillary Raimo:** Well, we only have 18 minutes left so....

**John Perkins:** You know Hillary, I have to say I don't like to talk about things I don't have personal experience, I have no inside information on 9-11. But what I will say is, I can not believe that a man with a walkie talkie standing in the cave in the Himalayas directed that operation. Nor can I understand why there was a huge hole put in the nations largest fortress, most important fortress, the pentagon. The hole was put there and no senior official lost their job. No general lost his job. That's amazing. And there's cameras all over the pentagon. Why has nobody ever produced a photograph of that plane hitting the pentagon? It's incredibly suspicious. I don't know who did it, and I don't believe the official story.

**Hillary Raimo:** So now that we have this open-ended kind of threat of terrorism going on in the world. Do you think that has given the corporatocracy, the American Empire a green card to go into whatever country they want? For example, what's going on with Iran right now? Is this an example of how an economic hit man would work because it seems to me that there was a lot of negotiation going on trying to get them to do certain things and now all of a sudden, it's escalating and feels kind of like what you describe in your books? Is that indeed what's going on?

**John Perkins:** It is. It's a huge deception. There is no such thing as terrorism. There are people performing acts of terror around the world. But there's no global terrorism. I know members of Al-Qaeda, I've interviewed them. I've interviewed members of Farc in Colombia. I've interviewed Somali pirates, they have nothing in common. It's not a global movement. This is not like Communism, not like Catholicism, it's not like Protestantism, there's a lot of ism's, but terrorism is not an ism. They are acts of terror, yes, but they are not united. There's no such thing as a war on terror.

And we bought into that somehow. The media has been extremely reluctant to really face the facts. The corporatocracy wants to convenience us that there's another war, like the war on Communism. But the war on terrorism is not the same thing at all. We simply bought into it, we bought into the fear around it. Most of the terrorists that I've interviewed, in fact I say all the one's that I've interviewed, are desperate people. They're starving. The Somali pirates, fisherman whose fishing waters were destroyed by basically by piracy from European and other foreign fishing vessels. And also, US Navy vessels dumping nuclear waste from Diego Garcia Island, where their base is there into fisherman's waters. For 20 years those fishermen complained to the UN and other international bodies. About the pirating of their seas and they can no longer fish. Their kids are starving. They turned to piracy. Every terrorist I've ever interviewed says I don't want to be a terrorist, it's a dangerous occupation. I just want to be able to provide a living for my kids.

Now, I'm not saying there aren't fanatics, there are. There are a lot of fanatics. There are people who are wealthy who are involved in acts of terror. This war on terror is a misnomer. There's no such thing as global terrorism. There are simply acts of terror. And the best way to deal with them for the most part is to help the economies in the regions where these people are being breed. Most people don't want to be terrorists. They won't follow the fanatic leaders unless they're desperate.

**Hillary Raimo:** Is this being used to manipulate the majority of people, to be complacent with the way we have set up our systems?

**John Perkins:** Yeah, we're buying into it, you know. It's easy for us to believe. We want to believe our country is a good place and that there are bad people out there that are behind all of this. And our economy is collapsing, I don't have a job because there's bad people out there, whatever. It's easy to believe that. It's seductive and it is a technique of economic hit men. It's been taken to a very, very large level now. But we the people need to stop buying that. And understand that yes, there are bad people we have to protect ourselves against. There's always going to be rapists and mass murderers and people with screws loose in their brains, but that's not saying there's an international movement of terrorism.

Movements like that, I mean organizations like Al-Qaeda can only exist on a large level because they are desperate people who are extremely angry about what we are doing in the Middle East and what we are doing in Indonesia with oil and exploitation of resources. And what we are doing many other places. You know you can go into Latin America, you can go into Barros very, very poor ghettos. In Caracas and other places in Latin America and see pictures of Osama Bin Ladin as a hero. It's not because these people are muslims, they're not.

They're Catholics, they don't like Islam, but they see Osama Bin Ladin as a kind of Robin Hood because he's standing up to what they see as a dangerous empire, the United States. And I think that's very sad, Hillary. I think we need to come into the world with a new vision.

Like I explained before, develop a new economy that's going to be aimed at helping starving people around the world. And cleaning up the impoverished planet. Let's come up with a really good picture that gets rid of terrorism, by getting rid of the root causes of it.

**Hillary Raimo:** How would you tell that to a young man growing up in the system like you did, going to school, trying to go forward in the career that may get tempted and seduced with money, power, and sex like you did? Is it just a dysfunctional kind of mechanism in the human being itself or is it just a matter of reaching deeper into people to really get them to understand that concept?

**John Perkins:** It's a matter of getting the word out. And I think that's been the problem. When I was in college for example, in high school and college, nobody was talking the way I am today about the system. There was a huge anti-communist movement. There was a big red scare. My father and mother were stanch conservative republicans who were very, very terrified of communism. I grew up with that. Television programs that scared the pants off of us about communists. We grew up with that and there was nobody else speaking like what we are talking right now.

The Vietnam War came along and there was a huge movement against it. I went to Boston University and Howard Zinn, who just recently released a, God Bless Him, a mentor and a very dear friend of mine, he was speaking out and Noam Chomsky and a number of other liberals against the Vietnam War, but at that time it was all oriented toward that one war. Not the bigger issues, and when the war ended we didn't go and examine the bigger issues. A few people did, Chomsky did, Zinn did to a certain degree. But not very many people were listening. Today I think more people are listening.

And so, I'm doing exactly what I think I'm suppose to do, which is I go around and speak at a lot of college campuses, a lot of MBA programs. I speak at business conferences. I want people to get this word. And there's a lot of others out there, there's a lot of good books, there's a lot of good movies that have come out, The Constant Gardner, Blood Diamond, Hotel Rwanda, The Al Gore movie on the environment. Many movies that are now opening people's minds.

**Hillary Raimo:** How does global warming play into all of this?

**John Perkins:** Well global warming is a fact, I think. I've seen the glaciers melting terribly and, in the Himalayas, and in the Andes. And also, in the United States and Canada. So, it's happening, there's no question that global warming is happening. And whether we humans caused it or not, who needs to argue that point. I happen to think we are, but so what if we are not. The fact of the matter is, something is happening on this planet and we need to look at this as an opportunity to change things. We need to look at this as an opportunity to conserve energy, to cut back on our oil use, to cut back on all energy use, to cut back on resource exploitation. To really become much more conscience and to realize that life is not about possessing more and more material goods. What makes us happy is not that. What makes us happy is decent living conditions, being taken care of in our old age, being loved, being taken care of as babies. It's pretty simple.

And we need to really focus on these things. And look at the fact of global warming as a wake-up call that we really need to change our relationship to the planet, to ourselves, and to each other. And the way we conduct our lives and run our institutions.

**Hillary Raimo:** David from Fort Collins writes in, he asks to play "Devil's Advocate" for a minute, and how does John think we can possibly convince most Americans that three SVU's and a 60-inch TV is not their God given birth right?

**John Perkins:** Well I think it's happening, to be honest. I really think people are beginning to get it. And they may not have acted accordingly yet, but it takes awhile. *Confessions of an Economic Hit Man* came out in late 2004, I was on an extensive college speaking tour most of 2005, including a lot of the MBA programs including Thornton,

Stanford, the famous MBA programs. Every time I spoke at one of these schools I arranged to have dinner with anywhere from a dozen to three dozen students before I spoke. And I would say to them, let's go around the table and I want to hear from each of you why are you at this school and why are you having dinner with me? What are your aspirations? Back in 2005 they were all of them talking about money and power, that's what they were there for. That's what they wanted.

Well this last year I did something very similar, went on the same basic tour of many of the same colleges in 2009 and then again in Spring of 2010. I didn't hear that at all. I heard a very different story from, basically the same, not the same individual students, but the same class of students. And now their saying they want to create a better world. That they realize that if they're going to have kids, they've got to create a better world. Many of them said they have big college loans, that they have to go to work for corporations to pay off those loans, but that's not why they are in these business schools. They're there because they want to become entrepreneurs and do things that will make a better world.

I think things, Hillary are changing. I think consciousness is changing. When you consider that's over a period of five years, and it may seem like a long time in our lives sometimes, five years, in history it's not even a blink. So, I hope that things are happening, but we have to keep pushing. People like you, this program, keep pushing, pushing, getting the word out. This is what's so important. We must educate ourselves and each other.

**Hillary Raimo:** John, you have an extensive background and experience in Shamanic cultures, indigenous cultures that you came across when you were working in these third world countries. Has that played a part in your coming out of this with such a drastically different perspective?

**John Perkins:** It absolutely did, Hillary. I thank these indigenous cultures and the Shamans. I still have a very strong connection. I have three god-children in the Amazon and Andes, where children are Shamans, elder teachers there. And one of the things they always teach is that change is possible. Anything is possible. All you have to do is change your dream. Change your consciousness. A book I wrote before *Confessions of an Economic Hit Man* was *The World Is As You Dream It*, it's still available at bookstores. You can get it at my website johnperkins.org, but it really addresses that the Shamans say when you have a dream, whether it's an individual or a cultural dream, you give it energy it manifests.

And we, in our culture, have given energy to a dream of big material success, lots of cars, big industry, lots of tall buildings. It manifested.

And now we are realizing it's destroying us. And it's threatening to destroy us. And so, we need to change that dream to a dream as I outlined before of living a life that's much more satisfying than a life that's solely based on materialism. So, we need to create a new dream. And Shamanism has taught me the incredible potential for doing that and that it can happen very quickly. Another book I wrote is Shape Shifting, which is about that. How you can change that energy and shape shift, an individual or a culture very quickly.

**Hillary Raimo:** Let's imagine someone who works in a corporate world whose job gives them a sense of hopelessness. How could they shape shift that sense of hopelessness?

**John Perkins:** Now I teach a workshop on that at the Omega Institute in upstate New York every summer in August. I suggest you come to it. Go to johnperkins.org. It's a process that's hard to describe in 5 minutes here, but I think the important thing here is to understand that shape shifting is all about energy. In fact, everything is energy. That's why it's so important to us, our main energy source. And everything we do is about energy. Eisenstein said matter and energy, that's what it's all about and so when we give our energy to a certain dream or certain idea we shape shift into that. And if we change that idea, that dream, that concept, that para dime, and we give energy to a new one. And we truly do it, it will manifest. It's eerie how that happens.

If you read the thoughts of most of the great people that have made a mark in history whether it's someone like a George Washington or Martha Washington, or someone like a Thomas Edison or Rosa Parks, or who ever, Eisenstein. You'll see that they are all about changing energy. Giving new energy to a new intent, a new dream, a new preset.

And in the case of Rosa Parks, for example, all she had to do was sit in front of the bus instead of the back. I say all she had to do and at the time that took a tremendous amount of courage. A tremendous amount of energy. Psychic and emotional as well as physical energy just to move from the back of the bus to the front. But it changed the world. It absolutely changed the world.

**Hillary Raimo:** What a beautiful example. Talking to John Perkins. You can go to his website to find out more about his upcoming events and his books johnperkins.org. So, John, you also do trips, I understand, to different sacred sites around the world. How did you get involved into doing that?

**John Perkins:** Well I've been doing it since 1991, when I saw the Amazon. I went down there and told them I wanted to help them save their forests. Then you've got to change the dream of your people. That's where the book *The World Is As You Dream It* came from. And they said so for one thing you could bring people down here to learn from us about shape shifting. I've probably taken a thousand people into the Amazon over the past 20 years to learn about that. And now that it's December I'm doing it with my co facilitator Lynn Roberts. To Guatemala to the Mayans, to really look into the 2012 prophecy.

And this Tipping Point Conference in Vancouver July 22 -28 is on the same thing, the Tipping Point Prophecies and they are the organizers of the December trip. Lynn and I let a trip of about 25 people last December to the Mayan to work with their Shamans, their elders. And explore the true meaning of 2012 and we're doing another one this December. It's a wonderful experience to be among these sacred sites, these huge pyramids, these amazing sites, do ceremony, do fire ceremonies late at night. Really get into the Shamanic vision and journey to really experience it and work with these extremely powerful Shamanic teachers, men and women. I enjoy it immensely and the people on the trips get a great deal out of it. It's very experiential, it's wonderful.

**Hillary Raimo:** You have to change the dream of your people. What is the message in that statement that you'd like to share with our listeners?

**John Perkins:** Well I think that we, first of all it's very easy to give up. It's very easy just throw up your hands and say oh the problems just to big, it's just too difficult. That doesn't accomplish anything. You know, thank God Rosa Parks didn't say that, or Rachel Carson didn't say that about DDT, instead she sat down and wrote a book, she had no idea whether it would be published or not. It became a silent spring that started a worldwide environmental movement. You can look at individuals throughout history, we mustn't throw our hands up and give up. Instead, we have to get on the internet or do whatever individuals most moved to do. Get on the streets, demonstrate, call people, do whatever. Take action, we have to take action. And when we start to take action and give energy to our new dream, it happens, it does manifest. And it's good to make it manifest to the new dream has to be about a sustainable just and peaceful for every child on the planet. And we all need to give that as much energy as we can.

**Hillary Raimo:** John Perkins, everybody. John thanks so much for joining me on the air, it's been a pleasure.

# 10

# DR. STEVEN GREER
# THE DISCLOSURE YEARS

*I first met Dr. Greer on one of his expeditions to Mt. Shasta in Northern California in 2010. At the time I was exploring the world of UFO's, alien agendas and Ufology in general on my show. Those eight nights under the stars changed my perspective on the entire genre. The majority of perspectives at the time revolved around the assumption that aliens are a threat, something we need to protect our world from, and with Hollywood's cooperation, that included a military preparedness with billions of dollars behind it. Dr. Greer was teaching a different story, that off world intelligences are actually friendly and seeking our cooperation. What I saw for myself on expedition guides my perspectives even to this day.*

RECORDED OCTOBER 21, 2010

**Hillary Raimo:** Dr. Steven Greer is an American physician, UFOlogist, author, lecturer, and founder of the Orion Project and the Disclosure Project. In 1990 Dr. Greer founded the center for the study of extraterrestrial intelligence, also known as CSETI, where he offers how-to training on initiating contact with extraterrestrial intelligence. CSETI is an international nonprofit scientific research and education organization dedicated to the furtherance of our understanding of extraterrestrial intelligence. CSETI's projects include the CE5 Initiative, also known as Close Encounter of the 5th Kind, which is characterized by mutual bilateral communication rather than unilateral contact.

Dr. Greer also teaches the use of meditation techniques that he claims allow attendees to remote view locations and times both past and present and develop what he calls cosmic consciousness and supernatural abilities such as precognition. Dr. Greer has founded the Disclosure Project claiming evidence of extraterrestrial visits to earth and a wide-ranging conspiracy among world governments. The Disclosure Project is a nonprofit research project working to fully disclose the facts about UFOs, extraterrestrial intelligence, and classified advanced energy and propulsion systems. He has over 400 government, military, and intelligence community witnesses testifying to their direct, personal first-hand experience with UFOs, ETs, ET technology, and the coverup that keeps this information secret.

Welcome Dr. Greer, thanks for being here.

**Steven Greer:** Thank you Hillary, I'm very glad to be on your show.

**Hillary Raimo:** On October 9th a global CSETI CE5 initiative took place with the direct intention or request set by the group to ask the ETs to form a triangular pattern similar to your CSETI logo, and in the days that followed we had sightings in triangular formation in New York City around October 13th, El Paso, Texas, I believe it was around October 15th, and then in Richmond, Virginia on October 17th. I'd like you to share the story of the CSETI logo, and what this event has meant to you both personally and for the group.

**Steven Greer:** I think to set the stage for this, people need to understand that the intelligences that we're dealing with are from civilizations that are obviously interstellar, and therefore moving faster than the speed of light. Any time you talk about technologies that cross the light barrier, I call it the crossing point of light, you enter into an area of physics that's been called transdimensional, or hyperdimensional. Those sciences also interface with consciousness, or mind. The technologies that are used by extraterrestrial civilizations for their own internal communications, but also with other civilizations, have an interface with consciousness and thought. They are electronic systems, but they're electronic systems that are extremely refined and are transdimensional, and interface with very clear coherent thought. Sort of like laser light is a coherent beam of light, where all the wavelengths sync up if it's green laser. The technologies we're talking about would be able to pick up very clear and coherent thought emanating from an expanded state of awareness.

This is sort of where the ancient teachings of the Vedas meet the space age if you will. We began doing this, I actually began doing this, when I was a child, when I was a young boy about 18 years old, and I had an encounter with an extraterrestrial being in North Carolina up on a mountaintop. I was hiking up there before sunset. It's a very long story, which I won't go into all of it here, but it's in the book Hidden Truth, Forbidden Knowledge, which you can get at DisclosureProject.org. This particular event was when the CE5, the Close Encounters of the 5th Kind initiative, was born. Because when I had this experience with this extraterrestrial civilization, and I had an onboard experience on this craft, we sort of procreated together this concept of how humans could contact them using consciousness and expanded awareness and remote viewing, where you see distant places in space and see into the future, not just the past and present, and can then connect their electronic telemetry system. Like we had a telemetry system that went to a lunar module that my uncle designed, that put the first man on the moon, they have telemetry systems that go beyond the speed of light that interface with consciousness and thought.

I think that this is very, very important, that people understand that this is why the CE5 protocols work. Fast-forward to when I formed CSETI 20 years ago, and shortly after that I began to organize people into these contact teams to go out and use these protocols that involved not only thought and consciousness and remote viewing, but also high-powered lights, lasers, and these electronic tones that we send out into space. These tones were recorded actually in a crop circle and then we got them from Colin Andrews back in 1991. I think that what we found was that there was an instant response from these extraterrestrial civilizations, and we began to have amazing contact events that are chronicled in the new book that just came out. It's called Contact Countdown: The Transformation. It's about 300 or 400 pages of accounts of our team's experiences over the last couple of decades, and it has a DVD that comes with it that has the images of these objects appearing.

One of the things that happened, in 1992, was that we went over to England, where we will actually go in the summer as well. People may want to go to CSETI.org and get on a list, we're going to do an expedition there this coming summer, again in 2011. We went there for the first time in 1992, and I was with Colin Andrews and some other folks. Colin Andrews, those of you who may know this, he coined the term "crop circle" and has provided a lot of the briefing information for the Royal Family of Britain.

We went up to this hill called Woodborough Hill that's on this 1,800-acre farm in Halton Barns in Wiltshire, and the group entered into a state of consciousness where we would go into deep silent awareness, remote view the ETs that were behind the crop circle phenomenon and send to them a specific form. We didn't know until we got up there together what it was going to be, and we discussed it, and we settled on an equilateral triangle made of three circles and connected by lines. You can see this logo at C-S-E-T-I dot organization, CSETI.org. When we did this, we all felt this connection had happened, and the next morning, a few hours later actually because we were out there probably at 1 in the morning, then about 4 or 5 in the morning a farmer in a field in direct line sight of where we were found exactly that crop circle in the field. All the studies that have been done on the crop itself that were in the circle showed the most amazing changes to the cell wall structure and electromagnetic changes.

It was an amazing crop circle. But it was really a CE5 crop circle, so now we're introducing another concept. That is a human cooperative and human interactive component to creating these big agroglyphs, or crop circles, which Colin Andrews has confirmed he had happen with Busty Tailor. As they were flying over a field once they had the thought, "Wow, I wish we could see a crop circle that could appear, that would look like all the ones we've seen up to this date." This was in the late 80s, early 90s, and exactly over the field where they were flying when they had that conversation, exactly that formation appeared and was found the next morning.

This kind of interactivity to the phenomenon, most people think of it as, it's something out there and we're passive observers. What the whole thrust of the CE5 initiative, which has now become this global movement of people from all over the world doing this, is that no, it's about us interacting actively and proactively with these interstellar visitors. That's really how the CSETI logo, or the triangle, came about. It was in an actual crop circle, and that is on our website. Also, some great video of it right after we found it, on this DVD that comes with the book, Contact Countdown: The Transformation. Interestingly, this of course, the meditation we refer to, was going on, we had 150 people or so, or 200 people, at Rio Rico this past couple of weeks, and we of course were doing a group meditation for contact, and around that same time very large triangular craft were seen outside Tucson where we were. This is the kind of thing that happens, and it is an interactive phenomenon.

I think this is taking the whole question of the UFOs from sort of a passive study of things that have already happened, what in science we would call retrospective research where you study things that happened in the past, to actually seeing that it's a living, ongoing encounter between human civilization and these other civilizations, which are obviously here to learn about us, and for us to learn about them. But it takes two to tango, and so what I've come up with is the set of protocols that we teach people at these training events that we do a few times a year around the world, and teach them how to do the meditative process, to remote view deep space, to make contact, and to invite the ETs to manifest in whatever ways it's safe for them to do so, in whatever environment we're in, and with whatever the group's readiness is.

We have found that we always have some kind of contact, whether it's through tones that come into the circle, whether we have objects that are seen, whether people will be touched by ETs that'll be partially dematerialized walking around the circle. All kinds of phenomena that sound like something out of a movie, except this is what you experience when you go out and do this, and it's because the ETs are very eager to find humans that are willing to make contact for peaceful purposes.

Because let's face it, over the last 60 years since the World War II era, the only response they've gotten has been either denial, official denial, or being shot at, or people looking at them passively. What we wanted to do was add another dimension to this, and that is the human cooperative diplomatic mission to these visitors for the purpose of peaceful contact. Because we think that's really, really essential, it's the thing that's been missing for decades.

It's not enough to just study things that have already happened, because this is not like studying the dinosaurs that are now extinct. This is an ongoing event where there are extraterrestrial vehicles and extraterrestrial civilizations obviously involved with planet Earth, concerned about the path we're on, and there has not been an appropriate response from the United Nations or the secretary of state or the foreign ministry of any country. What CSETI has done is form this ad hoc, admittedly, nothing official, but global citizens diplomatic response, and it has now become truly a global event.

**Hillary Raimo:** Could you speak a bit about what seems like a quickening of disclosure events? We have had reports of UFOs over China as I mentioned before, Manhattan, El Paso, Texas. The UN has recently assigned an extraterrestrial greeter, so to speak, and most recently Denver's Extraterrestrial Commission. I'd love to hear your thoughts or your take on all of this recent activity.

**Steven Greer:** Everything's quickening and contact itself is in ascendancy. The Disclosure Project, if you go to DisclosureProject.org, you'll see the events that launched about nine years ago in 2001, just before 9/11, a few months before 9/11. What we found was that, when we went forward with that, and we had at the time about 110 of these top-secret military and intelligence and corporate aerospace people who'd worked on this issue come forward, now we have over 550, to update your bio a little bit, what we find is that as we launched that, it began the entire worldwide disclosure movement. So much so that the mainstream media and *The Washington Post* refers to Disclosure as sort of a brand. That was something we started in 2001 and it's truly become global.

Since that time, we've seen massive releases of files from the French space agency, Japan, from the ministries of defense of Great Britain, Denmark, Chile. Mexico had a press conference last year, or earlier this year, where they had their pilots, air force pilots, showing their gun camera footage of these craft that they were tracking all over the world. Now of course the hardest nut to crack has been the United States, because this is the crown jewel of the military-industrial complex, and where the real projects are sitting in terms of the science that has resulted from the study of these extraterrestrial spacecraft.

Because let's face it, anyone who thinks about this just in a cursory way, once you see the evidence and you see that we're not alone, most scientists and certainly any physicist is going to say, "How are they getting from another star system to Earth?" The how they're getting here has within it a big part of the reason for the secrecy, because they're not using a solid rocket booster or Exxon Jet A fuel. They're using these transdimensional energy and propulsion systems that would, if disclosed, completely remove our dependence on oil and gas and nuclear power and create a sustainable civilization. Most people when they hear that say, "Then why isn't that out there?" It's because there's a $600 trillion interest group that deals with these commodities, and the petro dollar and the whole financial system, and the commodities trading, the futures trading, that would suddenly become rather obsolete, not to mention every public utility and every gas, oil, and power company.

This is a huge multi-trillion-dollar problem, but if we don't disclose this information, we're of course going to end up destroying the planet. Because wind and solar is not going to be able to get widespread enough in a cost-effective way to replace the current infrastructure of coal and oil. We have this huge crisis, and a lot of people can't connect, or haven't connected, the dots between the environmental crisis, world poverty, the wars in the Middle East, and the secrecy on the UFO issue. They don't really see that connection. It's our place to do that through disclosure.

Also, we have a separate project called TheOrionProject.org, which is an energy research and education project, that's a nonprofit, that we founded a couple of years ago, that is focusing on the energy and propulsion aspect of this, where a CSETI disclosure project is focusing on the UFO subject and the contact protocols through CSETI. These three projects, interestingly, make a nice little equilateral triangle, with CSETI being the initial one, and disclosure project being a project of CSETI, and then a spinoff being TheOrionProject.org. Those are the three main foci of our activities, because until that you really can't separate out ...

I know that when I briefed, for example, Bill Clinton's CIA director R. James Woolsey on this matter for nearly three hours, he didn't need convincing that UFOs were real. Most people who look into this matter even in a cursory way find enough evidence to know that they are out there, and the majority of the population in America, something like 50 to 60%, think so. More than that, two thirds of the public believe there's intelligent life somewhere out in the universe, so this is not hard to do. The problem is that when you're, say, a CIA director, or you're the president of the United States or the Chairman of the Senate Intelligence Committee, or House Intelligence Committee, and you suspect this is going on but you can't get anything through channels ...

This is what people don't understand, is that the secrecy is so highly compartmentalized that even a sitting CIA director, and I'm one of the few people that you'll ever interview who can say this with certainty, had been denied access to these projects. Lord Hill Norton, who is the head of the Ministry of Defense of Great Britain and had been the head of the military committee for NATO, and was a five-star admiral, what they used to call a Sea Lord, I met with him at his home and he told me point blank that he was never given information on this subject. It was only after he left that position and was in the House of Lords that he learned of the fact that this was real, but that he had been deceived on it and never provided information on it.

A lot of people don't realize that the way this secrecy has been maintained is that it's not a grand conspiracy. Most people conflate the fact that it's secret to the fact that there are tons of people involved in the secrecy, and this simply isn't the case. They're a relatively small number of people who control these operations in terms of having full knowledge of it. Just because you're the president, or just because you're the CIA director or the Secretary of Defense or the head of the Ministry of Defense, does not mean that you're going to be told about this or be told the truth about it. I think that one of the real problems that the Disclosure Project is trying to fix is that the public needs to know about this and needs to know about it in a way that's truthful and direct, and isn't sensationalistic and scary, which is most of what you see out there in the movies and the media. But the public officials who most Americans would think, "You're the top of the heap, you're the head of the pyramid ..."

I remember briefing personally the head of the Defense Intelligence Agency, the DIA, and it was just like the CIA within the Pentagon, and almost as many employees, it's a very huge intelligence operation. This three-star general was completely being deceived on this, and the military advisor for dispro.org as well as some of these top-secret witnesses, and Edgar Mitchell and a few of us had been at the Pentagon briefing people. This particular three-star general said to me he had made inquiries, but the only thing he had gotten for his inquiries through the chain of command was ... he went over to his book shelf, and this is in the E-ring, the outside ring of the Pentagon, he picked up a little ET doll and brought it over to me, he says ... It's something you get at a five-and-dime sort of a toy store. He said, "This is all I've gotten for my inquiries on this through my official inquiries." He was very upset about it.

A lot of people have to understand that, the public needs to understand, that this is a very dysfunctional situation, and it's the fulfillment of what Eisenhower meant when he said, "Beware the military industrial complex." He was not anti-military of course, Eisenhower was a five-star general, was General Eisenhower from World War II, but he had been deceived on this issue, and had been pushed out of the control of how the projects dealing with the ET and UFO issue were being handled. A young man who worked with him, Stephen Lovekin, who became an attorney in North Carolina who is the cousin of our science advisor, Dr. Ted Loder of the University of New Hampshire, worked with Eisenhower in the last couple years of that administration and testified publicly that he had heard the president talking about this, and also talking about the fact that he had been shoved aside, and that the corporate and financial and so-called military industrial complex had circled the wagons and shoved aside the control of the president.

This is a very, very serious problem constitutionally, and it has implications in many arenas. Number one, we're still using oil and gas for heating our houses and driving our cars when we don't need it. Number two, we are mired in the Middle East because of our dependence on oils. Number three, we have no official diplomatic contact without these extraterrestrial civilizations, and instead there's a rogue military operation that's transnational, not just US, that has been targeting, and actually has struck, these extraterrestrial vehicles using electromagnetic weapon systems, and have been doing so for many decades. This is a very dangerous existential threat to the peace of the planet. Then on top of it you have this obvious constitutional crisis of, what does it mean to live in a democracy if there are hundreds of billions or trillions of dollars over the years going into so-called black projects, that neither the president nor the Congress and the people's representatives have any control over. These are very large issues and problems that we're trying to address through these various projects.

**Hillary Raimo:** What is the ultimate agenda of these shadow groups, this small group of people? What would you say in a nutshell is the ultimate agenda.

**Steven Greer:** I think that it's evolved over the years. I think if you go back to the 1940s, they just didn't know what the heck they were dealing with. For example, a man who is a dear friend of mine, a medical doctor like myself, I'm an emergency doctor, he was a hematologist, pathologist in Denver, John Altschuler. Dr. Altschuler was the nephew of General Jimmy Doolittle, and General Doolittle, as most of your listeners probably may recall, was a very famous general in World War II. FDR, president Roosevelt, during World War II, sent Doolittle over to World

War II, the theater over in Europe, to investigate what had been called these foo fighters, or for fighters. That's what these objects were called that were making circles around our aircraft, and sometimes coming straight down the center of the craft as sort of a plasma ball of light. People didn't know what they were, and we thought initially it was a secret Nazi weapon. The Nazis were having the same thing happen, and they thought it was a secret allied weapon. Gen Doolittle came back to the White House and said to President Roosevelt that they were quote "interplanetary vehicles" investigating what we were doing in this massive war.

This is obviously in the early to mid 1940s. In the early days they didn't really know what they were dealing with, and so it was kept very secret during the Roosevelt and then Truman eras. After we had acquired some of the material from the crash in New Mexico, in Roswell, in the 1940s, and I'm not so sure we didn't have some material from the 1930s from China. I understand Douglas MacArthur may have actually retrieved an ET craft that had crashed there through some means back in the 30s. Certainly by the 40s we began to study this, but we didn't really understand the modules operandi, to use the quote of the top secret document from Canada that we have for Wilbur Smith, of these objects, and so a group put together by Dr. Vannevar Bush, who headed up the Manhattan Project, and Edward Teller was involved in this, and many of the early aerospace greats, Wernher Von Braun, began to study how these things might be working.

Of course, the Nazis had been working on anti-gravity, as had T. Townsend Brown beginning in the late 20s. What happened is that some of the electromagnetic sciences that we had breakthroughs in in the 20s and 30s and early 40s were then potentiated by the downing of these extraterrestrial vehicles that happened in the 40s and 50s and 60s, that then potentiated that whole area of scientific research. It wasn't that we didn't have a good handle on it, it's just that it was greatly augmented and potentiated by being able to study the materiel from these disowned extraterrestrial vehicles. Once they realized what they had, and this is the critical point, by 1954, and I can give you a date, October of 1954, is when all these projects dealing with anti-gravity and electromagnetic propulsion systems, things of this sort, went black. I have a person in the Department of Defense who's been in, quote, The Vault, and saw exactly when the lid was slammed down on all these things. That's when Eisenhower lost control of it.

The agenda has been to keep this stuff secret because, not for national security reasons, but because disclosing the information would upend the entire macroeconomic system we live under, which is tantamount to economic slavery. Let's face it, we have nearly 7 billion people on the planet, and there are a few hundred and 50 or so families and individuals that have half of the net worth of the world under their control. This is something that isn't sustainable for one, but number two, people who have that kind of power, or who feel they need to have that kind of power, don't like to let go of it. If you bring out these scientists and information, suddenly you're going to have all of China and Africa and Asia and India and all over the world, every village is going to blossom, because you're going to have free energy, you're going to have the means of manufacturing and electricity and refrigeration and clean water and irrigation and desalinization. Even the deserts will bloom, as it says in the Bible. But what you're going to have also is a relative dissipation of power from this super elite group of folks, and that's what they don't want to let go of.

It went initially from, "Gee, what are we dealing with here," to realizing, "Oh my God, this is what we have here, and here are the implications. I don't think it's an accident that the Rockefeller Commission of 1956, if you look it up, reorganized the Department of Defense and the CIA so that basically the President and the Congress would not be able to keep track of where all the billions and eventually trillions of dollars were going into these projects. This is what we uncovered follow through DisclosureProject.org, which, we have been putting information out there of course since the 1990s on this.

That's part of the agenda, is macroeconomic financial technology. Another part of it, and this is something that surprised me, because I was raised in a very nonreligious family. I was raised a Unitarian like Benjamin Franklin and Thomas Jefferson and a lot of the early founders of the country, and I didn't have a particular worldview that was orthodox at all. But there was a man, a scientist, at the Jet Propulsion Laboratories, who back some years ago, I was talking to him about these objects that had been imaged on mars and also on the moon that were very ancient. Those do exist, by the way. I've had multiple people confirm this too us.

He said, "The reason we can't show even that," it wouldn't be like a contemporary UFO event, but "The reason we can't even show these ancient structures is that it would become obvious that there is a connection to the origins of life on Earth and humanity to these ancient structures," some of which look like the pyramids on earth, some similar structures. This would, and I'm quoting here, "Collapse the orthodox belief systems of every organized religion on earth." To which is aid, well good, it's time for childhood's end. He says, "No, you don't understand the power of these groups." He says, "They do not want this formation out, because suddenly ..." I mean let's face it, I mean no offense to anyone listening, but the people who think that Earth is 6,000 years old and we rode dinosaurs with saddles on them like the museum in Kentucky shows, people who believe that would have a hard time. You'd have a lot of explaining to do. When a lot of this information would come out that's millions of years old, that shows an ancient, multi-million-year intelligent life that has existed in our solar system. This Jet Propulsion Lab scientist says flat out, he's a scientist, not a theologian, flat out told me that that was one of the reasons for the secrecy. Because the orthodox belief systems would be upended.

Then you have another layer, and that is the sort of unseen inertia, the momentum that builds around secrecy. That once a group paints itself in such a corner, it's very hard for them to come clean. Because if they come clean, how are they going to explain to the public that we still have a space program using the shuttle, where people get blown to smithereens, that we're still using fossil fuels, that we're doing all these wars in the Middle East unnecessarily. That both polar ice caps and the ice shelves of Greenland and Antarctica are calving off and melting. That we have all this poverty around the world, where 40% of the world's population literally doesn't have a pot to pee in. They don't have plumbing, they don't have anything. That's 2.8 billion people in the last UN report. How do you explain that when you say at the same time, for 60 years or more, we have had the ability to have free energy, anti-gravity propulsion, no pollution, abundance, et cetera and so on?

This is a very hard thing, so the secrecy becomes its own little black ball of inertia that's very hard to change course. This is one of the reasons why a lot of people say, "How have I gotten a way doing what I've done?" I say, "You know there are people at the CIA, and within this so-called group that's been called Majestic, or Majestic 12 in the early days, in the Truman era, that want me to get this information out, because they can't." I've had people at the CIA since the 90s say, "We really do want this information out, but we can't do it. We need someone to get the truth out about this, because we painted ourselves into a terrible black corner." This is a dynamic that sounds very strange to most people hearing it, but when you think about it, it makes sense, because what a scandal if this group were to come clean with this sort of high crimes, treason, murder, mayhem. The criminal activities that have gone on, and the killing of an entire planet. A few years ago, I coined the term planeticide, which is the deliberate, with malice and forethought, killing of an entire biosphere. Which is what we're in the process of doing, unnecessarily.

I think that this is something which is a very, very difficult thing for people to come clean on, and I think that this is why, in a sense, the Disclosure Project, which is now of course not only an American event, but has become this global event, is also potentiating this global contact phenomenon. Where now we have, through CSETI, and we do a few of these every year, you were recently at one at Mount Shasta, but it will be again at Joshua National Park November 7th through the 13th for your listeners who may want to join us, we're going to be there up in the high desert of California training people in what the protocols are. So that people can go back to their country, or to their home, and form a contact team and practice this.

We're getting reports, literally from Malaysia and from India and from China, and then from Africa and from Brazil, and all over the world where people are doing this, where they're having amazing contact happen. This is in and of itself a phenomenon, because it creates what Rupert Sheldrake would call a morphogenic field. The morphogenic field is when, it's sort of like the 100th monkey effect, where the more people begin to do something, particularly at a higher state of consciousness, and particularly with a unified purpose, it creates a momentum that transcends all the little games of secrecy and all the little games of suppression. This is really how things happen. It's a very empowering message to the public that are listening to your show, and that is you don't need to just sit on your hands and say, "Big Brother is lying to me." You can go out there and do this yourself. You can make contact. You can educate people about this and link them up to the Disclosure Project, DisclosureProject.org is the website, and you can help us find the people and the funding to put together a laboratory to bring out these technologies.

One of the things, The OrionProject.org has been working on is to, and we've just completed in the last couple of months, it's a $5.7 million budget proposed laboratory, where the scientists that we've identified from all over the world, and who've worked in these areas and understand the physics of this new energy, where you use very high-voltage systems to pull energy out of what's called the zero-point energy filed, the fabric of spacetime around us, that we want to open a lab that isn't associated with the government to do this work, and bring out these energy systems so that we can bring out at least a generation 1.0 prototype of something that would run your house or car, pulling energy out of this environmental space energy, rather than burning oil and gas and coal, or splitting the atom creating thousands of years of nuclear waste problems. I think that this is what we're wanting to do, and we actually are in the process of putting this proposal in front of some folks. But we also need the public to help. The public can go to

TheOrionProject.org and they can contribute, or they can help us network to people who might go to help us with this initial funding proposal.

**Hillary Raimo:** There's been some recent articles coming out saying that ETs have been known to disarm nuclear power plants. I know that you've spoken at some point on this, and I'm curious if this-

**Steven Greer:** They weren't nuclear power plants, they were nuclear missiles, which is a big difference.

**Hillary Raimo:** Thank you, the missiles, yes. If the ET's disarm missiles, this suggests they are peacemakers and trying to stop us from harming ourselves and the planet, yet Hollywood movies and mainstream perception makes us believe ET's are here to harm us, not help us. Is this kind of angle going to be used as an agenda to create the perception of ET's as a threat, and will it manipulate humanity into thinking and accepting we have to put all kinds of money into protecting this planet, and join together globally to fight them? What are your thoughts on that?

**Steven Greer:** I think that this is one of the real problems, is when people say disclosure I go, "Whose disclosure?" The cabals include, the foxes who've been guarding the henhouse, what will they say? We don't want the disclosure coming from those guys. The reason we don't is that they have a vested interest in war, what's Ben called SDI or Star Wars. That was never developed to target Soviet missiles, it was developed to target extraterrestrial vehicles. I have witnesses who date from the mid-60s who have testified that we have had platforms in space using, not normal missiles, but electromagnetic type weapon systems. A so-called Tesla type scaler electromagnetic equipment. Like, you saw the spiral over Norway, that happened about a year ago in November of 2009; that was a man-made scaler weapon demonstration while Obama was getting his Nobel Peace Prize in Norway, and it was a shot across his bow quite frankly. I knew about it a week before it happened, by the way.

The point I'm making is that we have very advanced weapon systems that have not been disclosed to the public that have been used to target extraterrestrial vehicles. People say, "Why would they do that?" I say, "It's because people want to provoke a war." The question would be, "Why?" I said, "The war profiteers. Who benefits from the $1 trillion a year war machine?" Certainly not the American public, and certainly not the people of the Earth, but the big military industrial complex interests that Eisenhower warned us about. Eisenhower was a very conservative, pro-military general, and the reason he made that warning is that he knew that there was this kind of manipulation going on, which had nothing to do with our national security as a people, but had everything to do with control, secret control, and the profiteering which goes along with it.

One of the things we have to be wary of is all this sort of ... Particularly in the UFO subculture, where if you were to go to a UFO conference, most people by the time they leave are so depressed, because all you hear about are about the marauding aliens that are coming to eat us for lunch, and this and that and the other thing. This is almost 100% disinformation, false information, that's been deliberately put out to the public to basically brainwash folks into the idea that there's a threat out in space. No less a figure than Wernher Von Braun, before he died in the 70s, told his spokeswoman, who's on our team, Carol Rosin, that in fact this has been the plan all along since the 50s. That is to try to present this issue in a way that would be frightening so eventually people would accept the costs of an interplanetary conflict. No less a figure than General Douglas MacArthur, in the well of the House of Representatives in his last speech to Congress, this is in the congressional record, that quote, "World War Three will be interplanetary." This is the crazy thinking of people who have an infinite view of expanding war and conflict, not only on Earth but into space. This is the madness that we've got to stop.

One of the things that you mentioned about the recent events with the people coming forward about the nuclear missiles being deactivated by the extraterrestrial vehicles, and that did happen. In fact, my group was the first group to bring out about a dozen of these people who had information about this. They told me, rather than the spin of, "The aliens are trying to take our nuclear weapons out," what they told me was that when this happened, during the height of the cold war, they felt that the ETs were trying to send a message to say, "Please don't blow up this beautiful planet, but if you go to mutual assured discussion," MAD, which was our defense posture basically, where if we sent off a missile or if the Soviets sent off a missile, everyone would send all of their missiles and Earth would be completely destroyed, and all life on Earth would be destroyed. That the ETs were saying, life on this planet is precious, and if you go to MAD, which was the defense posture, it was literally called mutually assured destruction, MAD, "We will intervene."

What people don't understand is that ABC news did a segment on this. They had the same thing happening in the Soviet Union, where their missiles were being deactivated. Because the ETs, I believe, have been involved with Earth and Earth's evolution and humanity's evolution for a long time, and they really don't want to see one generation, or in one person's lifespan, for us to go from a fairly primitive industrial society to annihilation. Which is the trajectory we're on if we don't get ahold of ourselves and change course. The ETs, being very compassionate, they didn't go and blow up these facilities, they just simply took electronic control of them to say, "Look, you need to not do this."

If you're someone who is wanting to view this in a xenophobic way, in a way that sees everything as a threat, which is how most military people think, you're going to view it that way. But in reality, it's quite clear than any civilization, and this is what's really key, let's take a big cosmic step backward for a minute, into space. If you have the ability to travel faster than the speed of light, with technologies that are hundreds of thousands to millions of years more developed than a thermonuclear weapon or rocket, if they were hostile, they could've come here the day we detonated the first atomic weapon, the Trinity site in New Mexico in 145 at White Sands, and they could've simply taken out all of our infrastructure, militarily and technologically. Obviously, this is not their intent.

If they were hostile that's what they would've done, no question about it. It doesn't mean that they're not concerned about our own militarism and hostility, because let's face it, we quickly went from detonating nuclear weapons, atomic weapons and then thermonuclear, in the 40s and 50s, to going into space. This would concern anyone who's watching this development. If you were watching Earth, and had been for a long time, and you pick up the signature of a nuclear weapon going off on this planet, and we're beginning to go into space, these civilizations can be excused, frankly, for being a little bit concerned that we've lost our minds here, that we are MAD, mutually assured destruction. And that not only are we a threat to ourselves, but we're a threat to other people in the universe.

If you came into my ER as someone who was a threat to yourself and a threat to others, this is how you get an involuntary commitment and get put into the mental hospital. Because you're about to kill yourself or kill someone else because you're mentally ill. In a sense our society has become mentally ill over the last 50 to 100 years, where we have gone so far off course, of welfare and secrecy and suppression of these technologies, to now we have 7 billion people, 40% of whom live in abject poverty, and all these sciences that are kept secret. At the same time, we have all these weapons of mass destruction, and we're going out into space.

Then you add to that the secret technologies that are in the so-called secret space programs and weapons programs that have started targeting extraterrestrial vehicles when they're coming near to the Earth to see what we're doing, and on a number of occasions, it doesn't happen every day, but on a number of occasions we have hit them and knocked them down. I know more than one person who has been on teams where they have seen the extraterrestrial vehicles or seen the ETs themselves that have been killed as a result of these hits. A lot of people say, "If they're that advanced, how does that happen?" I'm going well, the same way that at tribesman might throw a spear into the rotors of a Sikorsky helicopter. Your rate of success won't be very high, but eventually you hit it just right and bring the big helicopter down, even though you're a caveman era person throwing spears and stones and rocks.

The point I'm making here is that this is the kind of thing that the president and the UN Security Council and other heads of state need to know about, and that's one of the things that I'm doing. I put together a briefing for President Obama and for his new CIA director, Leon Panetta, and for the Secretary of defense Bob Gates, as well as the House Intelligence Committee Chairman, and I've also provided this briefing to other heads of state in other countries. In it, it clearly states that there is an attempt to deceived the public about an alien threat that does not exist, and that this is something that they need to be aware of so that they're not fooled, like they were on 9/11 frankly. Also, so that they don't get stampeded into a crazy response if somebody were to stage something that looked like an alien attack but was really being run out of a secret base out in an underground facility in Utah.

I think one of the problems is that people have to understand that there is an agenda here, the purpose of which is control of the masses of the world through fear, and to release the information on the ET issue within a matrix of fear, within a threat matrix as they call it. Which is completely concocted and false. Because anyone with a scintilla of common sense would know better. When Stephen Hawking said this summer, or last spring, I can't remember when, in the past year, that we shouldn't make contact with aliens because they could be a threat and try to colonize the Earth, I had to laugh. Because any civilization that can travel faster than the speed of light can materialize and dematerialize whatever they wish whenever they wish. They certainly have no need for anything that's on this planet. There are billions of Earth-like planets that probably have no intelligent life on them yet, or very little, scattered throughout our own galaxy, never mind the whole universe. If you can travel at multiples of the speed of light, why would you need to come to an armed camp like Earth to get something? This is a childish, xenophobic fantasy by paranoid people, and it says a lot more about the people making these claims than it does about the actual ET presence.

We have gone around, we're the longest standing ET contact diplomatic group on the planet today. We've been doing this 20 years, month in and month out, all over the world. We have never had anything but beautiful, peaceful experiences with these ET visitors. On the other hand, we've had lots of threatening things happen from military, or from humans. I think that people need to understand that the kind of negative imagery that comes with this whole subject, everything from cattle mutilations to abductions, much of that has been concocted, or presented in a form to be frightening, because they need people to have some new enemy to hate. It's just like, look, we created Saddam Hussein. Rumsfeld was in charge of selling him his first chemicals to make his chemical weapons, this is a matter of historical fact.

The point is that we have to keep creating enemies to justify the trillion dollars a year we're spending on military and other programs. But more than the money part of it is the control of people's minds. It's a mind control thing, where people get controlled through fear. What I'm saying to people is that, it's like that En Vogue song from the 90s, "Free Your Mind." You've got to free your mind, honey, and step out of this nonsense, and kind of see that this is all sort of like the movie "The Matrix," where it's this false thing that's been created that everyone is living through, and take a big step out of it, and think about this carefully. I've concluded that there's absolutely no threat from these extraterrestrial civilizations, but there's plenty of problems with them being presented as a threat.

One of the things that we're trying to do is to address this, not only through having thousands of people now going all over the world making contact peacefully through the CSETI protocols, and again I just want to mention, people who want to come to this event in Joshua Tree National Park, it's from November 7th through the 13th. We spend the afternoons talking about these issues and doing discussions about consciousness, and the applications of consciousness and meditation training, and then we go out every night under the stars and train people in how to observe, how do you identify something as a satellite versus a plain, versus maybe an ET object, and what other kind of phenomenon happening? What happens if an ET object is 20 feet away, but is there resonating faster than the speed of light? What's going to happen? You're going to have electronic discharges, you're going to have light discharges, you're going to have tone to come into the group.

If you go to CSETI.org you'll find out about some of the things that have happened recently. There's a photograph up there of an extraterrestrial being that was hovering right outside our circle at Joshua Tree National Park 11 months ago when we were there. We're going to the same place this year. This particular ET, we learned later, was from the Andromeda galaxy. I was there with a team of people whom, number of folks had heard the voices of them but they couldn't see them.

Someone took a photograph because she felt them and asked them to appear, and they flashed in in a fraction of a second, and there's a photograph of this ET literally hovering in sort of a transportation beam of a cone of light from an orb, right outside the circle, maybe five feet outside the circle or less. These are the sort of things that are happening, and it sounds like something out of science fiction, but it's happening.

People, not just our group, when I'm there training people, what's exciting for me is that I'm learning that people are doing this all over the world and are having amazing very close encounters that are close encounters of the 5th kind, which is when humans invite the encounter and do it for diplomatic purposes. This is something that has just taken on a huge momentum in the last few years.

**Hillary Raimo:** Thank you Dr. Greer. Are the commonly referred to reptilian and grays which have been labeled "negative" or "bad" aliens within UFO subculture being produced or made by the shadow groups in government and secret programs using bio and nanotechnology?

**Steven Greer:** Yes, we have a number of people who have worked in these projects, not only in Australia and the United States, but also in England, where we have manufactured these sorts of robotic things. They have integrated circuits in their neural complex, but they look biological, and they look alien, but they're man-made. These have been put on what would be called a flying saucer, an alien reproduction vehicle, which is manufactured by Lockheed Martin and Northrop and a few other companies. These have been used along with electromagnetic weapon systems and chemical weapon systems to do what the public would call abductions.

It's interesting, because there's this man in Denver who had some footage of this creature, which he calls "Boo." I went to his home and saw the footage, and it was interesting because he'd probably been in the Air Force, and someone had been calling him using a computerized animated voice, giving him information, who when after he got this footage of this and he had been quote "abducted," they said, "Stan, that's one of the fake ones." But neither he nor any of the UFO researchers who were with him knew what that meant. I said, "They're telling you it's one of these programmed life forms." He said, "What's a PLF," a programmed life form. I said, "These are man-made aliens. They're not ETs at all." This man had never heard of this. I said, "This is the big coverup within the UFO community, is that there are very advanced psychological welfare programs that involve the electromagnetic and biological and chemical systems as well as these things that look like a UFO but they're man-made. These are antigravity craft that we've been making since the late 50s and early 60s."

Unfortunately, people think everything that goes bump in the night is an alien, and in fact some of the things people are experiencing are completely man-made, and they're what are called stagecraft. Actually, I have a document that talks about the stagecraft used to hoax abduction and mutilations events so that it would scare people. This document is from a think tank involved with these issues, and it's interesting because this is something not talked about much. You don't see this in documentaries and at UFO conferences, and a man who first uncovered this in the 80s told me that if I were to go public with this, it would result in me being blacklisted from a number of programs and conferences because the people who are behind that do not want the truth out, that our classified programs have the ability to hoax a lot of these events. Sort of a cosmic 9/11 or a cosmic Gulf of Tonkin type event, where things can be exaggerated or a threat can be created, and that the technologies for this have been around for many decades, literally since the 50s.

I think that people have to understand that there's fool's gold and there's real gold and we've got to do an assay, and this has not been done, and we have to tighten up our research community. It's my conclusion that a great deal of what's bandied about as quote-unquote alien is entirely hoaxed and man-made because of its psychological welfare value to scare people, and if people are afraid they'll accept the cost of war. We have to awaken people to this issue and think rationally about how we approach civilizations that are here, that obviously aren't hostile. Because if they were hostile it would've been point, set, match, over back in 1945.

How do we approach this and sift through all this confusing information and obscuring and obfuscating information, and get to the truth of the matter? This is how we have to do it. We have to disclose the truth, we have to go make contact directly. Then TheOrionProject.org, I think the government won't come out with these technologies. We the people need to come together and figure out how we're going to fund a research program so that scientists and physicists who understand this new area of energy generation can come together and we can do this independent of the corrupting influence of big money and big power that you see so often in Washington and in corporations.

That's what we're working on, and I hope people will go to the websites and learn more about this, and also will join us in Joshua Tree or some of the upcoming ... We haven't yet published the 2011 schedule yet, but we will be going to England and Mount Shasta and Colorado and other places in 2011 for these week-long expeditions. If people want to sign up on those websites at C-S-E-T-I dot organization or DisclosureProject.org they'll get notified when we get the information about where we're going to be doing these programs.

**Hillary Raimo:** One last question for the show Dr. Greer, and I know it's going to be a big one, but my question is, time travel technology, HAARP, weather manipulation technology, is this reverse alien engineered technology?

**Steven Greer:** As I mentioned earlier, there are a lot of electromagnetic systems that deal with transdimensional technologies that have been developed by humans. One thing I always point out to people, the wonderful thing about science is, the laws of the universe and of nature are universal. Humans have begun to uncover some of this in the late 1800s and early 1900s. By the 1930s and 40s there were classified projects. People have heard of the Philadelphia experiment, that stuff really did happen. Time travel, teleportation. Humans have done classified experiments in that area for decades. Rumsfeld himself said that there's two or three trillion dollars missing out of the Department of Defense budget over the years. He said this right around 9/11. Rumsfeld himself, Bush's Secretary of Defense.

The point I'm making is that if you then take that, and then potentiate it with studying materials that we've retrieved from downing these extraterrestrial vehicles, then you have a really mighty combination of forces, because you have these really well-developed pedigree of secret electromagnetic research programs that then are potentiated further by studying these extraterrestrial materials and what have you. That's what is going on inside the black world, the classified world, the super secret world, that the President doesn't control and the Congress doesn't control. I think that that's why some of these other programs that people have heard about, you can't just say that it all came from SETI and ET technologies, and it's probably not true that it all just came from men creating them. I think what you have is a combination of people who understood these principles, began to experiment with them, and then that research got further augmented, or potentiated, by studying the extraterrestrial materials that we retrieved from downing these spacecraft from other star systems.

**Hillary Raimo:** Is it possible then that the ETs have developed the ability to time travel since they are going interplanetary? Could they be some form of us from the future?

**Steven Greer:** I think some form of them maybe in fact are, and I have learned that the Rendlesham Forest Bentwaters case in 1980 or 81 in England, that's one that we have at DisclosureProject.org, witnesses who testify to this, where there was a craft that landed near this Air Force base in England. The officers who were very close to that event have told us that the ETs that were there, they were extraterrestrial because they were from other star systems, but they were our descendants. They were from 500,000 years in the future, at which times humans had become highly enlightened and interstellar, and they were coming back to warn us about the dangers of the cold war and the nuclear base that was there. By the way, the Bentwaters RAF, Royal Air Force base, was a secret US nuclear base there in England, and it was not supposed by treaty to exist. They were warning of the dangers of the path we were on that could lead to global annihilation and destruction.

I understand that those were both ET and human descendants, because in the future we've gone out amongst the stars, and they were almost these luminous light beings that floated through the wall. It was a black, pyramid shaped craft that landed. In fact, when it came down through the trees it actually left traces, and left a landing mark where it landed, an indentation that was studied by the Ministry of Defense, and this has now been released by the British Ministry of Defense. I have spoken to a number of people, but a lot of people don't realize that those ETs were very likely our descendants 20,000 generations into the future, half a million years into the future.

**Hillary Raimo:** This is where I find your work to differ from other people's, is that you bring a quality of spiritual consciousness and interaction, and make that key point in the contact experience, and you use remote viewing and techniques of that such to enhance that experience. In closing I would like you to comment on your hope for people as we evolve through the time that we are here on this planet, and what that spiritual and higher consciousness value has.

**Steven Greer:** I think this really is a spiritual crisis that we're in, and it's going to be a spiritual solution, and that the study of higher states of consciousness, and the understanding that within each and every sentient being, every human and every ET that is conscious, is this light of awareness, and that the mind itself is a singularity. As Erwin Schrodinger said, who is the father of modern quantum mechanics and particle wave theory specifically, he said that the total number of minds in the universe is one, and that is that it's a singularity. This is literally true scientifically, but experientially.

One of the things, before I became a medical doctor and an emergency doctor, is that I was a meditation teacher, and I studied the Sanskrit Vedas, and the mantras and all this. This is, a lot of people don't realize when they come to these CSETI, we call them trainings, I basically give people a very intensive course in the Vedas and meditation along with all this other material. It's a bit much we cover, but we try to do the best we can. I think that the reason that's so important is that, if people understand that our true nature is that we are the cosmic mind itself, that it's folded within each of us. That we have the ability to do wonderful great things that are beyond just the ego and individual, and that also this is the common meeting ground where all peoples can gather, whether they're from another star system or another race or religion or whatever. That is in the sense of the fact that we are all one in spirit, that there is this essential aspect of ourselves that is this single light of awareness where we all have our home.

This is not only a very important spiritual concept, but it's an operational system, because it involves then the ability to go into that state of higher awareness and cosmic mind, see remote places, and see the future, and contact with these extraterrestrial civilizations, and make contact using these advanced concepts of technology that are the science of consciousness, as I call it. I think that this is really, really important for people to understand, that we really have that ability folded within us. There's a wonderful Sufi saying that goes, "Thinketh thyself a puny form, when within thee the universe is folded?" It's a rhetorical question. Basically, it's saying that the entire cosmos is folded within every individual through this sort of quantum hologram of consciousness and mind. Once you begin to experience that, you see that almost anything is possible.

**Hillary Raimo:**  Thank you so much for joining me Dr. Greer, it's been a pleasure.

**Steven Greer:**  Thank you very much, Hillary.

# 11

# PHIL CORSO JR
# THE DAY AFTER ROSWELL & REVERSE
# ENGINEERED TECHNOLOGY

*Philip Corso, Jr. parlayed his talent for mechanical engineering
into a career but his life was to take an extraordinary turn in 1997,
when, his father, US Army Colonel Philip J. Corso (ret.), published a
memoir written with William J. Birnes (an X-Conference speaker). That
memoir, The Day after Roswell, is easily one of the most controversial
and implicative books published in the 20th Century. Now Phil, Jr. has
an additional vocation - protecting, extending and validating his father's
legacy.*

RECORDED OCTOBER 28, 2010

**Hillary Raimo:** One of the most important milestones since the
disclosure process began in earnest, back in 1991, was the publishing of
*The Day After Roswell*, by Lieutenant Colonel Philip J. Corso in 1997.
The allegations in this book rocked the foundations of a longstanding and
deeply entrenched coverup. To this day, neither the Army, the
Department of Defense, nor any other agency of government has
formally responded to these allegations. In the book *The Day After
Roswell*, the colonel disclosed how he spearheaded the Army's super
secret reverse engineering project that seeded extraterrestrial technology
into American corporations such as IBM, Hughes Aircraft, Bell Labs and
Dow Corning, without their knowledge. He describes the devices found
aboard the Roswell craft and how they became the precursor for today's
integrated circuit chips, fiber optics, lasers, night vision equipment,
super-tenacity fibers; and classified discoveries, such as psychotropic
devices that can translate human thoughts into signals that control
machinery, stealth aircraft technology and Star Wars particle beam
devices.

He also discusses the role that extraterrestrial technology played in
shaping geopolitical policy and events, how it helped the United States
surpass the Russians in space, start up elaborate initiatives, such as the
Star Wars projects, Project Horizon, which was to place a military base
on the moon, and HAARP, and ultimately brought about the end of the
Cold War. Colonel Corso also said that captured UFOs were and are kept
at Norton Edwards Air Force Base. He continues that a working UFO

group was set up by President Truman in September of 1947, a group some call MJ-12, and that has functioned ever since. He continues to disclose that, in the 1950s, two crude prototypes of antigravity craft were constructed, but were powered by crude human nuclear fission generators, which were inefficient and leaked radiation.

He says, in his book, that the Star Wars program was always primarily created to prepare for war against ETs, in case of invasion. The military and political groups Corso Sr. allied with adopted the same outlook on the ET visitors, as some invasion force that had to be eliminated by a crash program of back-engineering Star Wars weapons from captured UFO technology. To his credit, he did not personally fall into that reactionary conservatism that viewed ETs as insidious potential invaders. During this next hour, his son, Philip Corso Jr., joins me on the air, live. At the end of the hour, we'll be presenting information, never before revealed to the public, right here on the show. Welcome, Phil.

**Phil Corso Jr:** Yeah, Hi, Hillary.

**Hillary Raimo:** Let's start with Time. What do ETs and UFOs and time changing technology have in common?

**Phil Corso Jr:** Well, I think they are one and the same, in my opinion. They all share a similar technology. As you were doing the introductory, there were many things there that we can elaborate on. This could go on for many hours, so I know we have to condense it into one. I think the best thing is probably you just ask me the questions, and I'll see how I can answer them. I have a few things that I would like to bring in, and then, of course, at the end, the letter that we've just received. The letter is going to be very important, I think, if it is real. Now I say if it is real because it still hasn't been verified. It does have some military codes on it, and the man that brought it forward wants to remain anonymous. It is very interesting, so we'll bring that, like you said, at the end. Go ahead and shoot. Ask me some more.

**Hillary Raimo:** Your father revealed information and technology regarding reverse engineering. Let's start there.

**Phil Corso Jr:** Well, the book got started, actually, by accident. In 1992, my father and I ran a small electronics company. Dad would sit at the desk and say like he said in his own words, "Hold down the fort," while I went out and worked on yachts. Well, he got bored sitting there, so I said, why don't you write your memoirs? Which he did. We got turned down, his memoirs, some, oh, I guess, a dozen times or more. Nobody wanted a colonel from World War II and what he did in the war. But there was one paragraph in there that was about ... Oh, I guess, just a short brief. It said, "When I was in R&D in 1960 with General Trudeau, I seeded alien artifacts." Well, ufologist, which we probably all know very well, George Knapp, in Arizona, picked up on it, called dad. Bill Burns got involved and some others. They said, why don't you elaborate on it? So hence the book was born. Never really meant to be.

Later on, dad said that he wrote the book, and he declassified the parts of the book himself because he was declassifying officer. He said he did it mainly for the youth. He says the youth can handle the truth, and they're entitled to the truth. Unfortunately, the book caused the family a lot of problems. We got sued by people we didn't even know. On my dad's death bed, he was really quite sorry that he had wrote the book, only for the reason that he said he had left a family in a mess. He wanted to stay. He wanted to help clean the mess up. I said, pop, don't worry. I'll take care of it. So, I'm hoping that people out there will realize this book did not come forth easily. Our family has paid a dear price to bring it forward.

**Hillary Raimo:** If this is such secret and devastating information to release to the public, how would it get published in the first place?

**Phil Corso Jr:** Well, the publishing also was done very quickly. Bill Birnes happened to be in the family of Simon & Schuster, through his wife, Nancy. It got published by a young publisher named Tish Corbin, and he was able to do it so quickly that my dad was not able to have a legal reading on it. He never did a proofreading. In fact, we have another book where he might say some of the book got a little bit of Hollywood in it, and he didn't like that. Anyway, that's how the book got written so quickly. If you remember, right after the book was revealed in 1997, the Air Force came out with their so-called, quote, final word on UFOs when they brought up the crash dummies and stuff. I myself think that was a rebuttal to the book. Also, we had Senator Thurman, which wrote the forward for it, and there was quite an upset over that. Senator Thurman, just to take you to the end of it and make a long story short, fired his whole staff over them trying to say that they were going to sue dad for falsely putting that in the book. The first 1,000 issues of the book have the General Trudeau's forward in it, and Tish Corbin, the editor, said that someday they may be collectors' items. If anybody out there can find one in an old bookstore, buy it.

**Hillary Raimo:** Are we still seeing the products of that reverse engineering pop up in our culture today?

**Phil Corso Jr:** Well, yes. We've had many scientists to the house after dad wrote the book. These guys said we knew something was up. They said because it came too fast, too quick. Now don't think that there were not lasers prior to dad introducing the little flashlight, which will be mentioned later in this letter. He called it a flashlight, but it was, of course, a laser. What took place there was already ... Night vision came from the Germans, which, by the way, dad said they had a craft too. So, when dad seeded this information along with General Trudeau and the funds and the artifact, only when they would begin to flounder did dad put the artifact in. They put it into companies that were already working in those areas. They told him, take the patents for it. Run with it with the civilian. Do whatever you want in the civilian culture with it, but the military gets first priority on it. They left no paper trail, which later on, this letter, if it is true or genuine, is probably the first piece of paperwork I have ever seen. It's probably a mistake on dad's part, and thank goodness for it, if it is real, again.

**Hillary Raimo:** Weather modification technology, the HAARP program, are these built on this reverse engineering alien technology?

**Phil Corso Jr:** Well, I think that you have to remember that, when the integrated circuit is introduced, it changes our world. It changed our world in such a way that General Trudeau, some of the German scientists that dad brought over in charge of Operation Paperclip for Eisenhower and such. They all said that it's 200 years advancement, and that's something I'd like to touch on also, is that, technologically, we are 200 years advanced from where we should be, if these gentlemen are right. But, morally, the religious issue, the economic issues and such, we are still far behind, and we haven't caught our technology. Dad and all of these powers to be and these very brave men were very worried that these technical items would be misused, and, indeed, they were. For instance, the stock market would not have been able to do what it did today without the computer. Actually, the computer was misused, but we do know that all great inventions is a two-sided sword.

As far as technology of today, yes, it all came from, basically, five different items. Some of the technology dad left notes on that I still have, and we plan to release these in the Corso files in the near future. For instance, I'll just give you one that is really something. The other part of the IC that was burned, after they did more research with it, Bell Laboratories, this is, they discovered that there was a fluid amplification, which, of course, is an oxymoron because we all know, from hydraulics, you cannot amplify fluid. Whatever you put in comes out at the other end. But on the atomic base, it can be done, and it was done on a molecular base with the other part of this integrated circuit. Just to prove that, dad took a brief to John Glenn, when he was senator, and said, here's a car that runs on four flashlight batteries. This is no little scooter. This was a regular car. Four flashlight batteries for one-year, constant running, by the way. So that technology no one knows about. I have never mentioned it before. But just the fact that we know it existed, it can be back engineered again.

**Hillary Raimo:** Regarding free energy technology, has it been weaponized?

**Phil Corso Jr:** Well, like I said, we have many issues we have to catch up on before you're going to have free technology. Dr. Steven Greer goes around, and he looks for a lot of this free energy. You might as well forget it because it's not going to happen again because our economic base has not caught up and is not ready for free energy. We first have to change our way of thinking, which is being done only because we fear the greenhouse effects and such like that, but we have to begin changing not based upon fear but based upon a common goal to increase our morals and to not let the economic system dictate to us what we need to be doing in the near future, especially in politics.

**Hillary Raimo:** Could we have this technology, and yet, biologically, not be caught up with that technology?

**Phil Corso Jr:** Well, that might be very true. My dad was ghostwriter for Jane Dickson, which is a very clairvoyant woman that passed away some 10 years ago. He was ghostwriter for her for 30 years. My father had a very keen insight into the future, and, yes, he said that she could, at will, change the timeline. Now does that timeline mean that it changed ... And this is the same timeline that many of the religions speak of, and the Hopi Indians. Do we have the power within our mind to do things? Well, you and I, Hillary, both know that, yes, it can be done. For instance, Steven Seagal flew him out to Vegas, and he only wanted to know one thing. He said, "I had a near accident just like you, and time slowed down. The car bent, and I want to know what happened." So, he and dad became friends. They told of that.

It's happened to me. It's happened to my sons, and it's probably happened to many people out there, when you see that car coming at you and it's going to smash into you. It seems like time does change, and, of course, we both know that time is relative, and it's relative to the human mind. You make a trip somewhere. It takes a long time going, and you're back in a second if you're busy in a car, talking, and having a good time and you're very happy. So, we know time is relative. So, the answer to that question, I believe, yes.

**Hillary Raimo:** Why is it so very remotely spoken of?

**Phil Corso Jr:** Yeah. Well, it's my best subject too. I love speaking of time. I see time myself as being more digital. What I mean by that is, to the human brain ... I have a very good friend that is a neurosurgeon, and he and I talk quite a bit. We believe that the human brain sees in icons. For instance, your birthday, when your child was born, and these are memories that you store away, and they're actually pictures. These pictures, when you recall them, if you could visualize more than time moving forward and back ... In other words, we have our timeline when we're born and when we pass away, so we see everything within that timeline. But, actually, I don't believe it's correct. I think it's more digitally with these icons sideways. In other words, Jesus is still dying on the cross right now. It's just our limited human brain that puts these limitations on it. The limitations are put on by us by our society too. As we begin educating, they say, well, here's a clock.

I talked to Edgar Mitchell recently. He says, "Yes, time is based upon the movement of the planets, and it always has been." He says, "We need some other standard to go by," and I'm not talking about atomic clocks or anything like that. I mean a new mental standard to go by. When you go by thinking this way, it opens up all new dimensions for you. Then you begin thinking the way that the scientist should think, and they think in M-theory and string theory and such like that. So, these are questions that people are bringing forward now and are beginning to understand, and more people, almost everyone you talk to, understands these things nowadays.

I myself, the popular belief for me, is that it's us taking care of ourselves. My dad said there's something awful about the human race, and he never really elaborated on it, but I have a feeling what it is. I think maybe the missing link is us. In other words, I think our future selves could come back and create us, create man. If you just think about that a second, it does make a lot of sense because maybe that's what all of these abductions are about. Maybe there are implants being put in, and these implants are probably changing the race.

Now one of the notes we're going to release in the Corso files is my dad wrote very disturbing notes, and these notes were what he called genetic bombs. Just to prove that he was right on with this, this was before the diseases of SARS and AIDS, and he has them in there. He actually calls them by their proper names years before they were out, so these genetic bombs were not necessarily for warfare, but they will change the human race, almost overnight, into something else. I do believe that there are certain people walking around that are indeed hybrids or changes, not necessarily from space aliens, but maybe from our future selves, just a theory. It's just a theory. I have no facts to back it up.

**Hillary Raimo:** If that is true, then these diseases, and perhaps even the vaccines to cure these diseases, could be considered the biggest atrocity to humanity. Is it a secret plot to change the genetic makeup of humanity? What agenda is this serving?

**Phil Corso Jr:** Yeah. For instance, with my three sons, I built the experimental aircraft. I would come home. My dad lived with us the last

201

five years of his life after my mom passed away, and I would come home full of fiberglass, sit on the floor, and say what are you writing about today. Well, one day, just like a kid would ask his dad, he said, "Well, who is God, anyway?" My dad looked at me, and he answers ... Still today, I wonder about it because he said, "Well, God is the intellect," so if God is the intellect and that is us. So, I know I'm going to get in trouble with a lot of religions here.

But, possibly, that's all we get is ourselves, possibly. I mean, it's just a theory, so don't anyone out there say Phil Corso's an atheist, and he doesn't believe in God. I do believe in an organization within the universe, and I do believe that we all bow to that organization.

**Hillary Raimo:** Is the spiritual advancement, the spiritual enlightenment of the human population and this planet, really, what we're trying to catch up with when it comes to technology?

**Phil Corso Jr:** Yes, yeah, absolutely. Just for the fact, I do believe in Jesus, and I do believe that he was a man from God that accepted the responsibility. I do believe that the religion ... The Bible is still being written, and I do believe that religion needs to upgrade itself. By upgrading itself, I mean the Bible is still being written. If it doesn't do that, my prediction is the younger people are not going to take it anymore. They're going to find their own way, which may not be the right way. The religious leaders need to address it. Of course, we know, in the recent past, it's been done. The Pope says he would like to baptize an ET. There is now an ambassador for the UN, and we also know that there's a possibility, very soon, we may have to deal with such an entity. Now when I say entity, I'm not lumping it in one basket. I'm saying there is dimensional travel, which my father has actually talked to one of them. He's had other encounters with one. I used to be very against him speaking about that, but I do see that people are changing, especially in the last 12 years since dad has passed away and you can talk about it more readily now.

**Hillary Raimo:** DNA bombs, now there is something to ponder. Is it safe for you to talk publicly about these topics?

**Phil Corso Jr:** Well, there's a hands-off policy with our family. I know that. I've been told that. I've been told that by some very important people on this planet in high positions. What we are, I guess, is an enigma, and that's fine. Leave it that way because I also have been told what to say and when to say and how to say, and there are certain areas that we do not talk about. My dad was senate internal investigator for the ... excuse me Senator Javits, which investigated the Warren Commission. My dad was in charge of that. It's still classified. I will not talk about it. I don't know anything about it, and I won't talk about anything that is classified, unless I've been told otherwise. We've had every agency, every sort of person come to our hanger, talk to us, spy on us, threaten us, give us gifts. We've been all through that, and I think that maybe we have reached an understanding, hopefully.

**Hillary Raimo:** Is it a slow leak process of disclosure to people?

**Phil Corso Jr:** It's a slow education, Hillary, right.

**Hillary Raimo:** Is it a slow leak for educational purposes, or on purpose because they don't want people's minds to be blown instantly and have everything collapse on them?

**Phil Corso Jr:** Well, of course, yeah, I agree with you. It's a slow education. You see, it's not up to us. In other words, ET or time travel or whatever, it's not that we are waiting for them to reveal themselves. They're waiting for us to grow up, and there's no doubt about that. Are we growing up? Well, I believe in the agnostic spark, that everybody has the achievement of God within them if they can only look for it and want to achieve it.

**Hillary Raimo:** Let's talk about the microchip agenda. Is this reverse engineered alien technology?

**Phil Corso Jr:** Oh, yeah. Dad and all the powers to be, the scientists and all, they said one of the things they were also worried about, by releasing the microchip, was that they believed it's a living entity. Now you're going to get a ... We'll get a lot of backlash on that. But look how fast it has developed. In fact, here's what dad said, every year in research and development, for the military, there's more advancements each year than there was the previous year before and all of the rest of the years in history. So, it's exponentially going up at a rate that we can't even imagine. Here we have an integrated circuit that was a little six transistor radio, 50 years ago, and now look what it is. It's an iPhone that does almost everything that needs to be done but put a holographic image out, which will be around the corner. In fact, when something comes out, we all know it's outdated by the time it arrives on the shelves.

**Hillary Raimo:** But nobody else does. The masses don't. They're in the dark delusional world of marketed consumerism and socialization programming. Can technology advance people spiritually?

**Phil Corso Jr:** Well, yes. I do believe that. I think that technology will grow into something that will help us all, if, again, we put it in the right direction. Are we putting it in the right direction right now? No, not really, because the economic system is dictating where it goes. The great military complex is dictating where it goes. I think we need to rethink some of that. I would like to see all political parties in the future being scientists. I don't think we need lawyers anymore. I know we're going to get some backlash from that too. A lawyer, to me, in politics, is no more than a person that couldn't make it in his own profession, so he sees this other horse and jumps on it. It's a shame, and there are some good ones out there, I'm sure. In any type of society, there's good and bad, so I'm not criticizing all lawyers. Mr. Kent, which is my lawyer, is a very decent, honest man. But we have to rethink our politics. I would like to see the science party as a third party. We look at the Republican and Democrat, and there's not much choice there, and I think everyone would admit that. But if we had scientists in there, I think that they would begin to move our planet and move our technology in a different direction, which needs to be done, based upon global warming and other problems.

**Hillary Raimo:** You often speak of benevolent intent, having a good intention and a higher spiritual connection, as being a part of a psychic protection and a way to move through using these technologies in a way that's a positive end. How does the Philadelphia Project fit into this discussion?

**Phil Corso Jr:** Well, the Philadelphia experiment was real. I held the brief in my hand before someone came in the house and took it from us. Dad revealed the Einstein worked on it, and dad was in charge of Operation Paperclip for Ike, brought the scientist here. He was not ... Now Mr. Freeman criticized my dad because he said he was MJ-12. No, he wasn't MJ-12. He was the one they reported to, and he reported to Eisenhower. My dad was very much in the know during these times. What were we talking about? I've lost my train of thought.

**Hillary Raimo:** The Philadelphia Project and how ...

**Phil Corso Jr:** Oh, yes, yeah.

**Hillary Raimo:** ... higher intentions.

**Phil Corso Jr:** Well, Einstein was part of it, and here's what it was for. It was not invisibility; that's completely wrong. What it was, the Eldridge was equipped with six revolving fields with the frequency of the earth. How do I know that? I met the man, Mr. Beckworth, over in Tampa. He's deceased last year, that actually built the transformers and worked on the Eldridge. Now he was very good friends with dad too. Now here's what it did. German's invented the magnetic mine. During the Battle of the Atlantic, it was coming up ... A magnetic mine allows the first two or three ships to pass over it. Then it pops up in the middle of the convoy and really raises havoc with several ships. So, we were losing the Battle of the Atlantic. They did this Philadelphia Experiment. They were actually very successful moving the mines 500 yards through time and space. There was an accident, dad said. The brief that I read said there was an accident. The soldiers really did have problems that are, pretty much, revealed in the Hollywood movie.

We have had time travel for a long time. That is time travel, by the way, and we have had it for a long time. We didn't have the sophistication to pinpoint it, where now we do. I've sat at a table with Pentagon, military officials, with religious officials, and at this table Mr. Beckworth, that actually makes all the transformers, mostly, for the military. He makes them for the HAARP program and such like that. By the way, try to build a transformer and see what happens. You can't do it because that's Tesla technology. I've sat at the table with these people, and Mr. Beckworth wanted to release ... He got up, and everybody went in another room, and he started up a small armature, like a motor spinning, and it disappeared. It just went away, and he wanted to release this technology to the universities.

We went back in the room. Everyone said no. Then the religious leaders said, "Why are you doing this?" Because they're coming back with excess baggage, the military is. So, they wanted to know, from me, what's going on. I said, well, it's very simple. My dad and I talked about it quite a bit. You don't just start up a time machine and move through time without having a benevolent reason. If you don't have a benevolent reason, the universe does not correct itself. For instance, you go back in time and the old paradox where you kill your parents and you don't exist anymore, well, that doesn't happen in a benevolent universe. What happens is you go back in time, and you can't return to this future. You grow forward in another future. Now you say, how does that help our future? If you grow forward in the other future with the proper benevolent reasons, well, there's a ripple effect. The ripple effect goes through the 11 membranes of the M-theory and such. I don't want to get too deep into this right now, just because it's very hard to follow. I would rather just stay on, like we've been doing, specific terms, if it's all right with you, Hillary.

**Hillary Raimo:** Of course, thank you. Are there two worlds converging? You have the UFO and alien activity and planetary hierarchy, masters, angels, guides, religious beliefs. Do you see them as converging, or are they the same?

**Phil Corso Jr:** Yeah. Well, let me say this. We see this. First of all, there's a level of government that we all learn in school, the judiciary, the Congress and so on, the president. You have this college level or entry level. The next one after that is the secret societies. They all think that they run things, that they have power over this other lower run. They're going to impose their will with their wealth and such like that. Then you have another third level there. You have the great military complex, which President Eisenhower warned about. Dad used to carry the orders over from Ike to the chiefs of staff, and he used to say, kind of, laughable, he used to say, "I was only a colonel, and here I'm telling a four-star general what the president wants to do. I wonder what I would ever do if they said no," and he said, "But they never did say no to him."

Anyway, you have this other level of the great military complex. Now above that, you have either time future or the alien agenda, and that opens up a lot of ... And, above that, you have God, of course. Now does the lower level know about the second one? Does the third level know about the second one? Does the second level believe that they are really in power when the great military complex is really in power? Once you begin to understand this, then you understand part of the reason why there is a coverup. By the way, when dad was called in by Ike, he originated or founded the liaison between Chiefs of Staff and, like I said, would carry the orders. But when Ike called him in, he said, "Where are they from, Phil?" And he says, "I don't know." He actually called him Corso. He says, "Where are they from, Corso?" He says, "We don't know," and he says, "What do they want?" He says, "Well, we don't know." He said, "Well, what do we know about it?" Dad said, "Well, they penetrated our airspace, and you and I are just old soldiers, so let's just say nothing," so hence the coverup began because everyone, CIA, everybody jumped on this bandwagon to coverup.

I've seen dad talk to some of these CIA people before his death and say, "Why are you still doing this?" They were retired, and one of them came forward once and said, "I don't know why I'm still doing this." Maybe they have to die off first. Harsh terms, maybe they have to die off first before anything else is going to come forward. I don't know. It's an old agenda, and it's not needed anymore. My dad had colonels come up at Air Force bases during the signings of the book and said, "Get this monkey off our back. We can't tell our wives. We can't tell our family anything of what we do." He says, "Your book is right on."

**Hillary Raimo:** Do you believe that ETs have a good, positive agenda, or have we missed the point by getting caught up in an us versus them mentality that's spread by mass perception and enforced by TV shows, like "The Event," and films and even children's cartoon shows. Is there a positive, good, bad thing going on?

**Phil Corso Jr:** Well, dad said this. Part of the coverup is how would you like to be in an Air Force, general, and know that these UFOs or whatever you want to call them come in and can disarm your missiles, can raise havoc with the Air Force, can take back crafts that have been crashed, and there's nothing you can do about it. But you're this big, bad Air Force. It has the latest, greatest stealth and this and that, and there's nothing you can do about it. It'd be very embarrassing if you admitted ET was doing these things, so you can simply say he doesn't exist. That's the way I see it. I mean, that's part of the coverup, in other words. That's probably going to get me in a lot of trouble, but I'm old enough now that maybe I can take a little bit of trouble.

**Hillary Raimo:** Understood. Let's move on to another subject. Can nuclear missiles be disarmed by ETs? Are ET's worried about humanities violent trend?

**Phil Corso Jr:** Dad was very good friends with President Reagan, and President Reagan used to call dad quite a bit, in running this marine electronics store. Dad would always stand at attention behind the desk when he would call so I knew who it was. President Reagan was, of course, we know, very aware of ET's. He said to Khrushchev, I believe, that ... or Gorbachev, he we may have to fight this war together. Well, dad did say that there was an actual war going on. In other words, it's a secret war, just like the Cold War, but there was a secret war where these creatures were actually raping us, abducting us, coming into military bases. He said they followed every single missile that has ever been shot. He said they interfered with a lot of our Mars probes. They interfere with everything.

So, there's actually a war going on, or has been a war. Now, here, dad went to Reagan, and he says, "We need a planetary defense system." That's what the SDI was about. It was a planetary defense system that's still in use right now, and there's been a famous shot from a shuttle where you actually see a UFO coming in and a laser beam, particle beam weapon comes up from the earth, and it turns 90 degrees and runs from it. This hot war with ET, you can see why the military would not want you to know it's going on because there's really not a lot that they could do about it.

**Hillary Raimo:** The fact that this disclosing has been more public lately thanks to alternative media and the brave people in it, do you feel that's because it's accelerating, or is it just getting harder to coverup with things like the internet and access to information?

**Phil Corso Jr:** No, because we're winning the war. Dad did say, "We have literally caught up with them in every technology except for biology." That's what dad said.

**Hillary Raimo:** When you say winning the war-

**Phil Corso Jr:** So that the war is beginning to be won, sure, now you can begin bragging a little bit.

**Hillary Raimo:** Is that how do you personally see this?

**Phil Corso Jr:** Oh, it's a war.

**Hillary Raimo:** I see.

**Phil Corso Jr:** I personally see it as a war.

**Hillary Raimo:** Is this something we have to protect ourselves against, or do you see some good coming out of this?

**Phil Corso Jr:** No, I see that we have to protect ourselves against it. My dad's exact words are, quote, "They play very rough."

**Hillary Raimo:** Have you had any personal experience with the ET phenomenon yourself? Did you interact with them on any level growing up or since?

**Phil Corso Jr:** Every time my father had an experience, I had an experience, yes.

**Hillary Raimo:** Does your own family have the same experiences now because of what you do?

**Phil Corso Jr:** They do.

**Hillary Raimo:** How do we know the difference between what we've created and what are real ETs?

**Phil Corso Jr:** Well, Hillary, that is exactly the double-sided sword. You remember Star Trek Five where they go back and get the whales and Scotty is standing there and he's giving them the matrix for the transparent aluminum and he begins talking to the computer and the computer doesn't talk back to him. He says, "Oh, you have to type," and he says, "Oh, very quaint." He begins giving the fellow the matrix, and he begins typing it in. What's one of the other guys? The Russian guy is standing there, and he's saying you're breaking the prime directive. Scotty looks at him and says, "Well, how do you know he didn't invent the damn stuff anyway?" You see, if you back engineer something, how do you know that you didn't invent it anyway. You have to think about that one for a minute, I'm sure. Everyone does.

**Hillary Raimo:** What do you feel is your purpose in all of this?

**Phil Corso Jr:** Well, sure. It's because we know we're headed down a path of no return. There's little question about that. We have had the technology for a long time. Hope that we can seed this technology into the right places, to where it can help us. There's technology out there that you and I cannot imagine. For instance, way back in the '60s, dad had an atomic reactor the size of a football. They put it up in Alaska and didn't touch the thing for five years, and produced so much reverse osmosis water, like thousands of gallons and such, and wasn't touched. Where is that device? Why hasn't it been put out to the public, the size of a table? The whole operation was the size of a table. Why don't we have these things? These atomics, we have been told, keep them out of space. We have been told to stay out of space. The Russians, the Berlin Wall came down, dad says, because the Russians put nukes in space, and they were told to close by ET, just a simple fact. Close down. You're finished. You see, maybe the fourth level has more influence than we think it does.

Yeah. Dad knew Albert really well, part of Operation Paperclip, worked on the atomic bomb, lived in Palm Beach. They talked often, and Albert said, "We should have known, Phil, after the first explosion, that the energy is missing, and it's in the other dimensions," so there you go. It's that simple. When we put off an atomic bomb, we disturb the other dimensions, and here they come. They're going to set us straight. Remember, if they want us gone, they have all the time in the world. They don't have to hurl a satellite or hurtle anything down here, I mean an asteroid. All they have to do is change our genetics, and we are finished. If you look at the sperm cell count, especially in England, it's down 20-something percent. The genetic bombs are a very scary thing.

**Hillary Raimo:** Is it part of population control? Is the New World Order conspiracy theory true?

**Phil Corso Jr:** Well, you live and you die, and you're going to die anyway, so I don't know the answer there. The only thing I can say is, if the world is to survive by reduced population, our future selves would certainly know that, and they would certainly be sowing the seed now to take care of that. I hope not, but I really don't know. It's just speculation.

**Hillary Raimo:** It's food for thought?

**Phil Corso Jr:** Hillary, that might be, but, on a closing note, let me just say this. If we were to grow up with the morals and the religion and the things that are missing, this Earth could sustain all of us, and we could have a wonderful future. Are we going to be able to do that? Well, that's what I would like to help with. If any way, shape or form my father, which I think was destined ... I don't think it was an accident that he came into all these positions in his life. He literally, at one time, knew every important person in the world, from the Russian KGB on through. It's just one of these things that I think, if we could get some common sense and stop the greed and move forward, I think we all could make it on this planet. I really do. We could possibly go to other places, not other planets. Forget other planets. Man can't travel in space, dad says, and NASA has known that for many years. But what we can do is go to other places, other dimensions, and that's where you go when you die anyway, so why hurry it up? Let's take care of this dimension here, and let's live within this dimension.

**Hillary Raimo:** Do you think that developing one's intuition, psychic abilities and learning techniques such as remote viewing help with the process of being able to time travel and work in different dimensions? communicate with other life forms on different levels of-

**Phil Corso Jr:** Oh, absolutely, oh, yeah. Dad was a great time traveler. He was a great remote viewer. If you do have these powers though, you have to be careful. You have to learn how to harness them, and you still have to live within this system here. Again, a two-sided sword. You have to live with these powers. You have to know how to use these powers, but, yes, it's an enlightenment. But as you talk to people nowadays, it's really amazing. Everyone understands it, and it's not a mystery anymore, just like everyone understands money now and how money is made and how you can make money and such. Well, 20 years, 50 years ago, people did not understand money. Now people are beginning to understand this new awakening or this new awareness. That's what I believe.

**Hillary Raimo:** Phil Corso Jr's website is HighSpeedComposites.com. Do you have any events coming up, Phil, where people can see you speak?

**Phil Corso Jr:** Well, yeah. We're going to have some big things possibly coming in the future. Right now, we just can't talk about them because they haven't happened yet. They're still being born. I would like to get some of my dad's notes out, and we would like to help the world, if it's possible, with some of my dad's notes. It's not that my dad is the savior of the world. It's that people are the savior of the world, and we already have these technologies, and let's begin using them. Let's begin applying them. Let's stop the greed, and let's just move forward with God.

# 12

# Dr. Carol Rosin
## Space Based weapons, Cosmic Agendas

*Dr. Rosin extended an offer for me to come onboard with her Peace in Space Treaty movement before this conversation was recorded. In the spirit of helping I agreed. After two years I resigned from the project. My decision however, doesn't alter the impact that Dr. Rosin has made in my life and the world. Dr. Carol Rosin was the first woman corporate manager of Fairchild Industries and was spokesperson for Wernher Von Braun, NASA's father of rocketry, in the last years of his life. She founded the Institute for Security and Cooperation in Outer Space in Washington DC and has testified before Congress on many occasions about space-based weapons.*

RECORDED MARCH 31, 2011

**Hillary Raimo:**  Dr. Carol Rosin was a witness in the Disclosure Project at the National Press Club in Washington DC in May of 2001, led by Dr. Steven Greer. She has since appeared in numerous media productions, interviews, and publications. She has served on technical and non-technical boards including the advisory board of the Exopolitics Institute. Among her awards included United Societies in Space Award for her 30 years of humanitarian work for the peaceful uses of space for peace on earth also.

She is founder of the Institute for Security and Cooperation in Outer Space. Dr. Rosin is leading an initiative to have a very important document signed by world leaders on this planet that would ban space weapons. Carol says that would cause a bridging of worlds for not only people here on this planet, but other worldly beings that are visiting here. Dr. Rosin joins me tonight to talk about the project.

**Dr. Carol Rosin:**  Thank you so much for having me and for making it possible to share all of this and with you.

**Hillary Raimo:**  Dr. Rosin, I want to start by discussing your background and work. You were an assistant to Dr. Wernher Von Braun, the father of rocketry, a Nazi scientist given asylum here in the United States who had visions of humanity colonizing Mars. Tell us about your time with him.

**Dr. Carol Rosin:**  I met Dr. Wernher Von Braun in 1974. I was actually invited to the Aerospace Industry Fairchild, because they were looking for a woman to be pushed up the corporate ranks of industry. I was teaching sixth grade, a child psychologist type. I was pretending that my classroom was in outer space, because these kids live in a very low socioeconomic area, and they wanted to figure out a way to learn, but they didn't want to be on the earth. Actually, the students created this way of setting up our classroom as though it was a space habitat. An article hit the press. It was really a fluke. It said that students were studying on spaceship earth. It was actually a satellite that was being launched, but it was misinterpreted by a lot of teachers. Most of us didn't know what a satellite was in those days.

I was invited up to Fairchild to explain what I was doing, because teachers were communicating with their child saying, "Can I launch my classroom? Can I communicate with the kids with pen pals if they're in outer space?" It was really funny, actually. I went to Fairchild, and I met some of the managers. They were interviewing, but actually, I was interviewing them to find out what was going on really in space since my students were pretending to be living and working there.

I was introduced to Wernher Von Braun as a gift. It was actually a gift they gave me. What was supposed to be a 10-minute meeting that lasted for over two hours. Von Braun, it turned out had a sense of humor, even though he was dying of cancer. He was being given just a few weeks to live at that time when he was cleaning out his office. He was shooing everybody away while I was sitting in front of his desk pretty much speechless, because I was talking to Von Braun. I knew he was a German. I didn't know too much about him. I knew that he was associated with what I thought were Nazis, of course they were. What I didn't know is that he had planned the escape from Peenemunde, from being under Hitler. He brought these, I think it was 118 scientists to the states. More than that went to Russia. He started telling me this whole story. At some point he tapped his finger on the desk, and he said "You will come to Fairchild. You will be here in three weeks. You must keep weapons out of space."

Then he went on. I remember saying something to him like, "No, teachers don't quit until June." This was February. Then we go on vacation and/or we take courses. I won't come to the aerospace company. I'm a teacher. This conversation just went on and on. The mesmerizing quality of the look in his eyes and the intention was absolutely impossible to say no to. At some point, I realized that he was dying. He assured me he was going to live for a few more years to teach me what the real game was, and he did. He lived another three and a half, almost four years. I was so lucky to have this relationship with him where I would give his speeches for him. Inevitably, my first speech was to 18,000 educators at the McCormick hall, which seats about 18,000 people. It was teachers. I was to introduce satellites as a teaching tool. It was quite an experience even then, because my first real speaking engagement was with Wernher Von Braun transmitting this speech into my left ear without a telephone.

You can imagine from there where this experience went. I had different roles in the entire military-industrial complex. My biography, when I look at it, it looks like the third person. It couldn't possibly be that I had done all that, but it's all underestimated in my bio. That was Von Braun. He really gave me this assignment. I've tried to quit several times.

This last one that we're working on now that I'm so happy to announce on your show that you and I are going to be working on together is to get a treaty signed called the Outer Space Security and Development Treaty of 2011. It's the most astonishing document, the most beautiful, intelligent, truthful, spiritually based, feasible, technologically, economically, politically, psychologically, socially, feasible treaty I have ever seen. I've read quite a few. That's really where I'm going with that Von Braun assignment, to keep weapons out of space and also to acknowledge the reality, the existence of what I call "all planet cultures." Some people call them ETs or aliens. In the treaty, they're referred to as cosmic cultures. It's a continuation, really, of what I know Von Braun would've been doing if he could have lived. He finally died of cancer in 1977. I went on an even more amazing journey. Thanks for asking about that.

I know Von Braun is controversial in a lot of circles, because he was a Nazi. I've even been accused of being one or a Nazi lover, because I worked with him. Anyone that knew him would tell you this is one of the most spectacular visionaries of our time. What a lucky thing this was for me. People who think that way, I feel sorry for them. I feel even more sorry that they didn't get a chance to meet him and understand where these rocket scientists, that's what they really are, were coming from and what their purpose is. It had nothing to do with war. That was their assignment. I worked with people working on the A10 bomb or airplane, but I'm not a warrior. I'm a full-time day and night for the last 37-year, peace activist and environmental activist.

A lot of us got caught up in these jobs. In his case, they would not have survived. They would have probably been killed or their families may have been if they didn't do their assignments over in Germany at that time. Then they came over here and got sucked up again in a missile program, but as soon as they could, they started working on the moon landing and on many other visionary pieces of technology that were just spectacular and still are the foundation for what we're doing in space that can have enormous benefits to earth.

**Hillary Raimo:** Would you care to talk about what agendas he shared with you?

**Dr. Carol Rosin:** In which aspect of it, Hillary?

**Hillary Raimo:** You mentioned in your testimony he had told you back in the late 1970s that there was an agenda with the Gulf War. First the Gulf War, then there would be terrorist, then asteroids and then an alien threat. Could you expand on that?

**Dr. Carol Rosin:** Yes, in fact, I testified with that. People can see it in clips on YouTube from the Disclosure Project. Thanks for identifying this, because he shared so much with me. Well, to bring this up, is one of the most profound pieces of information, I think, I ever had to digest. That is that these war games are planned so far in advance. It's hard for people to believe. They think that we're actually going into these different countries for some reason other than for security reasons, especially. I think people more and more are waking up to the fact that it isn't to defend us or our country or because somebody's jealous of all the good things we have, all the propaganda that we're told. Actually, these games continue to keep the whole military-industrial lab university, NASA, and other international space agencies, now the international organizations like NATO, this whole complex of government intelligence community going.

It's based on wars and drugs. This is something that ... Sorry, someone's calling me and I couldn't stop it on this Skype. This basis for war is fraudulent. It's a lie. We keep finding out more and more about this lie. We live under a canopy of lies and behind a veil of secrecy. I think more and more people, especially, probably your listeners, are becoming more and more intelligent that the fact is we just keep this war game going.

There are a number of reasons for it that Von Braun shared with me. Of course, the formula I mentioned was when I was starting out in this in '74, the Russians were the enemy. Then I could see what he said has come true now that we would identify third world country threats. We'll have nations of concern. Eventually, we'll look at asteroids. We have to protect our assets in space. There is a whole list of reasons like that that are given to us for why we are inevitably going to need space-based weapons. That's what they're aiming at. What are the space-based weapons for? To dominate and control the Earth from space and space from space. That's not me or Von Braun making it up. That's actually in the defense guidance plan to control the Earth from space and space from space.

Now, you're starting to see, even in the last two days we've seen more announcements of conferences that are starting to take place including in the UK and Europe and around the world where the topic of conversation is threats from space. That's actually the kind of titles that they're using. Of course, they're saying what other things there could be, maybe an asteroid threat or comet, who knows. We know what they're talking about. Von Braun knew. He talked to me between the lines. What they really don't want us to find out is who we really are in the universes, plural. The way we're going to find that out is when we are able to acknowledge officially that there are extraterrestrial beings that have been here, they are here. There are credible witnesses who have testified to this, military man has gone public at the National Press Club. Even more recently in 2010 September as you may have heard, Robert Salas, one of the military men say they've proven that they're not hostile. They've shown they can shut down our missiles. Their technology makes our weapons basically obsolete. This whole game is really, really ridiculous of war.

It's sad, because people are so suffering. It's to dominate and control the world in space so that we don't find out who we are. In some cases, it's because ... These are people I worked with, very high-level people who are Armageddon knights. They actually think that they will be saved, and it's okay. In fact, they're expecting. In fact, they may even be of the handful of them causing it in their minds, Armageddon to happen, so that they can be saved. It's almost a, not almost, it's a religious fanaticism in some of them. It's greed and money in another sector. It's about jobs and sending their kids to college or feeding their children and their wives or themselves. It's about selling books and tapes that people have bought into, the footnotes that keep getting passed along that the aliens are evil, which they're not. They're not dangerous. They're not coming to steal our ovaries and resources. In fact, they have stopped doing experiments on humans a few years ago when they actually started to realize that the reason that we're so different, that some humans holding the light and some humans killing each other, which is one of the things they were trying to find out when they were doing some experimenting according to my own visitation and what I've been told. The fact is, none of them are hostile.

This war machine is a farce. Your listeners, I know some of them are old enough to have seen the United States, which I unfortunately consider to be the most aggressive nation in this war machine, going from one country to the next country to the next with many different changes of reasons for who the enemy is and why we had to go into that country. I just turned 67 the other day in March, and I realize how many wars I have experienced.

I remember Timothy Leary wrote a book called *The Intelligence Agents*. He was identifying the genetic mutants he called "The Moo." We're all talking about this space issue. In the book, there were two pages that mapped out the world. On that world map were 37 wars going on at the same time. That was way back in the early '80s. Here we are in this generation of us who are listening to your show, how many wars have you seen the United States going to? In this one now, in Libya, they're saying, "Oh well, we're not doing it. We're just going along with what the other countries want to do." They've even found a new little slant to put on this one.

It's just you will keep hearing gobs of these lies. It's sickening really. What I've learned along the way having helped to start a movement, which I hear had a 50 million people in it that protested the weaponization of space, to stop Star Wars. I started the leaky umbrella campaign with people marching around the world with umbrellas with holes in them by presenting General Daniel Graham who introduced the space weapons programmed to Reagan with a leaky umbrella that the World War II veterans had given me outside of the studio of CNN. I remember saying to them, "I can't present this to General Graham." They said, "Yes, but it shows how the missiles will slip through. If they do, we're all going to die in this so-called shield." I remember saying to them, "Look, I'm a curly-haired woman in a short skirt. I mean, it's hard to debate a general here."

I did whip out the umbrella and open it. He put it over his shoulder. When he finally said to me what he had said in other debates, "Well Carol, the difference between us is you think nuclear bombs are bad. If you could hide behind a lilac bush, you can be safe." I went, "What? You just walk a couple of miles and hide behind a lilac bush and you'll be safe from a nuclear blast?" My eyeballs rolled. I remember pulling this umbrella out from under the seat.

I actually have worked on a lot of these movements. What I've learned from that that I'm getting at is it's great to uncover the coverups. It's great to find out what the secrets are and what the formulas and the plans are and what the lies are. There are just so many of them. That isn't changing anything. It is waking up people. That's all great. The protest movements, great, nice, makes us feel good. I want to participate in them. I've actually been cut out of some of the peace ones, because of some of the peace activist that think I'm a Nazi or a KGB agent or an FBI or a CIA agent. All these rumors around about me. It's pretty funny too. The protest movements are very valuable. It gets us together. It's an energy.

What I want to do with you and with anybody else that wants to make contact with us through your show or they can write to spacetreaty@gmail.com or they can go to the website, peaceinspace.com. I'll repeat those again later. That is something that people can do to let us know, to let you and me know that they are interested in working with us to get a treaty signed that will ban all weapons from space. When your listeners go to that website peaceinspace.com, I think they're going to be quite thrilled and surprised.

I know that they're going to get tapped into the highest frequency that this treaty is actually written in by the people just in the about us section. These are some men, the six men on the moon, some of your listeners probably know. They have Mitchell who founded the Institute of Noetic Sciences to study the brain and the mind and consciousness, because he had an out-of-body experience in space.

Scott Jones who's just fantastic. I knew him when he was a senior aide to Senator Claiborne Pell when they were studying things like life after life, alternative technologies. He's an amazing guy. He was also involved, like Ed was an all of these men were in one way or another, in the military or military industrial complex and the intelligence community.

Abe Kriger, just fantastic. He worked at Boeing for 37 years and part of what he did was work on what you and I would consider to be SDI, strategic defense initiative space weapons contracts at Boeing. These are all, now, senior men.

Commander Will Miller, who has been advisor to a number of us, to Steven Greer, Leslie Cane who has the best-selling book out now, to me on this extraterrestrial presence. To make sure that we don't go out of whack in the content that were presenting, he's just been a wonderful advisor for me. I'll speak for myself.

One other one that I want to mention that's the newest member of this website who is one of the most fantastic heroes on our planet. It's the Canadian former Minister of Defense Paul Hellyer. We just posted one of his speeches that's actually on YouTube. Here's a man from this high-level government position in Canada, in this case, who is willing to go public with the fact that there are extraterrestrial beings and that we need to sign this treaty to ban weapons from space so that they can come in safely and share with us what they know.

I mean, these are beings that have traveled these great distances and lived for how many years in a ship that Von Braun actually described to me without saying it was a ship. He said that we're going to have cars that have these thin skins. Humans can actually think their way to make them run. It was a whole thing that I'm now putting together and remembering that he said. It fits what the description is of these ships that they must be using, some of them, to get here. The telepathy, the psychotronic weapons that otherwise are going to be controlling all of our minds, are being experimented with right now. Some people know about harp, for example, which is a ground-based system. It's not based in space. The beams go up and come down. The system itself is based on the ground.

What we're going to be doing now is focusing on this treaty that will ban space-based weapons, allow these beings to come in safely. When they are invited in, imagine what we're going to learn from them. They have alternative energy, obviously, or they couldn't have gotten here. They're certainly not using oil or coal or nuclear anything. This is really important to the survival of the species, of our human species and all the other plants and animals and 500 million orphans, I hear, that are on the planet now. You see what's happening to the earth itself. There are solutions to this.

Many of us others who had been visited, we've all been told recently that none of them are hostile. Yes, there were some things in the past, but let's not keep promoting those footnotes. Let's get on with what's real now. Let's focus on the positives where there are enough negatives that can really get you depressed and down and even dysfunctional. You can talk to my husband about that. He introduced the Disclosure Project, and then at the end when one of the journalists said, "Well, if only one of your witnesses is telling a lie, then they're all discredited." My husband jumped up and said, "No. If only one of them is telling the truth." That's where this issue is. Some people will get it. Some won't.

My version is move on. Let's not try to convince anyone. I'm an educator, so I really want to educate people about this issue and that what I can do, for example, through your show. That's what you and I are going to be doing as we meet with world leaders, which is our plan. The grassroots are going to be given a great grand grassroots plan that will be announced within the next couple of weeks on that peaceinspace.com website. This treaty is, I'm talking about the benefits of the off-planet cultures, called cosmic cultures in the treaty, what it's going to do. What really, it's about is, to me, having come out of the belly of the beast as the first woman corporate manager of an aerospace defense company, a space and missile defense consultant, I really got pushed up the ranks because they didn't have any women.

I also had learned so much that I could probably talk military strategy to more top military people than you can imagine. In fact, I briefed the space command, the CIA. Space command is the combination of the Army, Navy, Air Force, Marines. I'm an honorary Marine. This goes on and on. The only peace act was that I was an honorary marine. Anyway, this is a plan of action for the grassroots. It's listed on the website right now in a very light form that, yes, you can please go and send this treaty if you have the gumption to do it to the world leaders with a letter saying, "Go sign it." At this point we're not asking, practically. We really have to be intensely focused with all of our intention and determination and commitment to getting this treaty signed into law.

The plan of action that we're going to be working, that's you and I included, will be two pronged. One for the grassroots to do. Hopefully, we'll get a more of a point and click kind of website where people can just point and send their letters, but for now we need to start this rolling with your show. Anyone that's interested can do this, or they can just make contact with us and wait until the formation of the plan of action is put into print on the website.

Then the second part will be for some of us to go to the world leaders themselves. We only need nine. According to the way this is written by these wonderful gentlemen on the website, this treaty, is to get nine world leaders to sign this treaty and ratify it, and we have a law. This is a real law. Yes, people are going to say, "Is it verifiable?" That's what stopped other treaties from actually getting signed or the U.S. from participating in it. Yes, it's verifiable. In '67 when the Outer Space Treaty was formed not all the countries that are involved in space even existed. They certainly didn't have the technology.

I put together the first telephone book of different countries that had telecommunications via satellite for an International Astronautical Federation Congress in Rome back in the '70s. By the '80s, there still were not that many people participating. In '67, the United States was definitely number one, blah, blah, blah, and Russia. Of course, the Cold War was going on, as I mentioned, when I got involved in this in the early '70s. Now we have many countries around the world are space faring nations. We know, you and I, I am sure you know this too, we will find nine leaders of countries that are going to sign and ratify this treaty.

I hope your listeners are really excited about this as I am. Nothing has gotten me excited in the few last years. I've actually been a recluse. I've been a recluse for the last two and a half years. I've just started to emerge, because these men were willing to come forward with all their credentials that are on the website and support and even work on every single word of this treaty. It's all based on truth. The technology that exists and the potential for our survival as well as for the benefits to all of us in terms of the real security. That's based on cooperation and collaboration. That's where the verification comes in in space.

Although people will tell you there are weapons in space, I have yet to find out one piece of evidence of it. Nobody that I know can prove that there are. You just have people say, "Oh, yes. I saw them when I was 20." No, this is not true. The fact of the matter is if there are any in space, this treaty will still ban them verifiably. The enforcement that we're going to use is what you can imagine based on cooperation and collaboration not on confrontation and more weapons. I still can hardly believe that so many people are so dumbed down in the human species, or as Ed Mitchell says that they're such a stupid species as part of it who believe that you need more weapons to make us more secure and we need to kill more people to make them safe. What? People put on their little uniforms and they go marching off. I guess they think they're going to be heroes whether they're dead or alive. I'm sorry, if it were my kid and it was a boy, he'd be wearing pink underwear.

**Hillary Raimo:** The frustration is real.

**Dr. Carol Rosin:** If it was a girl ...I just cannot believe ... I love pink underwear. It's just something ... We have to find ways of stopping our children from going into these wars. If they're going to play that old game, let's play it and not go. That's what needs to happen. In some of the countries, you see people protesting all over the world. They want what they think is democracy. I don't considerable what we have democracy, actually, because someone else is making the decisions for me. I'm sure not making them or the world wouldn't be run this way. I actually thought last night, I'll just sit down and run for president. I'll put Hillary in charge of media. We know enough people that we could get a great committee together. I don't really want to do this, but somebody needs to do it that actually isn't lying when they get up and present their platform.

We really need to come through with this treaty, because it's going to open up the truth. It's not confrontational in any way. It's not hokey. It's not a paranormal kind of thing that people can interpret us as being flakes. Uh-uh, can't happen. We have great people backing it. We have mature people coming into work on it. I've gotten over 4,000 Facebook friends within the last couple of months. I mean, I don't even know how this happened. I didn't even put my name on Facebook, someone else did it. I got this under my own control. Now, I'm trying to answer each and every person. I think you can only have 5,000, so I'll have to open up a new website. A young lady that's 21 from Indiana University named Aubrey Jean set up Cosmic Treaty and Ban Space-Based Weapons to other Facebook pages that she's answering. One of them has 700 people on it already. The other one has, I think she said close to 80. That's without any publicity at all. The treaty is posted in that. It's not in a very good format, because it's Facebook.

Again, on peaceinspace.com, people can actually download the treaty and really study. Teachers can use it in the schools to teach with. I know of an elementary school teacher who wrote to me that said that she's been using it to teach in the sixth grade. The kids are so excited about it. They want to travel. They want peace on the planet. They get that there are extraterrestrial beings. They don't want weapons over their head. Even some of them who have been watching and are so brainwashed by the TV and movies that are coming out of the evil aliens, they get that it's not true. The kids are not so dumbed down yet in the younger ages, unless they have parents that perhaps are supporting that idea or they've been watching too much TV.

**Hillary Raimo:** Carol, I want to ask you about that, because honestly, it seems like we're being feed these kinds of images. It's something that's consistent across the board. Hollywood is coming out with new movies now all based on us verse them themes. You can ask any gamer who plays video games what is the alien in a video game? It's the enemy. The goal is to kill it. They're taught to shoot it down. There is a really strong grassroots effort to plant a seed in people's minds that aliens are bad. What are your thoughts on this? Is this an agenda? Is this prophecy?

**Dr. Carol Rosin:** There is such a sense of urgency in my being that I got chills while you were saying that. What I know is that the largest research and development program in recorded history is now aimed at weaponizing space. They are accelerating that program beyond belief. Years ago, I testified before the Senate Armed Services Committee. I presented a document that was handed to me by a guy in a raincoat with sunglasses, if you can believe it, but said, "It came out of the Heritage Foundation." It had HF on it. What it was was a plan for educating the public. In it said, "We will steal the language of the arms-control community, regardless of the merits or non-merits of the system." Part of that plan was to educate the media, to put out productions of movies, television, radio that would be enough to continue building the momentum towards continuing this weapons game. This war game. Now, it was going into space. That's what I was testifying about.

It doesn't surprise me at all, and Von Braun also mentioned to me back when he was telling me about two movies that he consulted about going to Mars and going to Venus. They were even using the Mars rover that he designed as science fiction but that became fact. Isaac Asimov and Buckminster Fuller were my two board members when I originated this institute back in the early '80s. Both of them told me how science fiction can become fact. Von Braun used to say that the technology is just an extension of the mind. If that's what we're teaching our young people, and the young kids are actually being taken into rooms with rows of computers to supposedly teach them how to use computers. What are the games? Just what you described. Shoot them up, kill them down, space alien kind of games, monsters coming in. You see the movies with these horrible, ugly, craft and holographic images coming in now.

I'm really concerned about it. I think that fellas and ladies who are producing this stuff need psychological counseling, because they're producing a fear factor and an ugly image that is going to get created as we all go down and the human species gets obliterated in that vision of the consequences of actually building such a system. It's very disconcerting to me. There were parts of what you're saying that actually paralyzed me in a way, because I think it's just hopeless. We can't do anything. Until I started reading this treaty, which I really hope everyone will do. We don't have time to go over it line by line.

It will present another vision. That's why I suggested just to see if it would work to this one teacher to try it out on her elementary school teachers. It's working. I've now done it with several people. Let's start having our children draw positive visions. It must be very difficult for them, because that's not what they're being feed. I think it's time to involve the young people and have them present to us what they know. Let's dig it out of them, because they're losing the touch with their heart and spirit. It's very difficult, I know, for children to come from a place of love unless they happen to have one of those unusual families that have stayed together and really love them or a single parent who really loves and cares for them. There are some of those. There are also many, many children that don't come from that kind of environment. The cities around them, the communities are falling apart too. They're feeling the stretch of negativity that their parents are going through. Kids are very sensitive beings.

We need to start paying attention to these children that "they are the future." They're not going to have any future if we don't, as adults and people including children, students who can join in like in the Indiana University students have ... They're the only audience, by the way, of universities that I've addressed, because I have been in seclusion. They came through, these university students, and they got very up about what was possible in the world, because it's not La La land, let's all envision and everything is gonna be wonderful kind of talk. It's going to be wonderful if you get out there and make the changes, work for it in any field of interest at all, especially get into fields of technology and science, and get to the leaders.

I pretty much given up, unfortunately, on the U.S. Congress. I only met one congressperson that connected to this for the right reasons. It was Joe Moakley and he died, from Boston. I said, "Why aren't you going to introduce the first bill to ban space-based weapons?" He said, "Because I have starving, freezing seniors in the streets of Boston, and I know if the money goes into his enormous space-based weapons program, they're going to continue and it's going to get worse to suffer." Now, those who are politically oriented in the states, maybe can take this in and try to get a bill made out of it. I personally give up. That's why I've gone to the world level first.

I'm going along with what a man named Howard Kurtz who's also deceased now, founder of World Control Planners Inc., and Gary Davis who founded his version of The World Government of World Citizens for which I'm coordinator of the space commission having replaced Dr. Isaac Asimov. I've got all these titles and positions. I'm using everything I've got including Dr. Charles Merchia just appointed me to be World Space Ambassador. I'm sorry, World Peace Ambassador for the International Association of Educators for World Peace, which is consultative status with the UN Economic and Social Council.

If all us can get into any kind of position or just write letters to the media, get on the radio like I'm doing on your show, start to write letters, we all know how to do this and hand write them, because I remember hearing that maybe gets to people's hearts more. I don't think petitions actually work, but I think personal contact really does. That's my experience. I have helped to produce different amendments and bills and now this treaty. I believe that what Howard Kurtz and all of these other men I mentioned have told me is true, especially with the way the United States is headed. It's very frustrating to those of us who have tried so hard to work for the good in the states.

I think what we need to do is work at the world level, get the world leaders to sign this treaty, the first nine makes it law. As I said it's verifiable and enforceable by the nature of the cooperation and collaboration that we all are doing in space, sharing what we know and what we can do to pave ... The military has a role to play to pave the way into space and to help us get there safely and help the ETs come in safely. The corporations will be to create more jobs and profits than during any hot or cold war time. This expands the industry. It doesn't cut it down like swords to plowshares was sounding to the guys in the corporations. This is war to space but without space-based weapons. They are headed into space. We're only removing the mandate to weaponize it. We can do that. This is doable.

The laboratories, universities are going to get educational programs and funding for the research and development out of expanding our mind, our consciousness into creating technologies and information services that can be applied to solving the urgent and potential problems on this planet, man-made or natural, of which we are going into deeply right now. It's very scary. This nuclear one in Japan is just a bit of a hint to what's going to happen. Millions of people. A million people they already know died from Chernobyl. I was downwind of Three Mile Island.

It's going to induce cancers. We already know things like what's happening to the water, and we should know that just a millionth of a gram of plutonium or less can induce cancer and will induce cancer. Each of the reactors blowing up now has 250 kilos or 500 pounds of plutonium in it. I mean, we're in deep trouble, and we need to shut down these plants and go for the alternative energy. Every house should be using solar, wind, and all the other alternatives that are coming out with zero point that we will also free up mines and budgets for when the ETs come in and show us what we're capable of doing.

They've evolved. They've told me there's no guarantee, because of the human ego. If we can evolve it and this treaty is tapping people into this higher frequency, as I mentioned, we can stop these devastating incidents from happening. We can do it by creating another whole reality that we want. If they put these space-based weapons up there, basically we're screwed. We're not going to be able to stop it. The momentum and the inertia will become impossible to stop like it did on earth. This is a place where we can put a lid on it but allow the aerospace industries and the entire war game that's so interconnected with every aspect of work and life on this planet other than with the organizations and people who are working to put Band-Aids on these various issues that so need them, we can transform that by just getting a ban on the base part of it that's in space, the space-based weapons. This doesn't stop weapons on earth from developing. It does stop space-based weapons, puts a lid on it.

These guys are not stupid they are smart in the complex. They're going to look for what they can produce to keep their industries, labs, universities, the militaries, everybody going. We can do it without weapons in space to start. That's what this treaty is all about. By the way the treaty, one more thing, acknowledges not only ban space-based weapons, which is the bottom line of it, but it acknowledges and it allows the cosmic cultures and the indigenous nations to be parties to the treaty. In other words, to witness it. The first half of the treaty talks about that.

Then, of course, the nation state, the UN member nations are the signatories to any treaty. The leaders of the world know what to do. We just have to ask them to sign this treaty, make it ratified by their congress or parliament, whatever they have in that country, whether it's a president or prime minister, they know how to do it. They send it. The process is that they send it to the UN Secretary-General's office who is the treaty depositary. Again, the world leaders know how to do this. There are over 40,000 treaties in that office.

This one is the most unique one ever written, because it acknowledges the cosmic cultures. That's where the solutions are. Again, not many people are going to be able to grasp this, because it's a new concept and it's so tongue-in-cheek on mainstream news. In fact, it's a reality. For those of us who get it and can understand that, guess what? We're still here, so they haven't come to take us away off the planet or control us. There's no agenda to do that. It's proven by the fact that we're still here.

**Hillary Raimo:** Carol what do you say to the people who still haven't grasped ET life forms exist?

**Dr. Carol Rosin:** The first thing I do is send them to the Disclosure Project to look at these very credible witnesses and to the other ones. Leslie Cane did a National Press Club press conference with international experts. The military guys did, with Robert Salas, did a press conference in September. I think it was September 10, 2010 that actually proved that they're still here, that the craft had come in. They have not done anything to threaten or harm us. That is the proof right there. If people are going for the scientific proof like they did in the old paradigm, which is caused us all the problems that we're now seeing on the planet, this technological proof that anybody can prove most anything depending on who you hire to say what, the fact is it's obvious that they are not hostile. They're here. There's no evidence of hostility. There are a lot of stories, maybe some of them are true, maybe they're not from the past. In the last couple of years, it's become very obvious that none of them are hostile.

Some of us who have credentials that have gone public with that statement who know, people will either believe us or they won't. My other version is other than educating people with live witnesses who are alive today, and I know that there are others who are going to say, "Oh yes, but I've been plugged up. I've had these bad experiences." Well, okay. Good. I'm moving on myself. I want to hear from the people who get it, who really intuitively know it, spiritually know it, intellectually know it, whatever it takes for them to know, who are working on various issues or care about their future, because they know that we have to come up with solutions, for people who can understand that there's a whole lot to learn.

The problem is, that you're addressing, I think, at least one part of it is that we're taught to hate and fear. We don't trust people that look different, that have a different religion. We think it's okay to go in and murder a leader of some country, because maybe he's doing bad things. We don't communicate.

We don't have enough respect, enough awareness, enough of our evolutionary process to even go on to find other ways of functioning on this planet with humans. How can we expect that trickle down or up that certain people are ever going to believe that we can get along with extraterrestrial beings? I mean, they can't. They're totally exposed to this other vision like the children are that we were talking about. Yeah, they can see that children are suffering. You see these horrible visions of families that have no food, no water, no sanitary protection for themselves. We go in and bomb them.

We go in and bomb places and send in our drones now. They keep advancing the technologies where part of the country is drowning or in the middle of a drought, and we just bombed the crap out of the other ones. It's a continuation of the old mindset. I believe that some of these people, unfortunately, and I say this as a very sad educator, are not educable at this time. My husband who's an actor says that even if we had a landing, the people would say, "Oh, that's just Spielberg." There are people that actually believe we didn't go to the moon, because of that mistake on a video that these guys showed what they thought was better footage, but it showed shadows on the moons. Now people are convinced we didn't go to the moon. Others just don't believe it anyway.

There are going to be skeptics and nonbelievers. I actually understand it. I mean, I have a lot of compassion. I didn't get into the aerospace defense industry because I was a real peace activist. I thought I was doing something good for the country working on these missile systems. That's what you're taught. Somewhere along the line, I started listening to the people that I was supposed to be studying and educating with the lies, and I said, "Oh my god. These people are actually making more sense than where I am." Wernher Von Braun who had lived with and created weapons in wars and suffering was dedicating the last years of his life to try and to educate people. He was a religious guy with a Bible and all that. I'm not. He was. He would do anything that he could to try to present this positive vision of what could be in space. That's what I inherited.

I think that his influence on me, I hope, will spread my influence on others as an educator and yours too, because you do such positive healing work. That's what we should all be about now. I think that that's going to attract the first group of people, maybe in different levels of understanding and belief systems until they catch up to the fact that we

226

can truly live in peace and harmony on this planet. We can live in peace and harmony, as you said at the very beginning of the show, basically you were saying this, with the beings in space. They're from many different universes and galaxies. We have an opportunity to even have that happen in our lifetime.

It's not down the road in some other lifetime. It's going to happen within the next year or two. I'd say, within the next few months we should be able to get this treaty signed with people like you coming in and saying, "Okay, let's go get this done." And with other people who are working on the other vitally important issues. This isn't to take away from them, because we have a lot of Band-Aids to put on and a lot of environmental problems, a lot of health problems. It goes on every level of every being just like the belief systems that are so screwed up in people.

My bottom line to that is I'm looking to see who is attracted, who is tapped by this treaty and writes to spacetreaty@gmail.com or contacts you or goes through the website peaceinspace.com. Those are the first people. That's who I'm really more interested than hearing the negative news or the skeptics or the "You're full of crap" scenarios or you're an agent or a Nazi. I just don't care if they call me names anymore. I don't want to be hurt and hospitalized, like I was for doing this work. I don't want to be robbed anymore, like I was for doing this work. I've said to anybody that wants to do that just bring it on, because everybody knows now what we're about. We're about peace and love.

Dare, I say the word love? That's really what this is about. I love the children. I love animals. I love the beautiful environments that we can all be living in. There are too many people suffering on this planet. The suffering is being caused mostly by humans, not by ETs. None is being caused by ETs. That's another point to bring up to people. What we have to do now is find a place that we can all agree on. I have not got one single negative remark in over 4,000 Facebook friends about this treaty. I have got nothing. I mean, it shocks me, Hillary, nothing but positive statements and emails, thousands and thousands of emails. I have four email addresses and I can't keep track of them.

That's why I think with your listeners, if they would contact you and me through you or spacetreaty@gmail.com, we can start to collect the people who do get it. I think that's who we have to work with right now. I used to be much more all-inclusive. I've gotten to be a bit more discerning now, because I realized what you were mentioning so intelligently that there is a sense of urgency now. We really have to get this done fast or we're in deep problems that we won't be able to get out unless there's some spectacular thing that happens that I don't know about. I've been told that the ETs are going to leave if we set off a nuclear bomb or if we base weapons in space to shoot them down.

I believe that, because I have heard it from several other people who have had the same kind of contact I have. I've now gone public with that. I'm sure I'll be discredited by certain people for even announcing that I am in contact, I've had a meeting for an hour and a half with another man in the room with some extraterrestrial beings that walk through a wall. That's just the truth. I'm not a crazy ... Well, I might be crazy by the time I'm finished doing this. I'm not a crazy person. I have my credentials, and so did the other people who have gone public about these incidents. What we have to do now is sort and discern and see who is attracted and who will come to us and say, "What can I do?" We have enough assignments for every one of the thousands of people who will make contact with us. I know they will, because it's already started. That's why we were waiting to see what people's comments were.

We are working on a plan of action. Hillary,

**Hillary Raimo:** For more information go to peaceinspace.com there you can you can contact Carol directly. Thank you, Dr. Carol Rosin, so much for sharing your stories and information with me and my listeners

# 13

# Chad Marlow ACLU
## Data Privacy in a Digital Age

*We are more connected by technology than any other group of humans in the history of the world. With the good also comes the bad as more and more privacy issues and data breaches are making headlines every day. My conversation with Chad Marlow was not only eye opening but also a clear warning about protecting our personal information at all costs, and what the price tag is if we don't.*

RECORDED APRIL 30, 2016

**Hillary Raimo:** Every day your personal data gets swept up by location trackers, email, and social media apps and the devices and third-party software that you use at school, work, or home. And right now, there are too few legal limits protecting you from how your data gets used.

Your highly-sensitive personal data is up for grabs, the government has way too much access to it, and corporations are making billions of dollars mining it. That's why people are becoming more educated on how to #takectrl of their data, a new initiative movement started by the ACLU.

A bi-partisan coalition of legislatures in 16 states and the District of Columbia simultaneously announced legislation to boost privacy protections for students and employees to stop warrant-less invasions of your emails and text messages and safeguard you against location trafficking. The ACLU has been our nation's guardian of liberty, working imports, legislature in communities to defend and preserve the individual rights and liberties that the Constitution and the laws of the United States guarantee everyone in this country. Whether it's achieving school equality for everyone, establishing new privacy protections for our digital age of widespread government surveillance, ending mass incarceration, or preserving the right to vote, or the right to have an abortion, the ACLU takes up the toughest civil liberty cases and issues to defend all people from government abuse and overreach.

Joining me today is Chad Marlow. He is the advocacy and policy Council at the ACLU, where his focus is primarily on privacy and technology. Welcome.

**Chad Marlow:** Thank you so much, it's my pleasure.

**Hillary Raimo:** Most people when they think of this subject, mass government surveillance and data mining, they think in terms of the NSA and Edward Snowden. They get a little bit paranoid maybe, or so overwhelmed they shut down and ignore it. Where do we start when it comes to really understanding the facts?

**Chad Marlow:** That's a good question, and unfortunately, I think the place to start is to understand the problem you have to understand the full scope of it. Certainly, what the NSA and other federal agencies are doing in terms of mass surveillance of the American public is a major concern, and in and of itself, if that was all there was we would have a major problem on our hands. Unfortunately, the problem goes much deeper than that.

A lot of the surveillance that Americans encounter unknowingly on a daily basis is not necessarily coming from the NSA, but it's coming from state and local law enforcement agencies. So, when you walk down the street with your cell phone or drive down the street in your car your location may be being tracked by local law enforcement and you wouldn't even know it. In all likelihood, that is not being tracked by the NSA but it is being tracked by local law enforcement. When you send your kids off to school, and you think that's a safe place for them to be, you may not realize that the school is uploading enormous volumes of confidential information about your kids. The school and corporations in the Ed Tech Center are mining that data to figure out everything they can about your kids. From how they can advertise to your kids, to perhaps noting that they got two or three detentions this year, and so if they apply for a home loan or a student loan in several years, they make it a higher interest rate because there is a greater risk.

Obviously, when we go on social media and we choose to share information with a limited number of friends, that information is mined by corporations to learn everything they can about us in order to monetize information about us and the way that we live our lives.

Unfortunately, these incursions into our privacy are very broad-based. So, I think that when we first think about how we are going to address them, we have to think about the scope of them and realize that there is no magic bullet on privacy. That there is no single law or measure that can be taken that will solve all of these problems because we have actors on the federal, state, and local government levels, as well as private actors who are engaging in these incursions. So really, it's going to be, unfortunately, a broad-based, steady, incremental process as we continue to push back. If there is a silver lining in there it's that Americans are pushing back, they're increasingly pushing back, and we're starting to have victories to show for it.

**Hillary Raimo:** Can you expand on how local law enforcement is tracking people? Should this technology be disclosed to the public?

**Chad Marlow:** Do they disclose it? Sometimes. It takes groups like the ACLU and others to force them to disclose it. But there's lots of ways in which you're being tracked by local law enforcement. Again, it varies on how ... Where you live matters as much as you might think. For example, you live in a major metropolitan area, you might think that there might be some fairly active monitoring of local law enforcement for public safety purposes, but same thing goes for small towns in Connecticut, for example. It's really pretty pervasive.

So, I'll give you some examples. As I alluded to before, if you drive your car down the street in many cities and towns there is a likelihood that a technology called an Automatic License Plate Reader is going to look at your license plate, digitize it, and track where you've been. They may search your car, sometimes for legitimate purposes incidentally. If your car is stolen, or a subject of an Amber Alert, they're going to know about that, and that's good. But in other cases, they're just going to make note of where you were at that moment and keep that on file. So, over the course of time they may know what religious institutions you visit, what doctors you go to, what political meetings you go to.

Do you go to an AA meeting? These sort of private subjects about you, so that happens. If you're walking around with your cell phone there's devices called Stingrays or more generally cell fight simulators which work like the child's game of Marco Polo. They pretend to be a cell phone tower to yell out "Marco" and your phone has no choice but to reply with "Polo," and in saying "Polo" they reveal where you are and other data that is captured on your phone.

If you're using Facebook, or other social media, a lot of police departments and local law enforcement monitor what you do on social media to make conclusions about what things you're interested in and what activities you're engaged in. So, there is a lot of work going on, and those are just a couple of examples. I also alluded to if you send your kids to school there is a lot of people, even law enforcement, that are going to monitor what your kid is doing in school to see if they can draw some conclusions about what threats your kids may present to the community. It's happening in a lot of ways and it's happening in a way ... In so many ways that it's almost pervasive in our lives in the year 2016.

**Hillary Raimo:** Obviously, these kinds of systems did not pop up overnight. Can you talk to us about how this technology grew to be what it is today?

**Chad Marlow:** Sure, I think it happened in two ways that are not completely connected but are somewhat connected. The first is after 9/11 there was obviously a dramatic, understandable on some emotional levels, a strong push to do anything we could to protect ourselves. So, the idea at that moment was any sacrifice of privacy in the name of safety was justified. With that, there was a turn to technology to find every conceivable way that we could learn anything about the "bad guys." Unfortunately, when you don't know who the 'bad guys' are you have to get information on everybody. And so that's exactly what they did, that's exactly what the NSA did. They decided to get information on everybody, and in so doing, treated everyone like a potential criminal, a potential terrorist. So that's what they did. That's where that came from on the government side.

On the private business side, something totally different. The internet is exploding, it's becoming an incredible source of providing information to people, but there is a question. How do we monetize the internet? On the one hand, you have your basic commerce features where you're looking at 'let's sell you a sweater, let's sell you a CD,' and you make money off that. But a lot of smart people realize quickly that the real potential of the internet was not in what I sold you but, in the information, I can learn about you. And the more of that I can gather, the more I can compile and sell to others who are looking to sell you a product, or to motivate the way you vote, or to encourage where you might go on a vacation, or to influence you to watch a TV show, or listen to a radio show. And so, the private corporation had a completely different motive, which is "How do we take this amazing thing, the internet, and related technologies like cloud computing services where you can store information away from your actual hard drive on your computer, how can we maximize our profit off of this?"

Where these things potentially meet in the middle is that those companies who have the ability to develop advanced surveillance technologies can turn around and sell them to an eager government market who has the financial ability to pay billions of dollars to obtain that. I think that those three roads, that somewhat converge but somewhat don't, have all led us to this moment in time where people are finally waking up and looking at the landscape and saying in the words of the old Talking Heads song, "How did I get here?" And not being comfortable with where here is.

**Hillary Raimo:** There's an article Chad, back in July of 2015, about a mass surveillance infrastructure made out of light bulbs. Tell us about that.

**Chad Marlow:** In some respects, we're in an era where no surveillance can be too pervasive, or too stealthy.

It came to light, if you'll forgive the pun, that one way to create a larger ready-network of surveillance cameras in cities, airports, stores you may go to, would be by having this kind of dual pitch. Municipality or airport or company or... You could save a lot of money on your lighting bill if you switched from incandescent light bulbs to LED light bulbs to which most of us said "That makes a lot of sense," and they said "But let me tell you about our LED bulbs. Our LED bulbs not only is a light bulb, but we have the ability to put a surveillance camera and audio microphone inside the bulb, so that in this place that here before has just been a light socket to now be converted over into a light socket as well as a full surveillance video and audio camera for your use." The concept and pictures' been pushing ... I've seen this in a lot of locations. One such that has been publicly revealed is Newark Liberty Airport, but other cities are considering using them.

It's just a conversion over to these light bulbs. You look up and you see them and you think 'light bulb,' there's no reason to think looking at these things that these are in fact surveillance devices. And if you think about "What does the airport look like? What does the city look like?" Imagine the street lights in your city have been converted all into LED surveillance cameras.

As I talk about these things I like to think I have enough of a footstool grounded in the real world to know that sometimes talking about these things it sounds like "Oh, let's pack out the tin foil hats." The fact is that these things exist. They actually exist. The license plate readers, the Stingrays. There's things called Dirtboxes which are Stingrays that go on airplanes, Shotspotter, these things that sense gun shots, these things, LED surveillance light bulbs. They exist now, it's not science fiction it's science fact. This is one of the things that companies like GE are trying to roll out and push because they sense there's a market for them and I think that there is. Again, unless the public starts drawing lines in the sand and saying "You know what, this is too much of an incursion on our daily lives to be acceptable to us as the population."

So that's the situation with these incredibly stealthy, tricky, and as they're advertised, cost-effective in terms of the lighting bill, LED light bulbs that may, if we don't push back, be coming to a city or an airport or a store near you soon.

**Hillary Raimo:** Are we talking the LED lights in people's homes - the environmentally friendly way to participate in climate exchange efforts - or is this only done in public spaces or utility situations?

**Chad Marlow:** My best guess, and they tend to be a little secretive on that technology is theoretically it could be put into someone's home. Because I believe these light bulbs, they don't communicate through a direct plug-in wire feature, they would communicate through a through-air technology like Wi-Fi. So again, theoretically if they do that one could be stealthily put into someone's home, communicate by Wi-Fi to something outside your home and you'd never be the smarter for it. Certainly-

**Hillary Raimo:** Let's talk about the #takectrl project, how people can get involved, and why it matters.

**Chad Marlow:** Sure.

So, the first stage of the #takectrl effort ... Again, the hashtag is #takectrl. As it's written on your keyboard, so 'ctrl' is the hashtag. There's really three underlying concepts behind it.

First is: What is privacy about? Privacy, on some level, is about the protections we're entitled to under the Fourth Amendment, and I get that. But, on the other hand, really what privacy is about ... It's about you and I being able to make decisions about what information we want to share and with whom. All of us may have different places where we go to on that. I have a certain standard that I have for my privacy, Kim Kardashian has another standard, they are very, very different, but we all have lives. And what #takectrl is about the first instance is that individuals should be empowered to draw those lines. In effect right, now the government, and even more so corporations want to view your privacy the way you use it like an automobile; where they say "You are entitled to step on the accelerator, the sharing accelerator as much as you want, but you're not allowed to tap the brake." Really, what privacy is about is allowing everyone the power to hit the accelerator, that sharing accelerator as much as they want but also to tap the break as much as they want. So that's the first aspect of the #takectrl campaign.

The second is that there is a working theory that is largely accurate in this country right now. That Democrats and Republicans, progressives and conservatives, I even mean ultra-liberals and Tea Party people that we cannot work together on any issues. We are so discordant in this country that we can't come together on anything. While that is largely true, it is not true for issues of privacy. For issues of privacy you see groups like the ACLU, and the very conservative 10th Amendment Center marching arm and arm on these issues. Privacy is one issue where we can find many points of agreement. To not act to protect Americans privacy, given that it is one of the very few areas which we have broad, bipartisan, basically nonpartisan consensus would be even more of a shame. And fortunately, what we're seeing is there's becoming a broader recognition of that and Democrats and Republicans, and conservatives and progressives, are in fact working far more broadly on privacy then before, and I think that's going to continue to increase.

The third element of it is this: Consistently Americans have looked to the federal government, to Congress, to protect their rights broadly. Primarily, and logically because if Congress passes a bill it effects every single American. But at the same time, Americans are getting very frustrated with Congressional inaction, particularly on issues of great importance like privacy. And what #takectrl is about is it's saying "You know what? If Congress is not going to act to protect our privacy then the states will."

And granted, California, or New York, or Illinois, or Arkansas, or Alabama, can't pass the law that affects everyone, they're not going to sit back if their cities privacy is compromised and do nothing because Congress isn't acting. The states are going to step up, and they are going to take action to protect their citizens rights, and if Congress wants to sit back and watch, so be it. They're not going to sit on their hands anymore. What #takectrl did is in very broad areas from student data privacy, to location tracking, to personal data privacy ... 16 States and the District of Columbia all enacted legislation on the same day, at the same time, again, bipartisan support and pointed at each other saying "You know what? We're acting individually, but we are acting together to make a point that the United States is unified on this issue even if our federal government isn't acting. That we are going to take positive steps." Even already we already have three states, West Virginia, Virginia, and Nebraska, who have passed #takectrl privacy laws, and we have other states that are looking very good. So, again I think that the idea that Congress should act but if they won't the states and others will, I think it's the third, and perhaps in some ways the most powerful tenet of the take control effort.

**Hillary Raimo:** Now, with the elections coming up in the fall, none of the candidates have been discussing this matter of privacy and data mining. How does the ACLU see the establishment change affecting the legislation and the laws around this topic?

**Chad Marlow:** In the first instance, it's not that these issues have not come up at all. Senator Paul on the Republican side is very active when talking about privacy issues. Martin O'Malley and Bernie Sanders engaged in a pretty decent discussion during one of the Democratic debates.

In some respects, privacy is a challenging issue for the presidential campaign, particularly now that we're coming to the general election because Democrats and Republicans agree on it. The presidential election often is devolved into discussion of points of disagreement, and I think that that's unfortunate. I think it would be a value to the nation if the presidential candidates were pushed on issues of privacy both with respect to individuals and the government, and individuals and corporations, because I think they have a lot to say about it. But they're going to have to be prompted because in our 24-hour news cycle where something dramatic has to happen for them to cover it, but at the same time soundbyte where if something is a thoughtful point that doesn't necessarily scream of disagreement it doesn't get a lot of coverage, so it's a little bit challenging.

While I would hope getting the importance of this issue and getting the broad national agreement movement on the issue would be something the presidential candidates talk about, they're probably not going to do so without being prompted because it's not a place they can draw a line in the sand. Because as I said, there's really broad agreement on these issues. But moving from that agreement to actual tangible action is going to take conversation and moving this more into the forefront of the American consciousness.

**Hillary Raimo:** So much entanglement with government and corporations that are making billions of dollars off of the data mining. Is anything really private anymore? Have people kind of just given up on the subject of privacy because they've become so conditioned to the fact that they are always being watched?

**Chad Marlow:** I don't think so. I think it depends on how you talk about it. If you say to someone "What do you feel about protecting your privacy?" And you say it that way, people will say, "Oh, listen I don't have anything to hide, I'm not so concerned about privacy." But then, if you put it this way, "When you went on that beach vacation you shared photos of yourself and your family on the beach and you were in a bathing suit, right? You share that with your friends?" "Yeah." "How do you feel about your boss looking at those pictures?" "Whoa I don't want-" "Well, you know what? Maybe your employer is looking at your social media account."

One of the bills we have protects employee's social media privacy, so when you bring it to that level. "Did you send that cute wink, wink message to your spouse the other day?" "Yeah, I did." "Hey, what do you feel about the local police precinct looking at that picture?" "What?!" So, I think the thing with privacy is it doesn't resonate when you discuss it on a theoretical level, but when you bring it down to specific examples where it's happening I think people really do care about it, and they really do want a line drawn in the sand. That's really where the work revolves.

I would say one thing about federal action. I wouldn't write off at all action on the federal level, because Congressional legislations is like a lottery ticket now-a-days. You buy a lottery ticket, you don't expect to win, but if you win, oh you get a big win. You're going to get rich. That's kind of the way with federal privacy legislation. It's very, very hard to get it passed, but if you do get it passed, it's going to be a dramatic and huge win for the country.

One bill that's been stalled in Congress for a very, very long time involves electronic communications protection act. In short, the law that currently exists is so old it goes back to the 80's. And based on quirk on the way email worked in the 80's, you might be surprised, and your listeners might be surprised to learn that any email that you have on a server like Gmail or Yahoo that is over 180 days old, the government doesn't need a warrant to read it. Because it's considered abandoned by the standards of the 1980's. This outdated law actually has a majority of members of the Congress sponsoring it but it hasn't moved for basically political leadership reasons. But if we could get that bill to move that would be a major change for hundreds of millions of Americans. I certainly wouldn't give up on that, but I think the more important point is to say that we need to try to get our victories wherever we can. So, if that's the federal government, state government, local government, we need to be hitting in any place we have opportunities for victory because we have to take them where we can get them. That's the larger strategic point.

**Hillary Raimo:** Okay, people are listening, they want to do something to stop the over reach and invasion of their privacy. Where can people start?

**Chad Marlow:** All right, well in that ... Not to sound self-serving but one of the places you can start is you can go to ACLU.org, search for privacy or the #takectrl hashtag or even go to Twitter and search for the #takectrl hashtag and get yourself tied in to the movement and the work that's being done. Right now, when I look before me there are some critical bills dealing with issues of privacy that are active in many states. If you have listeners in Hawaii, or Illinois, or Connecticut, or in New York, Minnesota, all of these states, and quite frankly many, many more have active privacy bills which getting word out to your elected officials or writing a piece in your local newspaper is just the sort of thing that gives more attention to these bills and communicates to the people who can pass laws that the public actually cares about these issues. Surprisingly, it doesn't take a whole lot of that to give these bills the momentum they need to pass. That's want people can do to become informed and engaged at ACLU.org or in other places and they can participate in the process.

I certainly understand the theoretical concern that if you write something you're going to be more monitored but the bad news/good news is you're already being monitored so you don't have to worry about that so much unless you pop off and write something that's really threatening to somebody, chances are it's not going to get much worse for you.

I think it's like anything else. Become informed and get engaged. Let's just think ... I can tell you a story right now, we had a bill that dealt with social media privacy issues in West Virginia, and the bill, although it had broad bi-partisan support, it didn't seem certain that it was going to get a hearing in the committee that it was waiting before. The ACLU engaged our activists and others and ended up generating about 200 phone calls to the office to the committee chair and that was enough to get the bill moving, and it is now a law in West Virginia. 200 people, that's not a whole lot. So really there is a lot of power in individual action.

Again, if people can stay informed and become active with even a reasonably sized group of other people you can get a lot done. You'd be surprised.

**Hillary Raimo:** Yes. Thank you. Visit ACLU.org and find out more. #Takectrl, 'ctrl,' get to your social media networks and make a difference. You do count. Chad, thank you for joining us and for speaking to us about this important topic.

**Chad Marlow:** My pleasure, thank you so much for having me.

# 14

# WAYNE MADSEN
# THE EDWARD SNOWDEN YEARS

*At the time of this conversation, Edward Snowden was in the headlines. The biggest information leak to be reported had happened, and people were taking sides. The story was quickly managed and controlled by mainstream media outlets and the character assassination of Snowden had begun, as Snowden predicted it would. What he revealed was a massive over-reach of industry and Government power with digital spying on innocent civilians. Changes in privacy laws happened due to the events of 9/11 and in the name of finding terrorists and maintaining national security. This unleashed the massive network of search technology in place today.*

RECORDED JUNE 13, 2013

**Hillary Raimo:** Edward Snowden, a former contractor for the National Security Agency slipped out of the United States in late May last month traveling to Hong Kong with computers full of secret documents in order to expose what he called, "Horrifying U.S. government surveillance capabilities." He began in the shadows, leaking top secret files to *The Guardian* in the UK, and *The Washington Post*, but just a few days after the first stories broke, he stepped into the media spotlight himself, confessing to being the paper's source and telling viewers a little bit about himself. Since then, little by little, the details of Snowden's life, the parts he's left out, have emerged providing a picture of a smart kid who dropped out of high school only to embark on his own patchwork college education on his way to working for one of the most shadowy espionage agencies in the world. That's a direct quote from ABC News' website. Then, they continue to list in order, his timeline, going from one thing to another, highlighting what seems to be kind of a manufactured timeline, if you will, a piecing of some kind of troubled kid who just couldn't quite finish college and kept hopping around from place to place. Is it character assassination propaganda?

I recently finished a book by Sibel Edmonds, her story broke a few years after 9/11, and her book, *The Classified Woman*, came out in 2011. It was self-published and blew the lid off stories similar to hers and Edward Snowden's.

To help us better understand these events is my guest tonight Wayne

Madsen. He's a Washington D.C. based investigative journalist, author, and syndicated columnist. He's written for multiple publications all over the country. He's an author of *The Handbook of Personal Data Protection* and acclaimed reference book *International Data Protection Law*. Other books include co-authored *America's Nightmare: The Presidency of George Bush the Second*. Also, *Jaded Tasks: Brass Plates, Black Ops, & Big Oil*. As well as *The Manufacturing of a President: The CIA's Insertion of Barrack Obama, JR.* Into the White House.

He has been a major, regular contributor on RT and Press TV, a frequent political and national security commentator on Fox News. He has also appeared on ABC, NBC, CBS, PBS, CNN, BBC, Al Jazeera, and MSNBC. He's taken on big personalities such as Bill O'Reilly and Sean Hannity on their television shows. He has been invited to testify as a witness before the US House of Representatives, the UN Criminal Tribunal for Rwanda, and a terrorism investigation panel for the French government. He has some 20 years' experience in security issues. He's a US Naval officer, he managed one of the first computer security system programs for the United States Navy, and he also worked for the National Security Agency itself, and the Naval Data Automation Command and Department State, RCA Corporation, and Computer Services Corporation.

Welcome, Wayne. Thank you for being here.

**Wayne Madsen:** Hi, good to be with you.

**Hillary Raimo:** What do you think about the Edward Snowden situation?

**Wayne Madsen:** Well, I believe he actually is a whistleblower. Having dealt with a number of whistleblowers, especially from NSA, I can say that he certainly fits the bill, and I've dealt with whistleblowers from the CIA, as well. The only thing I find unusual is the fact that he tried to contact the mainstream media. I know other whistleblowers tried to do that in the past and they've gotten the short trip, and apparently, he did, too. At least from *The Washington Post*. But, nevertheless, we now know that the Post and *The Guardian* have in their position information that they decided they didn't want to release, because they consulted with the US Government. A long time ago, I stopped calling the US government for their opinion, because of stonewalling. I don't negotiate with the US government. I'm not surprised *The Washington Post* and *The Guardian* did. We saw the same thing happen of course with the WikiLeaks, the cable releases, State Department Cable's, deals were done, information redacted, information was taken out.

Having worked in the system, most classified information is classified merely to protect certain government officials from being embarrassed. It has nothing to do with national security. There are national secrets, absolutely. I've seen them, but when you look at the wide amount of information that's classified, the real secrets are probably 10% of less of all the classified information out there, as we know from the WikiLeaks, the State Department Cables. Most of that information could've been found in any local newspaper or on any radio talk show, depending on what country we're talking about, or in any diplomatic cocktail reception. That's the source. The intelligence community likes to say that there are sensitive sources and methods. There's nothing sensitive about going to a cocktail party and gossiping, and it's no intelligence method to go pick up and have translated the local tabloids at the local newspapers. So, this is what is called "Classified Information" today.

So, what Mr. Snowden had was the stamp to which the National Security Agency is routinely violating our privacy in the United States.

**Hillary Raimo:** Why did he choose Hong Kong? Why did he choose *The Guardian* and *The Post*? Is this being used as a distraction?

**Wayne Madsen:** I think it's blown up and with all this nonsense coming out now about him being a potential Chinese spy, that he had some people from the intelligence community today indicate that he took a thumb drive out of his working space and why, with all these documents, thousands of documents. We heard the same thing about Bradley Manning putting a quarter million State Department cables on a Lady Gaga CD. Having had some experience working in that, a sensitive department of information facility, there is no way you can put a thumb drive on these computer terminals for that very reason. If they allowed USB ports in terminals, they would have many, many more compromises of classified information. Same thing with CDROMS, whether it's a Lady Gaga CD or any other CD, you do not have the capability to introduce this type of portable recording media on these very secure systems. So, all these stories are faked by the government. But, the government knows that most people in the United States have never worked in one of these facilities and have no idea, they can learn all this propaganda about thumb drives and the compact discs, and DVD's, and all this other stuff, and people say "They must be like my home computer". No, they're not. They're very, very different.

So, why did he pick Hong Kong? I was a little surprised. The people were suggesting that Hong Kong is controlled by ... I heard people say they're in China. Every Cold War kook is coming out of the woodwork now. Unfortunately, they seem to be on Fox News and to some extent on CNN, but I've been to Hong Kong. Hong Kong is an international city. Yes, it used to be part of the UK until 1997, but they have a 50-year pact of basically giving them a special autonomy from The People's Republic of China and having spoken to senior Chinese officials, including Chinese intelligence officials, I can tell you they know to keep their hands off of Hong Kong and Macau, which is the former Portuguese colony. They do recognize the fact that these special autonomous regions and if they made any overt move in Hong Kong, that would send a shudder through the financial community of Hong Kong, because people are investing in Hong Kong and doing business in Hong Kong, because of its independence. So, these people are saying, "Oh, he went to Hong Kong" ... Like he defected to East Berlin during the Cold War, these are people who probably ... Their only experience with China is probably going to a Chinese restaurant.

**Hillary Raimo:** USA Today released an interesting article about how Hong Kong wants answers on Snowden's hacking claims.

What is it like being a whistleblower for the NSA Wayne? Do you have to engage in these intelligence games?

**Wayne Madsen:** I was working on mainly computer security programs and NSA, their computer security program at the time was in its infancy. Believe it or not, the Navy and the Air Force were further ahead than the National Security Agency in the area of applied computer security. Now, the NSA had a lot of theoretical stuff going on with the mathematicians and the cryptographers, but I got out of the Navy, I left the Navy, therefore I also left NSA. Now, NSA offered me a civilian job, but having worked there I said no, this is not my lifestyle. I do not want to be part of this type of organization. [inaudible 00:15:04] You're so constrained and travel, you have to get permission basically to do anything, and this was in the mid-80's, which makes me wonder too about what was going on. We know that Snowden sold his house and he was in Hawaii, and then he went off to Hong Kong. If that were Fort Meade, NSA's headquarters, there would've been alarms triggered with that move and he might not have gotten that far before being approached by some security people. So, I'm a little bit surprised that he was making all these lifestyle changes, and that's what they look for with their employees in NSA.

But, as some people have told me at the NSA outstations for example, like in Hawaii, that the security's not as strict as it is there, as it is back in Fort Meade.

**Hillary Raimo:** People are tired of the "War on Terror," I really believe that. I think you have a certain section of the population who really falls into "Yeah, let's go get him! We're doing the right thing!" But then, there's another bigger population that's growing and growing. They're tired of the economic drain, they're tired of this elusive enemy on the other side of the ocean that we keep hauling money and going into. The story just seems to be falling apart for a lot of Americans, and maybe that is a good thing.

**Wayne Madsen:** Yeah.

**Hillary Raimo:** Just like with the Wikileaks, we had the same competitive "Go team!" opposition. When programs such as Prism are exposed and you talk about people's information being gathered, phone calls being listened to, it does cause concern. I just assumed myself years ago that that was always happening anyway. I would just say, "Well, whatever. I have nothing to hide. If they want to listen, hey, how you doing?" Kind of thing. What difference does it make, really, in that sense? But is that a cop out and does it enable it to be ok and accepted as the norm?

**Wayne Madsen:** Yeah, I guess I'm one of the few around, I'm feeling my age. I can go back in the time machine to the 1980's and I know back in the 1980's what the senior people at NSA wanted, because I sat in those planning meetings, and they were talking about ... In those days. Now, this is as only the internet was coming in, we didn't have a World Wide Web, there was the internet or ARPANET as it was once known, the DOD network that expanded the universities and colleges, and research centers. But, they talked about, "We want totally hearability". In those days, NSA was listening to phone calls, any type of communication in the radio spectrum. So, they talked in terms of "We want total hearability", I remember that. It was stuck in my mind. My god, they want to hear everything! They said it and that was their plan. Now, when the internet started to gain popularity with people using email, in 1991, there was an NSA project called Nutcracker, which was really this metadata. Even then they were talking about collecting everything coming over the internet. So, fast forward this to the present time ... Oh, I should say that I was with a public advocacy in the early ... 1999/2000/2001 and Admiral John Poindexter of the Iran-Contra infamy came back to the Bush administration and was working for the Defense Advanced Research Project Agency on a system called The Total Information Awareness System.

And, you look at the logo, we all joked about it. It was a pyramid with the eye on top, the thing you find on the back of the dollar bill, looking down at the Earth. And, they made no bones about what they wanted. They wanted access to everything and there was a congress ... The organization that I was with, the Electronic Privacy Information Center, we sued under the Freedom of Information Act to get the documents on that and they finally ... We took it to court and Judge John Bates of the US District Court for the District of Columbia, ruled against the Pentagon, said you've got to release that information. Well, that said, a lot of things ... This was like, they want everything. They want access to all the databases and congress cut the funding, and we heard at the time it's okay, he cut the funding to the Pentagon, but it's going to reappear over at the NSA. It did and now we know that as Prism. NSA's got this huge data center. It's going to open up in September in Utah. 17 football fields in area. And, it's going to be able to process a number that most people would not find fathomable. It's called the yottabyte of data, that's one with ... A count with zeros after it.

So, they say ... So, the NSA and General Keith Alexander, the director, who is also the commander of US Cyber Command say we are not interested in everything, but they're collecting everything. So, if they're not interested in it, why are they collecting everything?

**Hillary Raimo:** Good question. Obama goes on TV and says "We don't want to listen to your phone calls", but yeah, they do. Right?

**Wayne Madsen:** Yeah, and the reason why is ... Google and Yahoo! And, all these other companies, Microsoft, All Fed. They were under pressure to store this information for the government to come and get, and they said no, it's a bottom line issue, right, to store that information, we've got to build data centers. We've got to store, it costs us money. It effects their bottom line, so what NSA did was come along and say, "We'll store it for you". It's like ... Would anyone who was going away for a month go to the police station and give them their key, and say, "Look. Just in case something happens, we want you guys to have a key." No. You get home, you come back, and you find out there's nothing left in your house.

Because, we say that's nice, Mr. Policeman, I stopped doing that when I was seven years old. My mother said, "You go to the police ..." I know better. The police aren't the people you want to go to in all cases. So, trust the government? Trust the government? I think it's just a ridiculous notion, but the thing about Snowden under attack, Snowden's getting attacked, everything about ... He dumped his girlfriend and he couldn't complete college, and he had all these jobs. Well, once place he worked was the US Mission to the UN in Geneva. I looked at this job, the Swiss government has confirmed he was an Acachete. So, he was under official cover by the State Department. It was a few years ago in Geneva, and that set off an alarm with me, because I have no reason to say that the Swiss government is wrong, because they have the diplomatic immunity. We have to declare those diplomats, so if they have that information, that means Mr. Snowden was probably working with the CIA and NSA, with an agency that's even more secretive than both agencies. It's called the Special Collections Service. It's headquartered in an office building in Beltsville, Maryland between Beltsville and Laurel, right off of Interstate 95.

It's connected, technically, by cable to the State Department's telecommunications system, which provides satellite communication for all the embassies around the world. So, what happens is NSA runs collection units in US and British, Canadian, Australian, New Zealand embassies. They would explain Mr. Snowden's kind of spotty resume, because he's been under ... He said he was working covertly. He was operating undercover, probably with false identities, false affiliations and whatnot. So, that would explain that. And, if he worked for the Special Collections Service, and he's sitting in Hong Kong right now, he is the most sensitive person to come forward in a long, long time. And, I can just see that President Obama and others really would want to get their hands on this guy. I'm not saying he's an agent or he's a defector to China. It's just that he knows an awful lot of things about breaking and entering, because this is what Special Collection Service does. Internally, in NSA, it's known as F6, and most people have never heard about that, and they want to keep it that way. So, if Snowden is singing like a canary, I would imagine there's people very, very worried about what information he has.

**Hillary Raimo:** There has been a massive response to his actions and an overpowering character assassination on the mainstream media here in the US. What you just exposed is pretty important for people to understand, that we have these agencies like the Special Collections Service in Maryland happening above the CIA, correct?

**Wayne Madsen:** Yes.

**Hillary Raimo:** Since 9/11 and the Patriot Act everything is now a matter of national security. That is all we hear on our news broadcasts here in the US. How do you see the United States post 9/11?

**Wayne Madsen:** Well, we became a surveillance state. The things we were worried about in the 90's when I was a privacy advocate in Washington, we argued all the time with the Clinton administration, who wanted The Justice Department, Attorney Janet Reno, and her Deputy who was Eric Holder, by the way, wanted all these powers, and we fought them tooth and nail. And, everything that's in the Patriot Act was basically their wish list in the 90's. We sat there and they said, "Well, in a perfect world, this is what we would like." We said, "You're never going to get that" and they did. After 9/11, they got that plus more. So, everything we were ... And, we were like ... Amongst the privacy advocates we were talking about this utopian future, enemy to Spain, and then the Gattica, and we would say, if we don't do our job, that's what's going to happen to this country. And, of course, movies aside, after 9/11, we did become like that. And, it's not getting any better, and Obama ... I supported Barrack Obama in 2008. He wasn't my first choice, but after eight years of Bush and Cheney, I figured we actually needed the change and I believed after seeing him in action.

Just in a couple of months, I said there's something wrong here. He's not governing any differently really than the Bush and Cheney and started looking at his background, found out after he graduated from Columbia back in the early 80's, he went to work for Business International Corporation, which was a well-known CIA front activity. So, again, we have a person in the presidency who is more beholden to the intelligent super state than he is to the people who elected him.

**Hillary Raimo:** What was your experience like when you first started talking against the agencies you worked for?

**Wayne Madsen:** When I left NSA and worked as a contractor at various places for a while and then when I got involved with the privacy work, that was in the 90's. I used to get together with these NSA people. Of course, they never liked what I was talking about, but you know what? We agreed to disagree. I didn't trust some of them as far as I could throw them. I did get in some spirited debates in public with some of them in Washington, it wasn't where you have to worry about ... Some people have been reporting there's been some intelligence people that would like to kill Snowden and kill Glenn Greenwald. I heard this, too. I heard this in Washington in the last ... Well, since 9/11, I've heard these types of threats, "Somebody ought to take these reporters out", this comes out of NSA security, and we didn't have that back in the 90's, but after 9/11, people became fascists, and they're not joking around. They shouldn't be working in security even with the thought of going out and killing somebody, but now I've heard this. Even Bob Woodward, *The Washington Post*, he's expressed some fear he said something critical of the Obama White House and he said he received a threat. He didn't say what kind of threat, but it sounded ominous, so yeah, I do know that the White House does threaten people, and so do their intelligence agencies.

I mean, we have a president who drones American citizens without a trial. I guess we can expect anything out of this administration.

**Hillary Raimo:** Thank you for your insight and thoughts.

**Wayne Madsen:** Sure.

**Hillary Raimo:** What has your experience with the mainstream media been like when you went on to talk about these topics?

**Wayne Madsen:** I'm basically the punching bag for people like Sean Hannity and Bill O'Reilly, because they need to have some "Liberal" on there to beat up. The thing is, I know these guys, and they are showman. They are not journalists. Fox News is an entertainment channel masquerading as a news network. And, we can say that they're all like that. Certainly, there's some ... I think CNN, I mean, Anderson Cooper is really more of an entertainer. He had a show on during the day, where it was no different than the Jerry Springer Show, so these are not real journalists. I'm falling into their trap. People in journalism, not the business, 'cause they're in the business, that's show business, that's the Hollywood term. They're in the business. They know that these people are not legitimate journalists. As long as people know that going in then they want ratings, they're entertainers, you just kind of keep it ... They want to fight, I fight. I gave them a spirited fight. It's just yelling at each other, it's ... You don't go in there thinking, "Wow, I'm really going to try to sell my idea, because if I convince the audience ...", no, no. That audience, you're never going to convince. You just go on there and do your thing. It's like getting in the boxing ring for a little bit and then getting back out and hopefully you're not bloody too much.

But, I really think ... I knew professional journalist television, radio people, and we all say the same thing. Those of those who are still with us. Many of my old colleagues have passed away, but the same thing. We just shake our heads and lament over what has happened to television and to some extent, radio news, or radio journalism. It's awful, because there's no one like Walter Cronkite or Chet Huntley. Even later on, some of the CNN people who were on in the 80's and the 90's, very few of them are left on the air.

**Hillary Raimo:** WayneMadsenReport.com.

**Wayne Madsen:** Yes, there's two sides. There's a public side and then there's the subscription side. That's just to allow me to keep it going, but basically what I did when I started the website in 2005, one of the resources that Washington lost many years ago, which I think was sorely needed, I was told by others we need something like this. There was a journalist named Jack Anderson who had a column called The Washington America Round, and before him, it was Drew Pierson. These were called muckraking journalists. And, muckraking is not a pejorative, it's like you dig, you dig at the bottom of the barrel and you see what comes out, and usually it's scandals. I thought that was sorely needed in a city where it's all ... The journalism, it's the White House Press corp is really the stenographer's corp. All they do is rewrite faxes and press releases from government officials. That's not journalism. And, when you see somebody with the press corp like Owen Thomas who says, "Hey, I'm going to stand up and say what happened to her? They fired her."

But, that's what I'm trying to do on the internet, to bring back the spirit of the muckraking journalists, and I've been able to break a few stories over the years. There's a State Department scandal now with a foreign ambassador, ambassador of Belgium being cited for being a pedophile. I broke the pedophile story in 2007 in the State Department and named an ambassador, not this guy, but somebody else. Usually when I write something, I have to wait five or six years to see it on the front page of *The Washington Post.*

**Hillary Raimo:** When kids go to school and they learn history and they go through government class and they come home and compare it to what they see on TV, online, or on YouTube it contradicts many common-sense sensibilities creating an intuitive conflict between knowing what feels right vs. what you are told to believe.

**Wayne Madsen:** Yeah, you're right.

**Hillary Raimo:** In theory the structures work, but in practical application corruption seeps in.

**Wayne Madsen:** Right. And, I've got to say, it does. It's all education. I've got to really thank my teachers in public school for teaching critical thinking, and I know it's not being taught now, the corporations don't want critical thinking taught, 'because they want us as the servant the group of consumers out there, but I remember in sixth grade, and seventh, eighth, and ninth grade, I was sitting in class and I had teachers who were critical of the Vietnam War, critical of President Johnson, critical of President Nixon, and really, these teachers ... And, the most critical ones weren't where you would expect to find them, in the history class. In my case, they were my math teachers and my science teachers, but everybody taught the students to be critical thinkers and that's just not happening today, and I really ... I shudder to think what these schools are turning out as far as people who don't question authority.

**Hillary Raimo:** Are there things you cannot talk about on radio and TV shows?

**Wayne Madsen:** No.

**Hillary Raimo:** No? So, as a former NSA agent you can talk about anything?

**Wayne Madsen:** Yeah, when I worked at NSA, it was in the mid-80's, we had the Soviet Union at the time, we had the Warsaw Pact, we had a China that was considered a military opponent of the United States. Well, things changed at the end of the 80's, so anything I knew back then has really been superseded by historical events. We no longer have three Soviet nuclear submarines heading in the Atlantic Ocean with a 15-minute window to fire their missiles and obliterate the Earth Washington, and a few other cities, but that's no longer the case.

**Hillary Raimo:** Do you start to notice red flags that pop up around stories of people like Snowden, and if so, how do you proceed to tell others?

**Wayne Madsen:** Yeah. Snowden, I know he's having this huge character assassination taking place. I've dealt with other whistleblowers like him. Actually, I was involved in a whistleblowing case in the Navy, and I was attacked, not so publicly, but within the chain of command I was attacked. And, this is what they do. This is the type of thing that happens to people who they say violate the chain of command or go public. So, the red flags that are popping up for me are the means that the government is using to try to destroy his credibility from these sock puppets on the internet posting these repetitious attacks to people attacking his girlfriend, because she was an acrobat, and they're saying 'because she did pole dancing, she must have been a stripper. I mean, see, this gets into the debasing of him. And, then there's a photograph of him wearing his pants around ... This is from 10 years ago, so they're going to find everything they can on this guy. So, yeah, I know what he's in store for, but I think from the interview they gave *The Guardian*, he knew what he was in for, too. 'Cause, obviously he knows about other whistleblowers like Tom Drake.

Tom Drake basically said the same thing as Mr. Snowden, and there were retirees who had served in NSA when I was there who came forward and talked about the abuses. There was William Benny, Kurt Levy, Mr. Loomis, and these people ... Tom Cannon who was the Justice Department Prosecutor, and they all got harassed by the FBI and NSA security for coming forward. So, it doesn't surprise me that he did, what surprises me is I think he has much more information than any of those other guys had, 'because I think he has working knowledge of targeted individuals by name and targeted offices and homes. In fact, as I suspect, he worked for the Special Collection Service, 'cause that's what they do. So, we may be in store for a lot more revelations, which I think will also increase the efforts to try to get him extradited from Hong Kong.

**Hillary Raimo:** You are suggesting we're dealing with somebody here who seems authentic, who has this training, has these really extravagant connections to various places. So, they really want him. They want him for probably a variety of reasons, like you've stated, and then we're dealing with somebody who also knows the game, knows how to work it, because he has seen it. It will be interesting to watch and track the updates as it all unfolds.

Wayne, don't you think that so many people at this point perhaps feel hopeless or powerless to be able to change this?

**Wayne Madsen:** Well, certainly, after 9/11 when they talk about the "New Normal", Some say, "Well, this is the way it's going to be and there's nothing you can do about it, so get used to it". But, you know. Looking at the members of congress just basically roll over and accept everything NSA's telling them, or the Obama administration's telling them, that we need these powers, we're able to stop a half dozen terrorist attacks, when in fact they gave no examples. They gave a few details and a few examples, but those attacks were probably stopped not because they were listening to everybody's phone calls, but because of good old fashion shoe leather on the ground giving intelligence. You know, you just wonder who are these members of congress really beholden to? And, it's both parties. It's democrats and republicans, and I think the only answer is that this two-party duopoly of power we have, it's an easier said than done, but we've got to get rid of it.

I remember we were talking about in the 90's, well we need a constitutional convention just to reform the government, and people went, "Well, we just have to make our current constitution work", then we found out that Bush called a "Expletive piece of paper", and apparently there's a radio interview that Mr. Obama gave in Chicago in 2001 where he called The US Constitution a Charter of Negative Rights. I don't know what that means, but I've never heard any president refer to the constitution as a charter of negative rights.

**Hillary Raimo:**  The charter of negative rights?

**Wayne Madsen:** Negative rights. What he was trying to say was the constitution says here's all the things government is prevented from doing, but it doesn't say what the government is allowed to do, like he would favor that. Like tapping everybody's cellphone and reading everybody's emails, is this what he's driving at? This is pretty scary, because he said he knew the professor of constitutional law at The University of Chicago, actually, it wasn't a full-time, it was one of these visiting people, so it's debatable how often he taught a class. It's pretty hard to find any student that actually took his class. Well, what in the world was he teaching while he was teaching that? That's highly suspicious as far as what he thinks about the US constitution. I would welcome ... I'm not a lawyer, I don't play one on TV, but I think I know enough about the constitution, I'd be very comfortable debating President Obama on that issue that a "Charter of negative rights".

**Hillary Raimo:**  Hm. "Charter of negative rights". Directly quoted from President Obama himself. We have a question submitted online from Joseph in Napa, California, he's asking, "Like to know what your thoughts are on Matt Drudge. He appears on the surface to be a muckraker, but with a post-modern flair for the overdramatic, but I question his veracity". Wayne?

**Wayne Madsen:** He's very political. He's very pro ... He's a republican and he puts out a lot of republican talking points. So, unlike ... I'm not tied to either party. I find them both disgusting and I also find some of the third parties ... They don't seem to ever get off the ground and they're like narcissistic, because they're centered around particular candidates. I don't want to mention any names and we know, you know the reform party, the green party, it was all candidate based, personality based. To do a muckraking, everybody's got to be fair game. And, Drudge goes after democrats, but he rarely goes after republicans, so I believe that's not true.

**Hillary Raimo:** Are we knocking on the edge of egos here and really asking people to say, "Hey, this isn't really what it's about, we need to move beyond that"... We have a couple minutes left in the show, what are your closing thoughts on where we need to focus our positive energy at this point?

**Wayne Madsen:** I have nothing to hide, why should I worry about anything, and you hear it a lot on TV. I don't have anything to hide from the government, and people give up ... People say "I give up my information to Facebook and I give my information to Match.com", and all these websites. The difference is they don't have the power to arrest you, to bring charges against you, to empanel a secret grand jury. These companies don't do that, but the government does. That is the major difference between people giving up their information to these .com operations and wanting to give it up unmasked to the federal government.

**Hillary Raimo:** There it is. Wayne Madsen. Thank you.

# 15

# STUART TRUSTY
# BITCOIN & THE DARK WEB

*Stuart taught me about the Bitcoin markets in 2014. He showed me how to open my first wallet, how to buy bitcoin, and how to set up mining contracts. As Bitcoin was beginning to bloom I watched the markets fluctuate and learned a lot. If I had questions, he would be kind enough to answer them, and finally we arranged to do a show together to help others understand what was happening with this new thing called cryptocurrency and blockchain. Crossing paths with Stuart Trusty has changed many things about my life, including my focus and where I put my energy now.*

RECORDED FEBRUARY 2, 2016

**Hillary Raimo:** Bitcoin, the facts and fictions, the reality of changing from a world banking system to a digital global currency. The pros and cons of what this means, and what every day people like you and I need to know. Tonight, we're going to have a philosophical discussion of ethics, realities, and myths.

Stuart Trusty is an engineer and architect of solutions for cutting edge cluster computing applications for industry and network applications. Stuart had the 3$^{rd}$ ISP in Seattle, Washington, and was the founding technologist for Alibaba. He is CEO and founder of Worldbit.com a new integrated hybrid crypto-currency augmented reality ecommerce system. Stuart, welcome to the show, and thanks for being here.

**Stuart Trusty:** Thank you. How would you like to start on this pack, it's a pretty broad set of subjects here, how would you like to narrow that down?

**Hillary Raimo:** How about starting with the deep web vs. the surface web, and how Bitcoin has come to thrive in it all. Cryptocurrency often brings to mind a dark and seedy picture that hovers off in a dark secretive web used by criminals and shady organizations. Is this true? Or is it misleading?

**Stuart Trusty:** Okay. Well there's reports that a majority of the internet is in this dark web where it's not accessible by your browser. To some extent that's exaggerated, I mean, there's a lot of company Internets out there, you can't go and access all of the content behind

Bank of America, for example, so really when we're talking about inaccessible content, I think they're kind of lumping that together. When we're talking about the dark web, we're talking about basically international vendors for contraband goods, and it's subject to the same weaknesses in interacting with these vendors, as with the Bitcoin system affords. I mean, basically everything is in Bitcoin.

When you're on your web browser and you access a website, that goes between your computer and their computer. What the dark web is, is it interposes a mesh network that's called Tor, which was developed by the military, and any person running the web browser through the system becomes kind of transparent, you can't really tell where the origin is. So, it breaks up the data so you can kind of have an anonymized, and I say kind of, it's kind of anonymized, connection, and then you can go and buy fake license plates or drugs. I mean, it's pretty much anything that you could get, it is there.

It is an important ... I don't know. I mean, certainly it's an unusual thing to have it just be very easily accessible by anybody. It's something you have to go looking for, and want to involve yourself in, and to explore, but it's actually a very easy, almost effortless thing to do with the right USB drive or CD to boot. It's very, very simple, any Mac or PC immediately can buy something from this network at will.

**Hillary Raimo:** I think when people hear about something like this they automatically assume that it's a place where people go to do bad things, and in fact, the Silk Road case that came up last year with Ross Ulbricht talked about these black markets and how Bitcoin was an anonymous type digital currency that allowed people to function in these black markets anonymously so that they could not be traced. So, when you talk about needing access to Tor and other types of software to get into it, and how anonymous that can be, and also how dangerous it can be if you really don't know what you're doing. I think it keeps people away from even looking, and they think, well this is just a dirty, dark place for people to do bad things, but in reality, we also have governments holding a vast amount of information in the deep web, universities, so there's a storage capacity to the deep web, yes?

**Stuart Trusty:** Yeah, and deep web probably can, I mean, it's unusual to me how this whole idea of this deep web, dark web, and all this content aggregating both the university and government labs, and all that data which is on private internet. With this dark web Tor phenomenon, because that content's not available through Tor, that's content that you have maybe a card reader, or you have a password, or whatever it takes to get behind these firewalls to get to the data. I mean, that's part and parcel of in this government agency, or that university, what, but it's not something you're going to find loading up Tor and tooling around with your Onion browser, which is what it's called. It's an entirely different world.

And I would say roughly, probably 80% of that deep web stuff is basically we're just talking about private Internets, we're not really talking about something that you're going to penetrate by exploring it in a different way. You actually have to be given access or break into it, but it's not going to give itself up by browsing around in a Tor browser.

**Hillary Raimo:** Thank you for explaining that. When we talk about the surface web, we're dealing with the typical Google search engines, Mozilla, Firefox. When I was researching this for the show, I was really almost shocked to read that we only access about 4% of total information on a typical search engine. When we do searches we think we're accessing this big vast database of the Internet and we're pulling everything out, but we only really have access to about 4%.

**Stuart Trusty:** I kind of qualify it like this. Let's say that we wanted to look at some case history of some lawsuit to try to get a class action together or something. And we can use Google to access the public records and the county records and some of the court records, and what not, and we could probably get a pretty good picture, but it's not like we have an account at LexisNexis and we can just log in and pinpoint what we want to find in a database so vast on legal topics that will pretty much dwarf the public available records, at least in a way that's organized and structured in a way you can actually punch in case history and what not.

So, I don't think it's that unusual that this content exists, and it's just a matter of how much information is this government agency holding, it's like USGS or NIH. Is the National Institute of Health, are they providing all of this technical lab information? I mean, there's so many different security clearances and ways that this information has to be validated as far who can access it, that I think it's pretty unsurprising that so much data is there. If you want to get it out, you have to go try and do a Freedom of Information act, like I'd like to know this piece of information.

But yeah, all of the money that's being spent on government research and et cetera, in private industry, all of this data is private data. So, it's not obscured data that can be accessed by non-standard means, it's private data help under nondisclosure, or some other intellectual property that make that threshold where virtually you can't get at it.

So, to me, it's not that surprising, if that helps clarify.

**Hillary Raimo:** Thank you for that. I also compare it to the human brain where we only have access to a certain small percentage of it so they say, we have this vast, large amount that we can't access. It kind of reminds me of the model that the deep web and surface web take. but-

**Stuart Trusty:** I mean, okay, I heard some information from a source, with a certain high-level security clearance, someone said I don't have my password to my email, and this person has such a high clearance that when we pulled up the information of the password of this private industry account, but all that users other passwords to all their other public accounts. And so, there are definitely people with high level of access that do have access to this information kind of willy nilly. It's just that the public doesn't have access to it. But the way that the system works, I mean we don't really know the inner protocols and the backbone of how this was all laid out.

Since inception almost of the fabricated internet, we don't know how many cards have always been built in so that this data is always accessible. We can look at it from our perspective and go, yeah, we've got this fishbowl approach to this data that you have. There's the office of Total Information Awareness was out for a while, and that was basically to try to get all the information aggregated in one place and accessible from a top down kind of a thing, and then were complaints about that, and that division was disbanded but the same technology continues, so if you're the right person, you have access to all kinds of information but everyone else doesn't have that full access level, I guess I could put it that way if that helps clarify.

**Hillary Raimo:** Yes, it does help clarify, and it also makes a lot of sense because information is power, and if you give that information to everybody you're giving a lot of power to the people so to speak.

Some might think that Bitcoin's just a fad, it's one of these things, it's a computer generation, it's something trendy for the younger people to get into, some say it will never do anything, won't ever really go anywhere, but in fact, recently PayPal just moved to make it a payment option, which to me signals that they're getting ready to move Bitcoin in to become more mainstream, and they've also released the first debit card that can be paid using Bitcoin as well.

For our listeners, why don't you explain what Bitcoin is exactly, and where you think it's going.

**Stuart Trusty:** Well, Bitcoin is basically ... You hear people talk about this blockchain, it's basically a Log file that everyone has their eyes on. It's a distributed Log file that's more or less a ledger, and it shows the creation of digital assets and numbers on a balance sheet, different addresses that are created, and it basically is just a log of transactions. You do a transaction, you take a part of that number, and you put it in a different account, and then you send it into this queue of all these other people doing the same thing, same transactions, and all these transactions occur over a certain period of time, and then there's an end of that block of transactions, and then it's kind of processed in a fancy way, and that's added to this chain of transactions on this public ledger that everyone sees, and becomes part of the next starting point for the next block of transactions.

So really, it's like basically if everyone had a spreadsheet open, and it was all being encrypted and what not. If someone moves a coin from one account to another, it shows up, and it's basically that kind of thing, but it's not actually any value associated with these objects except that people will take as payment, and the free market is deciding that.

What differentiates that from a digital currency is it's not a centralized system, it's private and occurs along private channels and what not. This is a very public, very visible infrastructure that anyone can just see at any time, it doesn't need to be audited, it's self-auditing. Everyone sees the audited file. So, when we're talk about digital currency, the words are important because some of this is digital fiat currency, and we're talking about central banks putting these numbers in balance sheets Private X25, banking at work et cetera. But this is something occurs in the public, and it's an encrypted channel. It's based on distrust, or any trusted party to make sure that the numbers are right. I mean, this is all occurring in real time by everyone, everyone's participating in this process, and that's kind of the dividing line between them.

**Hillary Raimo:** Does cryptocurrency have the power to take away the current banking system as it is set up with the World Bank, because it doesn't require a bank to approve your transactions, it's done real time between two people, the buyer and the seller, and there's no middle person?

**Stuart Trusty:** Oh absolutely. I mean, you could even take it one step farther, I mean you could take anybody's credit card number, and the expiration, and the little three-digit code, maybe your zip code, and you could use that as accordance to create a Bitcoin address, and you could actually just change the protocol on any card reading device, and have it go through the Bitcoin network rather than go through the banking network if the banking network were to fail.

So, it's just a matter of creating ... Where the Bitcoin is at right now, is that for something to be usable, it has to be usable at the, I don't know if it's the third-grade level or the three years or four-year-old level, but you have to be able to have this transaction take place and be able to go down and understand what it is, and go buy a piece of fruit or something for mom. It has to be understandable by everyone, and right now, like you said, now really that's come to be. I don't know about PayPal, but this card with Bitcoin denominated credit card's fantastic, I mean, anybody can use that.

But it is tied to, you know, you have to be using the Coinbase, digital currency aggregator, which is highly regulated and it's tied to your fiat bank account. You can certainly start using Bitcoin, but in the case of a total failure or a lacking the capability, or not wishing to use anything to do with the central banks. You still can't do that with the Shift card, it's not really independent of central banking system, but it's certainly possible to do completely independent transaction of any central bank and just use Bitcoin, absolutely.

**Hillary Raimo:** Does Bitcoin trade like Wall Street, does the value of it fluctuate up and down, and if so why?

**Stuart Trusty:** Well, since it's a smaller market with fewer transactions, I mean, it's considered a commodity now in that space, but it's very volatile, you'll have something as simple as one of the Bitcoin team come out and say, oh I'm very frustrated with this, it's going to go nowhere, and all of a sudden, the price drops very dramatically for a minute. If you heard that from maybe a Blue-Chip stock selling some disgruntled person, I mean, you may or may not see any impact on the stock price.

In this case, it's more volatile in the sense that there's fewer people using it, it's newer. It does have some real unknowns as far as what's going to happen when, so as the threshold is reached, how are we going to sell this problem? It could be very confusing, people will sell, or there could be a big drop. We've noticed last time there was a big drop, I think it was when Greece was about to not take the bail out, there was a big surge, but I think that was the way it went down.

But it's a little more volatile because it's a little more intangible. Everyone can understand the pros and cons for orange juice or wheat prices, or whatever, but Bitcoin is a little out there, and people are just starting to experiment with it, and it doesn't help that these central bank CEO's are trying steal the blockchain is important. There's really no blockchain without the digital currency itself, I mean that's just an absurd idea. I mean, anyone can have a log file, it's not exactly new technology.

I guess maybe that's how I'd answer that.

**Hillary Raimo:** Thank you. When I think about the current banking system, I think about how there's been a lot of war and a lot of things that have happened on this planet because of the current banking cartel of the current banking system and the way it's set up. It's not set up to help people, it's not set up to really benefit humanity. It's set up to be very controlling, it's set up to be very dominating, to make a lot of money off of people, so when I hear you say a comment like that, it makes me wonder, well, are the bank CEO's not wanting the blockchain, which is clearly associated with Bitcoin, because it takes some of that power out of their hands?

**Stuart Trusty:** Oh yeah, they're first trying to control opposition there, I mean there's absolutely no benefit that the bank could possibly have by making them lose control. They just want to pay homage to this idea, and somehow still think they can continue to print the money out of nothing, and then somehow become more innovative by using this distributive log idea and calling it blockchain and ignoring the fact that the blockchain is made of Bitcoin, or whatever digital currency.

And another feature of this, is that any transaction that is recorded can embed all kinds of information publicly. I mean, you can put your dissertation in, and conceivably by really complex transactions, but the blockchain can become this depository for any kind of text or message, or message in a bottle, or whatever might be desired, but it's not censorable. No government agency can go, "I'm filing an adjunction against Bitcoin to make sure that this information doesn't get put on the blockchain." I mean, it's over, it's done, it's never ever going to come off of that blockchain.

**Hillary Raimo:** Does that mean then that the blockchain is transparent in that aspect?

**Stuart Trusty:** Yeah, absolutely. And there's a site called Graffiti, I think. Look up graffiti and Bitcoin, anybody that wants to do that, but you can just write out your message, it can be as long as it wants to be, and it will encode it into a set of Bitcoin transactions that you spend the transaction and bang, it's in the blockchain forever. I mean, it's always going to be there, it will never vary, it can't be shutdown, it can't be not found if you go looking for it, so yeah, very definitely.

**Hillary Raimo:** Do you feel that Bitcoin is on the edge of coming out to be a global thing, and soon we will see the transition of every household over to using Bitcoin or to using some form of digital currency? Obviously going global would have to happen in stages.

**Stuart Trusty:** Okay, there are a couple things on that. So, we can look at how different governments approach the issue, and what is the extent to which they can control it or influence it, or whatever. And then the other thing is, what is on the surface of what's possible and what may actually be going on. So, I mean, first thing, so governments want to control et cetera, I mean, you can look at one of the earliest adopters to do a cryptocurrency on a national level was Aurora coin, that was

Iceland trying to get into that, and to do some special stuff.

One of the things that happened there very quickly, since it was not an established network, there was a lot of available computing power to do the 51% of hash power, that thing was forked several times from the moment pretty much out of the gate, weeks or months after, then it was dead. So basically, if one entity can get 51% of the computing power, they can subvert that whole batch of the currency.

Other governments have tried to ban it, other governments try to work with it, now under the commodity exchange rules here in the United States. But there's an internet black out button, there can be an order that's given that shuts the internet, but more importantly I would say that there's probably a button you could push to ... These Bitcoin transactions have a certain signature, they have a certain look and feel of the packets that are used to interact with them, whether you're anonymous or not, to where you could probably really mess with ... I mean, there's already been distributed service attacks against Bitcoin and other currencies, but there's certainly cyber warfare going on out there that can have a detrimental impact, and different agencies and governments are more or less interested in pursuing that.

We've had kind of a laissez fare kind of an attitude towards it that we see in the United States, and I don't think it's because the intelligence agencies, they're not going to take any chances or risks, I mean, the central banks, the way they're hand and glove with the government, I mean we don't know what's going on to a certain level.

And just to give you an example, we know right now pretty much in quantum computing, we know right now about the Google IBM quantum computer, and that's just many orders of magnitude faster than anything that's presently available. Now, that's just one we know about, and that's just one collaboration that we know about. So, in terms of this dark web, what's visible what's not, we know that there are huge, huge super computing facilities. To what degree you could turn that into cryptocurrency mining, I don't know, but I have a feeling that there's ways and means to where it's to certain governments or certain government alliances benefit to roll with it. Because if you give them point they can probably just turn up the volume, and then they have the 51%.

Now, I don't know if that's mathematically feasible right now, but we don't know how many of these big computers are out there, and how much processing power they can turn out or they will, but I think we just hit the Xabide or something. There's some milestone that was recently reached on the amount of total computing power that's being thrown at this Bitcoin network. I venture to say that there is vulnerability within the quantum computing in the hands of certain agencies working and they could probably, not only feasibly, but also very quietly, turn the tables.

And right now, there's a lot of press. I don't know what was with the guy that the Bitcoin author came out and said China controls all of the stuff now. Well maybe China does, and maybe China doesn't, but I think that there's a lot that's not known there, kind of this gray area, like this football field where there's going to be some scrimmages down here, and it's not exactly going to be visible though. It might be quite subtle, and no one knows who Yakomoto is, I mean, who was that? I mean, was that one person, was that an agency, was that a military operation? I mean, where did that come from?

So even though that the cryptography element may not be easily crackable, we really don't know what kind of conceptual vulnerabilities there might be in the whole apparatus, and that's something that is a matter of, you know, we're aggregating the best minds on these public forums, you know, and then sometimes they're being censored, and sometimes not, by certain individuals. One really has to do a lot of quantitative analysis to get to the heart of what the future is for this, and what the vulnerabilities are.

But in the mean time, without having to get too speculative, just to be able to go, okay, well, in the immediate future, Bitcoin's probably going this way, and we can probably use it, and if it does die, there's another one. I mean, there's plenty of them, there's hundreds of cryptocurrencies out there right now, and some are more transparent than others, but it's trivial to go from Bitcoin to another currency. Technologically it's very simple, you could go from the Shift card to another card, and all of a sudden, it's in Lite coin, or something like that.

No matter what happens in a certain branch of this, there's multiple redundant paths towards the same end, and depending on the mood of the people and the idea that's taken as to what creates the substantiality, or why that there's buy in to it. Any killer idea that everyone says yeah, let's do it this way, could be the golden ticket, and all of a sudden that's going to be the prevailing cryptocurrency, and that's a trivial matter. It could happen at any time.

**Hillary Raimo:** What is a quantum computer? Why should we care, and what are the potentials?

**Stuart Trusty:** With the quantum environment you're dealing with physical particles at a deeper level, you're not just dealing with on or off, you're dealing with quantum state. You can have something set as zero one, it's either basically on off, sideways, or something else, and it's more about the three-dimensional kind of approach to being able to do processing at every interval.

Okay, to just back up a sec, some processors run at two gigahertz, that means two billion analyses per second trapped in time. Here, we're going to do two billion of these processes of one or zero on these logic fields. This is not easy, I'm trying to talk very simple. Basically, anything that the computer's doing now, it's able to do it not only faster, but pretty much like a multi dimensional switching. So, it's able to do things at exponential several orders of magnitude faster and more robust. It's not a simple either-or decision, it can take in more features of every slice of time, every billionth of a second, you can get more bang for your bucks.

So, it's a way to do things that create possibilities for logic or analysis or artificial intelligence or et cetera, that previously possible just by sheer brute force required to do something like that. Like let's say you wanted to take one person's face and match immediately over the entire breadth of every single person in the world and find out who that was, I mean, those kind of instant realization, if you have a big enough memory, and big enough bandwidth for your system, you can access that in a quantum computer type of environment. Whereas, some simpler thing might have to have basically a memory array with a lot more fabric, a lot more storage. Not so much storage, but the linear way that approaches the problem makes some of the applications less feasible. That's the kind of stuff.

Even right now, on Sound Hound, you can play a little song and immediately it gets the signature of that and pulls through every last song that is in the musical database. Oh, it's this song, you know, obviously it's this song. But this type of technology was almost unheard of before that came out, well that kind of leap in computing power and just using it to ... I mean, what I see going on with that, so it's a lot of military analysis, a lot of behavioral analysis, a lot of meta file analysis of people's habits and psychological, social profiles of things, and going to huge lengths to just basically get in someone's head and basically use it as a command of control mechanism. I think that, that's a lot of really what's going on with that technology.

**Hillary Raimo:** We have cell phones, we log our whole lives from the time we get up to the time we go to bed, whether it's social media, texting, whatever app we're using. So, is this a possible way to store all the data collection? ... You know, you have the NSA, you have the big data facilities in Utah and elsewhere, and you have all of this data being gathering from cell phones, and it's going into these data farms. Is it really to just ultimately profile people to the point where they can be so understood that you can just press a button and manipulate their life to whatever degree, whatever, whoever, is pushing the button wants to?

**Stuart Trusty:** I don't think you need quantum computing to do that, but that is certainly almost definitely being done right now with Facebook. Anytime you like something, I mean, there's no benefit in you liking something, there's no benefit to the person who's having their stuff liked. That's creating profiles, and then on a law enforcement and command control level, it's an extremely intricate behavioral analysis and psychological profiling, that there's this constant spontaneously exploiting the data streams to find stuff you would not normally be able to go looking for, and then that's compounded and it's continued to do exactly what you're saying.

Yeah, to whatever extent that, that is being used for that purpose, we don't know, we don't really see any evidence so much of that, but I would say it's certainly the mechanism has already been created, I mean, it's already dumping this information.

What we can do right now with Facebook, I mean, okay I want to find Billy Joe Jim Bob I knew in third grade, I think he lives in Ontario. Well you can barely find that information, you could type Billy Joe Jim Bob in and you go through 16 pages of information, and they may or may not come up the same every time you do the search.

But I guarantee, if you're some three-letter alphabet soup agency you want to find Billy Joe Jim Bob in Ontario, you've got the back door into that database, you're going to find every last thing you want, including all the other behavioral and social analysis, and people's browsing habits, up to and including all the back door's, and all of the Trojans that have been put in people's systems that have been mining their data.

You can get a pretty comprehensive heartbeat on any individual, all their friends, all their habits, all their assets, all their bank accounts, all their passwords, it's all there for the taking, and it's already been taken because we've already given it a way. I mean, part of the terms and services of Facebook is that basically you're owned, the moment you log in, you're owned by Facebook, and your data, and you'll never get it back. All this information can and will be used against you, by not only court of law, but by every mom's basement dweller and Chinese hacker, and everybody else that just wants to get out there and just stir up the pot. So yeah, beware, I mean it's just-

**Hillary Raimo:** We've actually seen evidence of that happening in news cases in mainstream media here in the US, where they talk about somebody's post led to an arrest, or something like this, so that's already starting to happen. Or jobs can discriminate against people because of their social media profiles, and so on.

Cloning Facebook pages. Somebody mentioned that to me recently and I was quite perplexed by what that meant. Something about cloning someone's Facebook page and being able to basically see their page real time as if they're logged into it. Is that a reality?

**Stuart Trusty:** Yeah, I mean, that code is pretty easy. I mean you can write applications that dump ... There used to be a Unix shell-oriented Facebook client where you could pull up the different people's information up at the command line and what not, and they kind of shut that down relatively recently. But if you're a programmer and have some time on your hands or some avid interest, you can do a lot of things like that. But a lot of this is simply ... I've been approached by clone Facebook pages looking to friend me, and a sister or a kissing cousin of that is the mysterious people that appear in your friends list who you have no idea how they became your friend, but they're there for reason, and who knows what it is.

A lot of it is not as sinister as it is just mundane, I mean it's some kid in Lagos Nigeria that's part of a 419 crew that's just gone and copied someone's dating profile or whatever, has set up shop on Match.com, or Facebook, and is engaged in portraying themselves as you or somebody else. It's just look for a few books here and there, it's not really any mastermind, it's just someone that's exploiting some little vulnerability or hole in Facebook security. It's a free for all.

So yeah, not quite the problem that some of this other stuff is, but definitely annoying to be sure.

**Hillary Raimo:** So, it is possible, it's just amateur compared to some of the other things we're talking about.

Let's move on to conscious artificial intelligence. It's a constant question in circles of higher realms of technology. What does it mean for an artificial intelligence to be conscious? Is it a realty already, or is it something we're headed into?

**Stuart Trusty:** Consciousness, we usually apply that to bodies, like the symptom of consciousness is the body is moving around, and when the body stops moving around, we're pretty sure that the symptom is that, that body's no longer conscious. When we're talking about digital infrastructure, it's a little bit harder to find symptoms of consciousness. There's a Turing test which is some threshold of intelligence, you have managed to fool a certain percentile of intelligence into think that this is a sentient being. Something that can actually think on its own accord, it's always going to be based on rules that were programmed for it to analyze data from sensory input and to make decisions based on different criteria and from other sensory input.

So, when we talk about thinking in that sense, we're talking about assigning a stack of priorities to a server or a program, you're giving it certain priorities of input, like if something's really, really hot, like the house about to burn down, your priority is to call the fire department as opposed to bringing the systems admin his lunch.

And then there's interrupts that happen, and basically, we're talking about setting something up to have the trappings of being able to think, but the actual imparting of conscious is a hard thing to ascertain. I mean, this is a question that's philosophical along the spiritual lines, it's gone back thousands of years, especially into the Vedic system.

But actually, being able to see something that is sitting there conversing with you and that's learning not only new information but how to process that information and correlate it with the existing information to form more complex ideas or capabilities, and maybe increasing the scope of its ability to process its existing sensory input, or to aggregate or to expend its sensory apparatus.

I don't know what kind of program it would take to do something like that, I mean even in genetic material you have a body that is providing functions, but it doesn't mean it's alive. If something is stillborn, it has to be this concept of the soul. There's a soul, that there's the conscious entity that has intelligence and that it's controlling its mind and then its body, and its input and output to the senses are being utilized. So, unless there's an ability to create a bonafide conscious entity that somehow stands the bar of consciousness, not at the Turing test level, but at the same kind of features you'd find in a human being or even an animal.

It's going to be illusory, I think it's probably the new perpetual motion device, I mean, on times past that was the impossible to achieve feature, and then it eventually was. It was created, but hundreds of years later. I mean, that's kind of the pre-energy technology that we're seeing now.

But the artificial intelligence actual ability to create consciousness, I'm skeptical. I'm not really seeing any examples of any bonafide creation of actual consciousness so that it would to pass on a philosophical platform of consciousness You might have some complex natural process, but it's not going to actually possess consciousness, it's going to be a thinking machine.

**Hillary Raimo:** One could really understand and study human behavior almost to the point of mimicking perfectly, and in that mimic, we might actually be thinking we're seeing something that's conscious or has a soul, but doesn't really-

**Stuart Trusty:** Absolutely. That is totally correct, absolutely. You can mimic using this information, you could find a signature for F1's mind, and you can look at the words they're using and how they make what their habits are, or what not. If you didn't know someone in a foreign country and all of a sudden that person was taken out, and this emulator was put in place using all this aggregated stuff, you could probably fool someone for a very, very long period of time into thinking that they're interacting with a person, when in fact they were just using the energy signatures that were created from the log files, and the meta files, and et cetera, et cetera. I mean you probably could do that, that would be achievable quite easily.

**Hillary Raimo:** Well that is eye opening. So, someone can mimic someone and pretend to be someone else, while you interact and all your data is collected and studied. This information can be used in vast reaches. What could go wrong? What recourse do real people with real lives have? Is privacy dead?

**Stuart Trusty:** Yeah, privacy no longer exists. The only thing you can do is to delay certain information from being released for a certain period of time is by using current state of the art encryption protocols. Every last piece of information that you put out there is irrevocable, someone's got it somewhere. It will be used against you eventually, most likely. There's no place to hide, there's no place that you can't be heard. The thing is, is that there's been technology like remote viewing for a very long time, the demonstration where you can go around to someone's desk and read the manuscript on their desk without ever physically going there or eavesdropping equipment.

And just the idea that you could go into even at the metaphysical context or spiritual context, I mean if god is always knowing what you're doing, or if at some point your life is in these Akashic records or something and all this stuff is accessible, there was never been any privacy to begin with, it's always been just an illusion.

So, I guess I would just kind of, instead of being depressed about that, that there's no more illusory privacy, I mean if you have an audience that consists of these government agencies and whoever else, make your message a good one. Speak something that's going to create some positive change, and maybe influence the minds and hearts of the upper people listening to it, because that's really the only recourse at this point. I mean, you've got to make the words that you're saying and the things that you put out that worth listening to and doing, otherwise the forces that are doing the listening and the analysis are the ones that are getting charged, so to speak.

But listening doesn't make you in charge, but I'll explain it as this, and that is, let's say we want to develop a business plan and we're going to collaborate, and we're going to put that on Google Docs and we've got some original intellectual property and then some ideas, so we're going to collaborate on that. And the thing is, is that these contractors that are working for these agencies that are out there, they're going to be pulling that data down and they're look at that and they go, oh wow, Hillary's got some cool ideas, why don't we sell that to Joe in our pocket over here at this corporation. Hey, look at what Hillary's doing, why don't you guys see what you think of that.

And it's not like it's this, oh big brother's looking at me and trying to keep me down, this is like, no, I'm stealing your intellectual property and for personal gain, I'm giving it to a friend or scratching someone's back, and I'm breaching someone else's information without their consent, I'm not obeying any of the intellectual property laws or copyright, I'm just out right stealing the data. And the reason I'm doing this is because I can, and because it's there.

And while I'm at it, even though Hillary's running this red phone program, I'm just going to bust into that set up a private data stream before her information is encrypted, where every time she talks to Stuart with this red phone, this encrypted thing, I'm going to listen to everything they say. And that's going on constantly, and it's a real shame because it's very hard to have any privileged or private information with it being raped from the get go by anyone that wants to at that level of the game, because there's really no ethical behavior going on.

And the proof that there's no ethical behavior there is because if you look at, like, system administration, there's ethics involved. You don't break into someone's data, you don't break into their email, you don't go looking at their email, you don't use that for your own private enjoyment or purposes. If you see a virus, you erase it, if you see malware, you alert everyone and then you remove it. So what's going on now with this idea of how we use information, we're going to break into someone's email, we're going to watch what they're saying, we're going to put viruses of our own on their system, it's going to steal the data for us, and then we're going to look at it, we're going to do whatever we want with it, and if we can make money off of it, or whatever we want to do with it, we're going to do that.

And that's like the opposite of ethics. The epitome of exploitation.

**Hillary Raimo:** Yes.

**Stuart Trusty:** And government and our system administrators are doing it. It's absolutely the opposite of anything ethical or beneficial to everyone that's underneath that authority.

**Hillary Raimo:** Stuart, how can people reach you if they have questions?

**Stuart Trusty:** Sure, yeah, I'm available at stuart.trusty@gmail.com, and all that information will be just between me and them, and the NSA, and everyone else that's watching the Google server.

**Hillary Raimo:** Thank you for sharing your thoughts with my listeners and me. This has been a very informative show.

**Stuart Trusty:** Okay, thank you very much. I'll talk to you later, Hillary.

# 16

# HILARY CARTER
# THE 11:11 PHENOMENA & SYNCHRONICITY

*It was Hilary who helped me understand the number phenomena that had started to happen frequently to me at that time in my life. Numbers were aligning in mystery ways, and sequences were illuminating in ordinary places. Certain combinations of people could make it stronger or weaker. It was something I started to track months before I found my way to Hilary's work. Over the years Hilary participated in the Love, Breathe for Earth Meditations I organized from 2014- 2017. She would often tune in from inside a crop circle near her home in England. Her energy was helpful in raising the heart space of Earth over those years.*

RECORDED JULY 10, 2008

**Hillary Raimo:**  Have you ever looked at the clock, and been surprised at how often it says 11:11, or 2:22, or 3:33? The 11:11 Code tells the story of yoga teacher Hilary Carter, who was brave enough to follow the synchronicity around numbers to see what would happen in her life. To her amazement, the number signs lead her to buy an ancient convent in Spain, formerly a home to the Knights Templar.

According to Hilary, the building was haunted, and seemed to have a will of its own. Her exploration of synchronistic events, destiny, and past lives is an inspiring example of discovering meaning behind true events. After hearing this inspiring true story, you may never look at the world in the same way after again. Once you are awakened to the 11:11 code, there's no going back to sleep. Welcome Hilary.

**Hilary Carter:**  Hello, Hillary. Thank you.

**Hillary Raimo:**  Let's start with your story. How did you come across the convent in Spain?

**Hilary Carter:**  I came across the convent, I thought it was by accident, but in fact looking back I can see being strongly guided towards it. I'd gone down to Spain to buy a property that I could use as a yoga center, so I could run yoga courses for my students, and I'd gone to Spain because the property there is a lot cheaper than it is in England.

I found a house, a beautiful old house. It must've been about 14th century, but unfortunately the person with the key didn't turn up. So, I was led around the corner to a rather normal, ordinary looking building.

Very old, very decrepit. Above the door, was written old Franciscan convent. I thought, "Oh, that sounds like a rather nice place to teach yoga, an old convent. I thought, "It's going to be full of lovely light, and vibration, and prayer.

I was actually wrong, it wasn't. And it was very odd, because the moment that the estate agent put the key in the lock, all the bells in town went crazy, and it was split-second timing. It was to the second. Apparently, this happens in Spain at midday, so it must've been exactly midday. The place, I really didn't like. When I got inside, I immediately didn't like it, and in fact, I went back to England, and decided I wouldn't buy it. But then, I changed my mind.

**Hillary Raimo:**   How did 11:11 guide you to Spain?

**Hilary Carter:**   Well, 11:11 led me, not exactly to Spain, but directly to the convent, because once I got back to England, I was actually feeling quite despondent, because it wasn't easy for me to go all the way out to Spain. From England, it's several hours. I had to go to London from my home here in Dorset, and then I'd have to go all the way down to Spain. So, when I got back after this visit to the convent, I thought, "I wonder if it was really that bad. Could I consider this building?"

So, I actually started to draw a plan of the convent. The minute I started calling the plan, the bells here at my local church in Dorset began to go wild. And I thought that's very peculiar, because it's not midday. In fact, I looked at the clock, and it was 11:11. And at that very second, at 11:11, not only did the bells ring, but my telephone rang, and it was the estate agent who had told me that I had a buyer for my flat. So, I could actually raise the money for this convent.

So, having had those two things happen exactly at 11:11, I thought maybe I need to take note. So, I emailed the estate agent in Spain, and the next day, I got a reply, and her reply came through at 11:11 exactly. So, I thought, "Oh gosh, I really need to take note here." Obviously, I had a choice, I didn't have to follow the 11:11 sign. I could've just thought, "That was weird," and that was it. Or, I could take a leap of faith.

And I realized there was something peculiar going on, because I had the courage to take the leap of faith. And I did. I took the leap of faith, and I inquired about the price of the convent, because I didn't get that point, the price. Now fortunately, it was far too expensive. I couldn't afford it. So, I emailed back and said, "No, that's much too much. The most I could afford to pay is 100,000 euros."

So, the agent emailed back and said, "Well actually, they will drop a bit more. They've given me the price in pesetas, but work out the price in euros," which I did, and the price in euros was 111100.

**Hillary Raimo:** Wow.

**Hilary Carter:** I know, that's what I thought.

**Hillary Raimo:** Hilary, have you always had a history of numbers appearing as signs in your life?

**Hilary Carter:** Yes, I do. I had some incredible experiences around the number 23. Now, I don't know if in the states you have that film called *The Number 23*, do you? Have you heard of that film?

**Hillary Raimo:** Yes.

**Hilary Carter:** Okay, so it must've been the same film that we have here in England, and it's called *About Number 23*. Now, I'm going back at least 20 years, to 123 appeared in my life. I actually had a car accident. A small child ran in front of my car, playing chase in between the parked cars, and went flying through the air, and fractured his skull. It was very difficult time for me. After this had happened, I went off to the Mediterranean, for holiday.

When I got out there, I met a man called Martin, and he said a funny thing to me. He said, "You know, the number is 23." I said, "What number?" He said, "Just be aware that the number is 23." So, I got back to England after my holiday, and I was working in the east end of London, I was a teacher. I think it's equivalent, something like the Bronx in New York. Was a rough area.

As I walked into school, my headmistress came up to me with a massive great envelope, and on it was written 23. And she gave me this great big envelope. I said, "Why are you giving me this great big envelope with the number 23 on it?" She said, "It's the poster that you ordered for your classroom wall." I said, "But why have you put 23 on there?" She says, "Well, we're number 23 in the internal mail system."

Then, I went upstairs to my classroom, and I looked down the list of teachers, I was number 23. I looked at the date of the car accident I'd had, it was the 23rd. I added up my bank account, 23. I added up my passport number, 23. Everything came to 23. But in a way, the 23, that's when I hit a very low point in my life, because I didn't know whether this little boy, little two-year-old child was going to live or die. It was an awful thing to have to go through. Fortunately, he did live, but it was touch and go for quite a while.

And looking back now, I can see that actually 23 is the breakthrough number. So, if you're experiencing the number 23 in your life, it's as if you're breaking through into something new, into a new level of being.

**Hillary Raimo:** Extraordinary. Thank you for sharing that with us. If 23 is a breakthrough number, what is the number 11?

**Hilary Carter:**  Right, well 11, which could also appear as the K, which is the 11th letter of the alphabet, or as in your name, Hillary, the double L. I actually call that a hidden 11, because I see where it appears. So, that's three ways it appears, double L, the K, or the number 11, or one one one, or 11:11.

Now, the number 11, I believe, starts to appear in your life when you're ready for it. When you've worked on raising your consciousness to a certain level. I have spent, you know, almost 25 years doing meditation, tai chi, yoga, lots of consciousness-raising exercise, and then the 11 began to appear, and it came in a huge way. It wasn't just a case here or there, it was as if that 11 had to come into my life in a massive way to wake me up.

Because I believe it's the manifestation of a higher level of consciousness. It's where we our one consciousness of humanity. And as more and more of us recognize this fact, that my thoughts affect the entire world, as do yours, as do everybody's, then this language, the 11:11 will appear in your life to guide you to your place in the puzzle.

If we think of the life as a great big jigsaw puzzle, and we've all got a little piece to put into this puzzle. Every single person has got a piece to go into this puzzle. Because if there's one piece missing, that's the very place your eyes will be attracted to. So, never underestimate the power of one person's consciousness.

**Hillary Raimo:**  Beautiful message. Thank you. In your book, *The 11:11 Code: Secrets of the Convent,* you talk about your journey into the convent itself, how when you first experienced the convent, it wasn't such a positive experience. When you walked in there, you didn't like it, that you were repelled by the energy in it. Could you talk about this experience, and the paranormal activity that was taking place?

**Hilary Carter:**  Yes. When I first stepped into that convent, it was, as I described in my book, it was like walking into invisible cobwebs. And I always had the feeling that I was being watched. Very powerful feeling of being watched. I always felt uncomfortable. And my very first time in the convent on my own was the day of the fiesta, when the local saint was brought down my road. It's a Catholic saint, because it's very Roman Catholic.

The saint was brought down my road, and it just stopped, the whole crowd of people, the procession stopped right outside my convent, and I was eye to eye with this saint. And the band stopped playing, everyone was silent, and there was just a very odd feeling, as if I was being given a message, that I was here for a purpose. The occult activity in the convent, that began when they took the roof off. Up until then, it'd only been the uncomfortable feeling, but as soon as the roof came off, it's as if something was unleashed.

The woman opposite ... Now, you've got to imagine, this is a tiny Spanish town up in the mountains, 5000 feet above sea level. And it's very ancient, and the roads are very narrow, only about two meters wide. My neighbor on the other side of the road, two meters away from the convent, she had a little dog, a little, tiny little dog, a Yorkshire Terrier, called Boo. Little Boo began to get very, very nervous about going into the apartment opposite.

In fact, when my friend went in there, she found all her doors and windows were open. This is after the roof came off the convent. So, when that happened, stuff started to happen, mostly to her. I mean, it might've happened to me had I been living in the convent, but the convent was uninhabitable, it hadn't been inhabited for all but 70 years. 60 or 70 years.

**Hillary Raimo:** The paranormal activity started in the apartment across the way from the convent. Now, you also talk about, in your books, that there was perhaps a tunnel that connected that apartment to the convent, yes?

**Hilary Carter:** Yes. Well, when I arrived in town, obviously I stood out somewhat, because I don't look at all Spanish. I'm very English looking. When I arrived in town, I was sitting in a bar, having a cup of coffee, and an old gypsy man in the corner called me over. I ignored him, but then he called out, "Hey, you bought the convent?" So, I thought, "Hmm." Okay, I went over, and he told me of a hidden tunnel under the ground. So, I wasn't sure about this, whether it was true or not, and he did indicate that this was a secret.

It actually was true, because when my friend opposite, who had the occult activity, when she was putting in new drains, when new drains were being put in, they uncovered, the builders uncovered the arch of the tunnel. And as soon as they uncovered the arch of the tunnel, strange things started to happen to them. Their tools were moved, they heard noises, and they heard, as I heard, and as my friend opposite heard, we heard the chanting of monks from under the convent.

Eventually I discovered, through meeting the former chief of the police, he actually drew me a map of the tunnel system of the town, and there was an opening in my convent, there was one in the Hermitage at the entrance to town, there was one in the former headquarters of the.... and one in the Catholic Church. But, the Catholic Church used to be a mosque.

**Hillary Raimo:** When you talk about the energy that was there at the convent you call it a negative energy bleed. Could you talk to us about that? What that is, and share more of that experience as well?

**Hilary Carter:** Yes. When I arrived in town, I didn't know anybody. I was completely alone. I didn't know a soul. But strangely, and happily, I had a lot of people drawn to me, almost as if the universe was supporting me in this and drawing in the right people to help me in all sorts of ways. The first person that I met was called Psychic Sue.

When she lived in England, she was an English woman, when she lived in England, she used to work with the police, helping them on a psychic level. And as soon as she walked into the convent, it hit her, the strength, and the denseness of this energy. She said, really, "Hilary," she said, "It's very dense. It needs clearing. Would you like me to do a clearing ceremony?"

So, I said, "Yes, please," and we did a clearing ceremony, and it was after that that the activity in the apartment opposite, where the little Yorkshire Terrier lived, became just unbearable. It became dangerous. There were dark shadowy figures, and noises, and all the doors, even the main door, the windows onto the balcony, which had never, ever been opened, were open.

My friend, who lived there, she rang Psychic Sue, and Psychic Sue came down the mountain immediately, and she said, "This is a vortex of negative energy." She said, "I've only ever once come across this before." It's where the energy is so dense, and so clogged, because of what's going on there before ... It's a bit like a blocked drain. You know, you can carry on putting stuff down your drain, until gradually you slow down the flow of water, but there will come a point where you've got so much stuff down your drain, it'll be blocked.

And this is what had happened at the convent. There had been so much trauma, so much evil, so much pain and suffering and torture in that building that the darkness, the negative energy had built to such an extent that it was blocked.

**Hillary Raimo:** I'd like to talk more about your research into the blocked energy grids and how you came to associate your convent with the geometrical connections on the grid with other significant places, such as the Vatican. How you got to that point and when you began to realize that there were connections to other places?

**Hilary Carter:** I'd come back to England, and when I came back to England, there was quite a lot of media coverage of the Da Vinci Code film, which had just come out, and there were all sorts of strange programs on television about this sort of thing. So, I just began thinking about where my journey had started, because this time, I won't go into everything that happened to me, obviously, in Spain.

But, I came back after a very eventful time, and I came back to square one, and I had to leave the project behind completely. I had plenty of time to ponder on what had happened. I went back to where my journey had started. My original 11:11 journey had started in a tiny little country church in Dorset, on the border of Hampshire, and it was built on the site of a benediction priory.

It was only a tiny church, but its history was very ancient. And I just started playing around with the maps, and my rulers, and realized in fact that it lined up to lots of benediction sites here in England. And having lined up all of the sites in England, I thought, "Well, I wonder if these would line up to my convent?" And I was working very much with my intuition here, purely working on intuition.

And I was given lots of signs. I lived by signs. Not just the number 11:11, but I try to be in every moment. For example, if I'm speaking to somebody, and there's a rainbow on the phone, because my crystals caught the light, I'll take particular note of who I'm speaking to.

So, I lined up the English sites, and then I discovered that if I drew a line from the source of my journey, in Dorset, down to the convent, it linked exactly to the Vatican, exactly. And we have a 33-degree angle, or it's a 66-degree angle, which fits into 33:33, linking the source of my 11:11 journey, to the Spanish convent, to the Vatican.

I think it was Sabaran who actually said to me that he had had to clear the grid, the grid of light around the earth, he had had to clear, I believe it was 19 sites, as far afield as Egypt, Rome, southern France, and the convent also lines up perfectly, to point three of a kilometer. So, that is a very, very tight distance.

**Hillary Raimo:** Who do you purpose designed all of this?

**Hilary Carter:** Well, I was told that it was a Franciscan convent, and it dated back to the 1600s. But in fact, when I arrived in town, I was told by somebody who was born in the convent, that it actually dated back to the Knights Templars. Now, the Templars of course were around in the 12th century. I think the figure they give is about 1114, but I personally think it is 1111.

However, the town in Spain where the convent was located, it was very ancient. It had been inhabited by the Romans and I believe that my convent was built on the site of a Roman temple. I think it's very, very ancient.

**Hillary Raimo:** It has been said that most of the churches are built on much older sites, which brings us an interesting insight to the grid that you spoke of, and the original intent behind building these places on such specific locations. Who were the original creators of the grid?

**Hilary Carter:** Well, the strange thing was, of course, that towards the end of my journey in Spain, I found myself chanting. I found myself with some people from the Ashram in Germany, who I just happened to bump into, and the last time I was in the convent, we were chanting, and we were simply chanting the mantra, "Om," which is a clearing mantra. And certainly, after this, the energy did shift.

Now, I think these sites, these ancient sites are obviously key places, and I feel that whoever has control of these sites, what goes on in these ancient sites, affects the grid. And I think we actually go right down to the source of darkness and light, because as I say in the book, darkness is defined by light, because you won't know light without dark.

So, it could be, and I feel this is the case, that there has been both good and evil in my convent. And I'm sure it's the same with many, many of these ancient sites. I mean I was, I do remember being there when I was a Franciscan, and certainly my motives were pure, and good, and I was working to educate people. In fact, it was once a school of illustrious studies linked to the University of Granada.

But, I don't think it's that clear that, you know, it's always been light here, it's always been dark here. I think the crosses on the grid is where the struggle goes on. And this is where, in a way, the light of the place is the dark of the places. I mean, these are the more powerful places. And I come back to the Vatican here, I'm intrigued to know what goes on at the Vatican.

**Hillary Raimo:** One must wonder what goes on there, and how it is affecting the world. Could you talk about how the convent was built according to sacred geometry?

**Hilary Carter:** Yes. The convent was built in a traditional manner, built from earth, and stones, and rubble, with a facing of very small bricks. And these walls, they're incredibly thick. They're at least one meter thick. So, it's very difficult to knock down one of these walls. And frankly, the original walls were all in place. And when I measured the walls, the original walls, I saw at least two of the rooms downstairs where built according to the golden mean.

Now, the golden mean is pi, it's a ratio of one to one point six, and the fact that these rooms were built precisely to that measurement does indicate that whoever builds my convent, they had knowledge of sacred geometry. Not only that, the convent was built on a very strange angle, and I haven't gotten to the bottom of that one yet, but I'm pretty sure that there is reasoning behind the angle as well.

And the road it was in was called the Road of the Meridian. The Meridian, the midday. So, I think it must've been aligned to the sun, which takes us, of course, right back to the days of sun worship.

**Hillary Raimo:** In your book you speak about the feeling of scrolls being buried at your convent. Tell us about that.

**Hilary Carter:** Yes. Now, this was a message, that the universe obviously was very keen that I got this message, because from five different sources, I was told that there were scrolls buried beneath the convent. And these were unconnected sources, they hadn't spoken to each other, so I had to take note. Now, when I arrived in town, in Spain, into this mountain town, my neck immediately seized up. I really could hardly move it. I was given some cranial sacral therapy. Have you heard of cranial sacral?

**Hillary Raimo:** Yes. It's wonderful.

**Hilary Carter:** Oh. Well, I heard of it, but I've never had it. I thought, "Oh, for goodness sake, how can just gently pressing your skull have any effect?" That's before I'd experienced it. And I had a flashback, and it was more than a flashback, because I had a very, very detailed past life recall come to me from having cranial sacral therapy. And in this recall, the first thing that happened was I remembered what state I was in, emotionally.

I was in an absolute panic. My heart was thumping in my chest, as if ... And I was petrified, and I was in a hurry, because I had to hide something. And I had this metal chest, and I had to hide it. My life depended on it, and it mustn't, this metal container must not fall into the wrong hands. And so, I went down, I remembered the layout of the convent, I went down into the tunnel, I secreted this chest, and then I did something that I didn't even know existed, and I still don't know whether it exists, but I knew it in this life, I put a sealing spell on the scrolls. That's sealing, S-E-A-L.

And by using gestures, a bit like in yoga we use energy, we put our fingers in certain positions, and our body in certain positions to affect the flow of energy ... Well, in that life, I had detailed knowledge of how to use the flow of energy to control energy. So, I sealed these scrolls into the hiding place, knowing that nobody, absolutely nobody would ever be able to get those scrolls, because they were completely secreted. I didn't realize at the time, but it was going to be almost 1000 years before I went back for them, which is what I did.

**Hillary Raimo:** You talked about a beheading in your book. Was that that particular lifetime, or was that another connection?

**Hilary Carter:** Well, unfortunately, I had two violent deaths there. In one life, a life where I buried the scrolls, I was a Templar, and it was a Templar life. Do you, yourself, have you ever gone back into past life stuff?

**Hillary Raimo:** Yes. My first past life experience was when I was five years old by my grandfather Les Holloway, a brilliant psychic in his day. I returned to my life on a farm, with loving parents, horses and a special cat in England. I played the piano and died young.

In another, years later I was a priest who preformed exorcisms for Rome. I taught demonology to other priests. This lifetime was confirmed by another person who recalled me, as well as her own life within the Roman Catholic church.

My next one revealed my life as a Tibetan monk who lived in a valley between two mountain peaks, I returned to my small and humble temple there and the altar I had built inside of it. After cleaning off the dust, I took down some scrolls that I had written. As I read them I was able to walk down the mountain into the small village below. Here life was going on day by day, my appearance had changed and I was a homeless man. It was my job to check in on the realities of the common world to judge the progression of human consciousness.

**Hilary Carter:** Wow, okay. So, you understand that when you have the recall, you feel what it's like to be in another body, so you would've felt what it was like to be in that little child's body.

**Hillary Raimo:** Yes.

**Hilary Carter:** Because I felt what it was like to be in this male body of a Templar. This is when I buried the scrolls, and they wanted me to talk, they wanted me to reveal stuff, and I wouldn't, and I was tortured, and I was beheaded. And then again, I was there much more recently, in the 1600s, and there was a battle. In fact, there was a massacre in the convent, which is actually written down in the town's history. I was beheaded by the Moors, because this part of Spain was inhabited by the Muslims, the Moors. For many hundreds of years, it was the last stronghold of the Moors in Europe.

I was beheaded, as were my brothers in the Franciscan movement. We were all beheaded. I saw them beheaded. I recall that, and I remember that. Interestingly, I looked to the left, and I saw them, and it was the left part of my neck which would've taken the sword, and this was the part that I had the huge problems with.

Because, I died with a loss of faith, because my prayers hadn't been answered. I had such a faith in God, but my prayers hadn't been answered, and my faith died along with me in that moment. And that's probably why had to come back, because it was still unresolved.

**Hillary Raimo:** Did the problem in your neck clear when you did the clearing ceremony?

**Hilary Carter:** It did not clear 100 percent, thinking, "Oh no, where my going to be going next?" Because as you probably read at the end of the book, I'm going to another convent.

**Hillary Raimo:** So exciting. Has the 11:11 code led you to this one too?

**Hilary Carter:** Well, not quite so dramatic, because now I'm so tuned into that 11:11, that the universe doesn't have to be quite as heavy-handed with me. But, what happened with the French convent was, when I came back to England, I had very little money, and my sister said, "Well, don't worry," She said, "You can always go down to Southwestern France. It's very cheap down there."

So, in fact, I only had 90,000 euros, which is about 140,000 US dollars I think, tops. When I put that into a search engine on the Internet to find the property, there were only five that came up. There was a shop, a field, a barn, a ruin, and a little house. And it said, "This house was once part of an ancient convent."

**Hillary Raimo:** Wow.

**Hilary Carter:** So, I thought, "Hmm." So, I emailed to ask where it was, and when I looked it up on the map, the map reference was 111. I've got the map right here.

**Hillary Raimo:** Fascinating. Have you had any experiences in this house, that was similar to the one in Spain?

**Hilary Carter:** Well, I was prepared just to buy the house without actually going to see it, because I'm now so surrendered to the 11:11. Surrendering to the 11:11 is a surrendering of the ego. But, I was so surrendered that I would've bought it. But, I did go out to see it, and it has an outhouse with a medieval oven in it. The owner said, "Come in, and see the oven." And I didn't want to, but I stepped in, and immediately I stepped in I knew it was a mistake, I was crushed.

Within two hours, I was very, very ill, and I was very ill for three weeks. It was like someone had flicked a switch and said, "Produce a lot of mucus." It's just like I was put there, and just used to clear, and the darkness is clearing through mucus. That's the best way I can describe it.

I haven't been back since then. But I will have to go. I will have to go, and I'm waiting for the right moment, and I'll be given the signs when the right moment is. And then I will go. And I'm going to write my second book. I already know a lot about what's going on there. It's 10th century, this convent, but I believe obviously that it's even older than that.

**Hillary Raimo:** Do you think that this is part of your destiny in this lifetime, to go to these places?

**Hilary Carter:** Absolutely. I know that there's three. I know after France there's going to be Italy. And this is where the 11:11 actually puts you onto the path of your destiny, because Hilary, that's me, that's the little me, the ego that's got a name, Hillary, doesn't particularly want to go and live in France. You know, I don't particularly like France. And it's not even by the sea, and I love to live by the sea.

But, by following the 11:11 when it appears in your life, I believe it's your divine spark that's within each of us. It's the language of the divine spark saying, "Listen, your destiny is this direction, Hillary. Are you prepared to give up your own needs, desires, and wants, and follow your divine life?" It's a bit like, it doesn't matter if you don't, you know, because there are times I haven't followed it, but if you want to get from where you are to enlightenment, I think the 11:11 is a fast route, it's the motorway.

Of course, you could take the back route, along the little wind the roads, up and over the hills. You'll get there eventually, but it'll take you a lot longer. I think with the 11, it's a straight route.

**Hillary Raimo:** What a gift. Hillary Carter, author of *The 11:11 Code: Secrets of the Convent*. Hillary, thank you for listening to your heart and having faith to follow the signs.

**Hilary Carter:** Thank you, Hillary. Thank you.

# 17

# TOM CAMPBELL
## OUT OF BODY EXPERIENCES & MIND POWER

*Tom and I were cast members in a popular documentary series called The Path: Afterlife by Path11Productions. We met each other at one of the cast Q&A premieres in upstate NY, and then again in London. We enjoyed each other's answers to the questions from the audience, as Tom expressed the concepts very scientifically, and I from a place of intuition. Often the women in the audience understood what I said, and the men better understood him. He often referred to energy as data and over the next few years Tom and I would do a total of four shows together. His shows were well received by my audience, and he was frequently requested back.*

RECORDED FEBRUARY 1, 2010

**Hillary Raimo:** Tom Campbell, NASA physicist and author of the *My Big Toe Trilogy*, began researching altered states of consciousness with Bob Monroe at Monroe Laboratories in the early 1970s where he and a few others were instrumental in getting Monroe's laboratory for the study of consciousness up and running. These early drug-free consciousness pioneers helped design experiments, developed the technology for creating specific altered states and were the main subjects of study all at the same time. Campbell has been experimenting with and exploring the subjective and objective mind ever since. He joins us tonight to talk about a variety of topics that we're going to be exploring with higher consciousness. Welcome, Tom.

**Tom Campbell:** Yes, thanks, Hillary. My pleasure to be here.

**Hillary Raimo:** Why did you choose *"My Big TOE"* as the title for your book?

**Tom Campbell:** Well, *TOE* stands for *Theory of Everything*. It's a big picture theory of everything, which means not only does it have to explain science and things like quantum mechanics and relativity, which are physics, which is where the original word TOE came from it's a theory of everything. It was those trying to combine relativity and quantum mechanics under one description, one set of understandings. It does that, but it also does consciousness and metaphysics and other things so I called it a big TOE, and then I put the "my" in front of it because until it's your experience it can't be your knowledge. You can't really evolve your conscious. You can't understand at a profound level until it's your experience. If you just read about it in a book it's something you can believe or not believe, but it becomes your reality once it's your experience, so the my there is not to reflect, "Oh, it's mine, and I did it." The my there is to say that to make it your own experience is required.

**Hillary Raimo:** Is it also bringing the person experiencing life back to themselves as the creator of their experience as well?

**Tom Campbell:** Yeah, that's a good way to put it. We as consciousness in many ways create our own reality of silence.

There's lots of ways that we create our own reality. One is because our reality is basically data. All the things that come into our eyes and ears and touch and so on it's just nerve impulses and electrical signals and that kind of stuff, light, it's all information, it's all data, and we have to interpret the data and how we interpret that data is very individual. It depends on our experience. It depends on where we come from, our beliefs, our knowledge, all sorts of things, so how we interpret the data defines our reality, so yes, we do have some objective data, but then we have a lot of subjective interpretation. We also have feedback.

If we let's say are very kind and understanding and big-hearted people than we find that people like us and like to be around us and enjoy us, and if we're just the opposite if we're mean and unfriendly people than people don't treat us very well. They stay away from us or they say mean things about us so that way we create our own reality as well. There's several ways that we do that, but I guess the point is that each of us is walking around in our personal reality because of these subjective aspects to what we call reality, so we're all in our little reality though we also share certain aspects. It's a multiplayer game, so there are some things we share, but it's interesting to think that what we think is real out there is really our own interpretation.

**Hillary Raimo:** Describe for us how group dynamics effects consciousness.

**Tom Campbell:** We are all netted with each other. We all communicate with each other all the time, and particularly those people that we're associating with and interacting with, and all this is done in a nonverbal, and I don't mean body language. I mean non-physical when I say non-verbal as well, so when you have groups of people together these groups if they're all working on something reinforces each other. Whether it's good or bad they tend to pull each other up or drag each other down depending on which way they're headed, so you have a mob. That's kind of mob psychology. Everybody is dragging each other down to the lowest common denominator or you have a group of people working on world peace and love and caring and taking care of others and that sort of thing and they all just pull each other up. They all feel better and more successful at what they're doing by working together, so that's artifact of consciousness being netted we share. A group actually forms what's called a group consciousness, which is kind of a factor sum of all the individual consciousness that are in the group, and they encourage each other.

**Hillary Raimo:** How would one's individual consciousness in a group change and shift the group consciousness?

**Tom Campbell:** Well, they would do that by offering a better way of looking at something and just by being there by their example, by what they're doing and what they're saying they can influence that group. Their input, their thoughts are being traded back and forth all the time. They just have to make those thoughts appealing to the other members so that the other members kind of pick them up and go with them, so it's a matter like most things it depends not so much on what you have to say as it is on how you say it, how you present it. If it's something that the group likes and they resonate with it then the group will tend to move in that direction. If it's not it doesn't matter whether it's right or wrong or good or not good. If it's not something that group resonates they won't attach to it.

**Hillary Raimo:** Do you believe that certain forms or expressions of consciousness have higher and lower vibrations of energy?

**Tom Campbell:** Well, that gets into this word vibration. I think that's a metaphor. If we're talking metaphorically that's probably a good statement to make, but that's not actual. Consciousness isn't vibrating. Vibration is a word that's defined in physical matter reality. It's a physical word it means to move back and forth. It's not a word that really applies itself very well to consciousness in a literal sense, but yes, each person has a unique consciousness the subset of the larger consciousness, and each is in a process is evolving their consciousness, growing up if you will. You might say increasing the quality of their consciousness, becoming more spiritual. There's lots of ways to say that, becoming love.

In my books because I'm a physicist I also get technical with it and call that lowering the entropy of the consciousness. All of these things do make one consciousness different than another because there are different levels of this evolution, and the more evolved the lower the entropy, the more you are like love than the more influence the more power you have. Other people look up to you and they'll tend to follow your lead, so yes, it does make a difference. If you want to describe that as levels of vibration then that's a metaphor that works for a lot of people.

**Hillary Raimo:** Does the scientific and new age terminology conflict, or compliment each other?

**Tom Campbell:** The New Age community has to express their concepts and their ideas in the language that's common and the language that they understand. Science on the other hand tends to be a little more specific, a little more precise in the way they define things. It doesn't matter a whole lot in the sense that what matters most is that we communicate, so if I say, "How are your vibes?" or "You're raising the frequency of your understanding," or something, or use words that are not precise from a technical viewpoint. As long as you understand what I mean then we've communicated, so it's that sort of thing.

I won't say these words are wrong, and people shouldn't use them. They're fine as long as they're communicating, but the words tend to be fuzzy, and non-specific. They're metaphors and they give you an idea what's being talked about without really being specific. The problem is if people take them to be literal rather than understand them as metaphors then they get themselves kind of twisted up around a belief that just isn't true that says consciousness is vibrating. Consciousness is not physical. It doesn't move, there's no space, and it doesn't vibrate.

**Hillary Raimo:** Do you believe that non-human things have consciousness such as plants or rocks? Shamanic cultures talk about this as spiritual knowledge.

**Tom Campbell:** Well, when it comes to thinking beings, which would be almost all of what we find in the animal kingdom, right? Not only dogs and cats and monkeys, but things like bumble bees and squirrels and other things that we don't necessarily think of as perhaps with consciousness, but all of those animals have consciousness. They're all aware. They all interact. If you do one thing they react to that with something else. They have choices, maybe tiny choices. A clam doesn't necessarily have a whole lot of choices maybe other than to open up its shell, or they could split out or pull it in or something like that, but they do have some choices, and there's a tiny little bit of consciousness there it's not all just hardwired things. They can learn. They can do things a little differently, so if you have choices than you have consciousness.

Now when we talk about plants and rocks that's in a little different class. It's not the same thing. Rocks don't make choices and trees generally don't make choices either. They just kind of grow where they grow. They don't have a lot of choices to make, so it's a different kind of consciousness and I would say that we call the first consciousness that's what most people think of being conscious, having an intellect, being able to make decisions, and that the rocks and the trees have let's say a feeling other than intellectual consciousness how they're feeling consciousness so they can be associated with certain energy forms. They can have memory in the sense that things are associated with them, but it's not really not that the rock has memory it's that memory is associated with that rock so the rock and the memory can be associated in the larger database or records if you like. They do have kind of a very fundamental level of feeling awareness so I wouldn't really say they're conscious in the same sense that you and I are conscious or a dog or a bird is conscious.

**Hillary Raimo:** You wrote about an interesting experience that you had with Bob Monroe in a series of experiments where you did out-of-body meditations as you were separated in different rooms. Both of you had out-of-body experiences and then shared your experiences as you compared notes. Many of the experiences you had were very, very similar. Would you care to talk about that?

**Tom Campbell:** Yeah, I would be glad to share that and it didn't just happen one time. This was something that occurred with me and several other people, and then between those people other people as well. This was kind of a set of experiments we did for a while, while I was working with Bob Monroe at the labs. It was an idea of Bob's to do it. The person that I first had this experience with was Dennis Mennerich, and he and I were kind of Bob's scientists at large at his lab so we came up and very routinely like three or four days a week we would come out for four or five hours, six hours sometimes, and help Bob man and instrument his lab. He would then reward us for that would teach us what he knew about out-of-body.

After a couple of years of this Dennis and I were switching in and out-of-body pretty much at will and had been doing exploring and healing and reading numbers off of blackboards and other kinds of tests because testing was what was important. Bob had this idea that Dennis and I and he didn't discuss this ahead of time with us we just showed up at the lab one night and he said, "Hey, I want you both to get in your respective booths," and these booths were soundproof. He called them check units. They were just tiny little rooms with waterbeds in them, microphones suspended from the ceiling down over our mouths, and he had taught us. We'd train to be able to talk while we were in the out-of-body, so we could actually parallel process between the out-of-body state and the physical state and we'd go do something and we'd come back and tell Bob what we'd done, we'd go do something and that's how we reported because if you wait until after it's all done there's a whole lot that you forget. It's much better to talk as you go.

Some of our sessions would be several hours. Over several hours the details start to get lost, but anyway, Dennis and I were in these separate units. We could not hear each other. We each had microphones so Bob could hear us independently. He could talk to both of us at once, or he could talk to each of us independently and his instructions were that we should go out-of-body, go above the roof of the lab meet there, and then go off on our adventure together, but stay together. What he was doing meanwhile is he was asking each one of us independently what are you doing? What are you seeing? What are you interacting with? What's going on? He was asking me those questions and separately asking Dennis those questions and recording both of our answers on a cassette tape.

We went on an adventure kind of typical for us we were doing this pretty regularly with him then, and we met above the lab and we kind of went off together and we had conversations with each other. We had conversation with other non-physical beings. We saw things, went places, went to some other reality frames. It was a pretty eventful situation where there should have been a lot of evidence whether or not we were hearing, and seeing and doing the same thing, so afterwards probably, oh, at least an hour and a half, maybe two hours or so he ended the session and Dennis and I come staggering out of these booths. Of course, the light kind of nearly blinds you there for a few seconds. We went up to the control room and Bob looked at us and you have to know Bob Monroe, but he had kind of a sardonic humor and he looked at us with a kind of smile on his face and nodding his head said, "Do you two really think you were together?"

We kind of looked at each other and said, "Seemed like it to me." Dennis, "Yeah, well seemed like it too." He said, "Listen to this," and he flipped two switches at the same time for these two cassette tapes and there was my replies and Dennis replies to his questions playing back simultaneously and there we were talking to each other. We were having this conversation. First it would be Dennis and then it would be me. He was switching back and forth between us asking us things. Of course, we didn't know that he was doing that. We'd just know that he was asking us questions, so that was probably the most amazing thing that had happened to me up at that point.

You know, when you do this sort of thing there's a point where you have an experience that you cannot deny and also cannot explain. Now we had done a lot that defied statistics. We had done things, but then the statistics said were one in a thousand or one in a million or something like that. That it was random that we could have gotten the data, but that's all intellectual. When I did this it hit me below the intellectual belt to a place that's deeper and that was kind of a big turning point for me that I spent the next several weeks just kind of wandering around in a partial daze saying over and over to myself, "My God, this stuff is real" because there was no other explanation and until you get to that personal experience it is, "Oh, yeah, we can do things that are way off the statistical charts," but you just don't have a sense that the space at that level that it's really real. You still wonder.

This was a big turning point for me. It didn't turn out to be that big deal for Dennis. He remembers it pretty well, but it wasn't the big cathartic aha moment for him that it was me, and then I did the same thing maybe a couple of weeks later with who was then Nancy Lee Honeycutt that was Bob's stepdaughter whose now Nancy Lee McMoneagle, Joe McMoneagle's wife, and we had a similar kind of thing. We went up and met and went off and had experiences and then later the experiences just laid out perfectly. We were having the same conversations and seeing the same things, so it's a thing that you can do once you get proficient, or at least two of you are proficient in out-of-body status.

**Hillary Raimo:** Would you care to describe the technique that you use when you do this with another person?

**Tom Campbell:** Well, in this case our technique of going out of the body together was just to meet someplace, so we would just meet in out-of-body state and then once we were in the out-of-body state it was a matter of staying together and you just do that with your intent, and both of us intended to be with the other one so when we'd say something like let's go off and see what happens and we just kind of zing off into the great void there, but we'd stick together, and then we would see things and interact with things together just like we were together just like we felt we were.

What that does and the reason it hit me so hard is that tells you that the data that you're receiving it is your interpretation that's true, but there is objective data out there, and even though you have a subjective interpretation you could see that between Dennis and I that we would interpret things a little differently like people do and that was obvious, but it was also obvious that we were looking and describing very similar things, size and shapes, colors, function, all that kind of stuff was the same even though the details might have been a little different.

**Hillary Raimo:** Did the chosen place to meet have a common meaning to both of you or would it just be a random place? Would you use your mind go into a meditation state where you projected yourself at that place? Would you conversate between each other there in that place in the ethers or would you have the experience and then go back and talk about it after coming back into your body?

**Tom Campbell:** We actually would meet. Bob's instructions were meet above the lab so we just kind of floated up out of our bodies went up above the lab where we could look down and see the roof of the lab, and while we were floating up there we intended to connect and see each other, which we did so that's how we got together to begin with and from there we started, but it doesn't have to be that you meet someplace. You can go and kind of connect with another person just with the intention of doing so, and if that other person was also intending to meet with you than the two of you basically get together and you can do things together and you communicate with each other telepathically.

**Hillary Raimo:** How would somebody perceive that kind of communication who wasn't aware that it was being done on the other end?

**Tom Campbell:** It depends on where they are. Let's say they're not particularly aware at all. You're just going to visit somebody and they're not expecting you or whatever, they're not really aware. They're busy doing something else. Maybe they're busy playing a game of basketball or something that takes a lot of concentration on their part. They're not just sitting relaxed kind of dreamily wandering off in a meditation state, but they're doing something. Well, what would happen is that you would communicate with them. You could talk with them. You could carry on a conversation and they would get it. They would get the whole content of what it was you were saying, but they would sense it. If they were more sensitive they would sense it as their own intuition. It would be like a voice talking in their head and they'd assume that that was them that was their own talking to themselves, their own intuition talking to them.

If they were less aware they would just kind of get the idea. They'd get the big picture of what you were saying and that would now just kind of be an idea that they had and they would, of course, think that it was their own idea so they wouldn't be aware that you were talking to them, but they would take the information in, and you can do this basically with anyone that you wish to give information to you can have those kinds of conversations and they do get the information. If it's information they can use they often will act on it.

**Hillary Raimo:** Sometimes people will say, "Oh, I was just thinking about you," and then that person calls, or that person who has been crossing somebody's mind over and over could that be a result of that kind of phenomena?

**Tom Campbell:** Absolutely, and it doesn't have to be out-of-body. Like I say we are in communication with each other all the time, so if there's somebody you're particularly close to maybe a mother or father or son or daughter, or something like that, something very big happens in their life you're liable to know about it. You're liable to get this message that "Oh, I need to call my dad and see what's going on," and you call and you often find that there really was something going on you get that message.

Other people that just happen to kind of drift through your mind for no reason it's probably because that other person is thinking of you and that makes a connection or there's something there between the two of you that would be kind of significant for you to know or understand and you'll get that connection. You don't have to go out-of-body to do this. It's not an out-of-body phenomenon that you have to do to do this. It's just a matter of we're netted it's like everybody on the Internet we're netted whether we like it or not the switch is open and we send and receive.

**Hillary Raimo:** Does the intensity of the bond between two people effect the consciousness between them?

**Tom Campbell:** It can come from two different sources. If the connection is mostly coming from your end then, yes, it mainly has to do with kind of the attachment or the connection you have with that person. That attachment and connection you have with that person doesn't have to be just the connection that you have with them now here in this physical amount of reality. You may have been connected to that person in other reality frames at other times so it's not just that it has to be your son or your father or mother or something like that. It just could be somebody with whom you are connected with whom you have a resonance and you will pick that sort of thing up because you're sensitive to their energy to their being and what they're doing and if they're thinking about you might then start thinking about them.

They feel you thinking about them so then they think more about you so it tends to build on itself like that, so now it can go the other way that it's not necessarily you at all, but it's somebody else. Let's say I decide to talk with you about some kind of maybe shared problem or some issue that you're having or something like that and I would come and say, "Hey, Hillary, you know," we have this conversation. That would then you would get that message that I would give you. You may or may not know that I was giving it. It may just come across as your own thoughts, but that's me directing that at you because every person may be directing it at you and that's why you pick it up or it may be just you honing in on the fact that they exist and there's a resonance between you, so there's a couple of things going on there.

**Hillary Raimo:** At your workshop recently in London you had an interesting exercise for the group. You had a picture that nobody else in the audience saw. You asked everyone to connect and draw what they saw in their minds eye. Is that a skill that people can learn how to do? or is it just a natural talent that some have more then others?

**Tom Campbell:** Well, yeah, in a sense, and that's just a matter of how we define terms, but yes, we can say that these are communications that are not physical. You know there's no physical energy going back and forth. It's not electromagnetic waves or sound or light or anything like that it's just paranormal in the sense that it's outside of what's normal, but from another viewpoint it's perfect normal. When you understand the big picture, we are consciousness that is our nature. This is a perfectly normal thing for any consciousness to do, so yes, everybody can do this. It's not just special people who are born with the talent or special people who trained really hard it's just an artifact of being consciousness that you can communicate like this that's in remote view.

Most people aren't sensitive to it. They don't pay any attention to it. It's just noise in the background. Where the training comes in it isn't to learn how to do it it's basically to learn how to not block doing it because it's going on all the time anyway you're just not aware of it. You can become aware of it and typically when you do these kinds of exercises the remote viewing, the seeing the picture something like that it's best to do it very quickly because people in their first few seconds when they think about it they're not operating on it. The problem that prevents people from being successful here is their own analytical sense. They get an image and they say, "That doesn't make sense."

Like the other day I saw one that somebody else had done and they had this little apple core in their pocket. I guess it was Russell Targ did that and he asked somebody he said, "I have something in my pocket can you tell what it is?" Of course, the first thing the person did was he drew this picture of like a flower, which was sort of the way this thing actually looked except it was a flower inside a circle, but then, of course, one would think, well, flower he obviously doesn't have a flower in his pocket that doesn't make any sense, but then you kind of erase that and you try to do something else, but that's a problem.

We tend to get very analytical. We tend to think too much. We tend to have preconceived notions. We want to make sense out of it and that just is all the wrong things to do. You need to just have no preconceived notions, be open and see what happens, and then you just report what happened like a scientist. You don't try to say I'm only willing to report it if it makes sense. I don't want to look like a fool. You just report whatever happens, and if you do that enough you'll find that you can kind of get a sense of how it is you're doing it and making that connection and you can make the connection stronger so that's how people get better at it. It's just a matter of practicing, but the attitude is more important than anything else. Everybody can do this.

**Hillary Raimo:** I like that. Nobody is on a pedestal. A more natural way of communicating with each other. You talked about meeting other beings and "dimensions." Can you speak more about this?

**Tom Campbell:** The reality is a very big thing. Our reality here our universe is just a tiny little spec of it. We're not at the center of it and we're not by any means the larger part of it we're just a little spec. Reality as consciousness evolves and just like any evolving system it basically fills every niche that can be filled with anything that can be sustained in that niche. This is our little niche our universe, and it's a virtual reality, but there are a lot of others. There are many, many, many other reality frames besides this reality frame, and we visit some of them routinely like the dreaming frame that's another reality frame that we work in so that's two that most people get in and out of, but you'll find out that there's literally hundreds of these reality frames and some of them are what I call physical like which means they have constraints. They have rule sets that constrain them to being something like our physical reality. Things have a process. You have causality there that's obvious.

Then there are other reality frames and these are all virtual reality. Consciousness is the only thing that's fundamental. All these other frames are virtual frames. Our universe is a virtual frame, so you have other virtual frames like where we end up after we pass out of this frame is a virtual reality that is made particularly for transitioning from this reality there's a little part of that that we do, and then there's a larger frame that the out-of-body people travel around in and all of these are different frames, but they're all populated. Consciousness produces beings just like our environment produces animals, plants and other things. It fills almost every niche so you'll find all sorts of beings. You can interact with these beings. You can communicate with them. You can go to where they live. You can join them if you like in their reality frame, and you can do that either by just kind of telepathically communicating with them where it indicates your voice in their head, or you can actually manifest the body like theirs and go join them and interact with them in that way too.

It's just something that's available to everyone to do. Yes, a lot of people do it. That's what mediums are doing when they're talking to spirits or whatever they're connecting in that case probably to the database that has all the data in it if it's particular people who have been here, but you can just visit these places. The thing that's a little difficult about it I guess I should say is that it's your intent that gets you places. If you don't know that something exists how you can intend to go there? So, it's one of these things that you have to explore a little bit at a time.

It's just like any other exploration you don't know where you are or what's on the other side of that hill, but the only way to find out is you go and look. As you interact with other beings they take you places and then that becomes someplace you know, and then you make more friends and they take you places and that's another place you know. Eventually, I've been doing this for like 40 years you've kind of been around a bit and you have a lot of acquaintances, and you've seen a lot of things.

**Hillary Raimo:** Big circle of friends.

**Tom Campbell:** Yeah, big circle of friends so it does grow like that, and some of them actually become very good friends.

**Hillary Raimo:** It pays off to visit. We actually have a caller we have a question from Jane in Arizona. Hi Jane, thanks for waiting. You have a question for Tom?

**Jane:** I do. Thank you very much for taking my call. My question is about telepathic communicating with one another. I often find that I pick up on people's thoughts or people's messages people who just kind of like, "I want this or that or the other from Jane." I pick up on it and then before I know it I'm on the phone calling, and I'm saying, "Hey, I got this message that I was supposed to call you and do this, that and the other." It happens a lot, so a lot of times also I intuitively just pick up on, again, something that somebody may want from me or want me to do or think they need something from me.

Again, I intuitively pick up on it, but sometimes there are things that I don't want to connect with or don't want to hear so I'll sit there and have a telepathic conversation with whomever and I'll say, "Okay, cancel, clear, delete" because I don't want to have a conversation, but it happens a lot and I find that it's almost like an intuitive or an invasion of spiritual or intuitive invasion. I'm must be trying to figure out how do I work with that?

**Hillary Raimo:** That's a great question.

**Tom Campbell:** The way you work with that is you can open that channel up or you can close it down based on your intent. You don't have to receive those signals that you don't want to. You just have to form a very clear intent that anything that you are not interested in and you can kind of give a general description of what that is that you just don't want to hear about it, and it will shut that down. Now if you have an attachment to it, if you have a fear of it, if it's something that you think you cannot turn off then you probably won't be able to turn it off because that will be a belief and that belief will be fulfilled.

Again, we create our own reality, so just be steady in your

meditation, and when your mind is still and calm make a very clear statement about what it is you do not want to receive. If you keep that in your mind as you go through your day I think you'll find that those things will get fewer and fewer and then drop off. You can do the same thing with the things you want to receive. You have those in your mind and that signal will get clearer and stronger.

**Jane:** Yes, okay, I agree because there are times when I'll say, "Clear, clear, delete. I don't want to have a conversation with whomever. I don't want to talk about this subject," and a minute or two will go by and then it goes away, but then as soon as I'm in a different space or different energy all of a sudden I can feel like a person's energy come in and begin talking with me, and then I'll have to go through that whole process again that clear, clear, clear, delete, delete because so far that's the only way I've been able to clear out certain energies that I don't want to have a conversation with, but it happens lots.

**Tom Campbell:** You probably have created this little ritual with yourself of what you go through in order to vanish the communications you don't want and you don't really need that ritual. That's just something you've kind of gotten into because it works. You tried it and it works so then you do it again, and pretty soon you kind of get dependent on that. If you try other methods that are simpler and easier and last longer those will work as well, so don't get trapped in what just happened to work for you. There are ways that will be more efficient. You can set up a thing in your mind that will prevent that even from getting started.

**Jane:** Any suggestions?

**Tom Campbell:** It's like the affirmations that people use. They're start out when they're meditating and they'll say, "I don't want to communicate with anybody who doesn't have my best interests at heart," or some sort of thing like that. That wasn't very elegant, but you've heard these affirmations, something like that. You write up something that's very specific about what it is you don't want to hear and then you just put those thoughts in your mind and refuse you say just say, "I don't want to. I'm going to refuse anything that doesn't meet these criteria." That will work, and you can just write your own. It's a matter of intent. Intent is the active ingredient in all these things whether it's remote viewing or healing, or out-of-body intent is the driver that's what makes things happen.

**Jane:** Yes, you totally connected with me there and that's exactly what it ... That was going to be my next question is like describe intent because I feel like I'm putting the intention out there. I do my best to not push away anything. I try to stay open to everything because I feel like that which I push away is actually something I need to learn about so that I can evolve it, evolve my own consciousness so that I'm not like in this place of fear that I feel like those things that I push away are things that I'm saying, "I don't want to learn about that, that's yucky, unattractive," or I just don't want anything to do with it so I try to push it away, and instead of me pushing it away I'll say, "Okay, well, let me take a look at this try to understand it so that I can evolve it" instead of pushing it away because I feel like that's why it returns, so I try and face things so that I can have an understanding, but intention, yes, I need to understand intention.

**Tom Campbell:** Your intent has to be more specific. It has to be very clear and by that, I mean it has to have no noise and that's kind of now a different concept. When you meditate meditation is a tool that's all it is it's a tool. You generally use that tool to learn how to quiet your mind to get the noise out of your thoughts, otherwise, when you first try to meditate thoughts keep coming in all the time. Well, that's what I'm describing this noise it's all this stuff that your mind and your consciousness is doing. All the things you're thinking about operating on is noise. Once you get rid of all of that noise what you have left is just pure still consciousness. That's what I call the void state when all the noise is gone and you are sitting meditating. Your body is gone, this reality is gone, all the thoughts are gone, and you are a point of consciousness floating in the void.

Now at that point your intent what you want to do is a clear, pure signal, so that's one thing. You have to get rid of the noise otherwise your intent is jumping all over the place. You may be thinking something, but at the same time you got hundreds of thoughts buzzing around in your mind and it doesn't come out clear and therefore it doesn't carry much power, so that's one thing. You need to get rid of the noise so that your mind is focused. The second thing is your intent has to be very precise. It has to be clear. You can't be saying I want to be open to everything, but I don't want to be open to everything. If you have general intent like that conflict with each other than that's a problem.

You have to say, "I want to be open to these kinds of things." very specifically, what it is you want to be open to, and I don't want to be open to these things very specific exactly what that is. As long as you have general intent I intend to be open well then, you're going to be open because you follow intent. If you say, "I want to be closed off" than you may not get things you want. You need to be more specific than that, but first your intent has to be very clear and very focused without noise, otherwise, it doesn't carry as much power.

**Jane:** Yes, most definitely, and I totally align with the whole intent thing totally. I'm going to try that with the circle of light because, again, I can be meditating, I can be cooking or cleaning, or taking a drive from here to there and then all of a sudden I'll just have like this spiritual invasion of energy and it's like, "No, go away. I don't want to talk to you." So, I thought, "Okay, this is happening a little more often than I want it to happen," and I was trying to figure out how do I keep that. I don't want to have a telepathic conversation with someone and how can I keep that outside of calling up that person and saying, "Stop talking to me spiritually, intuitively because I don't want to talk with you," which I've done, but it happens lots and I'm trying to figure out where to go with this.

**Tom Campbell:** These things are tools the things just the circle of light. People can put a balloon, a light around them. People can erect walls that are barriers. All of these things are tools and what the tools do is they focus your intent. That's the purpose of the tools and you can make up your own tools. You can build a wall around yourself, or you can have a certain sign or symbol or something that wards off unwanted conversation. It doesn't matter the tool you use as long as that tool is something that you connect with and therefore it focuses your intent. Again, it comes right back to intent and many of us can't focus on intent without tools. We need these tools to give us a visualization, to give us some kind of feeling or something and that's fine nothing wrong with that, so make up tools. Make up whatever works, but find something that works for you, and what Hillary does might work for you or might not. You may have to experiment some until you find something that kind of resonates with you and that would be the best choice.

**Jane:** Fabulous.

**Hillary Raimo:** Great question, Jane. Thank you so much.

**Jane:** Thank you.

**Hillary Raimo:** Tom, what is your hope for the intention of your work as it reaches out across the world?

**Tom Campbell:** My main hope would be that people find it useful. I see it as news you can use not just theory that's there to name things, but this is ideas that you can put to work in your personal life understandings that will help you not only understand why you're here and what the point of your existence are, but how you're connected to everything else, so that's my hope is that people will find it useful and will go use it.

**Hillary Raimo:** If people want to find out more information about your work they can go to mbtevents.com. We are out of time.

**Tom Campbell:** An hour is so short.

**Hillary Raimo:** Thank you Tom.

## -18-

## ANGELA KAUFMAN
## HEALING THE AMERICAN SHADOW IN THE TRUMP AGE

*Angela Kaufman blends the mystical and the modern in her approach to helping women improve their relationships and their lives as an Intuitive Relationship & Empowerment Coach. Her article in Healing Springs Journal (2017) about understanding the American Shadow was a breath of fresh air in the drowning of the American spirit through the transfer of power to the Trump campaign. These were sad and dreary days filled with people fighting over opinions, beliefs and hating others for not raging the same way. After reading her article I contacted her to do a show. Our conversation sheds valuable light on the inner most workings of these times and offers a fantastic alternative perspective on how to see it all differently. It opens a gateway into a healing that is greatly needed in the West, and perhaps the whole world.*

Recorded May 30, 2017

**Hillary Raimo:** Tonight, we're going to be talking about collective energy, the shadow healing of the United States, current world situations, and how that all relates to each of us from a healing perspective.

I read an article that my guest had written back in January in Healing Springs Journal published out of Saratoga, New York, and I felt she had talked very intelligently and intuitively about this topic.

Angela Kaufman is an intuitive relationship and empowerment coach, specializing in helping women and others improve their relationships and themselves. In addition to being a clinical social worker, she is also an intuitive consultant and psychic medium, author and creator of the Discover Your Inner Queen, Mystical Path to Empowerment Program. Welcome, Angela.

**Angela Kaufman:** Oh, thank you so much. It's my pleasure.

**Hillary Raimo:** I want to start by reading the first paragraph of your article for our listeners.

"Regardless of political views or practices, this election cycle has brought significant undercurrents to the surface. We are confronting a shifting paradigm and, with it, being forced to face the Shadow on many levels. The Shadow is the aspect of ourselves which we prefer to deny. We may be unaware of it or try to suppress it. If the ego represents our outward personality, our 'shining star' selves, the aspect of who we are which we gladly portray to the world, then the Shadow is the dark side of the moon, the unknown, deep, primal, irrational self."

Powerful words. She goes on to compare some of the current social angst on the collective platform to having a kind of nemesis that creates a valuable lesson-like where it makes us grow. Some modern-day myths that carry this wisdom, for example, is the classic *Star Wars*, where Luke realizes he's linked to Darth Vader or in the *Harry Potter* series where we see a link created between Harry Potter and Voldemoort.

When I read that, it caught my attention right off the bat because I said, "Oh, this isn't just another I-hate-Trump article." This is asking us to look at something much more relevant and much deeper than just how much we hate him. I see a lot of people projecting all their victimization stuff on to him. He's such a good mirror for that.

Angela, where are we headed?

**Angela Kaufman:** Thank you. I appreciate your sharing it and your framing it in that way.

First of all, because we are talking about the Shadow, when the Shadow as a topic comes up, regardless of politics, I find that many times people have the thought in their mind of, "Well, how do I get rid of that?" or they might hear me say something about the Shadow and the illusion that is projected out there is that, somehow, I'm beyond all this because I wrote about it or because I speak about it or because I'm familiar with the concept, so I do just want to admit to myself right now that, yes, even having written this months ago back in December, I'm still knee-deep in mud today. And that is ok.

Last week, I was shoulder-deep in much, and it's one day at a time figuring it out because it is triggering so much, so, yeah, when we look at the Shadow it brings stuff up. There's a saying in recovery circles, when somebody's pointing the finger in one direction, if you're pointing your finger at somebody else, there's four fingers pointing back at you.

Over the past year or so as I'm following politics, and I'm following what's going on, and I'm human, so I'm having all my human reactions, anger, disgust, fear, shame, some brief moments of happiness here and there along the way, but most of it is not pleasant, but, at the same time, I'm looking at it like a social worker and, at the same time, I'm looking at it like a spiritual person, so I'm having all these conflicting views and interpretations of things.

It's been a fun trip, but I'm thinking back even ... I think the seed started to be planted for me actually spring of 2016. I don't remember what exactly put this in my mind in this framework at the time, other than perhaps that I was having a whole lot of reactions to everything I'm seeing and hearing about Donald Trump. Part of my training is that, at some point, I have to say to myself, "If I'm reacting all over the place, I got to look at what's being triggered in me."

Now, full disclosure, I will say that to myself, and I will sometimes still go months and months and months and not have looked in the mirror or I might look in the mirror and still only see what I'm willing to see at that moment. There is still a lot that's being unearthed.

I just want to be transparent about that because I don't want listeners to feel ... Sometimes, when we hear some of this really spiritual stuff, sometimes, folks feel a separation, and I hope that people don't feel a separation because, I'm telling you, I am right there with you.

Back about a little over a year ago, I was preparing for a presentation I was going to do on the Shadow for a networking group and then promoting it. It had nothing to do with politics specifically. It was how Shadow issues can affect your business and your marketing and how it can get in the way or how you can work with it, but I figured, "Okay, well, let me just, you know, let me just kind of promote this and get people come into this networking thing," so I posted in the group and said, "Hey, show up Thursday. You'll find out what Donald Trump and I have in common," and, of course, that's going to get people's attention, which right away tells you one thing that Trump and I have in common.

This realization or this awareness that anytime I try to make a dividing line between myself and someone else or between what I perceive my group to be and what I perceive another group to be, anytime I try to make that dividing line because my buttons are being pushed or because I don't like something or because I'm upset with something, I have to stop and slow down and remember that, spiritually speaking, if we are all one and if we are all here in this incarnation to bring whatever to the table that we bring to the table, and some of us are here as catalysts and some of us are here as healers and whatever our parts might be, that means that, and this is the real sort of bummer thing about walking a spiritual path, we don't get to cop out anymore.

We don't get to make that excuse anymore of just name-calling. It's still fun, and I do it from time to time, but I don't genuinely get to say that that's all there is to it because there's a part of us that, once you know better ... I don't want to say, "Know better." Once you know fuller, once you know a bigger picture of things, you don't get to go back and just pigeon hole things again.

I'm following these events that are happening through the primary and through the campaign and since the fall and, all along the way, I got to say to myself, "Okay, well, what is it that's being triggered in me?" number one.

Number two, "What is this that's being triggered saying about what I have not resolved?" because that's really what the Shadow is about, but, also, numbers three, four, five and into infinity, "What is it that other powers that be in or society recognize about how to trigger people and how to get reactions out of people, and am I playing into that, or am I thinking critically? Or am I paying attention to my intuition, or am I trying to be popular on Facebook? Or am I going with my heart and going with compassion, or am I looking for the easy fix of just slapping a label on somebody and, in doing so, denying that there is a piece of that me that I need to look at?"

I hope that kind of answered the question. I feel like I sort of went off a little bit. I do that sometimes; another thing Trump and I have in common.

**Hillary Raimo:** Thank you for that insight. It is really difficult watching the bashing that's taking place. It's like a never-ending waterfall of bashing energy, and it's name-calling and it's nasty and it's mean.

It's the same energy that many are calling Trump out on. Many are not even aware that they are participating in the same energy. If you know what energy is and you put yourself out there as a healer or somebody who talks about healing aspects, I think you have a responsibility to not do that. Angry hate energy, whether attached to Trump or Hillary, is still hate energy and you are spreading it by hating either way. Anger is an elemental catalyst for change.

Are most people just taking a side to take a side? I mean, aren't we done taking sides? Haven't we've ascended and learned what duality is, don't we know how to transcend it yet? We're all doing great, right, but then Trump comes along and tests us and perhaps we have some more learning to do. Otherwise why are we here?

Anytime somebody comes into our sphere of influence and triggers an emotional response that is deemed negative our unresolved stuff is triggered. Hello? This is a healing moment for you.

I think people are tired of listening to the rants, and the ones that are still ranting really just keep showing more clarity into the things that they have to deal with and face, unresolved victimization, unresolved traumas, unresolved wounds that's just are festering still, and Trump comes along to turn us into ourselves so that we can face this. A gateway into our micro-dimensions.

As we heal the micro, we heal the macro, and so if we really want to resist you have to ask yourself, "What are you really resisting? Are you resisting your own growth? Are you resisting a chance to look at your own healing process?

I mean, let's face it. He's our president, whether we like him or not. There comes a time when you've been going on and on for months about how bad his hair is and what a jerk he is and what a ... the list goes on and on, but are we really looking at this from a more evolved, higher awareness to heal and move on?

The election is over. We had the hundred days. They've come and gone. We've seen a lot of stuff happen, a lot of things to trigger anger, a lot of things to trigger a lot of things, and I just ... I worry about the environment and the health of our water. Big mirrors of the health of many things.

We should have been concerned when Obama when president. We should have been concerned when the Bushes were in offices, when the Clintons were in office, and the list goes on and on. Now, all of a sudden, Trump is here and he brings out so much for people.

You have this really great list in your article, and I'd like to go through this bit by bit to break this down for people. You mentioned a list of things that we need to kind of pay attention to, some bullet points. The first one says, "Get real with yourself. The emergence of the Shadow demands honesty."

Talk to us about that.

**Angela Kaufman:** Sure. Sure. This is sort of where, when you mentioned being triggered, this is where we need to get real, and it's really hard to do this. Even understanding, let me, again, be very transparent, even understanding this, it is still not pleasant.

There's a part of me that wants to hit fast forward till the end where we can roll credits and I can just sit back and eat peanut butter, because I do not want to be walking through this. It's really hard, but it means I have to admit to myself that the things that rile me about whether it's this person, this administration, other people, other things in the world that I do not think are fair, how am I a participant in this?

I know, when people are listening, when people hear this, the initial reaction, I'm following you, because the initial reaction could be, "I'm not a part of that. I don't do that. How could you say that?" I hear you, but just sit with me on this because I promise there's a connection here, because that's also what my reaction would be. We want to keep ourselves innocent. We want to make sure our hands are clean.

None of us have clean hands, and we've got to be real. Just like you said, why aren't we looking back at other administrations? This concept that, in a four-year period of time, all consequences of actions are wrapped up and there's a clean slate when the next person steps in is ludicrous, the fact that I can read Upton Sinclair's *The Jungle* that was written in 1906 and read it in 2016 and say, "Damn, nothing's changed here, and I am a part of this," I got to look at that.

I got to look at that. I may not like, I may not be an advocate for all of these things, but I am a part of this. The fact that, to give a real-life example, we all have our biases. We all have our prejudices, our knee-jerk reactions.

Back a couple of months ago when, you probably remember, we had like an entire Northeast season in like two days. We had this ridiculous snowstorm. We're all shoveling out the neighborhood, and there's this car that gets stuck. They declared a state of emergency. This car gets stuck on my little one-way street, middle of the road. The guy leaves it to go get a shovel, and my neighbor says, "Oh, this, this guy, whoever he is, he took my shovel off my porch and started digging out, and then he broke it and then he left."

Here I am digging out the neighborhood and just thinking, and I start thinking, "Well, who is this guy anyway? He's not from my neighborhood why is he in my neighborhood," and, "The nerve of him getting his ... You know, he comes out in the snow emergency. His car gets broken down. He takes my neighbor's shovel. He breaks it, and he's not even from my neighborhood," and I actually have to stop myself and say, "Wait a minute. What does this sound like?" because I got to be honest right now and say, "Here is my xenophobia. You're not from my neighborhood. What are you doing here?" Like here is my mistrust.

Maybe I'm not going out and saying, "Build a wall, and I don't want people from certain countries here," but here I am in my own damn neighborhood wondering why this car is stuck and who this person is and what business he has being there?"

I got to be honest about that reaction. If I'm honest about that reaction, then when I see somebody else jumping up and down and saying, "I don't want this person or that person here," I might not agree with them, but I understand the fear they're coming in with or I understand some aspects of the feeling they're coming in with.

In that moment, shoveling out, and I'm even taking it to that place, but I know who this guy voted for. Like it's going crazy in my head, and I got to be honest about that because, like you said, if we're talking about resistance, if we're talking about revolution, if we're talking about surviving as a civilization period, the dividing lines have to go, but they're not going to go unless I realized that there ... number one, there is not that big of a difference between myself as a human being and any other human being no matter what I want to say to protect myself or to

300

try to build up some kind of reputation.

Number two, even looking at the political sphere, I got to realize, when we really break it down, by the time somebody gets to the point that they have passed the primary, these days, there isn't that big of a difference between the two of them anyway.

That's a very uncomfortable truth because I really want to believe that there truly was some other alternative that would have made some kind of significant difference that would have ... but it's not going to come from the top. It's going to come from the bottom, but it's not going to come from the bottom if we're still fooling ourselves into believing that somehow, we don't participate in oppression, okay, because the other day when I go to Wal-Mart, I know that I'm buying stuff that's made by slaves, and I'm not proud of that, and I don't like that.

I don't consider myself pro-slavery, but out of laziness and inconvenienced and being cheap, I made that choice, and I have to live with that, and, someday, that will build up into my karma or, perhaps, it already has and that's part of what's going on, but I have to be honest with myself because, if I keep sticking my head in the sand and saying, "It's somebody else's fault and I'm just going to react to that person," we are not going to change anything.

Does that make sense?

**Hillary Raimo:** Yes, thank you. Some would say the danger lies not in the existence of the Shadow, but in excessive attempts to deny or suppress it. When we become out of touch with our Shadow side, we can't relate to other people about it.

I find that very powerful. Relating breeds compassion.

**Angela Kaufman:** I love that you make me flash back to when the real world was on TV and they said, "When people stop being nice and start being real." Absolutely.

What I'm learning, and I say "learning" because I want to be conscious of my own Shadow issue, I don't want to paint myself as if I've done all this and I'm just waiting on the mountaintop for everyone else to catch up, that's my own Shadow stuff, but what I'm continuously learning is that it really does begin with us because if I can handle, if I can sit with, if I can allow my own emotions, then I can allow somebody else.

If I can feel okay about the times when I need to cry, I can let somebody else cry instead of running and grabbing a tissue, which is sort of like a body language way of saying, "Stop doing that. It's sloppy. I don't want to see it." If I can be okay with the fact that I get angry, I can hear somebody else in their anger.

You're absolutely right because this, when we talk about the duality and how we believe that we can transcend duality, and we can, but we're also still human, so we have that sort of ego thing that sucks us back into it, but part of that duality is like we kind of split off. It's like things are good and bad, it's black and white, and the reality is that it's more of a paradox, but we've lost our tolerance for paradox.

Part of this, I look at how, for better or worse or indifferent, media has changed obviously and there's something to ... like when we ... We invest a lot in reading. There's a richness that can be allowed in a book that cannot ... Yeah, I'll say cannot. It cannot exist in television. It just can't. You have a half hour for a sitcom. Everything's got to be tied up and nice and neat and tidy by the time we cut to commercial. It doesn't allow for that same depth of paradox.

We go to social media. It really doesn't allow for that, and so we've got to really recognize as people, as participants in this current reality how are we going to keep in touch with that paradox so that we don't become one-dimensional, so that we don't allow ourselves to slip further into this mindset that is, like you said, everything has to be perfect and flawless and spotless.

We're not comfortable being exposed. We're not comfortable talking about how we're really feeling. There's like the Facebook version of reality and the real version of reality. For many of us, there's a very wide divide between the two, and then it becomes a shock to find out that somebody has stuff going on that is not being broadcast. It's like we don't know what to do with that.

We've got to get real about our own emotions because, if I can allow my emotions to be acceptable, including my resentment, indignation, outrage, anger, whatever, then I can sit and listen to somebody who doesn't ... who I don't agree with and doesn't agree with me, but they've got some outrage, and they're feeling betrayed, and they're feeling victimized, and they're feeling overlooked, and they're feeling like they're in competition to have their needs met, and I can at least hear them.

Even if I don't agree with them, I can at least hear them and not feel ... I think, sometimes, we feel threatened. Like emotions are going to be like a flu and I'm going to catch it from somebody. There is some work we have to do in order to kind of keep our own baseline and not get absorbed into other people's emotional realities, but it's work we would do anyway because in our relationships, in our families, I mean we would need to do this work anyway.

Right, this whole thing that's come up politically, it's kind of like pulling the curtain open on a bunch of stuff we thought we had buried. Some folks, like you said, we're all so burnt out of the fighting and the name-calling, and I totally get it, but it's worth doing this work and doing it with some sincerity because, ultimately, these are the same lessons.

I mean, we could think of this administration as ... If we want to go really far down the rabbit hole, we can think of this as a collective manifestation of somebody who's going to come into our world in a way that is hard to ignore and call us all to attention so that we don't have to keep bypassing the same lessons or missing the same opportunities and keeping things buried so that, 110 years from now, somebody doesn't read a book that was written in 2017 and say, "Oh, wow, nothing's changed." You know what I mean?

**Hillary Raimo:** (*giggle*) I had to laugh at that because it's true.

**Angela Kaufman:** That's okay. Humor is good. Humor helps with the Shadow.

**Hillary Raimo:** One of the things Angela and I were discussing prior to the show was the side-taking element to this and how it is the divisional process. It's what's dividing people into cliques and clichés of opinion and perspective, making people not speak to each other, having all kinds of shenanigans going on in social media, whether you block people or unfollow people or others who play these kinds of bait and trap games. People are making these kinds of decisions every day, which in a digital age has consequences. How are you being profiled through your anger?

If you have these kinds of actions happening to you, it can make you feel ashamed or make you shut your voice down because, "Oh, my God, I spoke up and expressed my anger, and, Sally, unfriended me and, now, she won't speak to me, and she is not coming to the picnic on Saturday," and so on and so forth, right?

These are very real reactions. Families are being divided. Relationships are being divided. I mean it's a divisional process. It's like if you take the extreme left or right, who says I have to go left or right? Why can't I just go straight or go backward, or some other direction?

I think we're really lifting the veil on the nuances within the healing process for the micro and the macro, collective, individual energetic scales. We're really taking a look at the fine-tuning triggers that we have to, and Trump has provided this mirror for us.

It could be so many things, and there's no shame and judgment in that. It's just an opportunity for us to heal and to say, "What do I still need to go back and take a look at? What still needs to be healed? What work do I still have to do on myself?" and, hallelujah, you found it. Now, you've done it. You've taken a look. You feel it, and how much better is your life because of it, and then you can take action on the things that you feel passionate about without being an emotional wreck.

In fact, number two of your bullet list says, "Create space and time for your emotions," and I'm going to actually read this. "If we don't deal with our emotions on an individual basis, whether we feel fear for our futures, concern for the environment or anger at injustices, we will be not only immobilized by our emotions, but run the risk of projecting our baggage onto others. Feel your feelings honestly. Sit with them. Acknowledge them."

Talk to us about why that's so important?

**Angela Kaufman:** Yes. Absolutely. Here in America, we love the idea of freedom. If we really ever want to be free, the ability to work with our own emotions is where that freedom is going to come from because if I have unresolved emotions, and this is something that I'm still, again, still processing, still aware of, it still comes up, it's not like we ... It's not like we work with the emotions and then we're done with them forever, unless you magically find a way to become a robot, and, even then, the way we're progressing with technology, pretty soon, they'll probably have feelings, too.

It's really important because what it is that, like you said, what it is that we're reaction to is a hot button issue that triggers the emotions within ourselves. If I don't have that under control or ... I don't want to say control as if ... We think of control as like, "Oh, I'm going to put the feeling in a corner and, that way, it won't, it won't affect me." That's not what I mean by control.

If we don't make some space to sort out my emotions from whatever else, here's what's going to happen. I'm going to turn on the news and I'm going to hear about whatever the latest tragedy is, and I'm going to be like up one side to myself and down another, and anxiety going and anger and fear and hatred and all of these different feelings that are caught up in me, and I'm going to lose sight of what is really my emotion? What is the button that's being pushed by somebody else and their agenda? I don't even mean politically. I mean, when we look at the power structure and who are the big messengers, who are the big puppeteers in this world right now?

We've got these wounds that we have through life, and this is what gets played on. Okay? When I say, 'Played on," I mean, if I'm trying to sell you Pepsi, you can rest assured I've got my marketing folks doing research, and they're researching what color are you going to react to, what fonts are you going to react to, what is the magic word that will make you crave that Pepsi, and what does it all come down to? Emotions.

On a day to day basis, if I'm not working with what are my

emotional things that I bring to the table originally, there's going to be this whole toxic mix of what other people are projecting onto me, what they're not projecting onto me, but I'm assigning to myself because I haven't dealt with my stuff.

It's really going to create this huge fog that I'm not going to be able to see my way through, except that I'm going to know in the back of my head that it's going to feel really good to yell and shout and call names and, like you said, unfriend everybody on Facebook, but where has that gotten me?

Because I'm going to go on to a different situation with a different group of people, in a matter of time, there will be a different set of leaders in this country, but all that stuff will be the same because I didn't learn a different way to recognize it and work with it.

**Hillary Raimo:** Brilliantly said, thank you. Number three says, "Hold space for the emotional process of others. This means not having all the answers and not trying to. It means not sweeping the pain of others under the rug."

When people go through the dark night of the soul, it's so important for people not to judge themselves or others and run away from yourself, or another person, because that just makes it that much more of an atrocity, but then again maybe that is what you are meant to go through.

I mean, I've been in that situation myself. I've seen other people be in that situation. When you have this fall apart shed moment, it's a time to hold space for whatever that person needs and however that person needs it. There is no judgment and shame in this. You talking about this in your article and how it really is important to not try to figure it all out and offer solutions too quickly because that in a way dishonors the person's journey and their own process of finding their own answers because, ultimately, healing is not about someone else healing you. It's about you healing yourself by figuring out what makes you tick and how you're triggered by stuff. Other people help by being mirrors, if you have an emotional reaction to someone, the mirror belongs to you.

Once you make and own those connections for yourself, then that empowers you and makes you a more whole and integrated person. It's a celebration all across the board. Each time a person goes down, it is our duty to be love, light of ... whatever we need to be for that person. It is not a time to slam the door in their face. It is not a time to label them with some kind of black sheep type label. It's a time for us to come together and be there for that person and hold them. You can change a person's life for the better this way, and in return it changes your own.

When someone is so stuck on the Trump issue that is has consumed their life, they can't stop complaining about it, ranting, going on emotionally just overflowing, how do we deal with that?

**Angela Kaufman:** This has been an issue for a while. There's a couple of things that come to mind about this. One thing I would throw out there, and, oh, my gosh, I wish I could remember which one of his books it was, but one of Michael Moore's books, he actually has a chapter, and it's something to the effect of "things we need to learn from your conservative brother-in-law," and he uses that as kind of a funny example, but his ... and this was years ago that he wrote this.

If you ever watch Michael Moore in *TrumpLand,* he sort of brings this up again. His point is that we really need to start building the bridge rather than pushing each other aside. One of the things he talks about in this chapter is, "We need to recognize the strengths coming from the people who differ from us ideologically."

He's kind of funny about it in his way, and he makes the example like, "Look, your conservative brother-in-law, he's probably up at 5:00 in the morning, and he exercises every day, and he never loses his keys." He's sort of generalizing in sort of a humorous way, but he's saying, "We need to, we need to listen and we need to appreciate. He brings something to the table. Now, we might not agree on what it is he's bringing to the table, but he brings something legitimate to the table."

Number one, this goes back to the self-honesty. I would say, please, please, please, we have plenty of time to fight later. Can we first look for some kind of common ground?

If you happen to see Michael Moore in *TrumpLand*, he goes into that where he talks about it... It's great. He's actually talking to a very conservative group of folks and trying to just create more bridges in terms of how we think about like ... and he says things like, "Well, what do we all want? We, we want access to healthcare. Um, we want to feel safe. Um, we want our kids to be educated. Uh, we want opportunities. Okay, we can agree on this stuff."

It sounds trivial, and he's got his way of sort of humorizing it, but it's serious. If I'm going to push somebody into a box and label them a monster or a fascist or a racist or a snowflake or a bleeding-heart Liberal or whatever, I've just taken their humanity away, and I missed an opportunity to see how we connect and where we connect, and if we don't have that connection, we're not going to move forward.

Number one goes back to how can we connect? Where is the common ground? How can I see myself in them? I know this is really hard because, remember, we're being exposed to constant, constant onslaught of information in media that has somewhat of a vested interest in captivating our attention at any cost, even at the cost of our own relationships.

For me, sometimes, keeping that in mind is the only thing that allows me to pause long enough to really hear and sit with when I want to react, and sometimes I mess up and I react anyway, so be patient with yourself. Be patient with the process.

Understand that when we don't agree on things, the sky is not going to fall down. There is nothing that's going to happen in that moment in probably 99.9% of situations. There is nothing that's going to happen in that moment because somebody has a different idea, and if we can connect with their feelings, their pain, if we can ask questions and listen instead of assuming.

One of the things that has really been a huge pet peeve of mine is the narrative going around that things are the way they are because poor, uneducated working class, so here we go again blaming the working class just like in 1906. Here we go again.

It's this narrative that comes about that we want to subscribe to, and there's narratives on all different aspects of the spectrum here, and it's the cliff notes, and it's ... God, it's not even the *Reader's Digest* version. It's the Twitter version of reality, and it breaks down to this real easy script that says, "If somebody did this, this or this, then they are this, this or that type of person."

My God, it's just so important. Please, can we ask questions? Can we try to hear? Even if we don't agree, can we try to hear why is it that somebody is feeling what they're feeling, believing what they're ... Can we just give them a space to speak because if we don't ... and there's a great fellow, I forget his real name, but his character name is Jonathan Pie. You can look up YouTube, Jonathan Pie, The Day After the Election." It is a rant, but that's sort of his style. He does this fake between the news, pretending he's talking to his producer and he goes on this political rant, but he makes this excellent point. We have portions of our society who have not felt heard.

When you have somebody, who does not feel heard, and not only people who voted for Trump, but also people in other segments of society who do not feel heard, when you have somebody who does not feel heard, what's going to happen is, someday, somebody's going to come along who's going to either listen or do a really good job pretending that they're listening and, either way, whether it's genuine or not, they're going to have that person's heart.

If we're feeling betrayed, if we're feeling like we've lost our way or lost our country or lost our whatever, maybe we need to start listening to get that heart back before we get to the point where we have that feeling that somebody else ... It actually reminds me ... Taking it out of the political realm, it reminds me of having a good friend who is in a relationship that maybe I feel is abusive or whatever, and I'm going to say to that person, "Yeah, but he's no good and he does this, and he hits you and he does that," and maybe this friend of mine is going to be like, "Yeah, but I can't picture life without this person."

What am I going to say? Am I going to write that person off and call her names ... or him ... call them names and downgrade them when they're already feeling downgraded, because the bottom line is, at the end of the day, that person has to make their own choices? One of the big ironies here is that there's a lot of silencing going on, and when we talk about being afraid of fascism and then we go about doing all of these things to silence each other, we got to take a look at that.

**Hillary Raimo:** You did a great job of covering number four, which is "don't assume," and you asked a good question in this paragraph. You say, "What if we took the time to really hear what they are concerned about before jumping to judgment?"

I'm going to give you a perfect example of this. In several of my online platforms, I have asked questions that are very neutral, very fact oriented, but not name-calling or side-taking. In those discussions, always, what happens is somebody will come in and make assumptions and assume I'm supporting Trump because I'm not bashing him. This is a perfect example.

If these people had taken the time to intelligently interact, not be so reactive emotionally, but yet be heard in their emotions clearly, but allow me to be heard in my emotions and my ... the way I'm putting information out and asking people to reflect, I think that's one of the big things is when we assume we just make asses out of each other, and we go in no direction, and we get nothing accomplished.

Then we move on to point five of your list here where you say, "Keep your friends close and give your enemies a new job title." Talk to us about that. How do we reconcile those who are our friends and those who are not our friends?

**Angela Kaufman:** Yeah, this is going back to the whole idea of the Shadow. Part of what I work with in coaching and has been a belief of mine for a while, and, again, I'm not saying I get this perfectly because I certainly don't, but that, similar to what you brought up earlier, when somebody comes in and they trigger these Shadow reactions when people talk about, even taking it out of politics for a moment, in relationships, we talk about, "Oh, the ex, they were horrible and they did this and this and this."

Okay, no, that was a really great teacher for you. That's a hard concept, again, when we've been increasingly taught to be one-dimensional and ignore paradox. It's a hard concept to understand that we're not talking about blaming a victim. We're talking about looking at the picture as there are no enemies. There are no bad guys. Nobody gets to be the hero here. It doesn't work that way. We want to sort of start to remake this whole script, and I hope that we can start to challenge the idea, like you said, with the assumptions, that if you say this, it means you're that.

Very fortunately, hey, the spirit works in really amazing ways. As I'm going through all of this personally and as I'm, personally, in my own life, being very, very much towards the left in many things, doesn't my partner of almost 10 years come home on election day and tell me he voted and tell me who he voted for, and don't I feel like my world just collapsed?

I'm very fortunate. I'm actually very grateful that this happened, that he voted for Trump and that he told me this because it forced me, as somebody who loves him and knows him to be a good and honorable and caring and loving and spiritual person, it forced me to set aside this script that, otherwise, I might be feeding into and say, "Wait a minute. That can't be right," because if I'm being told that people who voted for Trump are racist, misogynistic this and that, poor working class whatever, and yet I'm also looking around and saying, "Well, wait a minute. Here's my friend. Here's my family. Here is my lover. Well, something, something must be off here, and I'm not going to doubt my reality. I'm going to doubt the reality of somebody who's making a lot of money off of peddling this message that I need to hate people because they voted a certain way."

It's been tough. Don't get me wrong. It's been interesting here at our house, but it's a huge blessing because it's forced me to say, "Well, maybe I've been missing something and maybe I need to listen, because here's this person that I know to be intelligent and that I know to be, you know, a caring, loving person and that I know that when we go to the Indian grocery store and he stands and talks to people and says, 'You know, how do you say thank you,' and then he goes and says, 'Oh, shukriya,' and I know that he's worked in a profession his entire life that is female dominated, and he has no problem with women in authority because he's ... that's been his career."

It's forced me to say, "Well, wait a minute. There's something else going on here that I'm missing, that is not being brought up by some of these other sorts of default mainstream sources."

Don't get me wrong. It's challenging sometimes, but I also have a deeper appreciation. It's given me the opportunity to say, "Well, wait a minute. Maybe I need to not be calling names and bashing and whatever because then I'm saying that to him."

Does that make sense?

**Hillary Raimo:** Absolutely. In your article you wrote, "Look for common goals because most of us really want the same thing." You go on to say, "We just differ in our beliefs."

You continue, "Not only are Donald Trump and Hillary Clinton embodiments of our archetypal struggles which deeply trigger us all in positive or negative ways, but the entire election cycle spoke to our primal struggles as human beings, no wonder so many of us feel exhausted whether satisfied with the results or not. Trump's knack for speaking in ways which some find offensive and others liberating made him the spokesperson for the American Shadow. He did not create the tensions prevalent in our country, although his ability to instigate deep emotional reaction on both sides, another Shadow specialty, has forced our collective wounds out into the open. Like it or not, we can now let the healing begin."

How do we let the healing begin when he continues to do these things that continue to instigate? When we have a catalyst or a nemesis that is creating the triggers we need for the healing process, but just keeps triggering, where do we cross the line from the micro to the macro? Does it all matter?

In other words, when we're deep in our own healing process and looking at the mirror and going into our stuff and doing our work, he's still taking regulations off the environment, letting the oil companies go crazy and have their way, so where do we really make a difference in this?

Can you speak to the process of healing within each individual cell of the community to the effect of the larger collective? How is it going to make a difference?

**Angela Kaufman:** Yes. In fact, that's a question I was speaking about with someone earlier today. That's a very important question. Yes, I do want to make the distinction that I don't believe that it's our job to solely do internal work and say, "Well, I'm just going to, you know, sit behind my beaded curtain and, and look at myself in the mirror and love and light y'all, but, you know, I'm done with this political nonsense."

I don't feel like that's necessarily what, where the path ends, but it happens on a couple of levels, and there's a third part of it that I actually did not mention in this article specifically, but I'll bring it up as we're talking about it.

On the one level, I can only, just like in any relationship, whether it's family, partnership or workplace, whatever, I can only bring to the table what I straightened out for myself, or else I'm bringing my mess to the table with me.

Hey, if we want to have an America that's great, that's fine. Okay, so how am I going to act on an individual basis? Going back to this fellow whose car got stuck in the snow in my street, the fact that all the neighbors came out and were shoveling together, I mean, that's greatness. That's a choice to not get caught up in, "Oh, well, you know, and he calls like a middle-aged white guy, maybe he voted Trump. Screw him. He's on his own. He can shove out his own car." You know what I mean?

Getting past that stuff on the individual level, building community on the individual level or on the micro level, if the goal is greatness, if the goal is healing, if the goal is a sense of restoration and, for many of us, the goal is let's not just go backwards in the sense of greatness, let's go forward and figure out the pieces that we dropped off on the way, in other words, people in this country who have not yet had their Golden Age, we're going to work that out on the micro first.

This topic reminds me. There's a fascinating woman. She's a Haitian historian, and she talks about spirituality and culture and politics. Her name is Bayyinah Bello. She does this lecture on a YouTube video, and she talks about the same concept, although she talks about it much more eloquently than I can.

There's a concept actually in their spirituality where they talk about different forms of ... kind of like different forms of deity, and there's the one deity that will come in ... I'm calling it deity, and that's actually not the correct word. I apologize. It's sort of like what in other cultures we might call a demigod or like a spiritual influence, like a spirit that moves through a person who is here physically. There's two different names for them, and I'm forgetting both names, but the one is sort of like the trigger, the catalyst, and the other is the one who carries it out.

She speaks about this in terms of the Haitian Revolution and significant political figures in that process, but then she says this really amazing thing. She says, "Before, you know, if I'm feeling like there's something wrong with Duvalier," and she's talking about the leader at one point who was really not that nice of a guy she says, "Before I go out in the streets and start yelling about what's wrong with Duvalier, I got to look at what's wrong with Bayyinah," meaning, "I've got to look at what's wrong with me.

She's talking about the same concept, that we've got to clear it up in ourselves so that we can even go out into the world, like you said earlier, with the energy that we want to bring to it because, right, if we're ... if I'm mad at somebody for doing what I perceive as being hateful and it kicks up my hate and I'm fighting their hate with my hate, I'm just bringing more hate to the table, so we do have to work on it on the micro.

Another aspect I would say of working on it on a micro means that we need to expose ourselves to greater diversity, and I also mean diversity of ideas. I find it quite interesting that there are some folks who will be quick to champion the rights of all kinds of diverse people, and I'm not criticizing that, that's wonderful, but why can we not include in that diversity of ideologies? Why are we saying, "Okay, y'all Trump supporters, go off on an island? We'll build a wall around you and then we can have, you know, America for everybody else that, you know, who's been oppressed?"

Why are we turning around and oppressing people? You know what I mean? We've got to work it out individually even for that exposure because the exposure in and of itself does a great deal of healing.

**Hillary Raimo:** We have about a minute left in the show, and I wanted to end with your last piece, which is, "Honor the Shadow." If you could sum that up for me in 30 seconds?

**Angela Kaufman:** Oh, boy, in 30 seconds? The more you can do to acknowledge it and even be playful with, because when we take ourselves way too seriously, we're going to push that Shadow down, creativity is great for honoring and letting the Shadow in because we can do things in creativity that don't have to become like our "reality" part of ourselves.

**Hillary Raimo:** Thank you. Be sure to visit Angela's website intuitiveangela.com. Angela, thank you so much for being here.

**Angela Kaufman:** Oh, thank you. It was my pleasure.

**-19-**

# LYNN ANDREWS
# FINDING THE SACRED IN THE ORDINARY

*I spent 8 years working with Lynn. I entered her four-year mystery school shortly after giving birth to my first son. I found my way to her work the way all things do born of fate. I had things to heal in my life and I knew it. I also knew she could help, and I was right. I had to learn to stand in my own power, and to better understand the shamanic links to my own genetic makeup as a white woman. Lynn was able to help me better understand myself by learning about who my ancestors were. Through her I found a way into myself to access the genetic material I needed in order to do so. My time with her was magical, challenging and made me a better person. My shamanic training with Lynn changed the course of my life and the memories I have of our time in Joshua Tree, California and Ghost Ranch, New Mexico fills many journals. I was a good student all those years.*

*Leaving the nest was hard, but today I am thankful for it all.*

RECORDED AUGUST 7, 2008

**Hillary Raimo:** Lynn Andrews, author of 21 books, will be talking about her amazing adventures into the world of spirit this next hour. She is a New York Times bestselling author, and international speaker, spiritual leader, teacher and healer. Lynn is founder of the Lynn Andrews Center of Sacred Arts & Training (LACSAT), of which I am a graduate of myself.

Welcome Lynn.

**Lynn Andrews:** Hi Hillary, how are you? It's so good to talk to you.

**Hillary Raimo:** I am well, thank you Lynn. Would you mind starting with a prayer for all of us?

**Lynn Andrews:** I certainly will. If everybody would take a deep breath and close their eyes. Hopefully you're not driving. Great Spirit, Mother Earth, Powers of the Four Directions, our ancestors, the great and exquisite beings of light, who protect us and inspire us at this time, thank you for your inspiration and thank you for being with us on this wonderful show. In spirit, Namaste.

313

**Hillary Raimo:**  Thank you, Lynn. You're starting a writing school, and you have all kinds of fabulous things going on. Would you like to share with us about what you are doing now?

**Lynn Andrews:**  Absolutely. I began the course in my mind when I wrote Writing Spirit for Penguin Tarcher in New York. *Writing Spirit: Finding Your Creative Soul* was a book that came out about a year ago. Off of that book, will be the writing school. Of course, it will include aspects of that, but also finding your creative soul, not just for the writer, but for the artist, for the musician, for the person in search of truth and enlightenment in their life, in this lifetime. The course is really all about that. It's a year long course, and it is going to be online for now. We'll see where it takes us from there. I'm very excited about it. It'll start the first of next year, sometime probably in the early part of the year.

**Hillary Raimo:**  Lynn, if people are interested in signing up for your writing course, where should they go for more information?

**Lynn Andrews:**  On my website, which is www Lynn Andrews dot com.

**Hillary Raimo:**  I'd like to talk about your first book, *Medicine Woman*, and the significant of the marriage basket. Now, as you know, I picked up a copy of *Medicine Woman* years and years ago, probably about 12 or 13 years ago, and it changed the course of my life, as it has for so many people. How was the story born?

**Lynn Andrews:**  Gosh. That was a long, long time ago. I published *Medicine Woman* in 1980, and it was the first of 19 books that I have written along the line of the same series, which really is about my own life. They're all autobiographical. It started out in Beverly Hills. I was married to someone in the film business. I have a daughter. I was leading a life that most people would think, "Gosh. What a fabulous life to live. Why would you want to do anything else?" And I found myself tremendously empty in a spiritual way. I had had from the time I was born, I always had the ability to see lights around people, to see their energy field, to see when they were lying to me, when they were in pain, when they were in a state of illness in some way. And I discovered very early on that people were frightened by that. And so, I denied whole aspects of myself for a very long time into my twenties, actually. It was at that point that I realized that you cannot pretend to be something that you are not.

You cannot live a lie. You have to take a very, very close and profound look at yourself and take a look at the magic and the mystery that you live in. To make a very long story short, Medicine Woman is about this journey. Some very extraordinary things happened to me. I went to an art gallery opening, and this was a couple of years into my difficulty of trying to find a teacher, all over the world. And most of the people that I found were men. And they were wonderful and still remain great friends of mine. But I wanted to learn from a woman because I'm a woman. And I went into this art gallery one night with a friend and I saw a picture of this beautiful native-American basket. And it was a sepia print and I thought how unlike Eaglets who the exhibit was for to have done this kind of a photograph.

And I went up to it and I put my hands on the frame and I'll never forget it. I had a blast of northern air in my face and through my hair. And I looked down at the legend underneath the photograph and it said McKinley circa 18 something or another. And I said to my friend, "Oh my God. I've got to buy this photograph. Look at this beautiful basket. I've never seen anything like it." And he said, "Oh, for God's sake. Come back on your own time. I want to get out of here, blah, blah, blah." So, I left and that night I started a series of dreams that were to last for years. And it was always a series of different dreams of an ancient elder native woman proffering to me in her hands this beautiful basket. And I went down there the next day only to find that they'd never had any such photograph.

This was something that was occurring in a very different level of consciousness, and a parallel reality. So, I started my research of the marriage basket and it turned out to be a very sacred object that symbolizes the marriage of the male and female aspects that we all have within ourselves. And I of course, didn't know that at the time and nobody had every heard of the marriage basket. There were wedding baskets but not a marriage basket. So, a whole series of events happened that led me to the north of Canada, led me to the keeper of the basket, a woman named Agnes Whistling Elk. And another mentor, a very extraordinary woman of high degree, Ruby Plenty Chiefs. And when I met them, I knew instantly that these were my teachers and that my life would change forever in a very wonderful and magnificent way.

And I went into a place of apprenticeship to them for many, many long years. And I became part of a circle called the Sisterhood of the Shields, which they are part of. And I learned extraordinary things about ancient wisdom and knowledge and things that have been hidden for thousands of years and held faithfully by the women of different tribes of different nations. And the knowledge was passed down to other women and daughters and apprentices throughout time. And I'm the first person that has ever been able to come out publicly about these teachings. And they're held in scrolls and clay pots, and it took a long time for me to decipher them along with the rest of the women in the sisterhood. And I've written all of these books about it, and it has been an extraordinary journey of growth and of healing.

And then, I don't know about, about ten or eleven years ago, or twelve years ago I started this school, which Hillary you were a part of. And it's a school about sacred arts and training. And it's a Mystery School. It's based on these sacred teachings and it's an experiential process. And I think you would agree with me Hillary, it's not like any other school you've ever been to.

**Hillary Raimo:** No, it's not. It's an extraordinary experience. How would you explain a mystery school to someone in the 21$^{st}$ century?

**Lynn Andrews:** A Mystery School has many definitions. A Mystery School usually implies that it is sacred and secret, and that also, you learn to choreograph the energies in the universe on one level or dimension or level of reality that you can experience in a very, very tangible way. Egypt had mystery schools. Greece had mystery schools. The ancient Mystery Schools they say, of Atlantis. But there are Mystery Schools that have been hidden and held private only because people did not want power to get into the wrong hands and also because it wasn't time for people to hear certain things. And they say that in Tibet ... I wrote a book in Tibet called *Windhorse Woman*. And when I was trekking there in Nepal they told me, the old monks told me that you would walk along the paths and all of a sudden if it was your time langars or sacred writings, perhaps encased in something, in a pot, in a wok in something, would just fall in front of you on the trail. And you would pick them up and decipher them and it would be a process of great truth for you.

And I think with the Sisterhood of the Shields, the gathering of women, the circle that I belong to. There are 44 of us and the wisdom has been given now at a time when we so desperately need to grow and to move onto higher levels of consciousness. And you know there's this whole discussion on the end of calendars, of 2012, of what is going to happen when the calendars end. The Mayan calendars, the Hopi calendars and so forth and so on and even in China. And I think Armageddon that is spoken of in the bible. I think Armageddon and 2012 means an Armageddon in the sense that we're going to die to what we were. That the consciousness that we are is growing right now. Even though we're kicking and screaming going into a higher level of consciousness. I think many, many people are afraid of that. They're afraid of that wording. They don't want to hear this. They just want to keep things copacetic. They don't want things to get out of control. Human beings have a terror of change in any way, shape or form.

And yet, I'm sure there isn't a person listening who doesn't feel stressed and moved into higher energy right now. There's just no question about it. We're being moved at a much faster pace and often times we can't even describe it. We just know that we're running from beginning of the day to the end. And we keep doing it. And we're pressed almost, to keep doing it. And inside of that kind of an intent is the process of all of us becoming more than we ever have been. And capable of more. Capable of a greater perception. The Mystery Schools, to answer your question, are about understanding the levels of consciousness that maybe we don't experience in everyday life, or maybe we do.

But it has to do with being able to understand the harmony of nature for instance. We consume a great deal as human beings. We don't necessarily give away or pray to the animals that have given us life. We don't understand the balance of spirit in the physical body. That doesn't mean that you have to be a religious person. This is nothing to do with religion. It has to do with putting another chip in your computer so that you see more, are more, are able to do more. In the Mystery Schools you get a new chip in that computer brain of yours so that you can function at a higher rate of intelligence. And quantum physics is finally figuring that out, I think.

**Hillary Raimo:** It's interesting Lynn because your description of us moving into a higher-paced energy and feeling that fear is kind of what happened to me when I decided to join your school. I went through a series of, I don't know ... It was a fear. It was, oh I have so many other things to do. I just can't do this right now. But yet, there was a part of me that knew I had no choice, that I had to move into it and face it and go through it. I'm sure that's common among people who step out into trying to join the school. Saying, Okay I want to do this. I'm called to it. They find you and then what happens is that this fear sets in. What do you say to them?

**Lynn Andrews:** Fear sets in is usually the fear of someone finding that they're growing and not knowing what to do about it. It scares them because if you're growing that implies change. And change again, is something so hard for people to accept, to experience. We're afraid of it. We're so afraid to be out of control particularly if you happen to be a child of abuse in any way, emotional or physical abuse. Because if you've been abused you want to control the environment around you so that you won't be hit, so that you can be invisible. And you want to grow. You know that you're not getting any food for your spirit in your life. And yet. you're afraid of that. You would come to my school, say as an abused person, let's just say ... I'm not saying that all people who come to my school are abused.

But if you are an abused person you tend as part of that experience in life to be abused, usually means that you are a *puer aeternus* which is a Latin term to be an eternal child. And the eternal child usually tries to sabotage their adult life. If you find yourself doing that, sabotaging relationships, money situations, abundance situations, Sabotaging your education. Typical *puer aeternus* thing to do is to go to college and get up to just before you graduate and quit, that sort of thing. So, you sabotage yourself. You don't allow yourself to get the good thing at the end, the treasure, because you really unconsciously don't feel that you are worthy of that treasure.

Many people are going through that today. We don't feel worthy of the growth that is happening within us. We don't feel worthy of it and therefore we want to deny it. When you join a Mystery School ... A Mystery School is about learning how to use the mind, learning how to use your emotions for health. To heal situations of disease so that you're no longer in a vibrational area where disease can even exist. You learn how to think. You learn that if you are a puer, an eternal child, someone who's been abused, you don't even know what your dream was as a child. You were so busy trying to protect yourself from any kind of harm. I always tell people that have been abused, one wonderful thing about that situation is that you know how to be a magician. You know how to be a shaman. You know how to survive.

You can walk into a room and you absolutely understand the energy there in all four corners of that room and you know if you're in danger or not. And you're very, very careful. You're probably more careful than you need to be. But on the other hand, it's a tremendous training. So, the upside, probably the only upside of being abused is that you have that ability. And then you need to learn how to heal the scars and the wounds that are in there, that perhaps most people, I don't think know how to heal that. I don't think they know as therapists how to bridge the world of spirit truly and the world of the physical. Because most people, when we're dealing with the physical world we tend to learn a service or a technique or a school of thinking like Freudian therapy, Jungian therapy etc. And they're all fabulous and they're wonderful.

But I think along the line of that you have to put the spirit in there too. And it's hard to learn about the spirit. You do have to do as much study as you would do for a mental process like Freudian therapy or Adlerian for instance. So, you need to take responsibility for your spiritual life as well. And that's what we try to do in the Mystery Schools. We're trying to give you that kind of wisdom through the process of experience. So, it isn't just getting a series of books, reading them and doing a book report or being tested. You're actually being tested through the process of experience. Creating aesthetics, creating something of beauty, using colors and parts of nature and all of the elements of nature to help you to grow.

And there's a process for that. It sounds vast and it is vast, but there is also a process that leads you from point A to point B, to C. So that when you finally graduate, after four years, and by the way, the school is a school without walls so you can be anywhere in the world and go to the school.

**Hillary Raimo:** And it works. It's amazing how the tasks and the support that you have set up in your school, makes it possible to be literally anywhere in the world and have it work. And you do write papers. It is very academic as well.

**Lynn Andrews:** Yes, you do. You write papers, but you know why? Everybody used to gripe about papers. "I don't want to write that. I can't write. I don't know how to write. I can't type. I can't blah, blah, blah." The point about writing these specific papers is you're writing about ethics that mirror the innermost part of yourself, so when you write those papers you're building your intent. And that intent is invaluable for you in the world. And it's been very hard to exercise the intent. Shamans call it a dream body. And the dream body is accessing your ability to dream. In other words, you can dream at night Hillary, but you maybe cannot direct those dreams. But you can learn to be awake in those dreams so that you can direct where you want to go. And all of a sudden, you learn that there is the vessel of the physical body. But that the dream body can move out of the physical body into other levels of consciousness, into other realms of existence.

And since time only exists in the relative world as Einstein said, in the relative world of physical existence and relativity you can move out of that world into a timeless chamber of dreams. And it's there that so much is available to us in terms of higher lessons of wisdom. This has nothing to do with religion. It has nothing to do with whether you're a Buddhist, a Catholic, a Hindu, a whatever. It doesn't make any difference. Because in the higher esoteric levels of any religion, and people will argue with me about this, but I do think it's true that wherever you go in higher aspects of religion you find that there is a description of the dream body, of moving into levels of consciousness that we don't always experience in the everyday world.

Although, I think without a doubt that everybody experiences miracles every day. We just don't ... We just think, "Oh that was a coincidence." You pick up the phone and you know who's on the other end. "Oh, that's a coincidence. I was thinking about you." But you were accessing a part of your dream body or your brain that you don't usually access. It's that kind of thing.

You know, I'll tell you a little story. I was in Australia writing *Crystal Woman*. and I was living with the aboriginals in the outback and when my journey there was finished I wanted to give them something really wonderful as a gift and I had a radio ... I had a little radio that worked on batteries and stuff. And these people had never had any touch with the western world or the so-called civilized world. And so, I brought them this radio. I sat it down in the sand and I waited for everybody to be quiet. Everybody was sitting in a circle and laughing. We were having a wonderful time. And I turned the knob and all of a sudden Beethoven 5TH filled the place with music. And there was such a shock and such an excitement over this. They were so thrilled and often I have though that's just like the Mystery School. That's what it does. You're a radio. You're this incredible receptor. All of your life you've receiving all of these images and all of this instruction and conditioning, but you never learned how maybe how to just turn a knob and go to a whole other level of existence that is all around you.

You can't see those radio waves but, boy they are there.

**Hillary Raimo:** Denying any one aspect of your life leaves an unmistakable imbalance and feeling of un-fulfillment in one's life. Understanding that we are complex beings with complex natures allows forgiveness to become part of our everyday experience as we allow repressed elements of our life a chance to be born and to manifest, we begin living a life of self-actualization. If you are just joining us now, I am speaking with Lynn Andrews tonight and we're having a wonderful discussion on her adventures with the Sisterhood of the Shields. Lynn you were talking about an experience that you had with a radio, if you were to turn the channels to see how you connect into different stations and hear different things, it reminds mw of how consciousness is very much like that as well.

**Lynn Andrews:** Well, consciousness is very much like this radio. That's why I gave it to them, because it gives you an idea about the extraordinary unlimited quality of space around you. The interesting thing is that after these people, particularly the women of high degree, after they experienced this for a couple of days and talked about it and played with it and the whole thing, they decided not to keep it.

But it was incredible because they didn't want to keep it. And the reason they didn't want to keep it is because they didn't want to become addicted to it. They didn't want it to replace the sacred dream time, which is such a central practice and part of an aspect of their lives. And this dream time is something that they go into in ceremony and privately within their lives, all of their lives. And it is truly one of the more extraordinary experiences that I've ever had with people. To see that they understood the problems of addiction and how deeply they could be addicted into it within moments. And in a way, it would have changed their lifestyle. Do you see what I'm saying?

**Hillary Raimo:** Yes. It sounds a lot like today with all the high-tech stuff that we have. You know, I have two kids, two small kids and the imagination exercises of using their mind to daydream and to do all of those kinds of things is really replaced with PlayStations and video games and all kinds of high-tech stuff. And as they get older we move into the computer and the internet and all kinds of things. And it seems sad in a sense to me anyway, that we forget to get back to our original natures of the cyclic, of the moon and the planet rhythms and the things like that. And the imagination is dreaming. I've always considered it dreaming.

I've always been an avid daydreamer, an avid night dreamer. And you know, I have to always step back and step back out to non-technical places for me to really restore and rejuvenate that place. And I've always had to do that myself. But it's very interesting how when you take away that high-tech stuff, even though it's good. It has a purpose. We need it on some levels, but it does seem to take something away from the imaginations that we use.

How does technology and addiction affect dreaming?

**Lynn Andrews:** Well it's interesting. I heard on the news tonight that in 20 years every single American will be fat. Because of the video games. Because none of the kids are going out to play anymore. They stay in and they sit. And they're perhaps becoming very facile mentally, but physically there's a lot to be ... A lot that we could do, that we're not doing in terms of physical activity. And then, of course the whole fast food thing that everybody's been talking about. I just find it extraordinary in a way as how our world has progressed and did you ask me what that has to do with dreaming? Or how that affects dreaming?

**Hillary Raimo:** Yes. I wanted to know your thoughts on where we're headed as a society in general because you've had these extraordinary experiences with the shamanic world. And how does somebody in today's world connect with the shamanic world? I mean, when people hear the word shaman they just kind of cringe sometimes and say, "Oh. I don't believe in that."

**Lynn Andrews:** It has something to do with a belief structure. Shamanism is, well ... I think when people hear that word they think of some kind of anthropology and it is an anthropological term that originated out of Mongolia. But I really and truly ... Shamanism is about the balance of nature, spirit, emotions, physical world. All of it. It's about the sacred wheel of life. And when people say I don't believe that

... People should help them define what it really means. It has nothing to do what you believe in. It has to do with how you experience life, and health. And when you are tied to a computer or computer games or video games the imagination is yes, given to you. On the other hand, it is an almost three-dimensional vision of extraordinary things that you might not imagine for yourself. So, in a way it exercises your imagination.

And yet, it all is done for you. If you can take that and move into a place of your own dreaming, it's wonderful. And a lot of people do that. But unfortunately, an awful lot of people don't. They don't want to exercise their ability to learn more. To change, that wonderful word again, which is, oh God, being used too much. But yet, there's a truth to it. We're afraid of that change. We're afraid of growth. And yet, we want to become more intelligent because maybe we can play those games better. It's an odd time. I think it's a bridging time. It's a time when you're going to realize what is good for us and what is not.

You know, there are no schools to teach you how to be parents, how to handle family. And that's tragic. We don't learn the things in school, it seems, that we really need to learn. About financial things, as Hillary you and I have spoken about so often. We don't realize that how we deal with our finances is very symbolic of how we deal with life and our spiritual understanding. What do you think about that?

**Hillary Raimo:** I think it's really relevant. In fact, I just wrote a book called *Money Matters for Mind, Body and Spirit* that just came out last month and it talks all about the spiritual aspects of life and how it relates to money. And it's interesting because when people talk to me about the subject of money it's very often stocks, savings. It's very, very practical. But when I move them to asking them about spirituality or their mental relationship or their emotional relationship with money they kind of look at me like, "Ahh?" But when they start to talk about their relationship with money, I move into my own shamanic stance and I can see where they're leaking energy or where there are perhaps openings into other areas, which always end up leading into wounding or past ... Or some kind of relationship that they've had with perhaps their parent, or their dreams. If they don't have a relationship with spirit they're missing an element of something in their relationships, so when you talk about money it's almost like you're not really talking about money.

You're moving into somebody's deeper layers of the onion, so to speak. You're going into core issues. And once those issues are looked at, or the relationships, the strands of that web, so to speak, are looked at with the relationship to money they very often realize why they sabotage themselves with money. It is similar to when you spoke about before with being abused as a child and being an eternal child. Often unable to finish anything such as saving the $20,000 that they need to put down on a house. Often times, money issues are tied in with other relationship issues. If they have a dysfunctional relationship with money then they oftentimes have a dysfunctional relationship with other things. And they don't see the connection until it's oftentimes pointed out to them or they make that realization themselves. That's what I've experienced with the healing of the money.

**Lynn Andrews:** Well the money thing is very interesting because money is abundance and as you are above so you are below. If you have abundance of spirit then you have an aspect of self that expands and reaches out to the world with love. And you don't throw away or give that love in little drips and drabs. You open up completely and you are loved. And instead of just taking in abundance just in little bits, or giving it out in little bits, open up just as you do with love. And it flows through you and around you and its part of your beauty, part of your understanding of what is sacred. We have some funny idea in this world, I think coming out of, perhaps the Judeo-Christian ethic, that somehow, we have to conquer the beast and that money-lenders should be thrown out of the temples by Jesus. That money is the root of all evil.

Well, it's the misunderstanding of money that is the root of all evil. It's the obsession with money. It's what you do with money that is the root of all evil, not money itself. Money is the trade beads of the 21st, wherever we are, century.

So, money is an interesting gauge for how you are dealing with certain aspects of your life. It's a very important thing. And we talked about that very early on Hillary and I wanted to tell your listeners that you are a wonderful apprentice because you are able to take what you learned, kind of kicking and screaming part of the way, and then all of a sudden you just kind of got ahold of things and you just went. And if this didn't work, you'd go in another direction. If that didn't work, you'd move somewhere else. And you made it work for you. And you understand things, but then you act upon them. Often times we understand things. You have a school like I have. I've worked with thousands of people and they've healed their health. They've changed their lives from poverty, miserable into abundance and happy relationships and teaching in the world about wisdom and all kinds of wonderful things.

And I've seen it over and over again. I know that you can subscribe to some kind of a process like this. And you can grow from it and you can become healed. And I think you're a fabulous example of that. You've gone out into the world and you're making your way. And you're making your statement. You found your voice. In my writing school that you mentioned earlier, it's about finding your voice. You know writing is an engine light. You can write articles. You can write books. You can do all kinds of things, but if you haven't found your voice you're a writer that sits there and the more you put out, the emptier you feel. And if that's what's happening then you've got to realize that you're not getting food for your own spirit.

That somewhere along the way, you have sabotaged, maybe not in a very evident way, but maybe just in a way that sabotages your own happiness, your own joy. And it's a very, very important thing I think, as creative people to realize it. It's one of the reasons I'm giving the writing spirit because I feel that other people find these wonderful ways of expressing themselves. And yet oftentimes, it may bring you money, it may bring you success but maybe not food for your spirit. And if it's not bringing you food for your spirit you need to take a look at what you're doing to yourself. What is it that is holding you back from your total and complete happiness?

**Hillary Raimo:** Thank you, Lynn. I remember a conversation I had with you a long time ago about how I just never thought it was possible to get over wounds. I just didn't understand how some day they would be gone, and you said to me something very powerful. You said, "Some day those wounds will be scars and you will be able to run your hand over them and visit them as great teachers and great lessons in your life."

And at that point I understood that intellectually but I didn't believe it. And I wasn't sure I would ever get to that point. And something that has changed considerably in my life over the past few years is the fact that I understand what that means now. And I feel like I am now ready to move out and pursue my purpose for being here. And you know, if you had asked me years ago, even when I was going through the school, because one of the reasons I really joined the school was because I had stuff to heal from in my own life, in my own past.

And I knew that I had to do that and so when I joined the school it wasn't about having a fabulous place to go twice a year when we get together.

It was a real, get down, roll your sleeves up, do the work, get this done, heal it and move on. And once I did that, once I owned my responsibility with my own life and addressed those issues and being able to know, being able to rub my hand across those scars and help others to do the same, I knew healing was possible. I do take those wounds and rub my hand across them as scars now. And I have experienced many often times some of the things that the people who I work with in my practice come to me and talk to me about things that they've experienced, it's easy for me to go back and relate and pull from my own experience. And that's something that you've always taught me. That it's about taking your life and taking your experiences and figuring out what it's supposed to be for you, because we're all here with our own purpose.

And we're all here with our own experiences and our own spirit shields and we're imprinting them. But what happened for me was an extraordinary experience of taking back my power from a lifetime of giving it away to people, to different situations and circumstances. And I realized once I was at that point, now it was like, "Now what?" I kind of sat there and said, "Okay. Well, now what?" I feel like I've called back all of these pieces to myself and what I realized was, I have a purpose here. We all have a purpose here so now I've dedicated my life in going out into the world and bringing this knowledge out on a global level by doing the radio show, and when I say I dedicate this show to inspiring the human spirit, it's true.

Because what really helped me heal in my own life and what helps my clients heal now in my practice is that inspiration. It is the stories that we share with each other. Are the moments of life that are our own, like our gold nugget so to speak, that we can say, "Well, this is how I experienced it." And you're never really telling ... You're not telling other people how to heal. You're not healing other people. And that's one of the reasons that called me to work with you, was there's tons of people out there who say, "Tell me what to heal. Tell me how to heal. Tell me what to do." And it's like they hand you all of who they are on a silver platter and say, "Take it." And one of things that you've always taught me was ... You handed that platter back to me because I tried to give it to you several times....

**Lynn Andrews:** I said "Un-uh. Here you go darling."

**Hillary Raimo:** You sure did. And I think that was one of the biggest, profound moments for me. It's not about other people healing me. It's about me going inside and doing the work myself. And yes, along the way sometimes you need help and that's okay. And I think asking for help along the way during certain times was also another lesson in of itself, was saying, "You know what. I need help right now and I can't get through this point by myself." And discerning between the two is a really big lesson and it was one of the bigger ones for me. And now as a graduate and going back to Ghost Ranch with the kindred spirits as a mentor I am thankful to be able to help facilitate this process for others working through your school.

And it's just amazing how we've all grown in our own way and how we've come back and how we share that with each other in a wonderful,

wonderful way. Joshua Tree is an extraordinary opportunity for people who are interested in the school but maybe perhaps not yet quite ready to make the plunge into some deeper work. It is a yearly event that you do once a year at Ghost Ranch in New Mexico that is open to the public. People can come in and intermingle with people that are in the school if they wish, but It is a very relaxed setting and a chance to get a glimpse into what the school may be like.

**Lynn Andrews:** Well it's interesting. I think mostly when you're talking about things like this, people will think about studying and books and being confined to a school room. One of the reasons that I did this as a school without walls, so that you can study from anywhere. But we do come together at Joshua Tree. And Joshua Tree actually has moved from California now to Ghost Ranch outside of Santa Fe, New Mexico. It's a wonderful beautiful place to be. And we go there and we spend four or five days and we all stay on that particular property. And we do a whole course of study, depending on what it is that I'm trying to teach you.

I may be working on time, timing. I might be working on the fears that you hold within your body and where they live. I may be working on various different things, projects. And we do things physically. We paint or we have a beautiful band that has been with me for, gosh, it's going to be 19 years. And they are there. Scarlet plays for Bobby Dylan, a wonderful absolutely incredible musician. And they add to this experience that we have, so that we dance. We have incredible meditations. We do a lot of guided visualization processes that take us into other places of experience. I don't know to explain this event.

I keep it very low key and yet we learn great things. You know, it was incredible this year. We had the ... We had a big bonfire. We collect juniper and sacred wood and we collect it in a very sacred way. And we build a bonfire late at night, on Saturday night. And we do special things there that are really fun and very sacred. And if you where there this year, these three lights came over the valley and just sat there above the whole gathering. It was the darnedest thing. Everybody saw them. They were like triangular lights. And people thought they were UFOs. We didn't know what they were. You know, they were must there, and they hovered.

**Hillary Raimo:** If you would like more information about what we have discussed here you can visit lynnandrews.com.

**Lynn Andrews:** Thank you so much Hillary. Many blessings. Much love to you and all of your listeners.

# -20-

## CHUN ROSENKRANZ
## THE POWER OF KINDNESS

*When I first heard Chun's story I knew right away I had to do a show with him. In the middle of world chaos there was this beautiful beacon of light. Offering hope and kindness. Restoring faith in humanity and rebuilding trust across all matters of life. I believe kindness is the antidote to all the worlds' problems. Chun is an earth angel awakened and here to help. I was his first ever radio interview.*

Recorded May 17, 2016

**Hillary Raimo:** Chun Rosenkranz is the founder and the catalyst behind the *I'll Be There Project*. It's a kindness challenge. Illbethere.org random acts of kindness with Chun Rosenkranz. Thank you so much for being here. Welcome.

**Chun Rosenkranz:** Thank you so much for having me, Hillary.

**Hillary Raimo:** You were incarcerated due to an addiction to prescription pills. You were having what you call a dark night of the soul. And then a friend of yours did this beautiful act of kindness that changed your life. Tell me more about that.

**Chun Rosenkranz:** Perfect. Yes, as you said, I was incarcerated and I was completely broken, I had just kind of lost hope and self-worth or belief that my life could be any different from the way that it was. And during this time, the seventh Harry Potter book came out, and I am the biggest Harry Potter fan. I had read all of the books. I had waited outside of the bookstore at midnight when the new book would be released. And so, the seventh book is released, *The Deathly Hallows*. And incarcerated folks cannot receive hardcover books while in jail. And so, I pretty much just surrendered to the fact that I wasn't going to be able to read this book, heartbroken.

And my friend Jeannie, who I had met working at a wine and cheese bar in Gainesville, Florida, and we ended up being roommates, she went to Kinkos and xeroxed all 759 pages of the *Harry Potter* book and sent them to me in 200-page installments. She included a color copy of the cover. I had no idea. I was just going about business as usual. Like I said, subscribed to this belief that I had no self-worth or value to the world.

And in comes the first package of the xeroxed Harry Potter book that she surprised me with. And it essentially changed my entire world around. Not only did I get the gift of *Harry Potter*, which is magic in itself. It's the hero's journey, it's everything. It pierces the darkness. But it also gave me a sense of, like, that I was loved. Here's someone who loves me when I can't love myself, and does this incredible, unconditionally loving act for me. It gave me the hope that I needed to get through that time.

**Hillary Raimo:**  This was your *Deathly Hallows*, so to speak. Talk to us about what happened when you started to share those pages of the *Harry Potter* book around with the other inmates.

**Chun Rosenkranz:**  What was magical was that, before Jeannie had sent this, other people had sent me books. You know, they'd sent me in softcover copies of the *Harry Potter* books. And I would pass these all around to the other people who were experiencing incarceration in my block. And we would all read, and we would play chess, and discuss, and laugh about *Harry Potter*. And it's something that's so magical about those books, pardon the pun of magic, is that they do just transform you to another world. And you are able to smile, and you can feel. And, you know, these are guys who were also at the lowest point in their life.

And so, at night, I would pass the pages around, once I finished reading them. First my cellmate would read it, and then we would discuss. And then I would pass the packets around of 200 pages. And at night, I'd stay up a little later and you'd hear men who don't laugh, they would be in their cells, you know, laughing at the story. And it's something that everyone can relate to.

*Harry Potter*, I think why it is so relatable to everyone is that it's this mythical hero's journey. Where we all experience darkness, we all experience pain and suffering, and feelings of abandonment and loss. And questioning ourselves and our worth. And then the power of friendship, the power of kindness, the power of love, more than anything, being the strongest element in the universe to kind of transform us out of that space. And rise above and be victorious in the end.

So, these men, you know, who you ... Jail is not a place where you cry. It's also not a place where you often hear laughter. You know, for me to be able to cry reading this story, not only from the compassion that Jeannie showed me, but just from the magic of the words, the book, and the message. But to also see these other men who you would never see laugh or cry, be so moved by the story, and so touched that someone would do this. You know, it just kind of spread like a wave of light within the whole block. And you know, I did take the copy out when I was released from jail, so that my children would be able to read the seventh version in the way that Jeannie xeroxed it. But I left all the other Harry Potter books that were sent to me in there so that others, while they were in that period of their life, would have something to hold onto and some hope.

**Hillary Raimo:** What stops people from being kind?

**Chun Rosenkranz:** One is, I can relate. I mean, I think it's a little scary sometimes. You know, everyone is busy. But I think that there's also another thing that's combating that, which is this craving that people have for connection. And that we seem to have lost a little bit. I mean, social media's such a powerful tool for connection. But it also allows us to hide behind and remain kind of in this realm of disconnection from each other. Disconnection from real humanity and really seeing each other. So, what I would say to that is, I think, for me sometimes, I think something that blocks the intentional acts of kindness is that you think that maybe you're not really going to make a difference. That really, this won't really have any lasting meaning for someone.

And I mean, just as ... my story is my own. But so many other stories, where you hear this ... You never really know the ripple effect in someone's life. I also met a social worker when I was incarcerated, her name was Lois, who spent many hours with me. And had me write essays and tried to get me to believe that I was worth something. And you know, since being released, I have ... Now I went and got an undergraduate degree in social work from Florida State University. I got to play on the water polo team as a sober man, a 30-year-old man, never having played water polo in my life. I got a scholarship to travel to Prague to study human rights and social justice. And then got my master's degree last year from Columbia University, a master's in social work.

All of this ... I don't believe that Lois or Jeannie or anyone who does an act of kindness believes that the trajectory of that kindness will kind of take off. But really, I would not be where I am without the love and kindness of other human beings. So, if you're feeling like you're afraid to reach out, and you're feeling like it won't really make a difference, I am here to implore you that it does. And my life is living proof of that.

**Hillary Raimo:** Does some of the fear come from the thought that If you're nice to somebody, your kindness will be rejected?

**Chun Rosenkranz:** Sure. I mean, there's a myriad of reasons why we hesitate to do these acts. But I also think there are ... The reason, kind of, why *I'll Be There* went public in the way that it did was because I was seeing so much negativity with the political season on social media. So many warring factors, so many negative and vitriolic statements being made by people. And I was also keenly aware of the fact that all around me, so many people that I work with, in this office, I'd been doing social work, my friends, random strangers all around me are doing acts of kindness and love all over the place. And that stuff wasn't being seen.

So that was really why I'll Be There became a platform for people to share those and inspire each other, and kind of push back against the vitriolic hatred that's the other side, the darkness. As, you know, the Harry Potter and the hero's journey, this archetype of light against dark. Not that there's some sort of nefarious dark force out there, but that love and light will battle that. And that love is stronger than anything else out there. And that we can really push back against that.

**Hillary Raimo:** Do you feel that this really was a pivotal, fork in the road, life changing crossroads moment for you? Can you look back on those days of your life now and be grateful and thankful for everything that you have experienced to get you to this point?

**Chun Rosenkranz:** There's this Buddhist saying that wanting things to be different from the way they are is suffering. And I fundamentally ... I believe that. I have grown so much as a human, from that time of incarceration. I'm able to have empathy and relate to humans' experience, suffering, in a way that I never would have been able to before. This movement and the way that I try to live my life is founded in gratitude and I'm not sure that I would want my life to have been any other way. Absolutely, was that a terrible and awful a really difficult time to go through? Yes, of course. But it also saved my life. And it allowed me to change in a way that I'm not sure anything else would have woken my soul up quite like it did.

**Hillary Raimo:** Talk about the transition from getting out of jail and creating the movement that you've created. How was that for you?

**Chun Rosenkranz:** First, it was scary. I do much better behind the scenes. I've been doing these acts of kindness for eight years now. Since I've been released. Very quietly and wouldn't promote them at all. And it felt very organic and natural to me, to kind of offer this hope and this light, and make people believe that they are worthy of their dreams, even through the smallest acts.

But the thing is, how *I'll Be There* also, you know, not only in seeing the media headlines, but was ... I posted one thing one day. I took a chance and I posted a picture with a little story of my experience with a man experiencing homelessness. And my ability to go out and have a meal with him and talk with him and have him feel seen and heard. And just do an unconditional act of kindness. And it got a whole bunch of attention. And not attention like, oh hey look at me attention. It was attention as in, like, that's incredible, I want to do that too. And so, it kind of lit a fire in my soul to create I'll Be There in a way that would inspire not self-promotion, you know, not like narcissism. It's a way to inspire others, as a collective of humans, to go out and try and change the world.

And it doesn't always need to be some monumental 759-page xeroxing mission, it can be as simple as asking the toll booth operator, when you're on the highway, how their day is going. Or instead of just ordering your coffee in the morning, to look the barista in the eyes and tell them to have a beautiful day, or a good morning. It's connection. It's kindness. It's having people believe and seeing the humanity on other human beings. And offering that. Seeing the light in each other.

**Hillary Raimo:** Do you feel that the connectedness in technology has made that worse or made that better? Or is it a double-edged sword?

**Chun Rosenkranz:** Sure. I mean, I absolutely think it's the latter. I think it's a double-edged sword. I think I'm absolutely at fault of this too, of just being absorbed by my phone, and reading instead of being present in some moments. Instead of connecting with humans around me. So, I constantly am challenging myself to put my phone down. To look up. To see people. To look people in the eyes. To watch interactions on the subway. To watch a mother with her child playing in the park. To be present for humanity, so that I can catch those gems of a moment of human connection. That I can see people. That I can be seen. I do think social media's such a powerful tool. And, you know, you look at the Arab Spring. You look at any of the movements, Black Lives Matter, that are going on. And our ability to receive information at such an instant pace. And also, to spread hope and love. I mean, I think it's both an incredibly powerful tool and also such a distraction from our ability to be present and grounded in the moment.

**Hillary Raimo:** *I'll Be There*. Let's talk about how you're asking others to use social media and modern day digital technology to create a wave of human kindness.

**Chun Rosenkranz:** Sure. I started the *I'll Be There Project* as kind of like an overall umbrella organization. And one of the campaigns is this kindness challenge in which I'm asking everyone to participate in, and where you do an intentional act of kindness. And it can be as big, as small as you desire. You could take a picture of it. You could write a story about it. You could take a video. But you would upload it to social media with the hashtag #illbethereproject. And then you are going to challenge three friends to do the same. That way, you create this wave of love, this kind of pushback, that has the power to, you know, the ripple effect, to go all over the world.

**Hillary Raimo:** How do people get involved?

**Chun Rosenkranz:** Exactly. That's exactly right. One of the issues that we have is that status updates often are not public, they can only be seen by friends. So, using the hashtag #illbethereproject, we were hoping to be able to catalog, and all, you know, you would essentially, you're having a rough day, you're looking for inspiration. You look down and you see all of these simple acts that people are doing all over the world, to inspire you not only to be a better person but to just reach out and touch someone. Whether that is buying them a KIND bar as you're walking down the street and you see someone experiencing homelessness or buying a cup of coffee for the person behind you. Or just simply offering a smile and a hello, or your seat on the subway. It's to be inspired.

So, by using the hashtag #illbethereproject, we found it as a way to just catalog it all into one place and collect these stories. So that we can see what's happening. We can see the ripple effect. So, if you do an act of kindness, we invite you to post it as a public status, so that we all can join in on that inspiration.

**Hillary Raimo:** This is very easy to do.

**Chun Rosenkranz:** Absolutely. I mean, anyone can do it, no matter what religion or agnosticism you subscribe to, or atheism. I mean, it's not about separation. It's about a collective humanity, a collective consciousness that we all can tap into, that we all are inherently ... have inside of our hearts. Not only was I changed by what happened to me in jail, but Jeannie has also been changed. I mean, there's so much to be said for the receiver being changed. But there's also this fact of, like, when you give, I'm almost not able to articulate. Because it's this, like, intangible feeling inside of you where you connect to something deeper in you, that is, like, primal, and it is craving to be kind of scratched. It's this connection. This desire to love and be loved.

And I mean, it is almost addictive to offer acts of kindness. Once you ... That's why it encourages people. You know, get out there, try one. Take a risk. And you'll feel how it changes your day. It's almost impossible to have a terrible day when you're out there in a space of gratitude and a space of giving. And you're able to offer another human being that ... You know, there's that saying that, be kind, for everyone is fighting a battle that you know nothing about. And that's the thing. I mean, we have these opportunities every day, all day long, to be that one shining light in someone's day. You know, they might have just lost a job. They might have ... you know, many, many things could have happened to them that day. But you can be that one shining light in their day.

**Hillary Raimo:** It's a primal instinctual type of yearning to connect with somebody else in a positive, loving, light-filled way.

**Chun Rosenkranz:** Absolutely. Absolutely. I mean, I'm in constant contact with Jeannie, who, you know, Jeannie is the friend who did the Harry Potter act for me. When we talked about it, she had no idea that her simple act would have changed my life, and the trajectory that I've gone on since being released. But it is that spark, it is that light. You know, when humanity or when human beings are experiencing a low point, or the kind of dark hour, where you've lost that hope, it's such a simple concept to be of service and to be that light for somebody. And it just has such a profound effect. And we never know what that effect will be. There is, like you said, no agenda. It is just, you offer this to the universe, and the ripple effects are infinite.

**Hillary Raimo:** The acts of hate and anger, and the opposite of kindness can have a snowball effect as well. So, there's an opposite to the act of kindness, and it has the same kind of energetic effect. Would you say that's fair to say?

**Chun Rosenkranz:** Of course, absolutely. I mean, if there is anything that this project is trying to encompass, it is to be the opposite of the negativity and hatred. And you know, I'm keenly aware of the fact that random acts of kindness, it's not going to change structural oppression, or racism, or poverty, world hunger. Some of these really major issues that are plaguing the world right now. But what it does allow us to do is to see the humanity in people. You know, challenging racial bias, challenging the darkness inside of us that has kept us separate from other human beings. It allows us to become the human family that we were born to be before we were socialized any other way. Before we were taught hate and anger. You know, it is the opposite, it's the counterweight. It is the light to the dark.

It's ... kindness and love are really ... And I know it sounds cheesy, hyperbolic, the fact that kindness and love will change the world. But I know it to be true, fundamentally, inside of my being. I mean, I've seen what it has done for my own life. And I've seen the way it has changed other people's lives. It is a truth, it is a fact, it is a part of me that I now accept that love is stronger than anything else in the world, and that is what I'm trying to share with the world, is my love for humanity. The love that I received. I'm so inspired by, you know take Ellen for example. She's a platform and she has changed the world. She offers kindness and love and happiness. It's these human beings that reach out and offer and hand to other human beings. And offer a smile. I mean, it is so powerful. My heart's beating so fast right now talking about it. I just get so passionate. It's such a magical experience, to be both the giver and the receiver of love.

**Hillary Raimo:** I believe that kindness and love are the antidotes.

**Chun Rosenkranz:** Oh, I love that.

**Hillary Raimo:** Somebody like you, who has gone through a massive transformation, the before and after picture is a really stark difference, I guess, from what I hear from your story.

**Chun Rosenkranz:** Yeah.

**Hillary Raimo:** If you had changed your mind along the way at any point, we wouldn't be having this conversation right now. I wouldn't be staring at your website, and I wouldn't have watched your beautiful video. And I wouldn't have had this opportunity to hear you and to share and to have this conversation. So, thank you, first of all.

**Chun Rosenkranz:** Oh, thank you so much. That means so much. I'm truly grateful for having the opportunity to speak to you about my passion.

**Hillary Raimo:** Well, some people say once you come on my show, magical things happen. So, may this bless the whole project.

**Chun Rosenkranz:** I love that. I love it.

**Hillary Raimo:** What's your hope moving forward with the *I'll Be There* project? What are you guys working on now?

**Chun Rosenkranz:** There's the kindness challenge out there, and then I'm also now going to start looking for corporate sponsorships. You know, the KIND bar, KIND snacks organization, they do a great deal of humanitarian work and invest a good amount of money into people who are trying to spread kindness. So, I'm going to look into grants and ways to kind of do larger scale projects.

One thing right now, I just put up a GoFundMe last week, when I released the video. Already people have donated, and that money is going to go to larger scale projects such as, we're working with Hope and Heroes at the Columbia Hospital for children with pediatric cancer. We're going out and buying all the kids brand new toys. We originally were going to ... we had all these teddy bears that were brand new, bought from Amazon, but because of the immunity issue, they can't be teddy bears, they have to be prepackaged toys that can be sterilized. So, we are in the midst of, once that money comes is and is put into the account, we are going to go on a shopping spree and fill their closet up, because their toy closet is empty as of now.

We're also working on building gardens at low-income schools in the Bronx. That's another project that we're working on. We also are trying to do, with that money as well, is buy every LGBTQ homeless teen currently residing on one of the shelters in New York City a brand-new outfit, so that they can feel somewhat at home. So, we are going to look to get corporate sponsorships so that we can do some of these bigger projects that people can be involved in and then share that love as well with the community on the I'll Be There Project's Facebook page.

**Hillary Raimo:** It takes money, and a village.

**Chun Rosenkranz:** It does.

**Hillary Raimo:** Your father has passed. If you could say something to him now, what would you say?

**Chun Rosenkranz:** Well, he had an incredible heart. Still does, I believe his energy and his heart is still out there. And he was also an incredibly smart and articulate spokesperson. So, I just want him to know that I love him, and I hope that I'm making him proud. And to give me some of that articulation and spokesperson energy, as I try to transform this project, to be the biggest it can be, to affect as many lives as possible. And that I love him with every fiber of my soul.

Oh. And I think that it's like, you know, I'm not going to stop until ... It's going to be my life's work to spread as much love as possible, until my last breath. Have you ever read *The Alchemist* by Paulo Coelho?

**Hillary Raimo:** Yes, I have.

**Chun Rosenkranz:** I love that book. And there's a quote in it, when you really want something to happen, the whole universe will conspire that your wish comes true. And I truly believe that. I think that love and kindness are in alignment with what this universe wants and needs. And I believe that we will all conspire to make this happen. And this is not my movement. I don't own this. I'm just a piece of this greater collective of humanity, you know, trying to offer us another way to connect with each other, as opposed to this disconnect, this separation. I believe the universe is conspiring for this to happen.

**Hillary Raimo:** There's even science behind what you're doing.

**Chun Rosenkranz:** There is. There's research.

**Hillary Raimo:** And like *Harry Potter*, like his transformation through his journeys.

**Chun Rosenkranz:** I'm signed up for the adventure. And I love the story of J. K. Rowling. I mean, she was at a really low point in her life. She started writing *Harry Potter* on cocktail napkins. She was a single mother. And I believe she was struggling financially at the time. And now I believe she's richer than the Queen of England. And she changed the world through this magical story. She changed so many lives. Not only my own, but you're a fan. I mean, everyone I know, although there are some haters out there, everyone I know, essentially, loves Harry Potter. And so, here's is this like, the hero's journey. That she was struggling, she found herself, she believed in something. She believed in this boy and this adventure that she had in her mind. She believed in love. And this timeless story of light versus dark, and love being stronger than hate. And she put it out there. And it changed the world. It's magic.

**Hillary Raimo:** And if she hadn't done that, you would never have received that book in jail. You wouldn't have had that moment.

**Chun Rosenkranz:** It's the ripple effect.

**Hillary Raimo:** If you are meant to birth an idea or something, then that is your fate.

**Chun Rosenkranz:** Absolutely.

**Hillary Raimo:** When you have a destiny this big, you just cannot escape it.

**Chun Rosenkranz:** Absolutely. But sometimes you need someone to show you that you are worthy of your dreams. I mean, sometimes, you need someone to be there for you when you're in fear. When you're not following your destiny. Where you do feel lost. And that's where this project comes in. That's where Harry Potter comes is. That's where the million of acts of kindness that people do for each other every day, all over the world. They all play a huge part in having people believe that they are worthy of following their dreams. They are meant to do something, whatever is it on this earth, and they are meant to do it from their heart space with passion, with creativity, in whatever way they want to offer that to the universe. But we need to support them when they are in that space of fear or hurting. When they are not connected to that source power. And that's what we're trying to do.

**Hillary Raimo:** I am glad you said that. Thank you because I see way too much of that happening.

**Chun Rosenkranz:** Absolutely.

**Hillary Raimo:** You can't really know what love is until you know what hate is, and vice versa.

**Chun Rosenkranz:** Sure. I do social work during the day, and I mainly work with people experiencing incarceration in the Bronx and try to humanize them. And get DAs and judges to see the humanity and this belief that we are more than, as Bryan Stevenson says, we are more than our worst mistake. It's heartbreaking, but it's such a profound environment, to see what we have been, the stories that we have been told about our worth, and the ability for humanity ... Just like that social worker was, in jail, for me. And just like Jeannie was, in jail, for me. The ability for humans and humanity to sweep in and allow that person to create a new story for themselves. That they are worthy of their dreams. They can do whatever they want.

You know, there are absolutely structural barriers in the way, but, like, to just connect with another human being. And offer love. And just to be there and listen. And to see them, and to see that humanity, as opposed to see the crime they're charged with. It is humbling in a place that I, again, can't really articulate. And then to have my story involved there, and to see myself in them. I mean, that is the truth about empathy, is our ability to see ourselves in someone else and their suffering. And then also their joy. It's to share that. So, Jeannie saw me in my darkest hour. She really saw me, and she was there for me. And now she also gets to share in all of the magic that has happened since I've been released. It's this idea that we can make others believe that they are worthy of their dreams.

And you spoke earlier about hope and I think that is one of the most powerful ... Hope and love almost being synonymous. And that, like, when you love someone you offer them hope. Hope of change. Hope of a new life. Hope of their worth. And hope that someone else cares about them. And I think that is the essence of this project. Love and hope.

**Hillary Raimo:** It's like hope is the same thing. It's a taint of a color or hue, within that beauty.

**Chun Rosenkranz:** Yeah. You're instantly bathed in the sunlight of kindness and love. And I think it changes you on a cellular level. Even if you can't recognize it in the moment. Even if you go about your day, and it's not until you get into bed later on that you realize, like, wow. That person got up, you know, they saw that I was having a rough day, or they saw that I had my kid with me, and they got up from the subway seat and allowed me to sit down. Like, these little gems of moments that happen all over place. Everywhere. You know, they are known, and they are recognized, not only within the spirit, but in a physical way within the body.

**Hillary Raimo:** When we feel love, we start a domino effect inside of our body on a biochemical level that begins to stimulate the natural world around us.

**Chun Rosenkranz:** Right.

**Hillary Raimo:** You know the difference between a conversation that is illuminating your mind and stimulating your love, and stimulating your intellect, and you have all kinds of a-ha moments and synchronistic events happen. And you walk away from that conversation feeling completely different than when you have a conversation where things are negative, gossipy, boring, heavy kind of conversations. Right? You've noticed that?

**Chun Rosenkranz:** Oh my gosh, yes. Absolutely. You know, it's such a different texture. And you absolutely feel it. You know, it sits in my stomach when I leave a conversation in which there's negativity present, versus one where it's positive, it's uplifting, it's from a strength perspective, which is something that we talk about in social work. You know, it's a completely different feeling. And like you were saying, on this biochemical level, it's like, I can feel it. You know? And so, if I can walk into every space, if all of us can walk into every space trying to leave that space a bit lighter, those human beings bit happier than they were before we got there, then we have done our jobs as humans.

So often I look to these societal goals as realms of success, and it's like, none of that stuff is really lasting. And I know that's very easy to say, right now. But, you know, when I have to pay rent next month it'll be another story. But it is how we make people feel. It is how we change the world through love. It is who we are as humans that is our legacy. It's not these material possessions. It's those conversations that you have where we engage in positivity and strength building. And building people up versus tearing them down with gossip. And we all engage in gossip. But we are seeking to fight back against that with love, with connection, with positivity, with inspiration, with hope. With all of those really, really feel-good words that absolutely mean something so profoundly deep within our souls.

**Hillary Raimo:** I hope you're putting some of these thoughts down on a blog or paper somewhere.

**Chun Rosenkranz:** No, I haven't started one yet. I know, I know. I need more hours in the day.

**Hillary Raimo:** I just read an interesting article, last week I believe it was. It was about how Tylenol, that if taken long enough, actually decreases people's ability to have empathy. However, what we're also doing is consuming things that are taking essential, vital human aspects out of the human body. Like empathy. If you don't have empathy, how do you do a random act of kindness? You don't care what other people feel.

**Chun Rosenkranz:** Right. That is extremely interesting and also profoundly terrifying, what you just said. I mean, I'm also ... I'm a big believer in organic gardening and connecting back to the earth, and that we have lost that piece with all of the processed foods that are being kind of forced down our throats. But to hear that empathy can be absent from taking an over-the-counter drug is absolutely terrifying. So, all the more reason to kind of invite folks to join this project. Because I think without empathy, like you said, we are lost.

**Hillary Raimo:** Without empathy, we are in the zombie apocalypse.

**Chun Rosenkranz:** Absolutely. Yeah. I absolutely invite anyone listening to participate in the challenge. Not so much to proclaim that you are not a zombie, but to reclaim your humanity. To reclaim your place on this earth as a human being that cares about each other. That cares about what happens to other human beings. To be able to walk down the street and see someone experiencing homelessness, and even if you don't have money to buy them a cup of coffee or food, to look them in the eye and to see that suffering. To be present for someone else's life, and to be awake. Every day I'm trying to awake a little bit more. I'm absolutely nowhere near an awake human being, but I am, we are all on this path together. We are all on this planet together. It's the only planet that we have. And during my time here, I just want to connect with as many human beings as possible, and to offer as much love to anyone who is not feeling worthy of their dreams or doesn't feel like they are worthy of love. I am proof of what love can do, and how love changes lives. So, as opposed to being a zombie, let's just be human.

**Hillary Raimo:** Don't be a zombie.

**Chun Rosenkranz:** Yeah, don't.

**Hillary Raimo:** Chun, take a little credit there, buddy, for being a really cool person and doing wonderful, kind things. I mean, ego doesn't exist when there's no agenda.

**Chun Rosenkranz:** Well thank you so much for saying that.

**Hillary Raimo:** I'd like you to give a special shout out to your partner. He won a very special award last night.

**Chun Rosenkranz:** Oh, he did. He did. My boyfriend, Paul McGill, he won the Astaire Award for best choreography in an Off-Broadway play. And I am insanely proud of him. He wasn't even there to pick up his award because he is right now in Berlin, choreographing a circus called Filament. Yeah, so I'm insanely proud of him and his artistry, and the way that he moves through this world as a graceful, loving man. I just love him to death.

**Hillary Raimo:** What does he think about what you're doing?

**Chun Rosenkranz:** Oh, he has been incredibly supportive. He shares all of my posts. And then the moments of fear, before talking to you, before posting the video, you know, he is a rock of support and love. And guidance as well. So, he is a magical partner to be dancing down this path with.

**Hillary Raimo:** Thank you so much for sharing your story, it's been a pleasure and an honor to speak to you today.

**Chun Rosenkranz:** Thank you so much for having me, Hillary. Yeah, it's been an honor to talk to you. Such beautiful energy.

# ACKNOWLEDGMENTS

I would like to acknowledge everyone who has ever listened to one of my radio shows all my years on the air. I was the #1 show on Achieve Radio for multiple years thanks to you. I am especially thankful for all of the incredible people, places and experiences I have had because of my radio career. My family for supporting me through it, especially my life partner Anthony & my sons Michael & Anthony. I would like to thank Grandfather Whitewolf for blessing this project from the start. If it weren't for the ease and total support of my producer Bill Schreiner at Achieve Radio, none of what has transpired over the last decade would've been the same, his unconditional support and green light on my freedom of speech was instrumental in my radio career. Special thanks to Michael Habernig of Path 11 Productions whose unwavering loyalty and help set me on my path today. The team at MBT Events - Keith Warner & Donna Aveni, Tom & Pamela Campbell. My mentors Lynn V. Andrews, Robert Bauval and Barbara Hand Clow. To Jane Morrison who taught me how to seek the next level in all I do and was my first and only ever radio sponsor. Thank you to everyone who believed in me: Lauren Reamon, Karen Woodin, Vera Lopez, Cathy Torlina, Gail Swanson, Betsy Peerless, Lisa Osina, Katrina Clay, Alison Phelan, Mary Jo Gardner, Phil Chavez, Flo & Sal Yepa, Dineen Nazarian, Tehvul Garcia, Miriam & Leslie Holloway. To all of my guests over the years whose conversations has made me a better person, I am grateful for the journey.

I would like to thank John St. Augustine who always reminds me my voice matters even when I myself forget. A big thank you to Barbara Hand Clow for reading through the manuscript and offering her critique. It was a positive experience and made the book what it is, an offering of a piece of time and information documenting a progression of technology and human consciousness. I would like to thank all of the people who came in and out of my life over my years on the airwaves, you made me who I am today. To Liza Mannarino and Mia Mendez, who restored my faith in the goodness of humanity, and remind me often to see the world through the child's eye. Finally, my greatest acknowledgement goes to nature, whom I am forever in love with.